ARCHITECTURE AND GLOBALISATION
IN THE PERSIAN GULF REGION

The Persian Gulf, possessing half of the world's total oil reserves, has over the centuries become a major centre of global attention and conflict. Recent architectural and urban development in the Gulf has been equally dramatic. The so-called culture of 'Dubaisation' in the last decade or so is now ringing alarm bells among different professions. A 'free-for-all' approach to architectural development is seen by many as creating surreal cityscapes which deny real reference to place, climate or cultural identity.

This is the first book ever to examine the architecture and urbanism of the Persian Gulf as a complete entity, dealing equally with conditions on the eastern Iranian shoreline as in Arabic countries on the western side. By inviting a range of architects and scholars to write about historical and contemporary influences on 14 cities along both Gulf coastlines, the book traces the changes in architecture and human settlement in relation to environmental factors and particularity of place. It provides an innovative contribution to the study of architecture and globalisation through a detailed investigation of this particular region, investigating how buildings and cities are being shaped as a result.

A set of thematic essays at the end offer important insights into issues of globalisation, urbanism and environmental design, drawing from the experience of the Persian Gulf. The outcome is a unique record of the Gulf in the early-21st century at a point when global capitalism is making major inroads and yet questions of architectural design, climate change, ecological sustainability, cultural identity and so-called 'Facebook Democracy' are likewise shaking up the Middle Eastern region. The book thus offers a fresh reading of the architecture and urbanism of a fascinating and often contradictory region, while also showing how globalisation can be analysed in a more engaged and integrated manner.

Architecture and Globalisation in the Persian Gulf Region

Edited by

Murray Fraser
University College London, UK

Nasser Golzari
University of Westminster, UK

Routledge
Taylor & Francis Group

LONDON AND NEW YORK

First published 2013 by Ashgate Publishing

2 Park Square, Milton Park, Abingdon, Oxon OX14 4RN
711 Third Avenue, New York, NY 10017, USA

Routledge is an imprint of the Taylor & Francis Group, an informa business

First issued in paperback 2016

British Library Cataloguing in Publication Data
A catalogue record for this book is available from the British Library.

Library of Congress Cataloging-in-Publication Data
Architecture and globalisation in the Persian Gulf Region / [edited by] by Murray Fraser and Nasser Golzari.
     p. cm.
   Architecture and globalisation in the Persian Gulf Region
   Includes bibliographical references and index.
   ISBN 978-1-4094-4314-8 (hardback : alk. paper)
     1. Architecture and globalisation--Persian Gulf Region. 2. Group identity--Persian Gulf Region. 3. City planning--Persian Gulf Region. I. Fraser, Murray, editor of compilation. II. Golzari, Nasser, editor of compilation. III. Title: Architecture and globalisation in the Persian Gulf Region.

   NA2543.G46A69 2013
   720.953'09051--dc23
                                                                              2013020840

ISBN 978-1-4094-4314-8 (hbk)
ISBN 978-1-138-24562-4 (pbk)

Contents

Illustrations

BLACK AND WHITE FIGURES

1   Introduction

7   Abu Dhabi, UAE

Tables

Contributors

Robert Adam is co-founder of ADAM Architecture, the largest traditional practice in the world, and a Visiting Professor of Urban Design at Strathclyde University in Glasgow, UK. His contribution to the classical tradition is internationally acknowledged, and he has recently written *The Globalisation of Modern Architecture* (Cambridge Scholars Publishing, 2012).

Ali A. Alraouf is Professor of Architecture, Urban Design and Planning Theories in the Department of Humanities at Qatar University in Doha. He is the Principal of Environmental Design Group, and has contributed extensively on Gulf architecture and urbanism. He is also the co-editor of *Knowledge Cities* (Scholar Press, 2007).

Nader Ardalan is an architect and planner with over four decades of award-winning international experience. He is President of Ardalan Associates and an expert in environmentally sustainable design. He is also Senior Research Associate and Co-Editor of the *Gulf Encyclopedia for Sustainable Urbanism* at Harvard University in Cambridge, Massachusetts, USA.

Semra Aydinli is a Professor in the Faculty of Architecture at Istanbul Technical University, Turkey, where she teaches design studio and architectural theory. She has written widely on her research interests, which include design education and philosophy, aesthetic experience, cultural identity, and critical issues related to interdisciplinary studies in architecture.

Widari Bahrin is an architect at DP Architects in Singapore and the co-author of *The Dubai Mall: Sand to Spectacle* (DP Architects, 2012). She studied at the Architectural Association, London, and took the MA in Architecture, Cultural Identity and Globalisation in the Department of Architecture at the University of Westminster.

Olivia Duncan is an Associate Urban Designer in the Abu Dhabi Urban Planning Council, UAE, where she has been working extensively with large scale master-plans and planning policies since 2009. She is a qualified architect and recently completed a MSc in Sustainable Urban Development from the University of Oxford, UK.

Murray Fraser is Professor of Architecture and Global Culture at the Bartlett School of Architecture at University College London, and currently serves as the Faculty's Vice-Dean of Research. He has published extensively on design, architectural history and theory, urbanism, and cultural studies, including *Architecture and the 'Special Relationship'* (Routledge, 2008).

Nasser Golzari is a Director of Golzari Sharif Architects in London, UK, and a senior lecturer at the University of Westminster, and leads a design studio in the Department of Architecture at Oxford Brookes University. He has also set up the Palestine Regeneration Team (PART) with Murray Fraser and Yara Sharif.

Susannah Hagan is Director of R_E_D (Research into Environment + Design) and also the Research Leader in the School of Architecture at the Royal College of Art, London, UK. Her books include *Taking Shape* (Architectural Press, 2001) and *Digitalia* (Routledge, 2008), and her current research is on urbanism and ecology.

Tanis Hinchcliffe was until recently Reader in Architecture in the Department of Architecture at the University of Westminster, London, UK. Now retired, she continues to be the author of books and essays on a wide variety of architectural themes, including, along with John Bold, *Discovering London's Buildings* (Frances Lincoln, 2009).

Nicholas Jewell is a practicing architect in London, UK, and recently completed a PhD at the Bartlett School of Architecture, UCL, on shopping malls and urbanism in China. He won the RIBA Dissertation Prize in 2000 for an essay on British malls, subsequently published in *The Journal of Architecture* (2001).

Gwyn Lloyd Jones works for Weston Williamson Architects in London, UK, and is completing a PhD at Westminster University on the influence of Frank Lloyd Wright outside America. He won the RIBA Dissertation Medal in 2001 for an essay which retraced Wright's annual pilgrimage from Taliesin North to Taliesin West.

Avsar Karababa is a PhD student at Istanbul Technical University, Turkey, and she also works as a senior architect at ETUD Architecture. Previously she was an architect at SE Architecture, and has carried out research into topics that include cultural and power relations as manifested in architecture and urban space.

Tim Makower is the principal of Makower Architects, a practice specializing in large-scale urban projects, with offices in London and Doha. A former partner of

Allies and Morrison, his work has included the King's Cross masterplan, Bankside 123, Liverpool 1, St Andrew's Bow, and Msheireb and Sidra Village in Doha.

Kevin Mitchell is an Associate Professor of Architecture in the School of Architecture and Design and currently serves as Vice Provost for Undergraduate Affairs and Instruction at the American University of Sharjah (AUS) in the United Arab Emirates. He is well known for his extensive writing on Dubai's recent urban development.

Mashary Al-Naim is Professor in the College of Architecture and Planning in King Faisal University in Dammam, Saudi Arabia, and was formerly the Chair of the Department of Architecture there. He is currently also Vice-Rector for Business Development at the Prince Mohammed University, and writes about Saudi architecture and urbanism.

Hassan Radoine is Chair of the Department of Architectural Engineering in the University of Sharjah, UAE. He is a consultant on urban heritage development, and has written on Islamic architecture and urban design topics, including an essay in *Planning Perspectives* (2011) on the planning of old medinas in Arab cities.

Reza Shafaei is an Iranian architect currently living in the UK. After studying at the Art University of Tehran, he took the MA in Architecture, Cultural Identity and Globalisation in the Department of Architecture at the University of Westminster. His main research interest is in socio-cultural aspects of sustainable architecture.

Sonny Tomic is an award-winning urban designer, policy maker and educator with extensive experience in large scale planning projects in Europe, Canada, the Caribbean and the UAE. He is currently a Manager of the Centre City Planning and Implementation Division in Calgary, Canada, where he oversees policy and development applications.

Acknowledgements

This book started from a conference that we organised at the Royal Institute of British Architects back in September 2009, and from a process of fieldwork research carried out since then. In terms of the RIBA conference, we were extremely grateful for the input of UN-Habitat, International Art and Architecture Research Association in Tehran, and the University of Westminster. Jeremy Till, then Dean of Westminster's School of Architecture and the Built Environment, was especially encouraging of our project. It also helped up greatly that we had such an excellent organising team for the RIBA conference, consisting of Filiz Erol, Mahnaz Golzari, Sabba Khan and Yara Sharif.

Gratitude for the research stage must all go to the researchers who so diligently visited their allocated cities along both coastlines of the Persian Gulf. Those authors whose essays have now been included in this book will be easy enough to indentify. However, it was regrettably not possible to include all of the researchers' essays when turning our project into an edited book, and so we extend our gratitude to Ranjith Dayaratne, Wafa Al-Ghatam, Kelly Hutzell, Layla Karajica, Yasser Mahgoub, Torange Khonsari, Rami el Samahy and Jasper Startup. Others who had given excellent talks at the 2009 RIBA conference but who also unfortunately could not be included were Peter Barber, Diana Coramazana (UN-Habitat), Nabeel Hamdi, Ibrahim Al-Jaidah, Paul Finch, George Katodrytis, Tony Lloyd Jones, Souheil El-Masri, Pirouz Mojtahedzadeh, Aylin Orbasli, Samia Rab, Mohammad Radfar, Abeer Al-Saud, Nazaneen Shafaie, Peter Sharratt, Mohammad Tabarra and Nicholas You (UN-Habitat). We would also like to thank all the mayors, municipal officials, scholars, librarians and ordinary citizens who helped our researchers to carry out their studies around the Persian Gulf: however, there are too many of them to mention individually here.

In broader terms, there are also a number of people whom we would like to thank. Our unending appreciation goes to Valerie Rose, Publisher at Ashgate, who is responsible for their excellent emerging architectural list, and to her editorial team who worked on this book, led by Jacqui Cornish. We would also like to take this chance to say how much our loved ones have helped us during the lengthy process of producing this book. In the case of Murray Fraser, this applies to Eva Branscome and to his sons, Callum and Liam; while in the case of Nasser Golzari, he is, as ever, deeply indebted to Yara Sharif.

Murray Fraser and Nasser Golzari

1

Introduction

Murray Fraser

This collection of essays addresses pivotal issues of architecture, urbanism, cultural identity and globalisation, and in doing so offers two original lines of investigation. Firstly, it is the first book in English (or any language) to look critically at the buildings and cities located around the entire perimeter of the Persian Gulf, not only from one perspective. This might seem a curious point to make, so is worth spelling out. Previous studies have tended to discuss the Gulf either from its western Arabic side or its eastern Iranian side. Cultural variants, ethnic divides and other enmities currently divide the two sides of the Persian Gulf – and yet, equally, it has been a singular entity for most of human history. Hence this book is innovative in that it examines the architectural and urban patterns along both coastlines, giving no pre-eminence to either. Instead the aim is to provide a vivid snapshot of the complex changes now occurring as result of cultural exchanges across the Persian Gulf and the wider processes of globalisation. The essays stem from a conference that I, along with my co-editor, Nasser Golzari, organised at the Royal Institute of British Architects in London in September 2009, as well as from fieldwork research since then. As in the RIBA conference, the book provides an inclusive overview of geographic, economic, political and cultural factors which have shaped, and are still shaping, the built environment around the Persian Gulf.

The book's second innovation is in the way it treats the concept of architectural globalisation, with this term being usually translated into Arabic as *'al-'awlama'* and into Farsi as *jahani shodan*. The historiography of architectural globalisation will be discussed later, but it is worth pointing out here that this book presents a different kind of analysis – one that is deliberately not focussed on any one particular country, or particular type of architects, or particular building type. Instead, each of the authors has been invited to study a specific town or city on the Persian Gulf within a broader cultural continuum which retains strong urban differentiations. Too much writing about architectural globalisation tends to be overly hysterical, or else merely repeats ideological themes laid down by the operations of global capital. This book also wishes to sidestep the limitations in the notion of 'critical regionalism', which, as Adrian Forty points out, is merely a new form of 19th-century architectural nationalism.[1] If anything, the book's approach is much closer to what is referred to as 'area studies', in which different disciplines drawn from across the social sciences and humanities examine together a specific geographical or cultural region of the world, with the aim of revealing underlying systems and forces. Previous writers have pointed out that the Persian Gulf 'provides a laboratory par excellence to assess and fine tune the theories of globalization'.[2] This is precisely our intention.

As with any cross-disciplinary investigation, however, there are some obvious problems with the 'area studies' approach.[3] Perhaps the key criticism of many 'area studies' scholars is that they appear to think they can come up with a simple coherent summation of a given part of the world. Thankfully, there can be little chance of that mistake being made when looking at the Persian Gulf region. For a start, even the naming of the water channel is deeply controversial, reflecting the contrasting views of the countries around it.[4] From the Iranian perspective, there is no question that it is Persian Gulf, whereas people on the Arabic side have from the 1960s referred to it as the Gulf, or sometimes the Arabian Gulf (somewhat confusingly, given that term has also long been used for the Red Sea on the western side of the Arabian peninsula). Other variants include the Arabo-Persian Gulf, Islamic Gulf, and Gulf of Basra. Google has recently got itself into serious trouble with Iran for dropping the name of the water channel entirely from its maps, so that clearly isn't an option either. We realise how sensitive this issue is for those involved, but for both the RIBA conference, and this book, we have reverted to United Nations nomenclature as that is the official neutral source – hence our predominant use of the term Persian Gulf, albeit alternating at times with the Gulf for brevity.

1.1   Map of the Persian Gulf showing the countries and cities covered in the book

We are keen not to take any fixed position in relation to these political controversies. The essays in this volume seek not to praise or condemn any part of the Persian Gulf region; rather, they hope to demonstrate that it is just as complex, contradictory and fascinating as any other part of the globe. There is no tendentious spouting about a 'clash of civilisations'. If anything, in the region around the Persian Gulf – where religion is still seen as central to social value systems – it is the ideological and cultural differences between the Sunni-majority Islamic countries on the Arabic side and the Shi'a dominance in Iran which are most notable. Today, increased involvement by new Asian economic giants like China and India is likewise beginning to problematise the geo-politics of the Gulf, reviving memories of the 'Silk Road' which was once so important for Europe and the Far East. Also highly significant are the tensions in the Middle East (and Northern Africa) which began to be expressed during the 'Arab Spring' in 2010–2011, revealing deeply varying views between generations and social groups about the role and purpose of the state, religious institutions, and other agencies.

Turning now to the geography of the Persian Gulf, there are eight countries which can be mentioned: Iran along the east and for much of the short northern coastline, where it abuts Iraq, and then the Arabic nations of Kuwait, Saudi Arabia, Bahrain, Qatar, United Arab Emirates (UAE) and Oman along the western side. However, the great bulk of Oman 'belongs' to the Gulf of Oman, Arabian Sea, and Indian Ocean beyond, and thus it is more oceanic in location. Oman is not economically dependent on the Persian Gulf, and only the tip of the Musandam Peninsula actually abuts onto it. Iraq does have a coastline on the northern Gulf, but it is an extremely small one with little human settlement. In this sense, Iraq's

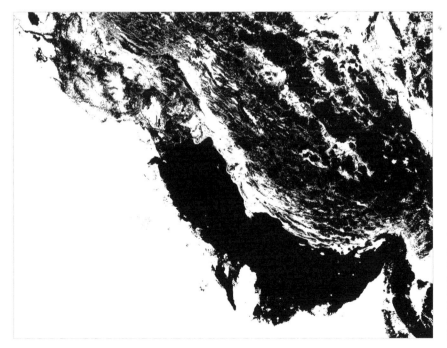

1.2   Relief map showing the mountainous eastern side in Iran contrasted with the flat desert-like Arabic side to the west

1.3   Reminder of an older way of life, close-up of an Iranian *dhow* in Dubai Creek

hinterland is much further inland to the north. For these reasons, this book focuses on analysing the key coastal cities in the six countries that possess substantial Gulf coastlines.

These six countries are united in that they face each other across the Persian Gulf. While mountainous and greener on the eastern Iranian side, the western shoreline is flat and desert-like. The Gulf itself runs in a direction from north-west to south-east, and on plan it is crescent-shaped, even banana-shaped. As a water channel it varies from 200–300 km in width, and is 989 km in length, creating a surface area of 251,000 km². This makes it roughly the same size (but not the shame shape) as Romania or Ghana or the United Kingdom. Indeed, it's a useful comparison to get into one's head that the UK would more or less fit straight into the Persian Gulf. Seasonal water temperatures of between 16–32°C make the Gulf one of the very warmest seas in the world, plus it is also one of the saltiest. At the southern end of the Persian Gulf, the celebrated Strait of Hormuz acts as a de facto entry chamber, or lobby, from the Gulf of Oman (which then drops into the Arabian Sea before widening out even further as it joins the Indian Ocean). As a consequence of its geographical location, it is no surprise that the Persian Gulf has for millennia been of vital strategic and military importance. That role continues today: the US Navy 5th Fleet is based in Bahrain and the US Air Force runs a base with 9,000 personnel in Qatar, largely to offer protection to Arabian oil states and as part of an ongoing diplomatic stand-off with Iran on other side.

But of course it would be wrong to reduce the Persian Gulf to merely a strategic or military entity, given that it has other important facets. Most fundamentally of

1.4   View across Dubai Creek to the heavily Iranian district of Deira

all, it acts as the drain for the mighty Tigris and Euphrates Rivers, thus making it part of what is often referred to as the 'cradle of civilisation' (or at least one of the 'cradles' around the globe). The first settlements in the Gulf region are estimated to have been born around 3,200 BC.[5] Soon it became a major trading route with ships heading in both directions to and from the Indian Ocean, setting up astonishingly rich networks of commercial exchange with Africa, India and the Far East. For its indigenous people, and the numerous immigrant communities who have come to live there, the Persian Gulf has long served as a metaphorical 'table' over which tribes and other cultural groupings on both sides can trade goods and services, share customs and diets, and at times fight each other outright. Indeed, a key function of the Gulf has often been to offer a route of refuge from conditions on the other side, such as in the case of the discontented Iranian merchants who sailed over to set up business in the 'free port' of Dubai. Cultural interchange has been profound. 'The result today is that the coastal populations of both sides of the Gulf contain a mixture of Arabs and Persians', as one commentator observes.[6] For instance, there are now an estimated 10,000 Iranian businesses in Dubai, and the annual flows of money from Iran to Dubai (estimated at $15 billion in 2007) easily make the latter Iran's biggest trading partner.[7]

In terms of environmental features, the Persian Gulf hosts a number of important natural habitats: the reed marshes of southern Iraq, harsh dry deserts along its western side, fertile mountain ranges close to the western shores of Iran, and an abundant collection of marine life and coral formations in what is a relatively shallow body of water. The Persian Gulf is only 90m at its deepest, with 50m being the average depth (although it suddenly gets far deeper once one has left through the 'lobby' of the Strait of Hormuz). Today, however, the Gulf faces many ecological problems. It is one of the most polluted seas in world, with an estimated 66 per cent of its coral reefs and hundreds of its marine species now at risk. Causes of this heavy pollution include the presence of oil and gas industries along the Arabian side (on land and offshore), discharges from coastal desalination and power plants, residues from wars in the form of shipwrecks/ oil spills/oilwell fires, unchecked sewage waste, aggressive 'alien' marine species brought in inadvertently by international tankers, and – not least of all – the rapid urban development of cities like Abu Dhabi, Dubai, Doha or Kuwait City, each of which contains a staggering 80–90 per cent of their country's population. Given the need for copious cooling of buildings in this hot and dry part of the world – summer temperatures regularly rise over 40°C and there is virtually no rain for six months of the year – the demands placed on air conditioning and other building services, or for heavily cooled car transport, is immense. In 2008 it was estimated that the UAE, with an ecological footprint of 2.5 hectares per person, had at last ousted America as the largest consumer per capita of natural resources and the worst producer of carbon emissions.[8]

Politically and culturally, the countries along both sides of the Persian Gulf have long experienced phases of colonisation by imperial armies led by Persians, Ottomans, Portuguese, Safavids, British, Americans, etc. Each has left a lasting legacy. As one vivid example, every year more than 1 million people from Britain alone, mostly tourists, visit Dubai.[9] As another concomitant of this complex history of colonisation in the Gulf region, for centuries there have been volatile relations between the largely Shi'a Persian and Sunni Arabic sides of the Gulf. Following the discovery of oil resources, a situation has arisen whereby American interests now prevail. Present-day intervention by western powers – generally neo-imperialist in intent and led by the USA with British backing – has over the past few decades maintained a status quo in the Persian Gulf to protect oil supplies. Historians duly point out that the previous 'Pax Britannica' has given way to a new 'Pax Americana'.[10] As such, since the 1980s the region has experienced three major wars involving Iraq, one of them directly with Iran, the other two with America and its allies. Today there is widespread hostility to Iran from those on the Arabic side of the Gulf, not least because of the Iran's shift towards a Shi'ite theocracy after the 1979 Islamic Revolution, which makes it (at least officially) opposed to western capitalism and materialist values. The latest worry in the Gulf region, voiced largely by Israel as America's main ally in the Middle East, is that Iran is secretly building nuclear weapons to use on Israel. Iran has indeed opened its first nuclear-powered electricity station near to the city of Bushehr, amidst fears from some observers that its real purpose – somewhat ironically, given that this would follow the lead set by Israel's nuclear power station – is to produce enriched uranium for nuclear missiles.[11] In response to concerns about Iran's nuclear ambitions, a series of economic sanctions have been imposed by the USA and European Union, which are now creating serious hardship and political instability in Iran.[12]

Meanwhile, the traditional economic activities once carried out by people in the Persian Gulf (pearl diving, fishing, trading, farming, craft industries, etc) have been changed dramatically by the impact of western-style capitalism. With the advent of oil and gas extraction, surplus capital now abounds. In a clear example of the process described by David Harvey, there is immense competition for this surplus capital to be invested back into new showcase buildings in cities on the western coastline, most conspicuously in Abu Dhabi and Dubai in the United Arab Emirates, Doha in Qatar, Manama in Bahrain, and Kuwait City[13] (see Plates 1 and 2). These development pressures are noticeably less intense in Iranian coastal cities, even if similar trends can be seen there too. Such differentials only add to the older rift between Persian and Arabian cultures. This is not to forget that there are deep social divisions inside Iran, as well as between Arabic nations despite the frequent expressions of pan-Arab sentiments. As an example of the latter aspiration, the Cooperation Council for the Arab States of the Gulf – usually shortened to the Gulf Cooperation Council – was founded in Abu Dhabi in 1981. It has had variable success since then. Disputes within the Arabic countries are often tribally based, with the presence of extended clans ruled by sheikhs remaining a strong social feature. On top, there persist tensions between nomadic Bedouin tribes and the settled majority population. The changes engendered were brilliantly captured in the *Cities of Salt* novels by Abdul Rahman Munif, as published from the 1980s. However, it should also be pointed out that divisions amongst the Arabic Gulf countries are no greater than those found between much of Europe or elsewhere around the globe.

The natural resources offered by the Persian Gulf represent significant economic assets, as it were one giant feeding bowl. Originally it was all about fish and pearls, more recently oil and gas reserves. Oil fields, which were first detected in Iran and Iraq in the early-twentieth century by British oil companies, and later developed on a far greater scale by US firms after the Second World War, have transformed life along both coasts of the Persian Gulf. As in other places like Texas, but in an even more intense and exceptional manner, oil became 'black gold' for many of the Arabic countries involved. As a consequence, from the late-1950s the Persian Gulf has served as the main petrol pump which fuels the world's automobiles. Staggering wealth fell upon Saudi Arabia, Kuwait, Qatar and the UAE, leading to increased global political power for their rulers after the Organization of the Petroleum Exporting Countries (OPEC) was created in September 1960. Of course there have been many historical ups-and-downs since then, such as the 'Oil Crisis' of 1973–1974, during which the Gulf nations were portrayed as greedily holding western economies to ransom. Following that was a period of steady growth that lasted until a noticeable tail-off in the early-1990s. The situation has since become more complicated, with oil output still rising slowly in Gulf countries and yet being heavily supplemented by the extraction of liquefied gas. Today, the Arabic countries of the Persian Gulf, taken together with Iran and Iraq, own around 62 per cent of the world's known crude oil reserves; in terms of natural gas reserves, Iran and Qatar are the second and third largest holders after Russia.[14] Widespread fears about 'peak oil' syndrome is, however, prompting serious efforts by Kuwait, Bahrain, Qatar and the UAE to diversify economically in a search for a post-oil future.

It is worth citing the sheer amount of oil and gas wealth that has now accumulated. If one takes the World Bank's estimates of Gross National Income (GNI) per capita in 2010, then Qatar sits in 5th place globally, with the UAE in 12th place and Kuwait in 13th place. There is then a drop to Bahrain, which is 48th, and Saudi Arabia in 61st position. More strikingly, there is a huge divide between western and eastern coasts of the Gulf, with Iran ranking 114th amongst nations in terms of GNI per capita. In terms of actual sums, Qatar earns around $80,000 per person per annum; UAE and Kuwait both earn close to £55,000; Bahrain is $25,000; Saudi Arabia is $17,000; and Iran is just $4,500 (for comparison, the USA lies at 18th with $47,000, Australia sits at 23rd with around $44,000, and Britain is 32nd with $38,500).[15] Similar results can be found by looking instead at the figures for Gross Domestic Product (GDP) per capita, which can be done by taking an average of three differing estimates, also for 2011, by the International Monetary Fund, World Bank and CIA World Factbook. In those terms, Qatar is rated as 4th in the world, UAE is 11th, Kuwait is 12th, Bahrain is 39th, Saudi Arabia is 40th, and Iran is 89th. Numerically, the average of the GDP figures places Qatar at $94,910 per capita per annum; UAE at $60,853; Kuwait at $59,542; Bahrain at $21,005; Saudi Arabia at $20,915; and Iran at $5,695 (again for comparison, Australia is 8th at £64,840, the USA is 16th at $48,410, and Britain is 25th at $39,003).[16] Hence both forms of statistics give the same ranking of economic performance amongst Persian Gulf countries, as well as drawing a picture of extreme wealth in which Qatar belongs amongst the world's wealthiest countries like Luxembourg, Norway, Lichtenstein, Switzerland and Monaco, with the UAE and Kuwait close behind. Saudi Arabia must also of course be regarded as a very important oil-rich economic nation, given that its population of around 27,130,000 citizens makes it the 44th most populous country in the world – thus it is far larger than neighbouring countries such as the UAE (c.8,265,000 people), Kuwait (c.3,580,000), Qatar (c.1,700,000), and Bahrain (c.1,235,000).[17] Once again the contrast with Iran is stark: the latter has a population of around 75,150,000 – the 17th highest in the world – and yet its economic figures look weak compared to the countries across the Persian Gulf.

Worryingly, the pool of extreme wealth in oil-and-gas-rich Arabic Gulf countries is by no means shared equally amongst the indigenous populations. Enormous differentials persist among social classes. Native-born Qataris, Emiratis and Kuwaitis are provided with social and economic incentives (some would say perks) from out of the oil-and-gas income to mitigate the worst effects of the huge wealth divide, yet this creates an anomalous lifestyle. Indigenous citizens, or certainly the male component, can readily take state-funded jobs which have higher salaries and fewer demands than in the private sector. The result is that, for instance, only 1 per cent of Kuwaitis work in private-sector companies even though their country purportedly operates on the capitalist economic model. This artificial padding within oil-rich countries can for some lead to lethargy, lingering resentment and indeed extreme anger amongst the native-born population. The most notorious case of this was the wealthy Saudi citizen, Osama bin Laden, later credited with forming the Al-Qaeda terrorist organisation which spectacularly flew two commercial planes into New York's World Trade Center on 11th September 2001.

Even more disturbing is the widespread exploitation within Arabic Gulf countries of the vast armies of poor labourers who come mainly from the Indian subcontinent and South-East Asia, and who don't have proper legal rights or financial stability in their lives. Hence the other pillar for economic success on the Gulf's western coastline is created by importing low-wage 'guest workers' from Asia. In the Arabic Gulf nations, these labourers comprise about 70 per cent of all expatriates, sending back home something in the region of $30 billion per year; there is also a smaller number of better paid and more advantaged workers from western countries, who generally get to enjoy perks like paying no tax on their income.[18] In most of the Arabic Gulf cities there are at least as many expatriates as indigenous citizens, and in the most vibrant economic centres such as Abu Dhabi, Dubai and Doha, the proportion soars to five expatriates for every native resident. For Saudi Arabia, these large numbers of expatriates are confined to a few coastal settlements along the Gulf like Dammam. The same is true for Iran, although it has a twist in that its free-trade zones on the Persian Gulf, such as Kish Island – which is now also an important domestic tourist destination – the locally-born population is heavily outnumbered. The vast majority of Kish's residents are now thus from elsewhere in Iran, with only 12.5 per cent born locally. This high degree of cultural interaction also means that rapid social changes are on the horizon along both sides of the Persian Gulf. An obvious example is the recent stirring of so-called 'Facebook Democracy', causing disruptions for political elites not only in Tunisia, Libya and Egypt, but also in Gulf countries like Bahrain, where the ruling government faces considerable opposition and unrest. No-one can predict how such changes will pan out in future, but it certainly poses the question of what ought to be done by cities around the Persian Gulf to enhance opportunities for freer social and political interchange.

It is these crucial social and cultural themes that this book touches upon, even if it cannot possibly hope to give definitive answers. By looking at the Persian Gulf as a 'solid' entity which binds together a wide range of countries on its coastlines, we take inspiration from Fernand Braudel's magnificent history of the Mediterranean region.[19] However, this book is not intended as a grand Annales-style academic investigation spanning over centuries. Instead it seeks to convey the latest cultural, architectural and urban influences around the Persian Gulf. As such, the Gulf is treated not as a mere sea, or as a gap between land masses, but as a cohesive land/sea entity (a similar case could, say, be made for the Indian Ocean as a 'solid sea' linking Africa, India, South-East Asia and Australasia). In the case of the Persian Gulf, this very act of joining together by a 'solid sea' also highlights the real distinctions amongst the countries that surround it. These differences can be portrayed clearly in terms of geology, climate, ethnography, ideology, cultural practice, and not least of all in architecture and urbanism. Traditional forms of architecture are especially strong on the eastern side of the Gulf, in Iran, as a nation which invented wind-catchers and erected so many finely vaulted buildings. In contrast, there are fewer examples of architectural heritage on the western coastline, where more important were the tented traditions of

1.5   Typical old streetscape in Bushehr in Iran

Bedouin tribes or, later on, the inroads made by Ottoman tastes during their period of rule. Even today, given the differential adoption of capitalism around the Persian Gulf region, there is a greater sense of architectural continuity on the Iranian side and a veritable global melting pot along the western Arabic coastline (albeit with pockets of cultural reaction as shown in several of this book's essays).

Many fascinating urban initiatives are being born in the Persian Gulf out of this complex mixture of geographic, climatic, economic and cultural influences. One of the most striking trends is that, despite the availability of huge extents of empty (albeit arid) land just inland from the coast, many of the Arabic countries seem to prefer to fill in the Gulf with newly formed, or else augmented, peninsulas and islands. These infill projects blur even further the land/sea continuum of the Persian Gulf, and provide distinctive additions to cities in Bahrain, Qatar and the UAE. The most famous examples are the Palm Islands and Dubai World in Dubai and Saadiyat Island in Abu Dhabi. However a similar infilling process can also be found elsewhere, such as on Kish Island in Iran. It prompts the speculation about whether the Persian Gulf might ever eventually be completely built over, a worry which preys on present fears of it being a threatened natural resource. Yet there is nothing inherently wrong about land reclamation: after all, countries like the Netherlands and Britain have been doing it for centuries, whether at home or in colonies like Hong Kong, with such actions being regarded simply as part of a 'rational' spirit of economic development. What then is any different, for example,

1.6   Iranian-style wind-catchers in buildings in Deira district of Dubai

1.7 Hotel developments on Kish Island, Iran

about the Palm Islands in Dubai? The answer is that today we are far more ecologically aware. As a highly saline and contained body of slowly circulating water, which sits in one of the global regions with the highest radiant heat gain, the Persian Gulf is already experiencing a significant loss of biodiversity and micro-organisms in its shallow intertidal zones. Land reclamation only worsens the decline of marine life and the spread of coral erosion. All these problems were reported clearly in the State of the Marine Environment Report 2003 by the Regional Organization for the Protection of the Marine Environment (ROPME), a research body run by the UN and founded in Kuwait in 1978 by all eight countries in the Persian Gulf region.[20]

These justifiable concerns about what is happening in the Persian Gulf stem largely from the rapid pace of urban change in Dubai and other cities as a direct consequence of globalisation. Exponents of 'critical regionalism' such as Liane Lefaivre and Alexander Tzonis warn us that such changes are flattening out the more nuanced cultural topography that previously existed around the world.[21] Yet in many regards what is happening in the Persian Gulf, and the worries it creates, are nothing new. In a telling quote from 1908 in the *Cairo Scientific Journal*, an 'orientalist' British architect who had designed a series of romantic mud-brick houses in Egypt wrote:

> *Unfortunately, the craze for novelty's sake has invaded Egypt. Things are sought for, not because they are sensible, but simply because they are novelties. This has been especially the case as regards building. The old type of [Egyptian] house, so well suited to the exigencies of the climate, gives way to the most ridiculous, bastard Europeanisms.*[22]

(*left*)
1.8   Aerial sketch of the old urban fabric of Bushehr

(*right*)
1.9   Sketch of the layering of urban development in Kharaba Street in Doha, Qatar

It is precisely these sorts of tensions that are explored in the essays in this book, albeit hopefully in a richer and subtler manner. When conceiving the initial RIBA conference, we were explicitly taking exception to the hysterical accounts of 'runaway' urban development in the Persian Gulf as epitomised by Rem Koolhaas and his AMO colleagues in their *Al-Manakh* volumes.[23] Not content with having produced such a messy pudding with their first volume in 2007, which embarrassingly predicted the continuation of uncontrollable speedy building in Dubai – an entirely erroneous prediction given the massive recession which hit the world economy the following year and slowed down Dubai's building to a snail's pace – Koolhaas and his team rushed out a second volume in 2010. It was as far off the point as the first one. One can characterise Koolhaas's compulsive fascination with discovering feverish hotspots of development around the world (e.g. Shenzhen, Lagos, Dubai) as that of 'ambulance-chasing urbanism' – i.e. an activity that seriously distorts whatever insights might come through research enquiry by the endless portrayal of processes of urban growth as the product of ego. More intellectual, but suffering from the absolute certainties favoured by denunciatory preachers, are the polemical

blasts – of the Albert-Speer-meets-Disney clichéd variety – from left-wing American critics such as Mike Davis and Michael Sorkin. They rail against what they see as elitist and exploitative 'feudal' developments in Arabic Gulf countries. It was Davis who suggested links to Speer and Disney in his tub-thumping essay in *New Left Review* in 2006, tellingly titled as 'Fear and Money in Dubai'.[24] As even Rem Koolhaas has written about this kind of stock 'Disneyland' jibe:

1.10   Aerial sketch of the urban texture in Khobar in the Dammam Metropolitan Region, Saudi Arabia

> In truth, the constant return of this Disney fatwa says more about the stagnation of the West's critical imagination than about the cities on the Gulf.[25]

A more responsive treatment of architectural and urban development in the Persian Gulf – although written mostly about the western Arabic coastline – can however be found in other books on cities such as Dubai and Abu Dhabi, or indeed from architects and scholars writing about architectural heritage and contemporary urbanism. This more balanced approach is represented by figures like Ibrahim Jaidah or Yasser Elsheshtawy, or by some western expatriates in the Gulf region, such edited book by George Katodrytis on Dubai's architecture, or in various essays by his colleague at the American University of Sharjah, Kevin Mitchell.[26] Michael Dumper and Bruce Stanley have assembled a useful encyclopedia of Middle Eastern and North African cities, including several in the Gulf, although the entries tell one little about architecture or urban form.[27] Other general books on the history and socio-economic developments in the Persian Gulf region have also been invaluable for framing this book.[28] Now a major research project, and indeed one that was triggered by participation in our 2009 RIBA conference, is underway by Nader Ardalan and his team at the Harvard University Graduate School of Design. Together they are working on the 'Gulf Sustainable Urbanism Research Programme'. This project is being funded largely through Qatari money.[29] In this way we are delighted that our initiative to link scholarship on architecture and urbanism across both sides of the Persian Gulf is already bearing such fruit.

What this brief survey of existing writings on Gulf architecture and urbanism reveals is the need for more systematic and integrated analysis. Hence this book is the first attempt to investigate the cities and individual buildings of the region

1.11   Sketch from a car driving along the Sheikh Zayed Highway in Dubai

1.12   New office towers along the Sheikh Zayed Highway in Dubai

1.13   Aerial view of the new blocks and landscaping around the Burj Khalifa in Dubai

as a whole, both historically and contemporaneously. It is an approach which is especially important given there is not much discussion between the Iranian and Arabic sides. Likewise, the over-attention by western analysts to the Arabic Gulf coastline, raised to an absurd level in the Koolhaas volumes, only serves to the detriment of Iran. As such, it has to be regarded as an invidious new form of imperialism. This is why this book places a continual emphasis on the need to treat the Persian Gulf as an interconnected region, a 'solid sea', and to combine positive readings of its architectural and urban patterns with open criticisms of these conditions wherever appropriate.

1.14   The Dubai Mall next to the Burj Khalifa

In order to transform the RIBA conference into this edited book, we deliberately chose a broad range of contributors to carry out the urban research, with the aim of achieving a greater sense of balance. The authors are hence a selection of architects and scholars from the Persian Gulf and elsewhere in the Middle East, as well as expatriates and writers based in the west. We also adopted a gender balance and mixed younger architectural writers with more experienced ones. Whatever their background, each author was required to bring a broad and tolerant approach to their study, and collectively they were asked to build up a rounded picture of architecture and urban development in the Persian Gulf, with a particular emphasis on conveying what these towns and cities are like to live in today. Having picked our authors, each of them was allocated a specific town or city to research and analyse. The principle for selecting these settlements was that they had to sit on or be as close as possible to the Gulf coastline, and be significant centres of habitation. A total of 14 towns or cities were chosen, of varying size, and with half of them on the Arabic coastline and the others on the Iranian side.

After the analyses of these individual centres, which constitute the main bulk of the book, we have included a final section of essays to discuss the wider ramifications from four different perspectives: sustainability, cultural identity in architecture, urban design, and globalisation theory.

Table 1.1   Outline information on the 14 selected towns or cities

Town or City	Country	Population in metropolitan area (estimated)	Share of national population (%)	Proportion of foreign residents (%)
Kuwait City	Kuwait	2,380,000	90	55
Dammam	Saudi Arabia	1,244,000	5	40
Manama	Bahrain	329,500	27	50
Doha	Qatar	1,450,000	80	80
Abu Dhabi	UAE	970,000	60 (Abu Dhabi Emirate)	80
Dubai	UAE	1,900,000	92 (Dubai Emirate)	83
Sharjah	UAE	890,000	90 (Sharjah Emirate)	80
Abadan / Khorramshar	Iran	220,000 / 124,000	negligible	negligible
Bushehr	Iran	225,000	negligible	negligible
Kangan / Banak	Iran	25,000 / 9,000	negligible	negligible
Kish	Iran	25,000	negligible	negligible
Bandar Abbas	Iran	367,500	negligible	negligible

Source: Murray Fraser, using data from the various essays in this book

The book's approach cannot of course claim to be entirely systematic, nor indeed fully comprehensive. Nonetheless we believe that a remarkable portrait emerges of the buildings and cities around the Persian Gulf, and of how local people currently inhabit them. It is perhaps worth noting again the obvious omissions from the book. Given the emphasis on coastal settlements, we decided not to include any Iraqi cities, since the part of Iraq facing onto the Persian Gulf is so tiny (just 15 km wide). Kuwait effectively blocks off Iraq from the Gulf, which was one of the reasons why Saddam Hussein was so eager to invade the country, thereby igniting the First Gulf War in 1990–1991. Given that Basra is the only sizeable Iraqi city in the Marsh Arab region, and lies some 80 km away from the Gulf, we felt it could not be included. Furthermore, my co-editor Nasser Golzari was already writing an essay on the Iranian cities of Abadan and Khorramshahr, which sit downriver from Basra and thus are closer to the Persian Gulf. Likewise, we decided not to have any Omani cities since so little of that country sits on the Gulf, nor indeed are there any substantive settlements in Oman's Gulf territory. Readers will also notice that we have deliberately not tried to include detailed maps of the towns and cities being analysed. This decision was taken because of the sheer ubiquitousness today of online maps on the Internet, such as Google Maps, which give a level of zoomable detail and interactivity not possible in a printed book of this size.

These caveats aside, the contributions of our authors raise important themes of tradition, cultural identity, urban change, and globalising pressures (both positive and negative) in the Persian Gulf. It all makes for a fascinating regional kaleidoscope, as well as a vivid introduction to the architectural and urban richness found along both Gulf coastlines. In wider terms, the book prompts each of us to look at our own part of the world as a myriad of local connections and globalised influences, with these operating together in a complex manner, and never as simple polar opposites. Hopefully the book will encourage other scholars to provide more nuanced and balanced studies of the impact of globalisation, while also adding to our knowledge about buildings and cities around the world. Indeed, we see the strength of this book as willingly holding both these aims at the same time. It does so precisely because the Persian Gulf is an exemplar of a region that is now so deeply implicated in contemporary processes of urbanization that it has become – within a relatively short period of time – an essential part of the production of architectural culture at a global level.

NOTES

1   Comment made by Adrian Forty as a respondent at the 'Globalisation or Regionalism?' symposium, Bartlett School of Architecture, University College London, UK, 27 April 2012.

2   John Fox, Nada Mourtada-Sabba & Mohammed Al-Murtawa (eds), *Globalization and the Gulf* (London/New York: Routledge, 2006), p. 3.

3   See, for example, the analysis in Hans Kuijper, 'Area Studies versus Disciplines: Towards an interdisciplinary, systemic country approach', *The International Journal of Interdisciplinary Social Sciences*, vol. 3, no. 7 (2008): 205–216. Viewable at http://www.asvj91.dsl.pipex.com/Hans_KUIJPER/AREA_STUDIES_Vs_DISCIPLINES_Hans_KUIJPER.pdf (accessed 12 September 2011).

4   'Persian Gulf naming dispute', Wikipedia website, http://en.wikipedia.org/wiki/Persian_Gulf_naming_dispute (accessed 12 September 2012).

5   Fox, Mourtada-Sabba & Al-Murtawa, *Globalization and the Gulf*, pp. 270–271.

6   Rosemary Said Zahlan, *The Making of the Modern Gulf States: Kuwair, Bahrain, Qatar, the United Arab Emirates and Oman* (2nd Edition, Reading: Garner Publishing, 1989/98), p. 8.

7   Jim Kane, *City of Gold: Dubai and the Dream of Capitalism* (New York: St Martin's Press, 2009), p. 25.

8   Ibid., pp. 223–227.

9   'United Arab Emirates', Foreign and Commonwealth Office website, http://www.fco.gov.uk/en/travel-and-living-abroad/travel-advice-by-country/middle-east-north-africa/united-arab-emirates (accessed 14 June 2012).

10 Zahlan, *The Making of the Modern Gulf States*, p. 1.

11 Jonathan Marcus, 'Will fuelling the Bushehr reactor give Iran the bomb?', 21 August 2012, BBC News Online website, http://www.bbc.co.uk/news/world-middle-east-11045291 (accessed 2 January 2012); 'Israel's Netanyahu urges "red line" over nuclear Iran', 27 September 2012, BBC News Online website, http://www.bbc.co.uk/news/world-middle-east-19746994 (accessed 28 September 2012); Uzi Mahnaimi, 'Israelis to shut nuclear plant in Iran's sights', *Sunday Times*, 8 January 2012, p. 26; Nick Hopkins, 'Britain rebuffs US on military aid against Iran', *The Guardian*, 26 October 2012, pp. 1–2.

12 Uzi Mahanimi & David Jones, 'Iran calls troops home as hardship bites', *Sunday Times*, 7 October 2012, p. 30.

13 The argument about reinvestment of surplus profit in overt architectural display, used by many other cited writers such as Mike Davis and Michael Sorkin, was set out best in David Harvey, *The Condition of Postmodernity: An Enquiry into the Origins of Cultural Change* (Oxford: Basil Blackwell, 1991).

14 Mehran Kamrava (ed.), *International Politics of the Persian Gulf* (Syracuse, NY: Syracuse University Press, 2011), p. 3.

15 'Gross national income per capita 2010, Atlas method and PPP', World Bank website, http://siteresources.worldbank.org/DATASTATISTICS/Resources/GNIPC.pdf (accessed 12 September 2012).

16 'List of countries by GDP (nominal) per capita', Wikipedia website, http://en.wikipedia.org/wiki/List_of_countries_by_GDP_(nominal)_per_capita (accessed 12 September 2012).

17 'List of countries by population size', Wikipedia website, http://en.wikipedia.org/wiki/List_of_countries_by_population (accessed 12 September 2012).

18 Kamrava, *International Politics of the Persian Gulf*, p. 3.

19 Fernand Braudel, *La Mediterranee et le Monde Mediterraneen a la époque de Philippe II* (3 vols, Paris: Armand Colin, 1966).

20 ROPME, *State of the Marine Environment Report 2003* (Kuwait: Regional Organization for Protection of Marine Environment, 2004).

21 Lefaivre, Liane and Tzonis, Alexander, *Architecture of Regionalism in the Age of Globalization: Peaks and Valleys in the Flat World* (London/New York: Routledge, 2012).

22 Somers Clarke, 'The Use of Mud-Brick in Egypt', *Cairo Scientific Journal*, vol. 2, no. 21 (June 1908), p. 211.

23 Ole Bouman, Mitra Khoubrou & Rem Koolhaas (eds), *Volume 12 – Al Manakh: DUBAI GUIDE; GULF SURVEY; GLOBAL AGENDA* (UAE: Stichting Archis, 2007); AMO et al., *Al-Manakh 2: Gulf Continued, Archis, Volume*, no. 23 (2010).

24 Davis, Mike, 'Fear and Money in Dubai', *New Left Review*, no. 41 (September/October 2006), viewable at the *New Left Review* website, http://newleftreview.org/II/41/mike-davis-fear-and-money-in-dubai (accessed 12 June 2012); Michael Sorkin, 'Connect the dots: Dubai, labor, urbanism, sustainability, and the education of architects',

Architectural Record, August 2009, viewable at *Architectural Record* website, http://archrecord.construction.com/features/critique/0908critique-1.asp (accessed 14 June 2012).

25 'Rem Koolhaas: An Obsessive Compulsion towards the Spectacular', quote taken from interview in *Der Spiegel*, 18 July /2008, viewable at the *Der Spiegel* Online International website, http://www.spiegel.de/international/world/rem-koolhaas-an-obsessive-compulsion-towards-the-spectacular-a-566655.html (accessed 16 November 2009).

26 Examples of this richer and far more balanced strand of urban and architectural scholarship in the Persian Gulf include: Nader Ardalan (ed.), 'Gulf Research Project on Sustainable Design', *2A Architecture & Art Magazine*, no. 7 (2008); Elisabeth Blum & Peter Neitzke, *Dubai: Stadt aus dem Nichts (Bauwelt Fundamente)* (Basel: Birkhauser, 2009); Steven Caton & Nader Ardalan, 'New Arab Urbanism: The challenge to sustainability and culture in the Gulf', Final Report for the Kuwait Program Research Fund, John F. Kennedy School of Government, Harvard University, 2 December 2012, viewable at http://belfercenter.hks.harvard.edu/files/uploads/05_%20New_Arab_urbanism.pdf (accessed 12 September 2012); Cynthia M. Davidson, *Dubai: The Vulnerability of Success* (London: Hurst & Company, 2008); Brian Edwards, Magda Sibley, Mohamad Hakmi & Peter Land (eds), *Courtyard Housing: Past, Present and Future* (Abingdon: Taylor and Francis, 2005); Yasser Elsheshtawy (ed.), *Planning Middle Eastern Cities: An Urban Kaleidoscope in a Globalizing World* (London/New York: Routledge, 2004); Yasser Elsheshtawy (ed.), *The Evolving Arab City: Tradition, Modernity and Urban Development* (London/New York: Routledge, 2008); Ibrahim M. Jaidah & Malika Bourennane, *The History of Qatari Architecture from 1800 to 1950* (Milan: Skira Editore, 2009); George Katodrytis (ed.), *Dubai: Growing through Architecture* (London: Thames and Hudson, 2008); Nartano Lim & Widari Bahrin, *The Dubai Mall: Sand to Spectacle* (Singapore: DP Architects PTE, 2012); Sandra Piesik, *Arish: Palm Leaf Architecture* (London: Thames & Hudson, 2012); Nasser O. Rabbat, *The Courtyard House* (Farnham, UK & Burlington, VT: Ashgate, 2010); Ashraf Salama & Florian Weidmann, *Demystifying Doha: On Architecture and Urbanism in an Emerging City* (Farnham, UK & Burlington, VT: Ashgate, 2013). See also the brief but fascinating study by the Middle East Institute, *Viewpoints Special Edition No. 9: Architecture and Urbanism in the Middle East* (Washington, DC: Middle East Institute, 2008), viewable at Prince Mohammad Bin Fahd University website: http://www.pmu.edu.sa/downloads/AU%20in%20the%20Middle%20East.pdf)/. Furthermore, an interesting body of slightly older texts on Arabic architecture and urbanism, which either directly or indirectly covers the Persian Gulf region, includes: Stefano Bianca, *Urban Form in the Arab World* (London: Thames & Hudson, 2000); Paolo M. Costa, *Studies in Arabian Architecture* (London: Variorium, 1994); Kenneth Frampton, Charles Correa & David Robson (eds), *Modernity and Community: Architecture in the Islamic World* (London: Thames & Hudson/Aga Khan Awards for Architecture, 2001); Mustafa M. Hejazi, *Historical Buildings of Iran: Their Architecture and Structure* (Southampton/Boston: Computational Mechanics Publications, 1997); Antony Hutt & Leonard Harrow, *Islamic Architecture: Iran 1* (London: Scorpion Publications, 1977); Antony Hutt & Leonard Harrow, *Islamic Architecture: Iran 2* (London: Scorpion Publications, 1978); Udo Kultermann, *Contemporary Architecture in the Arab States: Renaissance of a Region* (New York/London: McGraw-Hill, 1999); Ronald Lewcock & Zahra Freeth, *Traditional Architecture in Kuwait and the Northern Gulf* (London: Art and Archaeology Research Papers, 1978); George Michell (ed.), *Architecture of the Islamic World: Its History and Social Meaning* (London: Thames & Hudson, 1978); Azim Nanji (ed.), *The Aga Khan Award for Architecture: Building for Tomorrow* (London: AD Academy Editions, 1994).

27 Michael Dumper & Bruce E. Stanley, *Cities of the Middle East and North Africa: A Historical Encyclopaedia* (California: ABC-CLIO, 2006).

28   These more general sources on the Persian Gulf include, but are not limited to: Allen J. Fromherz, *Qatar: A Modern History* (Washington, DC: Georgetown University Press, 2012); Halim Barakat, *The Arabic World: Society, Culture and State* (London: University of California Press, 1993); Christopher de Bellaigue, *Patriot of Persia: Muhammad Mossadegh and a Very British Coup* (London: Bodley Head, 2011); David Chaddock (ed.), *Qatar* (Northampton, MA: Interlink Publishing Group, 2008); Nelida Fuccaro, *Urban History of Bahrain* (Bahrain: Excess University, 1999); Fred Halliday, *Arabia without Sultans* (London: Saqi Books, 2002); Colbert C. Held, *Middle East Patterns: Places, Peoples and Politics* (Colorado: Perseus, 2001); Sandy Isenstadt & Kishwar Rizvi (eds), *Modernism and the Middle East* (Seattle, WA: University of Washington Press, 2008); Bernard Lewis, *What Went Wrong? The Clash between Islam and Modernity in the Middle East* (Oxford/ New York: Oxford University Press, 2003); Mehran Kamrava (ed.), *International Politics of the Persian Gulf* (Syracuse, NY: Syracuse University Press, 2011); Ahmed Kanna, *Dubai: The City as Corporation* (Minneapolis, MN: University of Minnesota Press, 2011); Shirley Kay & Damish Zandi, *Arab Heritage of the Gulf* (Dubai/London: Motivate, 1991); Peter Mansfield, *A History of the Middle East* (London: Penguin, 2003); Samuel B. Miles, *The Countries and Tribes of the Persian Gulf* (London: Ithaca Press, 1919); Saba George Shiber, *Recent Arab City Growth* (Kuwait: Government Printing Press, 1967); Jo Tatchell, *Diamond in the Desert: Behind the Scenes in the World's Richest City* (London: Sceptre, 2009); Richard Trench, *Arab Gulf Cities* (Slough: Archive Editions, 1994).

29   GSD to study Persian Gulf, *The Harvard Crimson* website, http://www.thecrimson. com/article/2011/5/24/project-region-gulf-world/ (accessed 12 September 2012); 'Gulf Encyclopedia for Sustainable Urbanism', Ardalan Associates website, http:// ardalanassociates.com/research/gulf-encyclopedia-for-sustainable-urbanism-gesu/ (accessed 12 September 2012).

PART I

WESTERN COASTLINE OF PERSIAN GULF

2

British Architects in the Gulf, 1950–1980

Tanis Hinchcliffe

In the July 1977 issue of *Building* magazine, there was a report on an RIBA conference on the Gulf States, and in the same issue readers were treated to an artist's impression of a £3 million multi-storey tower complex in Doha, Qatar by a consortium consisting of White Young and Partners of Qatar and London, Arabian Design Associates of Doha, assisted by Hughes and Polkinghorne of Norwich.[1] Leafing through the architectural magazines, particularly those of the 1970s, it is not unusual to find articles chronicling the activities of numerous British firms working in the Gulf, and it could be claimed that this work kept the architectural profession in this country afloat, especially during the recurring periods of recession in the post-war era. My intention here is to investigate the activities of British and American architects in the Gulf from the 1950s through to the late-1970s, and to ask whether the work done in this region was a feature of an incipient global market in building, or a prolongation of colonialism in what has been historically a contested location. Furthermore, has this regional building history set precedents which are difficult to discard even today?

With the break-up of the Ottoman Empire in the early decades of the 20th century, Britain and France established Mandates which were intended as temporary administrations until such time that it was deemed prudent to allow the indigenous peoples within the old Ottoman Empire to rule themselves. France took control of Lebanon and Syria, while Britain took control of Iraq, Iran and the areas around the coast of Arabia. Britain's interest was primarily the transport route to India, but after 1912, when the Royal Navy switched from coal to oil in order to fuel its ships, the supply of oil assumed an increasing importance. Mindful of their increasing reliance on oil, in 1914 the British government bought the controlling interest in Iran's Anglo-Persian Oil Company.[2] Both Iran and Iraq resented British interference in their internal affairs, and this was especially true of Iraq, which in 1920 was not really one state, but in fact three distinct regions with little to hold them together. After an armed intervention which cost lives and money, and alienated the population further, Britain continued its control of Iraq at arm's length – until the Second

World War when it placed Iraq under military occupation.[3] Iran meanwhile suffered from its strategic position between the British and the Russians. During the Second World War, Iran became a vital supply route for the Soviet Union in its fight against Nazism, and when the Shah showed pro-German leanings, the two powers invaded the country.[4] Saudi Arabia and the Gulf States were able to maintain more equable relations with Britain, largely because their populations were small, plus a series of treaties with the ruling sheikhs around the Gulf ensured that Britain could maintain the required stability along the coast, and direct control of the all-important Aden Protectorate.[5] Given that oil was discovered in Saudi Arabia only in 1938, the great wealth of that country became apparent only after the end of the Second World War.

Given the complex pre-war history of the Gulf countries, particularly those of Iraq and Iran, it is a wonder that British architects made any headway there at all during the 1950s. It says something for the strength of the local desire to modernise the material fabric of these countries, that western engineers and designers were encouraged. In post-war Britain itself there was the will to modernise, a task in which architects would take an active part, but in the immediate post-war years the draconian cancellation of America's 'Lend-Lease' agreements in 1945, led to a crippling lack of cash for the post-war Attlee government, especially for public sector work.[6] The architect Raglan Squire recounted that in the 1950s, when his practice needed a boost, he read a paper which commented on the fact that there were 22,000 fully qualified architects in England, while in the Commonwealth countries the numbers could still be counted on the fingers of one hand.[7] Convinced that the opportunities overseas were immense, he opened an office in Baghdad in 1955. City plans and infrastructural schemes were undertaken by British firms, along with architectural work, and as Squire noted, the planning of Baghdad was given to Minoprio and Spencely, Basra to Max Lock, and Squire himself got Mosul – not that any of them had time to do much work on their plans before the revolution in Iraq in 1958.[8] During the next administration, the Greek architect Constantinos Doxiadis was given the task of producing an urban design for Baghdad. Like the English architects before, he seemed to make little distinction between the different ethnic and religious areas – and in fact his *Ekistics* approach was supposed to erase differences through the application of a rationalist mentality.[9]

It might well have been asked, besides Max Lock, how much experience the British architects had in planning large urban areas. In the March 1957 issue of *Architectural Design* devoted to the Middle East, Raglan Squire made the point that all the plans of these important centres were by British consultants, which he considered appropriate, since 'it has been England who has led the world in town planning'.[10] But this claim was modified by the warning that: 'A planning consultant can find himself in the difficult position of trying to explain a plan to an audience who have little or no conception of what town planning, as it is practised in highly-developed countries, really means.'[11] This clash of cultures became a *leitmotif* in the journals as time went on, and as the projects funded by the increasing oil revenues became ever larger and more ambitious.

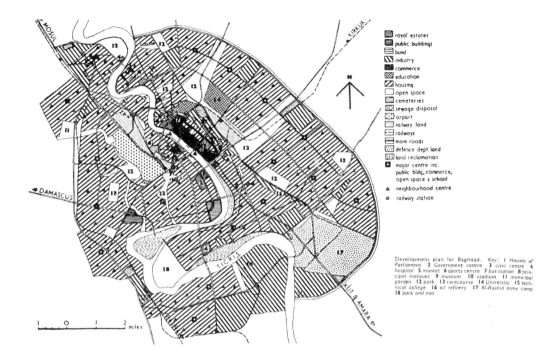

royal estates
public buildings
bund
industry
commerce
education
housing
open space
cemeteries
sewage disposal
airport
railway land
railways
main roads
defence dept. land
land reclamation
major centre inc.
 public bldg, commerce,
 open space & school
neighbourhood centre
railway station

Development plan for Baghdad. Key: 1 Houses of Parliament 2 Government centre 3 civic centre 4 hospital 5 market 6 sports centre 7 bus station 8 principal mosques 9 museum 10 stadium 11 municipal garden 12 park 13 racecourse 14 University 15 technical college 16 oil refinery 17 Al-Rashid army camp 18 park and zoo

2.1 Plan of Baghdad by Minoprio and Spencely and F.W. Macfarlane

As mentioned previously, it had been important for Britain to keep the Gulf region on its side while India remained such a vital part of the Empire, but it was the discovery of oil which kept the British there after 1947. The Gulf States assumed inordinate importance to the British economy, with Kuwait in 1967 becoming the single largest foreign holder of sterling.[12] Suddenly, rather poor and neglected territories in the Middle East acquired a degree of importance far beyond anything they had experienced before. Areas which had managed with almost no infrastructure up till then were transformed with roads, oil wells, refineries and desalination plants. Buildings for schools and hospitals, previously more or less unknown, were required along with commercial spaces. Not having needed these buildings before, the Gulf States had not developed a profession of designers, and therefore it was understandable that they would have to look outwards for professionals who were more expert in producing buildings of all types.

Many young British architects, fresh from architectural schools or war service, were looking for work in an overcrowded profession when suddenly competitions began to appear for work in the Gulf States. In 1952, an RIBA competition for the Doha State Hospital in Qatar was won by the young husband-and-wife team of John R. Harris and Jill Rowe, fresh graduates of the Architectural Association in London. When they won the competition, they had already worked on the Building Research Laboratories in Kuwait, but they still had to figure out from first principles how to design what was possible as well as what was appropriate.[13] Their innovations extended to contract and management, so that, for example, the foundations of the Doha hospital could go ahead and be built while the London office was still producing the working drawings – thus demonstrating to the Qatari population the political point that a new

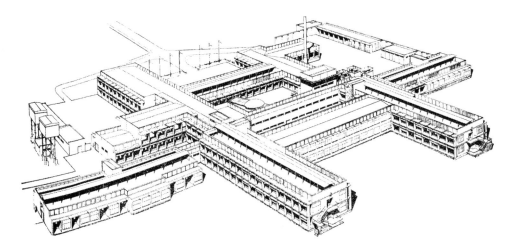

2.2   Doha State Hospital in Qatar, bird's-eye view, by John R. Harris and Jill Rowe

2.3   Doha State Hospital, main entrance view

hospital was immanent.[14] This was just the beginning of a long association of John R. Harris Architects with the Middle East. In 1958 they produced a plan for Dubai and subsequently designed six hospitals there. They opened an office in Kuwait and also in Tehran for the work they undertook for the National Iranian Oil Company. In 1961 they produced the first development plan for Abu Dhabi, and then they went on to do work in Bahrain, Sharjah and Oman. Harris's success came as a result of chance, since his office's decision to enter the Doha competition had been weighed against the possibility of entering the competition for Coventry Cathedral; nonetheless, the Qatar commission also ensured that a struggling young practice survived the adverse post-war economic conditions.[15]

Those architects who ventured into the Gulf found a building environment totally different from anything that most of them had previously encountered, with excess heat and sunlight a factor in early designs, while the procurement of materials and equipment was a perennial concern, even compared to the difficult conditions back in Britain. However, even in the 1950s there was an awareness that the issue of cultural specificity was important, although it was not always clear what this meant. In the 1957 issue of *Architectural Design* devoted to the Middle East, it was noted: 'Serious architects seek to develop a regional style: perhaps within the next decade they will have found the way.'[16] There were dark suggestions in the journals that some architects ignored local sensibilities, but it was never the actual architects who were under discussion, always 'someone else'. Whether it was a town plan or the design of a hospital or school, there was a consideration of how local tradition and culture could be accommodated in building types and plans unfamiliar in the region. This was particularly the case in the Gulf region. It was possible to take a very functional approach, which suited those buildings needed for strictly utilitarian purposes such as desalination plants. More difficult were buildings such as hospitals where functionalism needed to be tempered with some degree of cultural sensibility.

The desire for modern building and technology had provided a strong incentive since the 19th century for the regions of the Middle East to engage with the west. Their desire for modern technology did not always coincide with a preference for western culture or politics, which may have been a misconception laboured under by developed western nations. By the middle of the 20th century, the idea of 'modernity' carried a certain prestige, and countries coming into sudden wealth could be expected to seek some of that prestige for themselves.[17] It should be remembered, however, that at the same time the Middle East was seeking to transform its physical fabric with modern buildings, America – and to a certain extent Europe – were also changing the face of their own cities. The Gulf States were not trying to keep up with an already well-established modernism, but with a contemporary process that was happening all around the world at that time. In other words, they were not playing catch-up, but regarded themselves also as the present or even the future. This was reflected in the title of a 1975 feature in the *Architectural Record*, which asked if the Middle East was indeed the 'new frontier'.[18]

However, there was a lot of building needed in the Gulf States, and much of it involved infrastructure undertaken by large contractors such as the British firms Taylor Woodrow, Laing and Costain. Architectural work, on the other hand, was

2.4   Tehran Hilton Hotel by Raglan Squire Architects

2.5   Bahrain Hilton Hotel by Raglan Squire Architects

varied, and needed to satisfy the demands of a wide variety of clients. For example, Raglan Squire and Partners became involved with Hilton Hotels, which along with Intercontinental Hotels and Holiday Inn were building extensively in developing countries in the Middle East, Far East and Caribbean. Squire claimed that every Hilton Hotel was different, and his personal experience of these hotels ranged from Tehran and Bahrain to Cyprus and Tunis and to Jakarta.[19] But as Annabel Wharton has pointed out in her book, *Building the Cold War: Hilton International Hotels and Modern Architecture*, there was also a formula which incorporated the accepted luxury of contemporary America with just a modicum of regional decoration.[20] The Hiltons provided a comfortable familiarity for wealthy western visitors, but they also satisfied the desire for a palpable modernity from the ruling elites in the cities where they were built, sometimes in the face of great difficulty and expense. Wharton makes the telling point that Conrad Hilton actually did not pay for his new hotels, but relied on local investment, thus ensuring the support of the financial community at any rate for the shiny new buildings – which with their monumental scale often dramatically changed the urban landscape, and served to emphasise the 'shabbiness' of the traditional fabric.[21]

There were also buildings commissioned by Middle Eastern governments which could produce interesting work beyond the accepted modernist formula. In 1966 Trevor Dannatt won a limited international competition organized by the International Union of Architects on behalf of the Saudi government for a conference centre and hotel in Riyadh. This large project was completed in the mid-1970s, but the generosity of the spaces and the simple forms give the

2.6   Conference Centre and Hotel in Riyadh, Saudi Arabia, by Trevor Dannatt and Partners

2.7   Conference Centre and Hotel in Riyadh, Saudi Arabia, by Trevor Dannatt and Partners

complex a timeless quality.[22] Anglo-American architects are often uncomfortable with religion, or at least they have been in the recent past; hence many of them found the omnipresence of Islam and the other religions of the region a struggle. Nonetheless, Sherban Cantacuzino attributed the success of the Riyadh Conference Centre to 'Trevor Dannatt's nonconformist background and his understanding of Wahabi puritanism'.[23] Be this as it may, it is noticeable that from Dannatt's design are absent those pointed arches, decorative tiles and grills which seemed to be the limit of regional references for many new buildings in the Gulf at this time.

While building work in the Middle East continued to grow during the 1950s and 1960s, it was after the 'oil crisis' of 1973–1974 that the region's impact on architectural practice reached a global scale. In 1976 Edmund Dell, the British Secretary of State for Trade, compared the expansion of the Arab countries as 'the nearest modern industrial equivalent to the booming days of the American gold-rush'.[24] We have become used over the past years to take in our stride references to billions of dollars, but in 1975 the Central Planning Organization of Saudi Arabia was already forecasting that their government would be spending $27 billion a year on construction by 1980.[25] The resulting interest was enormous, since the very crisis which brought such wealth to the oil-producing countries was also pushing the industrial countries into recession. Dispiriting statistics continued to appear in the architectural press in the mid-to-late 1970s chronicling the fall in new commissions for British architects at home.[26]

It thus became more common for the architectural journals to cover work in the Middle East, and even to devote whole issues to working in the region. In January 1976 a brand new journal, *Middle East Construction*, was launched with a quotation from Le Corbusier on its cover and a remit to circulate itself free-of-charge to 'qualified readers' in the whole Gulf region. From the early issues of the journal it became clear that construction was viewed as a vital element in the British government's export drive, especially as it was considered that Britain was falling behind other countries such as America, Japan and Germany.[27] The stiff competition between industrialized countries for work in the oil-rich areas of the Middle East signals the change in the balance of power between those commissioning the work and the providers of design and construction services.

Although Britain was historically the major colonial power in the Gulf region, America had by the 1970s built up a long history of involvement in the area, especially since their interest in oil pre-dated the Second World War. Saudi Arabia's first oil concession in 1933 went to what became the Arabian American Oil Company (ARAMCO), and when oil was discovered in Dhahran in 1938, it was that company which took control of the refining, marketing and pricing of the oil. They also developed the area with their own infrastructure, and established in effect an American company town for its workers. Indeed, the US government fostered Saudi Arabia as their particular ally in the area, and one of their ministers even likened the Kingdom in the 1940s to 'a gigantic aircraft carrier, astride the Middle East'.[28] Subsequently, American architects and engineers began to undertake a significant amount of work in the Middle East, a fact reflected in the June 1975 issue of *Architectural Record*, which was devoted to opportunities for US designers in the area and chronicled the experience of architects already working there. The Americans were also much more upfront than the British about the cultural conflicts incipient in the relations between Gulf clients and western designers. They recognized the resentment felt at the 'demeaning' attitudes of many Americans, but they also noted that: 'These leaders are also conscious of their image, and the superficial image that many want – for better or for worse – is that of America.'[29] The efficiency of American methods was appreciated, especially since time was regarded as of supreme importance. There was very much a concern among leaders in the Gulf that building, along with diversification, should take place while the oil revenues lasted, so that the region would not ever sink back into obscurity when it could no longer provide oil to the industrialized economies.

The *Architectural Record* gave advice on how to get commissions, and mentioned the need for a reliable agent who would be able to set up face-to-face meetings with Middle Eastern clients. Sometimes western architects might have to wait around for weeks before their all-important meeting, and, as they were reminded, this was without benefit of alcohol or the usual kind of western entertainments such as movies.[30] When it came to the contract, many westerners found that the timescale expected for the necessary design and building work was unexpectedly tight, and the expense of building was beyond what they were used to. Scarcity of materials and transport costs were a major consideration, and, as one architect asked half-jokingly, how do you mix concrete when the water temperature is 100°F?[31]

As mentioned before, even in the 1950s there was awareness that instant modernisation could wipe out any previous cultural traditions in the Gulf region. By the mid-1970s, and the oil boom that was happening, this situation seemed even more likely. Hans Neumann of Perkins & Will International described a sensitive plan for a new town near Tehran which had been rejected out of hand by the clients because it included traditional elements: 'They didn't want to hear the word bazaar. It was a shopping center.'[32] On the other hand, Charles Hoyt criticised much of the recent work by westerners as being 'poorly planned and built, and its designers have copied the appearance of (for example) Miami in the 1950s', while Neumann remarked that the regions in the Middle East 'need an immediate warning before they destroy their heritage.'[33] This growing concern from the late-1970s coincides of course with the discovery of the importance of 'built heritage' in America and Britain, and could reflect western preoccupations just as much as international modernism had done twenty years before.

British architects too were increasingly aware of the cultural dimension of their activities in the Gulf region. Scott Brownrigg and Turner made a calculated decision in 1974 to get involved in Middle Eastern projects, and opened offices in Doha and Dubai. When they came to design the Abu Dhabi Trade Centre, as a spokesman explained, their architect had 'completely misread the client's requirements', lazily assuming the client's interest lay in prestige and hence their desire was for ostentation and wealth. The wry comment was that 'SBT see a danger in being excessively conditioned by UK press and propaganda about Arab excess.'[34]

Times may be changing,

but we're still a little old fashioned.

2.8
Advertisement
for Syston Rolling
Shutters

Some of the advertisements to be found in the architectural press at this time are as telling as the comments made by the architects involved. An advert from the *RIBA Journal* in 1977 for Syston Rolling Shutters presents a whole dramatic scenario which speaks volumes.[35] An Arab millionaire, the former colonial subject, emerges from his limousine to be greeted by a smiling commissionaire, the uniformed representative of British colonialism, since hotel commissionaires then were largely staffed by former army personnel. 'Times may be changing' stated the text, and we must remember that this was when people from the Middle East were seen as 'flooding' London's West End, eager to spend some of their oil wealth. The text went on to say that: 'We care about maintaining standards, we never cut corners. We care about the personal touch, we're never slow to respond to your needs and problems'. This suggests that there are others who will do all these things, especially if they are dealing with Middle East clients whom they think they can fleece.

In the July 1983 issue of the *RIBA Journal*, which was dedicated to 'Architecture Overseas', Hal Higgins of Higgins, Ney and Partners made the comment that: 'The mistake that many western architects have made is to come into the Middle East with set western notions and to construct buildings which are unsuitable in a traditional sense. This attitude shows a certain contempt for the place in which they are building.'[36] A second advertisement, appearing in the journal *The Architect* in December 1976, reflects something of this attitude.[37] The advert is based on that old schoolboy joke, how do you make a Venetian blind? [Answer: You poke his eyes out!] The crudely drawn cartoon of a cigar-smoking Arab, with a set of blinds as eye shades, is posed in front of some oil derricks, and the text concluded with the phrase: 'If you have to blind an Arab, try our service. It doesn't hurt at all'. Much less subtle than the previous advert and perhaps so over-the-top as to become innocuous, it did after all appear in a special issue of *The Architect* devoted to the Middle East, with translations into Arabic.

If nothing else, these advertisements demonstrate the ambivalence of those in the British construction industry to working in the Middle East in the second half of the 20th century. Architectural firms such as Scott Brownrigg and Turner attributed their continuing existence during a period of severe recession to their work in the Gulf region. And for many British architects, it was an opportunity to work on a scale they could never dream of at home. On the other hand, Middle Eastern countries with new untold wealth sought to satisfy their desire for modernity without often really understanding the implications of this move. But when it came to thinking about architectural heritage, which countries in the west finally got around to doing in the late-1970s, it could be asked whose heritage: that of the ruling elite, or of the indigenous people? Or was it perhaps even the great mass of foreign workers drafted into a country such as Kuwait, where already by the mid-1980s some 60 per cent of the population was made up of outsiders, mostly Palestinians?[38]

In May 1977 the *RIBA Journal* assessed the past 25 years of British architects in developing countries such as those in the Gulf region, and the conclusion of Michael Austin-Smith was that architectural assistance was not enough, since undiluted western architecture could be inappropriate. As Austin-Smith said, 'It is no good building a dozen hospitals or schools if there is no way of producing the necessary medical or teaching staff'.[39] Then he went on to add:

> There is therefore a great opportunity which is opening up for a whole range of British expertise to be applied to a large number of building programmes in a way which will ensure that our knowledge and expertise is used to solve the problems of the countries concerned and not to saddle them with inappropriate buildings.

And here we can see that the British were off again on another quest to run other peoples' lives for them. Much of course has happened since in the Middle East in the way of regime change and revolution, shifts in balance of regional power, and the politics of oil. But when we regard the present condition of architecture within the Gulf States, it is good to remember that where we are now began in the post-war rush to modernity, and came from the self-interested involvement of western architects.

NOTES

1   *Building,* vol. 224, no. 6779 (1 July 1977): 42, 81; *RIBA Journal*, vol. 84, no. 5 (May 1977): 229.

2   W. Taylor Fain, *American Ascendance and British Retreat in the Persian Gulf Region* (New York: Palgrave & Macmillan, 2008), p. 15.

3   William L. Cleveland & Martin Bunton, *A History of the Modern Middle East* (4th Edition, Boulder, CO: Westview Press, 2009), p. 212.

4   Ibid., p. 190.

5   Ibid., p. 231.

6   Fain, *American Ascendance*, p. 22.

7   Raglan Squire, *Portrait of an Architect* (Gerrards Cross: Colin Smythe, 1984), p. 147.

8   Ibid., p. 198.

9   Panayiota I. Pyla, 'Baghdad's Urban Regeneration, 1958: Aesthetics and the Politics of Nation Building', in Sandy Isenstadt & Kishwar Rizvi, *Modernism and the Middle East: Architecture and Politics in the Twentieth Century* (Seattle, WA/London: University of Washington Press, 2008), p. 99.

10   *Architectural Design*, vol. 27, no. 3 (March 1957): 74.

11   Ibid.

12   Fain, *American Ascendance*, p. 3.

13   A.E.J. Morris, *John R. Harris Architects* (Westerham, Kent: Hurtwood Press, 1984), p. 5.

14   *The Architect*, vol. 122, no. 12 (December 1976): 30.

15   Morris, *John R. Harris Architects,* pp. 2–3.

16   *Architectural Design*, vol. 27, no. 3 (March 1957): 72.

17   *RIBA Journal*, vol. 84, no. 5 (May 1977): 198.

18   *Architectural Record,* vol. 157, no. 6 (June 1975): 101–108.

19   Squire, *Portrait of an Architect*, p. 205.

20   Annabel J. Wharton, *Building the Cold War: Hilton International Hotels and Modern Architecture* (Chicago, IL: University of Chicago Press, 2001), p. 4.

21   Ibid., p. 7.

22   *Architectural Review*, vol. 157, no. 938 (April 1975): 194–219.

23   Ibid., 216.

24   As quoted in *The Architect*, vol. 122, no. 12 (December 1976): 25.

25   *Architectural Record*, vol. 157, no. 6 (June 1975): 105.

26   See, for example, *RIBA Journal*, vol. 84, no. 10 (October 1977): 447.

27   *Middle East Construction*, vol. 1, no. 3 (March 1976): 5.

28   Fain, *American Ascendance*, p. 22.

29   *Architectural Record*, vol. 157, no. 6 (June 1975): 102.

30   Ibid., p. 103.

31   Ibid., p. 106.

32   Ibid.

33   Ibid., p. 108.

34   *The Architect*, vol. 122, no. 12 (December 1976): 37.

35 *RIBA Journal*, vol. 84, no. 10 (October 1977): opposite p. 437.

36 *RIBA Journal*, vol. 90, no. 7 (July 1983): 4.

37 *The Architect*, vol. 122, no. 12 (December 1976): 62.

38 Cleveland & Bunton, *Modern Middle East*, p. 467.

39 *RIBA Journal*, vol. 84, no. 5 (May 1977), p. 198.

3

Kuwait City, Kuwait

Gwyn Lloyd Jones

This chapter explores the urban identity of Kuwait City in light of the proto-globalised architectural figure of Frank Lloyd Wright and his mythical projects in and around the Persian Gulf. It might seem curious to use Wright's influence within the Gulf region as a starting point, but as this chapter will show, he was someone who claimed to respect the architecture of the region even if he often muddled his way between Arabian and Persian precedents. For instance, in his 1937 book, *Architecture and Modern Life*, he mused: 'the opulent Arab wandered, striking his splendid, gorgeous tents to roam elsewhere. He learned much from the Persian; the Hindu, learning from the same origins.'[1] In addition, Wright frequently quoted his admiration for *The Arabian Nights* tales, and indeed within Wright's home in Oak Park, Chicago there was an illustration from 'The Fisherman and the Genii' in his children's playroom. Wright was so captivated by these tales that he identified himself as 'the young Aladdin' in *An Autobiography*.[2] Wright therefore equated his own powers of creativity with Aladdin's, and the idea of the rubbing of the lamp became a symbolic expression of his imagination.[3] So when Wright was invited to Iraq to design an Opera House for Baghdad in January 1957, it was his chance to prove, unequivocally, his creative genius. The brief for the Opera House was typically inflated by Wright into the need for a much grander 'Cultural Quarter' for the city – an unrealisable personal fantasy, but also prophetic of the fantastical projects and the search for cultural identity currently being undertaken on a lavish scale within the Gulf States.

As is well known, Kuwait has experienced a remarkable growth since the Second World War due to its natural oil wealth; indeed, the country changed beyond all recognition from the original settlement dependent on sea trading and pearl fishing. Kuwait City serves as its capital and by far the largest urban conglomeration, possessing in 2012 an estimated 2.38 million people in its metropolitan area (around 90 per cent of the total population). Only a half of the population are Kuwaitis, although most of the non-resident workers come from other Arabic countries and so the ethnic divisions are not as noticeable as in, say, the United Arab Emirates. In this chapter, a brief historical overview will first provide

3.1   Postcard
of Kuwait City

a regional context that considers the influence of Islam, globalising European empires, and post-colonial nation building. Questions will be raised about 'orientalist' perceptions of the region as captured in a number of colonial literary texts that portrayed an imagined and exotic Middle East. The mechanisms for planning rapid urbanisation that were adopted in Kuwait will then be discussed and local reactions considered. The relationship between place, culture and architecture within the domain of globalisation will be at the heart of the discussion throughout.

The later text in this chapter is organised around a number of taxi journeys to specific sites which provided me with a narrative about Kuwait and Frank Lloyd Wright's influence. My research involved conversations with academics, residents and expatriate immigrants alike; I also collected souvenirs and wrote postcards home, and visited sites in the city centre and in the peripheral suburbs. The act of journeying has long been an inherent part of inspiring and constructing architecture, and in this spirit I will reflect upon my own experience and Wright's recollections. My observations can only be preliminary and speculative, yet they shed a different view to the contemporary bombastic architecture in so many cities on the western coastline of the Persian Gulf.

THE ARABIAN PENINSULA

Situated at the centre of the region named the Middle East by Eurocentric nations, the Arabian Peninsula was the home of several ancient civilisations and trading routes that helped to foster early global encounters. Lying to the north, the cities of Mesopotamia and Babylon were part of the 'fertile crescent' that linked the Persian Gulf to the Mediterranean Sea, and there was evidence of an advanced Mesopotamian civilisation on Failaka Island, near Kuwait, around 3,000 BC.[4] The Arabian race as such were first noted in 850 BC by Assyrian writers, who described them as a 'nomadic people of the North Arabian desert'; these were of the Adnanais stock, whilst there was also another fairly settled grouping called the Qahtanis to the south and west of the peninsula.[5] Alexander the Great famously expanded his Greek Empire eastwards during the 3rd century BC, establishing a fortress on Failaka. The Romans later took command of the whole region at the start of the 1st century AD, and they remained dominant over the next three centuries, protecting their pre-modern trade route – the 'Silk Route' – which linked Asia and Europe. The

Roman Empire was succeeded in turn by Byzantine and Persian dynasties, with the latter of course predominating on the eastern side of the Persian Gulf.

The Prophet Mohammed was born in 570 or 571 AD in Mecca, and as a result, the peninsula came to have a lasting religious and cultural impact on the surrounding region, and globally. The Prophet established the Islamic faith, which Muslims believe to be 'the ultimate faith, which completes and perfects the two other heavenly religions – Judaism and Christianity'.[6] Islam propagated quickly and by the time of his death in 636 AD, the Prophet Mohammed 'had succeeded in welding the scatter and idolatrous tribes of the peninsula into one nation worshiping a single, all-powerful god'.[7] Thereafter, various caliphates expanded the Islamic faith, and by 711 AD its dominance extended from Spain to Persia. Grube identifies two general concepts that epitomise Islamic architecture: a concentration on the design of interior space, and the absence of specific forms for specific functions.[8] He notes, consequently, that 'Islamic architecture is given to hiding its principal features behind an unrevealing exterior'.[9]

Similarly, a number of scholars have identified the internal spatial concentration within Frank Lloyd Wright's architecture, especially in his non-residential designs, most of which was derived from Japanese architecture.[10] However, Wright also at times used thick enveloping masonry walls to separate occupants from the city, and to define the internal spaces, and in this regard there are obvious spatial similarities to traditional Islamic architecture – even if Wright never acknowledged any such link. Nonetheless, when reflecting on past ages of architecture, Wright plotted a history of masonry construction in which he expressed his admiration for the 'low, heavy, stone dome'[11] found in Byzantine architecture, and in particular the Hagia Sophia in Istanbul.[12] He proceeded to note that in 'the domed buildings of Persia we see the Byzantine arch still at work'.[13] What pleased Wright so much was that these domes managed to resist their outward thrust without the need for concealed chains or a corniced ring beam. He remarked approvingly that their 'masonry dome was erected as an organic part of the whole structure'.[14]

Defeat at the hands of the Crusaders in the 11th century, and later attack from Mongols to the east in the 13th century, made Arabians withdraw into a period of comparative 'retreat and isolation'.[15] However, another great Muslim empire, this time founded by Turkish warrior princes, was begun in the 13th century and conquered the last remnants of the Byzantine Empire before proceeding to annex Persia and the coastal Arabian states. For Arabians, the four centuries of Ottoman rule were doubly disappointing, since they had lost their status as rulers of the Islamic world and Arabic culture was no longer seen as dominant.[16]

A number of 'orientalist' narratives emerged during the 19th century as European empires sought to justify their own expansionist agenda in the Middle East. As noted by Edensor, 'the exotic remains tethered to those consistent themes that emerged under colonial conditions, an imagined, alluring non-Western alterity embodied in styles of clothing, music, dance, art, architecture, and food'.[17] This confrontation between western and Ottoman cultures propagated the supposed 'otherness' of the region, with Sir Richard Burton being a prototypical example of a colonial adventurer whose roles included those of 'explorer, spy, linguist, sexologist, translator and a writer.'[18] In addition, Burton was responsible for translating and compiling *The Arabian Nights: Tales from a Thousand and One Nights*, thereby transplanting into the minds of millions of children (such as Frank Lloyd Wright) the mythical world of Aladdin and his Genie. Other colonial writers such as Gustav Flaubert contributed to the exotic perception of the region; nowadays he would be regarded as a predatory sex tourist. T. E. Lawrence originally set out as an archaeologist to survey a number of Crusader castles in the region, but his mapping and linguistic skills made him an ideal British spy and leader of the Arab counter-insurgency against the Ottoman Empire in 1916–1918. Again the colonial script of *Seven Pillars of Wisdom* and *Revolt in the Desert* was the basis for *Lawrence of Arabia* (1962), a later iconic film that only embellished the myth.[19] Finally, Wilfred Thesiger travelled extensively in the Empty Quarter of the Arabia Pensinsula, documenting the vanishing life of the Bedouins in his book, *Arabian Sands* (1959); in doing so, he confronted the colonial legacy that was increasingly commodifying the region by recording the traditional everyday activities of desert dwellers.

There was also a sense of 'orientalism' within western architectural culture. Frampton identifies the importance of *The Grammar of Ornament* (1856) by Owen Jones in disseminating 'other' cultures to a wider audience of aesthetic thinkers and producers. The book was hence a 'transcultural, imperialist sweep through the world of ornament demonstrated by implication the relative inferiority of the European/Greco-Roman/medieval legacy compared with the riches of the Orient'.[20] Furthermore, there was a link from Owen Jones to Louis Sullivan and Frank Lloyd Wright as Celtic 'outsiders' who 'searched for an "other" culture with which to overcome the spiritual bankruptcy of the West', given that it was commonly believed that Celtic art had originated in the Middle East.[21] According to Frampton, Sullivan and Wright shared an 'implicit theology of their work … a conscious fusion of nature and culture'.[22] He noted that 'in Islamic architecture, the written, the woven, and the tectonically inscribed are frequently fused together', and indeed Wright's work sought such an integrated ideal.[23] Frampton concludes by claiming that Wright's 'text-tile tectonic' was to reach its pinnacle in the layout of Broadacre City, 'an infinite "oriental rug" as a cross-cultural, ecological tapestry writ large, as an oriental paradise garden combined with the Cartesian grid of the occident.'[24]

KUWAIT'S BACKGROUND

Despite the importance of Failaka Island in the history of the Persian Gulf, it is known that Kuwait City – which sits opposite Failaka on the mainland – developed separately and also much later on. Its name was derived from the Arabic for 'a small fort'.[25] In 1756, a Danish explorer reported that Kuwait City had 10,000 inhabitants 'who live on the produce of peals and fishing', with a fleet of 800 sailing boats.[26] By the late-18th century the British were active as maritime invaders keen to protecting their emerging Indian interests, focussing on trade with Basra in southern Iraq. In 1859, Kuwait had signed a pact with the Ottoman Empire, but were somewhat wary of the latter's power; thus in 1899 it signed a new treaty with Britain which gave greater protection to Kuwait's sea trade.

The defeat in the First World War of Germany and fellow Axis powers led to the break-up of the already declining Ottoman Empire. Mansfield identifies two contrary trends in the following years among Arabs: on the one hand, there was desire to develop a sense of territorial nationalism to support the countries newly freed from Ottoman rule, and on the other a contrasting demand for ethnic 'protection and unity', particularly in light of the emerging Zionist movement in Palestine.[27] Whilst Kuwait's borders were already fairly defined and strongly supported by Britain by this point, its newer neighbours tended to consist of amalgamations of different tribes and alliances within national borders which had simply never existed previously. These new nations – Iraq, Iran and Saudi Arabia – had been engineered largely by the British Empire as an attempt to dilute Arab influence, a solution which unsurprisingly has not led to long-term peace in the region. As early as 1920, Kuwait came under attack from neighbouring tribes, requiring the building of a new city wall to control the access to its capital from the west. There have been three successive Gulf conflicts rooted in the contradictory aspirations of separate national identity and the concept of a pan-Arabic state. Kuwait has suffered badly in all three conflicts, being occupied by Saddam Hussein's Iraqi forces in 1990–1991 under the premise of creating a wider Ba'athist Arabic movement.[28] A coalition of forces led by 'Pax America' liberated Kuwait, and, conveniently for the western powers, managed to restore the agreed boundaries and the all-important distribution of oil reserves.

Oil had been first discovered in Kuwait in 1934, but it was not commercially extracted until after the Second World War. Kuwait City had hitherto been an excellent example of an integrated desert settlement with a protective outer wall, an organically ordered town plan formed by layers of accretion, close-knit low-rise buildings with narrow lanes, and a visibly democratic city of generally no higher than two-storey structures. However, by 1950 Kuwait City's population had leapt to 150,000, of which almost a half were now immigrant workers, and traffic congestion was becoming acute. This led the Kuwaiti government in 1951 to commission Minoprio, Spencely and Macfarlane to prepare a master-plan. This new vision for Kuwait City was based on the British New Town precedent, with a comprehensive road network, clear zoning for different uses, and a protective 'green belt'. The British firm had recently completed the plan for Crawley in West Sussex, with Minoprio admitting: 'We didn't know anything much about the Muslim world and the Kuwaitis wanted … a new city'.[29] Gardiner noted that the proposal 'was primarily a road plan – [which] arose from the five gateways of the wall'.[30] Or as Jamal wrote acidly in the Architects' Journal in 1973, this first master-plan 'was simply the imposition of western technology onto an established Arab society'.[31]

Kuwait City gained independence along with the rest of the country in 1961, and its urban growth continued; by 1970 the population had soared to 733,000, of which only 47 per cent were Kuwaiti. A second master-plan was commissioned, this time from another British practice, Colin Buchanan and Partners.[32] However, neither the design process nor the resulting master-plan proved at all successful, given that indigenous Kuwaiti architects and planners were by now beginning to question the wisdom of bringing in foreign consultants. The debate highlighted a growing sense of cultural confrontation. In the same *Architects' Journal* article, when discussing the second master-plan, Jamal identified the major flaws in western thinking about urbanisation in the Persian Gulf:

> 'Rapid urban growth resulting from implementation of the plan will speed
> up material changes in the society without compatible cultural change.
> Traditional Kuwaiti character will not be reflected in the new urban and physical
> environment, while the traditional environment will deteriorate further ...
> Generally speaking, Kuwait should not assume that economic growth equals, or
> automatically brings, personal social happiness. The Kuwaitis' way of life should
> not be geared to consumption or wasteful living as seen in the West.[33]

Colin Buchanan's firm published a subsequent rebuttal in the *Architects' Journal* in May 1974.[34] However, a third article on the subject in the same magazine, published in October 1974, dismissed their master-plan as a failure. It noted that 'all copies of the plan have been lying locked up ... for the past three years' on the grounds that it couldn't be understood, approved or thus implemented by Kuwait City's planning authority.[35] Additional master-plans were prepared by western consultants in 1977 and 1983, and then by the Kuwait Municipality itself in 1993. The most recent master-plan, drawn up in 2003, was produced in collaboration between the Kuwait Engineering Group and Colin Buchanan and Partners.[36] Despite all these official efforts towards planning, however, the destruction of the old building fabric in Kuwait City simply continued – and hence the passionate cry for cultural reflection by Jamal in the mid-1970s was never heeded.

ARRIVAL

Using the internet I had booked a room at the Ghani Palace Hotel by Saleh Al Mutawa, which opened in 2002 (see Plate 3). The hotel is modelled on a conventional Yemeni town house, with whitewashed walls, insets of coloured glass, intricately detailed timber screens and balconies, and projecting timber joists and water spouts. Inside, the hotel's thin atrium made allusion to a traditional alleyway, with an open arcade of shops and projecting balconies giving another Arabic cultural representation. A local expert, Yasser Mahgoub, told me that Al Mutawa's work embodies 'Kuwaiti traditional architecture in his buildings', while also pointing out that of course such forms are also part of a wider Arabic consciousness.[37] From my hotel room on the sixth floor, I could see Kuwait City in its confrontation with the Persian Gulf – albeit with a six-lane motorway mediating the connection as a legacy of a city re-designed for the highway.

After a short rest, I met with Omar Kattab at the University of Kuwait in the afternoon, and we discussed a number of ideas concerning Frank Lloyd Wright. It seems that although Wright's projects for (adjacent) Iraq and Iran are well known within the Gulf region, there isn't any record of him ever visiting Kuwait,

3.2   Ghani Palace Hotel (2002) by Saleh Al Mutawa

3.3   Interior atrium of the Ghani Palace Hotel

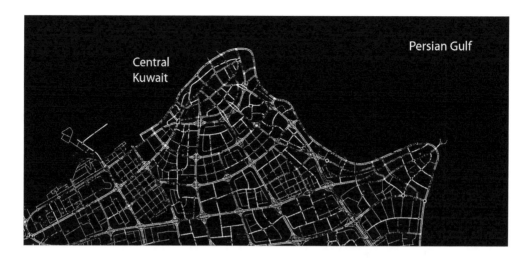

3.4   Sketch map of the road network of Kuwait City

3.5   View of the skyline of Kuwait City

3.6   View of remnant of old fort wall on Al Soor Street

or having designed anything in the city. Undeterred, we went for a drive towards the city centre, progressing down one of the main radial thoroughfares. At one set of traffic lights, we paused to view the impressive neo-capitalist skyline of tower blocks gleaming against the blue sky. Kostof argues that the skyline acts as the 'shorthand of urban identity … when the city centre ends up an aggregate of tall office buildings, we recognise that the city image has succumbed to the advertising urges of private enterprise.'[38] Further on, we slowed down at Al Soor Street, the site of the former city wall, where a remnant from the 1920s fort now lies within a roundabout. The mythical 'green belt' of the 1950s Minoprio master-plan was in reality a strip of desert, with little planting or shade, just a memory of the old lost town.

IDENTITY

In the evening I caught a taxi to the northern edge of Kuwait to visit the Water Towers, completed in 1979. I travelled along the Arabian Gulf Road and experienced the two identities of Kuwait, the dusty oil-rich commercial city to the south and the hazy blue waters of the Persian Gulf to the north. I was impressed by the futuristic design of the Water Towers. It is claimed that the design was inspired by an Arab perfume burner with a long tall neck and spherical reservoir for its base; this seems a plausible enough connection, and now it would seem that perfume burners are being made in the image of Kuwait Towers! It is also a design that clearly fulfils the role of international icon, and yet is immensely practical. At 180m in height the observation tower was the tallest structure in

3.7   Kuwait Water
Towers (1979) by
VVB, a Swedish
engineering
company

the Gulf region for several decades after its completion in 1977. Kultermann has commented on this progression from architectural function to cultural expression: 'the water towers in … Kuwait … are significant signs of a shift from technology and its dominating negative impact on the human environment towards a positive use for necessities, entertainment and beautification.'[39] I entered the larger of the two towers and got into a golden lift carriage which took me up 120m to the observation level, which was entirely glazed within a triangulated space frame. From this level I could see the whole of Kuwait City and much of the Persian Gulf beyond. It was twilight and city was now illuminated by its tall office towers. Being the festival of Ramadan, the fading light also brought respite for residents from the day's fast, and at 82m I too found a welcoming restaurant serving a hot buffet. Predictably, most of the diners were well-dressed Kuwaitis whilst most of the servants were Indian or Filipino.

Gardiner identified an 'architectural plan' for Kuwait City from the 1960s that was jointly directed by two architects: the Englishman, Leslie Martin, and the Italian, Franco Albini.[40] Essentially they wished to give the city a stronger architectural identity, and so they asked four internationally-known architectural practices to analyse the existing city plan and work up designs for specific case studies. Together, they summarised their key architectural principles under five points: maintaining the waterfront as a recreational area; turning the area around the Seif Palace into a special historical site; reintroducing residential areas to the city; preserving and expanding the traditional *souks* and bazaars; and maintaining the old city wall as a 'green belt' zone.[41] The design by Alison and Peter Smithson for the Kuwait Government Buildings was a poetic vision and also critique of the new architecture within the city and the Persian Gulf generally.

3.8   Viewing platform in the Kuwait Water Towers

They proposed instead an open urban fabric based on a gridded 'mat' that was orientated towards existing mosques, low buildings and overhanging roofs to provide shade for pedestrians beneath.[42] The dramatic rise in oil prices after the 1973–1974 'Oil Crisis' boosted Kuwait's income further, allowing a number of the case studies to be progressed – but not sadly the Smithson's rather intimate proposal.

Frank Lloyd Wright's unbuilt project for a 'Cultural Quarter' in Baghdad (1957–1959) represented a singular vision for the identity of that city. Although had been invited with other modernist 'masters' to participate in Baghdad's development, Wright assumed the mantle of cultural arbiter as his original brief for an Opera House turned into a full-blown Arabian myth. When introducing his scheme in a 1957 issue of *Architectural Forum*, Wright proclaimed 'that a great culture deserves not only an architecture of its time, but of its own'.[43] Rhetorically he cited the ancient cities of Mesopotamia and Babylon, the original Garden of Eden, the circular 'City of Peace' by al-Mansur, and the imaginary court of Harun ar-Rashid in *The Arabian Nights*. No doubt these cultural references pleased the regime of King Faysal II, a Hashemite ruler who was not even an Iraqi. The centrepiece of the 'Cultural Quarter' was to be the Grand Opera and Civic Auditorium; it was based on the intersection of two circles, one for a revolving stage and other for an auditorium with 1,600 seats to hold an opera performance, or an additional 3,700 seats for 'conventions or patriotic celebrations'.[44] Wright designed a symbolically expressive crescent-arch to support the proscenium, which was then to be 'decorated with metal-sculptured scenes from *A Thousand and One Nights*'.[45] And at roof level, directly above the centre of the auditorium was to be the figure of 'Aladdin [Wright] and his wonderful lamp'.

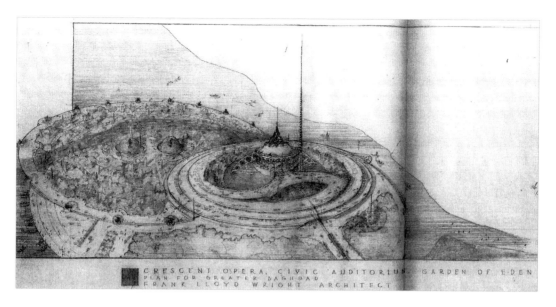

CRESCENT OPERA, CIVIC AUDITORIUM, GARDEN OF EDEN
PLAN FOR GREATER BAGHDAD
FRANK LLOYD WRIGHT ARCHITECT

3.9   Crescent Opera House for Baghdad by Frank Lloyd Wright (1957–1959)

The modern-day implications of Wright's form-making are not too hard to spot. In the Gulf State of Abu Dhabi, part of the United Arab Emirates, the Saadiyat Island scheme attempts to create a 'cultural quarter' for the 21st century with four contemporary masters of the architectural universe: Frank Gehry, Jean Nouvel, Tadao Ando and Zaha Hadid. Interestingly, Hadid was born in Baghdad, and she was charged with producing a new Performing Arts Centre in Abu Dhabi as another expression of western culture – Arabian states seemingly can't get enough opera! Hadid says that her Performing Arts Centre's 'organic design will have five theatres, a music hall, opera house, drama theatre and a flexible theatre with a combined seating capacity of 6,300.'[46] Furthermore, she explains the concept as 'a growing organism that sprouts a network of successive branches … [and] performance spaces, which spring from the structure like fruits on a vine.'[47] However, as Charles Jencks commented on the Baghdad project: 'Wright loses control of his geometry and allows it to contradict function, material, construction, structure, freedom [and] … organic architecture.'[48] Likewise the gratuitous form-making of Hadid may be considered sensual and 'organically' inspired, but it also lacks functional and material integrity. For Wright, his 'Cultural Quarter' was intended as a continuation of imagined cities from the past, whereas Hadid's scheme engages with one city's aspirations for the future.

I took a short walk along Arabian Gulf Street at the end of the day, with the heat now gradually waning, to take a closer look at the impressive National Assembly Building (1978–1982), by the esteemed Danish architect, Jorn Utzon (see Plate 4). Kuwait did not dream of chimerical opera houses but rather built a National Assembly to project a progressive and democratic identity for the country and the region. Historically, an informal means of democracy had existed alongside the ruling Kuwaiti family of Al Sabah, with the local merchant class forming a 'majlis, or advisory council' to discuss affairs of state.[49] But this delicate balance or power was altered significantly once oil revenue began to be directed solely through the Emir and his ruling family. Consequently, a quasi-welfarist model was established in the 1950s to try to redistribute some of the oil wealth by building new schools and improving the infrastructure. As noted earlier, this process only caused resentment among Kuwaitis, and so they demanded greater participation in government as a reaffirmation of their national identity.[50] Kuwait duly became independent in 1961, with the Emir as a constitutional monarch, thus establishing a paternalistic ruling dynasty since copied in other Gulf States. In 1962, Kuwait's first elections were held for its 50 seat National Assembly, which was charged with checking legislation proposed by the Prime Minister. However, this 'democratic' Assembly has had fitful existence, having been disbanded by the Emir on a number of occasions.

Utzon's design for the National Assembly sought to reflect a number of Arabic features, and yet Vale notes a number of contradictions, For example; is the bold sweeping entry canopy just a simplistic western reference to an Arabic tent?[51] Or is it a subtle acknowledgement of the Emir's Bedouin past? But then again, tents are transitory elements, usually black or brown in colour, not a ponderous white concrete construction.[52] Yet within the National Assembly, gradual change has been achieved: in 2005 women were allowed to vote; in 2006 the roles of Crown Prince and Prime Minister were separated; and in 2009 the first three women Members of Parliament were elected. The voting base has expanded, but even so only about 10 per cent of Kuwait's population of c.3.5 million is allowed to vote. The recent 'Arab Spring' resulted in a number of demonstrations with some calling for a new Prime Minister, although not a change of regime, and Bedouins called for

3.10   National Assembly Building (1978–1982) by Jorn Utzon

improved rights.[53] The protests were appeased by legislators who promised to look again at civil rights, so seemingly democracy does function within Kuwait.

Interestingly, Utzon's original design for the National Assembly Building had a mosque placed beside the main entry, thus giving the sweeping entrance canopy far more relevance as a place of congregation. But now the reconceived 'Bedouin tent' is merely a 'monumental carport ... [where] leaders meet their chauffeurs.'[54] Just a short walk along the Arabian Gulf Road are the Seif Palace, Foreign Ministry, Grand Mosque and Stock Exchange. The old Seif Palace was built in the early years of the 20th century with a striking neo-Arabic watch tower, and its neighbouring replacement looks a rather fascinating low structure with abundant Islamic surface decoration, although I couldn't get to see much further, since it was as heavily fortified as other public institutions here. It is disappointing that these state buildings are so detached from each other and from ordinary Kuwaitis. Any future uprising in Kuwait would need to reclaim the road, a symbol of the city, and a means of divide-and-rule. When I got to the Foreign Ministry, however, the guards outside were preparing a small feast because the sun was now setting, and they kindly offered me to join them for a drink. So I shared some Vimto and dates, and we chatted briefly, but since my Arabic is not that good, my observations were mostly restricted to the climate – i.e. complaining that I found it very hot. They wanted to know where I came from and whether I liked Kuwait, before asking: 'Do you like Muslims?'[55] It was a rather personal enquiry, but one that reflects an ongoing sense of tension between western countries and the Middle East.

BEYOND THE CITY CENTRE

The next day I met with Yasser Mahgoub, who works at Kuwait University, at the classically inspired Central Mall which sits next to the Ghani Palace Hotel. We then drove together to the Tareq Rajab Museum, passing a number of water towers along the 5th Circular Road: the towers were designed as giant representations of palm trees, often grouped together as if to form an oasis. It is a brilliant idea for retaining water, creating a genuine architectural presence in their conception and scale, and I was

thrilled to see them next to the roadside. Gardiner has claimed that there is a passing reference to Wright's dendriform (tree-like) columns in the Johnson Wax Administration Building, which is true enough – except that Wright's columns had pin joints at their base and so would topple over in Kuwait![56] The basement museum is located in the Jabriya district, on Street 5/Block 12, and we got lost for a short time whilst negotiating that suburb. We discussed Wright's legacy as we walked around the museum, and I asked about why his appeal in the Gulf region seems so strong

3.12 View from car of suburban dwellings in Kuwait City

> **Gwyn Lloyd Jones:** *Do you think that the planning outside the city centre here, with its dispersed motorised suburbs, bears any relation to Wright's Broadacre City?*
>
> **Yasser Mahgoub:** *No, not at all; here the city planning was based on the Garden City typology, and not Broadacre. But I think that the Mile High Tower*

3.13 Tareq Rajab Museum

by Wright was a concept that has caught on in the Gulf with the Burj Dubai [Khalifa], and now there is a 1001-metre tower proposed for the new Silk City scheme [across the bay from Kuwait City]. The size of that tower is inspired by the 1001 Tales from the Arabian Nights.

Gwyn Lloyd Jones: *That's really fascinating. Wright talked a great deal about The Arabian Nights while doing his Baghdad project, so there is clearly a link.*[57]

Most of the suburban villas that I passed belonged to Kuwaiti nationals, as only they are allowed to own property. The houses displayed a number of styles: Arabic, classical Palladian, quasi-modernist. Given that the inspiration for expanding Kuwait City was Britain's post-war New Towns, with their car-based principles – as Fraser shows, heavily influenced by America – then it is this model which can be seen all around.[58] Kuwait's capital was developed as a typical 'City on the Highway' possessing all of the 'four main foundations' for a motorised suburb: new roads to open up more land, zoned land uses, government-provided mortgages, and a population boom.[59] Wright often eulogised the virtues of America's road network, declaring that 'along these grand roads as through veins and arteries comes and goes the throng of building and living in the Broadacre City of the Twentieth Century.'[60] His vision for Broadacre was based on a decentralised mode of settlement that was part-prophetic and part-trend planning of the kind which already existed in Los Angeles in the 1920s and 1930s. As such, it represented a particularly American viewpoint about travel, democracy, freedom, and architecture's role within all those things. Wright proclaimed that the city of the future could be 'everywhere and nowhere'[61] – and I would contend that Kuwait is now similarly affected by possessing a suburban condition lacking any identity specific to its geographical location or environmental conditions.

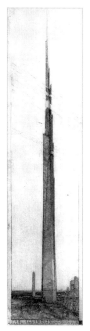

Frank Lloyd Wright is also undoubtedly prophetic of the present desire to build ever-taller towers. As Yasser Mahgoub had told me, some developers in Kuwait have for a few years now been planning a 1001-metre-high tower – designed by another American architect, Eric Kuhne – while in Saudi Arabia a genuine Mile High Tower is apparently being proposed on the Red Sea, near to the city of Jeddah. Not far away in Dubai, the Burj Khalifa Tower already stands at over 820m tall, the ultimate expression to date of global identity branding. It too was designed by a global American architectural practice, SOM, built by migrant labourers from poor emerging nations, and constructed in the Middle East for offices and apartments that may well be occupied by a multitude of nationalities. It's a contemporary Tower of Babel built on sand! Having the world's tallest building carries a certain status that Dubai obviously craves, but what else does the tower tell us about architectural identity? The Burj Khalifa is certainly similar to

3.14 Mile-High Tower by Frank Lloyd Wright (1956)

Wright's own scheme for a Mile High Tower (1956), with its triangulated plan, diminishing mass and stepped profile. It is said that Wright's initial brief had been to design a television antennae, but that he had developed it into a tower that could contain 'all Illinois state government offices and consolidate commercial, governmental, and civic functions'.[62] Furthermore, Wright claimed it 'would mop up what now remains of urbanism to leave us free to do Broadacre'.[63] I would suggest that the tower was a typical Wright edifice, although pushed to what to him must have seemed like the ultimate dimension of one mile, and it was conceived more for its imagery then its function. Interestingly enough, the novelist A.S. Byatt writes that '... the *Thousand and One Nights* is itself a symbol of infinity ... the addition of the extra 'one' to the round thousand ... suggests a way to mathematical infinity.'[64] Yet again the links between Wright and Aladdin seem rather close.

ALADDIN'S HOMECOMING

In the evening, Salmiya was busy with shoppers and a young crowd of Kuwaitis relaxing in the coffee shops, as a 21st-century *diwaniya* (gathering). It offered me a chance to reflect on my investigation into the influence of Frank Lloyd Wright. Kuwait has proven to be a resilient and progressive force within the Persian Gulf region, yet its precarious geo-political situation seems to dwell on its psyche – it appears to be a city on the edge of a nervous breakdown. Contrary to Wright's views, I would advocate that the disjointed city centre needs to be reclaimed through infill spaces that connect better to one another and to the Gulf coastline; no doubt Wright would have advocated instead a relentless suburban existence into the desert. Kuwait's discreet and egalitarian development should continue to be its focus, with wider reforms to embrace its enlarged population.

My own short trip to Kuwait and then along the western coast of the Persian Gulf has itself helped to contribute to the myth of Frank Lloyd Wright within a part of the world where he attempted to secure his legacy with a truly fantastical vision for Baghdad. As Frampton observes, there was a universal tendency in Wright's work, and he definitely did not adapt his architecture to engage with different environments. Instead, the failed scheme for an Opera House in Baghdad was realised in Arizona, making the latter Aladdin's second home! Yet, Wright's idea for developing cultural identity through architecture was prophetic of what is now being undertaken in the Persian Gulf. The mythical paradise based on an idealised Broadacre suburb has possibly reached its ultimate conclusion with the Palm Jumeirah in Dubai, but that reality is an exclusive society not a democratic one. And the technological and financial commitment to build a Mile High Tower is now only being bandied around the oil-and-gas-rich Persian Gulf. But it would be a purely symbolic edifice and its function would be secondary: the ultimate myth of eternity.

NOTES

1   Frank Lloyd Wright, as quoted in Bruce Pfeiffer (ed.), *The Essential Frank Lloyd Wright: Critical Writings on Architecture* (Princeton, NJ: Princeton University Press, 2008), p. 283.

2   Frank Lloyd Wright, *An Autobiography* (London: Faber and Faber, 1945), p. 38.

3   Donald W. Hoppen, *The Seven Ages of Frank Lloyd Wright* (Santa Barbara, CA: Carpa Press, 1993), p. 43.

4   Ronald Lewcock & Zahra Freeth, *Traditional Architecture in Kuwait and the Northern Gulf* (London: Art and Archaeology Research Papers, 1978), p. 12.

5   Peter Mansfield, *A History of the Middle East* (London: Penguin, 2003), p. 6.

6   Ibid., p. 13.

7   Ibid., p. 14.

8   Ernst Grube & George Michell, *Architecture of the Islamic World: its History and Social Meaning* (London: Thames & Hudson, 1978), pp. 10–13.

9   Ibid., pp. 12–13.

10 Jonathan Lipman's chapter in Robert McCarter (ed.), *On and By Frank Lloyd Wright: A Primer of Architectural Principles* (London: Phaidon, 2005), pp. 264–285; Kevin Nute, *Frank Lloyd Wright and Japan* (London: Chapman Hall, 1993), pp. 40–41.

11 Quoted in Pfeiffer (ed.), *The Essential Frank Lloyd Wright*, p. 282.

12 Ibid.

13 Ibid.

14 Ibid.

15 Mansfield, *A History of the Middle East*, p. 21.

16 Ibid., p. 26.

17 Tim Edensor's chapter in Joan Ockman & Salomon Frausto (eds), *Architourism: Authentic, Escapist, Exotic and Spectacular* (Munich: Prestel, 2005), p. 98.

18 Author profile in Richard Burton, *To the Holy Shrines* (London: Penguin, 1853/2007), p. i.

19 David Lean, *Lawrence of Arabia* (London: Horizon Pictures, 1962).

20 Kenneth Frampton's chapter in Ockman & Frausto (eds), *Architourism*, p. 173.

21 Ibid., p. 174.

22 Ibid., p. 176.

23 Ibid.

24 Ibid., p. 189.

25 Lewcock & Freeth, *Traditional Architecture in Kuwait*, p. 12.

26 Ibid.

27 Mansfield, *A History of the Middle East*, p. 229.

28 Ibid., pp. 229–230.

29 Stephen Gardiner, *Kuwait: The Making of a City* (London: Longman, 1983), p. 35.

30   Ibid., p. 37.

31   Karim Jamal, 'Kuwait: A Salutary Tale', *The Architects' Journal*, vol. 158, no. 50 (12 December 1973): 1453.

32   Ibid., 1454.

33   Ibid., 1456.

34   Colin Buchanan, 'Planning: Kuwait', *The Architects' Journal*, vol. 159, no. 21 (22 May 1974): 1131–1132.

35   Ghazi Sultan, 'Kuwait', *The Architects' Journal*, vol. 160, no. 40 (2 October 1974): 792–794.

36   Yasser Mahgoub, 'Globalization and the built environment in Kuwait', *Habitat International*, vol. 28, no. 5 (2004): 509.

37   Ibid., 514.

38   Spiro Kostof, *The City Shaped: Urban Patterns and Meanings through History* (London: Thames & Hudson, 1991), p. 296.

39   Udo Kultermann, 'Water for Arabia', *Domus*, no. 595 (June 1976): 6.

40   Gardiner, *Kuwait*, p. 67.

41   'Proposals for Restructuring Kuwait', *Architectural Review*, vol. 156, no. 931 (September 1974): 180–181.

42   Ibid., 183–190.

43   Anon., 'Wright to Design Baghdad Opera', *Architectural Forum*, vol. 106, no. 3 (March 1957): 89.

44   Ibid., 93.

45   Ibid.

46   Francesco Poli, 'The museums of the island of happiness: Saadiyat Island, Abu Dhabi', special issue on 'Performing Museums', *Lotus*, no. 134 (May 2008): 6.

47   Ibid.

48   Charles Jencks, *Modern Movements in Architecture* (London: Penguin, 1973/85), p. 137.

49   Rosemary Said Zahlan, *The Making of the Modern Gulf States: Kuwair, Bahrain, Qatar, the United Arab Emirates and Oman (2nd Edition)* (Reading: Garner Publishing, 1989/98), p. 34.

50   Ibid., pp. 42–44.

51   Lawrence Vale, *Architecture, Power, and National Identity* (New Haven, CT: Yale University Press, 1992), p. 224.

52   Ibid.

53   Mark Tran, 'Arab League states: a recent history of protests', *The Guardian* website, 22 March 2011, http://www.guardian.co.uk/world/2011/mar/22/arab-league-states (accessed 27 October 2011).

54   Vale, *Architecture, Power and National Identity*, p. 231.

55   Conversation between author and guards outside the Foreign Ministry, Kuwait City, 20 September 2009.

56   Gardiner, *Kuwait*, p. 88.

57   Yasser Mahgoub, interview with the author in the Tareq Rajab Museum, Kuwait City, 18
     September 2009.

58   Murray Fraser (with Joe Kerr), *Architecture and the 'Special Relationship': The
     American Influence on Post-war British Architecture* (London/New York: Routledge,
     2007), pp. 148–183; see also Gardiner, *Kuwait*, p. 37.

59   Peter Hall, *Cities of Tomorrow* (Oxford: Blackwell Publishing, 2005), p. 316.

60   Frank Lloyd Wright, 'Disappearing City' (1932), in Bruce Pfeiffer (ed.), *The Collected
     Writings of Frank Lloyd Wright: Vol. 2, 1930–1932* (New York: Rizzoli, 1992), p. 94.

61   Ibid., p. 85.

62   'Frank Lloyd Wright: Selected Projects, Mile High Tower', Bilbao Guggenheim website,
     http://www.guggenheimbilbao.es/microsites/frank_lloyd_wright/secciones/frank_
     lloyd_wright/proyectos_seleccionados/torre_oficinas_mile_high.php?idioma=en
     (accessed 10 November 2009).

63   Frank Lloyd Wright, as quoted in Brendan Gill, *Many Masks: A Life of Frank Lloyd Wright*
     (London: Heinemann, 1988), p. 477.

64   A.S. Byatt (Dame Antonia Susan Duffy), *The Arabian Nights: Tales from a Thousand and
     One Nights* (New York: Modern Library, 2001), p. xiii.

4

Dammam, Saudi Arabia

Mashary Al-Naim

The Dammam Metropolitan area is located in eastern Saudi Arabia along the Gulf seashore, in the most oil-rich region in the world. Today it comprises a number of cities, including Dammam, Khobar, Dhahran and Qatif, as well as a cluster of smaller towns and villages. This new urban conglomeration sits on the coast just to the north-west of the island archipelago which forms Bahrain. Indeed, Dammam itself was only formed in 1923 when a group from the Al-Dawaser tribe decided to move from Bahrain to the mainland, where King Abdulaziz allowed them to settle. They split into two groups and created separate fishing villages in Dammam and adjacent Khobar. These two villages began with slow development until 1938 when Saudi Arabia started exporting oil in commercial quantities (the county's formation into a modern kingdom had only happened in 1932).

As a result, the Dammam region witnessed continuous urban growth in the second half of the 20th century, even if initially it wasn't enough to bring all the urban centres together. Just two decades ago, the cities and towns in the region still remained scattered and a sense of urban connectivity did not really exist. The term 'Dammam Metropolitan' has therefore emerged due to the huge developments that have taken place since the 1990s, especially after the municipality decided to build a unified seafront along the whole shoreline. Now it is difficult for anyone to identify the boundaries between Dammam and its neighbouring centres: the area has become a large urban mass connected by major highways and real estate projects which all make it look and feel as if it is just one big city (see Plate 5).

The urban structure of the area can thus be considered as young, because all of its cities – excluding Hofuf and Qatif (along with a few older villages) – only really got started in the fourth and fifth decades of the 20th century. Indeed, it could be said that the origin of contemporary settlement in this part of Saudi Arabia stems from when Aramco (the Arabian-American Oil Company, now Saudi Aramco) built its initial housing projects in 'camps' for oil workers in the eastern part of the country from 1938–1944; the first ever was in Dhahran, close to Dammam.[1] These estates introduced for the first time a new concept of space and a new image of the Saudi home. It is possible to say that this early intervention had a deep, if not immediate, effect on the native population: it certainly made them question what they knew and how they should behave in their domestic environments. In other words, this initial change can be seen as the first motive for social resistance to new urban forms and imagery within the contemporary Saudi built environment. We should also mention here the impact of the railway which was constructed in 1951 to connect Dammam with Riyadh through Al-Hassa. That project was crucial because it encouraged many people from central Saudi Arabia to move to the under-populated Dammam region and build up their businesses there.

The significant impact of this experience presented itself in conflicts between the old and new in local Dammam society. Threats from interfering outside elements to social and physical identity created for the first time in Saudi Arabia a social reaction towards the physical environment. The conflict between traditional cultural values and the introduction of western forms and images was limited at the beginning of the period of modernisation; indigenous people followed what they already knew and tried to continue to implement it in their daily lives, including their homes. However, this emerging contrast between traditional images and newer westernised images in the minds of local people can also be considered the beginning of important physical and social changes in the Saudi built environment.

This chapter therefore tells the story of development in this eastern part of Saudi Arabia. Its main goal is to investigate how urban identity in the region has gone through transition during recent decades, and how this has influenced the 'acceptance' and 'use' of urban structures. The text here will concentrate on people's lifestyles within their home environment in relation to the wider transformation of urban structures. For this purpose, I have for many years been conducting fieldwork studies to trace urban changes in Dammam and find out how people respond to them. Social, economic and political changes must all be seen as major factors in the analysis of the impact of urban change on cultural identity.

4.1 Dwellings in the Dhahran 'camp' formed by the Aramco oil company

4.2   House in the Dhahran 'camp'

4.3   House in the Dhahran 'camp'

FORMATION OF THE 'DAMMAM METROPOLITAN' REGION

The first indication of a conflict between local culture and western culture can be ascribed to Solon T. Kimball, who visited the Aramco headquarters in 1956. He described how the senior staff members at the (American) 'camp' in Dhahran were completely imported from United States:

> *Not one westerner would have difficulty in identifying the senior staff "camp" as a settlement built by Americans in our southwestern tradition of town planning. It is an area of single-story dwellings for employees and their families. Each house is surrounded by a small grassed yard usually enclosed by a hedge.*[2]

This American camp, intended for senior oil workers, and which introduced its own new spatial concepts, contrasted strongly with the surrounding home environments found in the existing old cities in the region, Hofuf and Qatif.

In face of such developments, native Saudi people still persisted with their own spatial concepts and images, tending to resist the imported ones. They considered the latter as strange things. Therefore, whenever Saudi workers and their relatives 'moved in, they took over any empty land available and erected basic shelters and fences of locally available material, separated from each other by narrow irregular footpaths.'[3] This created 'a community of mud-brick and timber houses, built in a traditional and comfortable way.'[4] During his visit in the mid-1950s, Kimball noticed this alternative community growing up, and described the Saudi camp built adjacent to the senior staff camp as 'neither planned nor welcomed … these settlements represent the attempt by Arabs to establish a type of community life with which they are familiar.' Kimball openly recognised the insistence of native people on their own identity through his description of the Saudi camp as 'an emerging indigenous community life.'[5]

4.4   General view of the city of Dammam

4.5   General view of the city of Khobar

We should mention here that in the first two decades of change a number of alterations appeared in local Saudi people's attitudes towards their homes. What Kimball observed was the stance of the native population at their first point of direct contact with western culture. Saudi people, at this stage, refused to accept change and simply stuck with what they knew. This is not to say that the new westernised images did not also influence people; however, they were still in the process of developing a new attitude towards how they lived in their homes. An attitude had not yet been formed to reflect just how deeply the new forms and images broke the old idea of the Saudi home.

The Saudi government and the Aramco oil company were not at all happy with the presence of the alternative traditional-style settlements in the oilfield areas.[6] Even as early as 1947 the government had asked Aramco, which employed American engineers and surveyors, to try to control the growth of the unwanted settlements. This led to the first planned cities in Saudi Arabia, carried out on a grid-iron pattern, in Dammam and Khobar.[7] The spatial concepts and building forms which were introduced into these two planned cities accelerated the impact of westernised modern architecture on local people, not just in these two new developments, but also in surrounding older cities in the Dammam region.

The main characteristics of urban development in Dammam and Khobar were, as noted, based on the western principles of grid-iron land subdivision. These two cities were divided into a number of almost-square blocks surrounded by wide streets, as a form of 'domino planning'. The blocks were generally around 40–60 metres in either direction, and in the city centre areas at least were orientated in a north-south direction. Both the new street pattern and structures built on them were totally new, and as such they shocked local people; yet at the same time it

4.6   Apartment block with shops below on King Saud Street, Dammam

4.7   Apartment block on King Saud Street

4.8   Close-up view of apartment balconies on King Saud Street

started a transformative urban era which led in time to complete urban and social change. The Saudi government allocated some entire blocks to extended families that moved into the new cities and built new neighbourhoods within the planned urban structure. It is difficult now to track precisely how the social urban identity of the new developments were formed, but what certainly happened is that a mix of old and new values and lifestyles came to be created in these areas. We can thus attribute the sense of urban identity of the Dammam Metropolitan region today to this formation of a modernised fabric from the late-1940s and 1950s.

As mentioned earlier, the new type of house that was built, which became widely known as a 'villa', was imported originally from western countries and built on oil bases. But it was a type which developed further in the 1950s when the Aramco Home Ownership Program compelled local Saudi workers to submit designs for their houses in order to qualify for a building loan from the company.[8] People had to rely upon Aramco's architects and engineers to design their new houses because there were so few architects in Saudi Arabia at that time.[9] In order to speed up the approval process, Aramco's architects and engineers developed several standard design alternatives for employees to choose from. However, all these designs adopted a style loosely described as the 'international Mediterranean detached house'.[10]

This hybrid kind of villa house soon spread into the two new planned cities in the eastern region, Dammam and Khobar, especially in neighbourhoods which constituted the original historic settlements.[11] To give one example, Al-Said has studied the growth of the old Al-Dawaser neighbourhood of Dammam.[12] He found that, between 1930 and 1970, this neighbourhood grew from 56 to 250 residential units, and that these were 'mostly typical courtyard residential units as a result of contentious house subdivision and room addition'.[13] The situation was similar in Khobar, where the house style was more influenced by the prevailing traditional styles in the region. So even though many modern developments appeared in these two planned cities due to Aramco's programmes in the 1950s and 1960s, many residents, especially in the older settlement areas, insisted on using a more traditional variant of the house form.[14]

It can be argued that Saudi people, in that period, were still strongly influenced by their previous cultural experience, and were able to express this loyalty very easily since the full force of modern building regulations was not yet being applied. This meant that people had greater flexibility to decide the form of their houses. It is important to note here that most Saudi Arabians still retained a strong connection with their social, physical and aesthetic traditions, all of which were then strongly reflected in their domestic environment.

The new architectural image that spread through the planned cities was mainly of concrete buildings with neat crisp facades and balconies. Three-, four- and five-storey buildings appeared rapidly on the main streets – such as King Khalid Street in Khobar and King Saud Street in Dammam – during the 1950s and 1960s. The new urban form was very striking to local people compared to what they had been used to in the older cities. Furthermore, from 1960 to 1980 an entire range of abstract westernised building forms was developed in the Dammam region, often for very commercial purposes. The urban and architectural developments of the time created a real crisis of architectural identity which became one of the main issues debated amongst Saudi intellectuals by the 1980s.

THE SPREAD OF A MODERN BUILT ENVIRONMENT

The desire to create a modern country in a short period of time therefore brought about total physical change to most Saudi cities.[15] As in other Middle Eastern countries, the process of modernisation in Saudi Arabia 'is largely physical and heavily imitative of the western model's external departments and lifestyles'.[16] This is today manifested in unified governmental planning policies throughout the Saudi kingdom. However, prior to the 1960s, most attempts to regulate and control the growth of Saudi cities were partial and had limited impact.[17] By 1960, however, the first proper building regulations were issued in the form of a circular by the Deputy Ministry of Interior for Municipalities.[18] This circular, as Al-Said mentions, was:

> … the turning point in Saudi Arabian contemporary built environment physical pattern and regulations. It required planning of the land, subdivision with cement poles, obtaining an approval for this from the municipality, prohibited further land subdivision, controlled the height of the buildings, the square ratio of the built [area], required set-backs, [and so on].[19]

Still, such regulations took a further fifteen years until they came to be regularly applied in all Saudi cities. This can be clearly seen in the configuration of the master-plans that were initiated for all Saudi regions between 1968 and 1978.[20]

One example was the first master-plan for Riyadh as executed by Constantinos Doxiadis from 1968–1973.[21] His scheme reinforced the existence of the set-back regulations and applied a rigid planning system similar to what had been used already in Dammam and Khobar. Doxiadis therefore confirmed the notion of the grid as the most desirable pattern to be followed, not just for the planning of Riyadh, but for all other cities in the country.

Despite the fact that the Saudi built environment witnessed the gradual imposition of tighter building regulations from the 1960s, their actual impact didn't at first really influence the forms of houses or their surrounding urban spaces. This was because the authorities had not as yet developed proper institutions to follow up on the regulations.[22] However, with the establishment of the Ministry of Municipal and Rural Affairs (MOMRA)[23] and the Real Estate Development Fund (REDF) in 1975, the Saudi government demonstrated that it was aware of the need to monitor the construction of private houses which benefited from state loans.[24] In practice, the strict application of the building regulations through such measures 'institutionalised' the hybridised villa as being the only acceptable house type in Saudi Arabia.[25]

We can also now see in retrospect that steps being taken by the Saudi government to control urban spread in the new planned cities of Dammam and Khobar led in 1975 to the commissioning of Candilis Metra International Consultants to update the proposals for the region. This entailed the reinforcement of the original grid-iron urban pattern, and sent a clear message to the population in the adjacent older cities, Hofuf and Qatif, that Dammam was now the 'free place' where they could acquire new lifestyles in a modern urban image. This led many people to move to newer areas to establish their own lives away from complicated traditional social values and ties. From 1975 through to 2000, constant waves of migrants from these surrounding cities and from different parts of Saudi Arabia brought in the people needed to occupy the growing mega-urban structure of the Dammam Metropolitan region.

It is important at this point to consider the position of Saudi people in relation to such rapid developments in the built environment. If we go back to the beginning of this period of change, we can argue that Aramco's oil bases in the eastern region, in general, and the company's home ownership programme, in particular, should be considered as the origin of the formal and cultural contradictions that appeared later in Saudi people's home environments. The housing style imposed by Aramco's programme from the 1950s continued to have a powerful impact through to the 1970s, especially once Saudi building regulations were working to support and indeed encourage it. This could be seen clearly by the fact that owning a new detached 'villa' in Saudi Arabia became an important social symbol of personal and social identity.[26] There was also a similar consolidation of building materials towards more western materials, as shown in the table opposite.

We can attribute this emergence of a new symbolic role for the villa-type house to the appearance of a substantial Saudi middle class in the 1950s. This class included a mixed group of people from all over the kingdom, but

Table 4.1   Construction materials used by Aramco's employees in 1962 and 1968[27]

Type of material (percentage)	1962	1968
Cement block	70.8	84.3
Mud brick	15.0	9.1
Barasti (palm leaves)	5.1	3.4
Tent	1.2	0
Furush (sea stone)	0.8	1.7
Company portable	0.4	0
Other (mostly timber)	6.7	1.5

Source: Mashary Al-Naim

in the main they were employees either of Aramco or the Saudi government. These people were characterised by their level of literacy and experience of modern materialist culture.[28] As a middle-class group, they 'brought about cultural contact between Saudi society and the Western world',[29] and tended to express their new-found status by residing in the latest dwelling type, i.e. the westernised villa.[30] Due to their greater contact with other cultures, members of the Saudi middle classes were strongly influenced by the villa-type housing which had spread throughout the Middle East during the colonial era, and which was thus associated with people at the highest levels of administration[31] (see Plate 6).

The villa hence represented an image of modernity, and Saudi middle-class attitudes were based on 'the stylistic association that "modern", as expressed in the modern villa style, is "good", by virtue of being modern'.[32] The villa's ability to present a sense of individual identity and originality through the seeming uniqueness of design may also have led to its rise in popularity, given that the conformist habits of traditional society were beginning to be seen as 'backward'. In this mindset, any statement about individualism was regarded as 'modern' and therefore intrinsically 'good'. Jomah has noted the sense of formal individualism that distinguished house design in the cities of Mecca, Jeddah and Medina from the mid-20th century onwards. He considers these styles to be representative of a shift from a 'tradition-directed' to a 'self-directed' pattern of social organisation.[33] In his view, 'the concept of home was … reduced from the traditional spiritual home to the modern physical and spatial one'.[34]

4.9   Luxury villa-type dwelling in Dammam

4.10   Villa-type dwelling in Dhahran

A NEW URBAN IDENTITY FOR DAMMAM

Throughout all human societies, people surround themselves with specific objects to communicate with other members of their community. The need to express a common meaning through one's home environment encouraged the villa type to become the device which enabled Saudi middle-class families to express their new social status. In that sense, the home can be seen as a dynamic dialectic between individuals and their community.[35] While the Saudi middle-class family expressed its wealth and modernity by owning and living in a villa, they also used the uniqueness of their villa form to represent their own personalities.[36] People from different regions of Saudi Arabia who have settled in Dammam often recall images from their region of origin. This also reflects the desperation of designers to create a sense of continuity within the contemporary built environment in Saudi Arabia.

Our general desire to recreate traditional images has been discussed by Rybczynski. He writes: 'This acute awareness of tradition is a modern phenomenon that reflects a desire for custom and routine in a world characterized by constant change and innovation.'[37] The impact of external forms on people's self-image is a result of the strong connection between what the eye sees and how the perceived environment is interpreted. People tend to evaluate the visual quality of the surrounding environment according to their past experiences. In that sense, the sentimental reaction towards traditional images in Saudi Arabia can be attributed to the sadness and emptiness felt by people at the loss of these images, rather than as an expression of their actual cultural identity.

Another important issue is that the planned Saudi cities from the late-1940s, typified by Dammam and Khobar, passed through huge transformations that altered the form, height and styles of buildings found in them. Many blocks also passed through a series of changes of ownership, and as such were divided into smaller parcels. This shows two streams of urban identity working side-by-side in Dammam: one searching to retain a historical image, the other tending to reinforce the idea of modern urban identity. What has happened on the ground in the region in the last two decades has only increased this cultural and architectural conflict.

4.11
Dammam's urban development along the coastline

4.12 General urban development in Dammam

4.13 High-rise apartment blocks in Dammam

More recently still, a surge in development in the region has led, as noted, to an ever wider urban expansion. Plenty of new neighbourhoods were constructed in the last two decades to meet the population growth. Compared to the surrounding older cities, especially Qatif, urban and social identity has undergone incredible transition in Dammam. The different cultural backgrounds of newcomers to the area, along with the presence of huge number of expatriate labourers, have heightened this crisis of identity. For example, it is rare today that we find local Saudi people walking in the centres of these cities; those who are on the streets are mainly Asian workers collected together in huge numbers, which gives a very different impression to any visitors to Dammam or Khobar. What is especially interesting, and different, is that the older cities in the region have also been transformed from an urban perspective, but to a much greater extent they maintain their traditional social structure, ending up

4.14   Western-style supermarket in Dammam

Table 4.2   Population statistics for the Dammam Metropolitan region (2007), based on data from the Central Office of Statistics and fieldwork by the author

City	Population	Saudi	Non Saudi	No. of Workers	No. of Houses
Dammam	314,051	Varied	Varied	70,065	129,891
Qatif	474,573	Varied	Varied	51,826	68,553
Khobar	455,541	Varied	Varied	45,126	88,751
Total	1,244,165	736,929	507,236	167,017	287,195

Source: Mashary Al-Naim

4.15   New office
block under
construction
in Dammam

as a clear visual contradiction.[38] In these older centres, people have insisted on expressing their previous value systems even if they also ended up transforming their houses. It is also noticeable that there are relatively fewer overseas workers in the older settlements such as Qatif, when compared to Dammam and Khobar.

Urban projects in the Dammam Metropolitan region in the last two decades, including the seafront development and the construction of major freeways, have created very different lifestyles even since the 1980s. These buildings alter the whole structure of Dammam and Khobar, while contributing greatly to the new urban identity. Contemporary architectural practices show a tendency to commercialize the skyline of the cities by encouraging high-rise buildings spread along main highways and in the urban centres. This phenomenon has been associated with the economic prosperity of the last decade caused by the steady increase of global oil prices. We cannot deny also the impact of Dubai, which has influenced most Arab cities, including those in the Saudi Gulf region, to build upwards.[39] Competing with Dubai means for many officials in cities such as Dammam that the building of high-rise towers becomes the way to show their cities are equally as developed and modernised as Dubai.

The impact of the current global financial crisis – which has proved so dramatic for Dubai – has however been very limited in Dammam. This was because those involved in urban development in Saudi Arabia were very alert to the financial problems, and because urban growth has been more measured compared to that

4.16   Recently
completed
housing blocks
in Dammam

4.17   Zamil House office block in Khobar

4.18   Another
new office block
complex in Khobar

in other Arab Gulf cities. Although urban development was expedited because of the rising oil prices, the process nonetheless remained relatively controlled in Saudi Arabia. This has helped the 'Dammam Metropolitan' region to absorb this latest financial crisis, as reflected in its urban activities. Not a single project was cancelled or delayed in Dammam, and new projects are still being commissioned. Saudi people still clearly believe in investing in property, and real-estate projects have thus continued.

CONCLUSION

The Dammam Metropolitan region can be considered as the main gateway for Saudi Arabia onto the Gulf. It is therefore also the base for the country's oil industry, providing it with an important role within the Saudi and international economies. This part of the Gulf region must be seen as new, with its history not really stretching back beyond seven decades. This sense of novelty has also been reflected in the absorption of new forms and images in cities like Dammam, and a very different urban identity has been formed as a result. However, a continuing crisis of cultural and architectural identity is still being felt by local people, even if this was never as harsh in Dammam as in older cities like Qatif, or indeed elsewhere in Saudi Arabia. Rapid growth clearly contributed to what we can call an 'image instability' which has weakened the sense of urban memory. This is what has led to continuous tension between historical collective memory in Saudi Arabia and the pressure to adopt a more modern image.

The relatively youthful age of the urban structure of the 'Dammam Metropolitan' region makes it more possible for inhabitants to accept social change, and the new architectural images that accompany it, and so the city has shown very low 'resistance' to these forces. This can be seen as a positive dimension that allows the city to take a lead in urban modernization in Saudi Arabia. What has happened in the past few decades shows how Dammam can go along with new forms and images, precisely because its urban structure is a product of western modernist planning and land subdivision. Dammam's ability to renew its urban identity in such a short period of time should be considered an important hidden potentiality within its urban structure. Ever since its new urban structure was first introduced in the late-1940s, the city has undergone many changes, and every time it extends its urban fabric without difficulty. Today, new towers are growing up easily within the urban structure. However, many visual contradictions and tensions do continue to appear, especially in residential neighbourhoods, due often to the mix of cultural backgrounds of residents who come from different parts of Saudi Arabia or from other countries in the world. It all makes for a richer social and architectural combination.

NOTES

1   Aramco built its first camp in Dhahran in 1938, followed by one in Ras-Tanura in 1939, and Abqaiq in 1944. See: Saba George Shiber, 'Report on City Growth in the Eastern Province, Saudi Arabia', in Saba George Shiber, *Recent Arab City Growth* (Kuwait: Government Printing Press, 1967), p. 428.

2   Solon T. Kimball, 'American Culture in Saudi Arabia', *Transactions of the New York Academy of Sciences*, vol. 18, no. 5 (1956): 472.

3   Shiber, *Recent Arab City Growth*, p. 430.

4   David Shirreff, 'Housing – Ideas Differ on what People Want', in John Andrews & David Shirreff (eds), *Middle East Annual Review 1980* (Essex: World of Information, 1979), pp. 59–62. Saleh Al-Hathloul has also said: 'The initial growth of Dammam and Al-Khobar in the late 1350s[H]/1930s and early 1360s[H]/1940s was not planned in an orderly fashion. As the population grew, people took over any available land and erected basic shelters and fences of local materials. Following the traditional pattern of Arab-Muslim cities, the streets were narrow and irregular.' See: Saleh Al-Hathloul, 'Tradition, Continuity and Change in the Physical Environment: The Arab-Muslim City' (Unpublished PhD Thesis, MIT, Cambridge, MA, 1981), pp. 145–146.

5   Kimball, 'American Culture in Saudi Arabia', p. 472.

6   Ibid., p. 473.

7   Shiber, *Recent Arab City Growth*, p. 430. He describes the plan of Khobar thus: 'It covered only about one quarter square mile north of the company pier head storage yard. The blocks averaged 130 by 200 feet with separating streets of 40 and 60 foot widths.' Moreover, he indicated how the new plan ignored the existing Saudi settlements: 'Here again, the gridiron pattern was oriented north-south. No consideration was given to the mushroom growth of temporary structures and those were demolished to open the new streets.' See also: Al-Hathloul, 'Tradition, Continuity and Change', p. 146.

8   Roy Lebkicher et al., *Aramco Handbook* (New York: Arabian American Oil Corporation, 1960), pp. 212–216; Shiber, *Recent Arab City Growth*, p. 431; Al-Hathloul, 'Tradition, Continuity and Change', p. 167.

9   Al-Hathloul, 'Tradition, Continuity and Change', p. 167.

10   Saleh Al-Hathloul & Mohamed Anis-ur-Rahmaam, 'The Evolution of Urban and Regional Planning in Saudi Arabia', *Ekistics*, vol. 52, no. 312 (May/June 1985): 206–212.

11   In the 1920s, two small fishing settlements were established in Dammam and Khobar and occupied by members of the Al-Dawaser tribe. See: Fahad Al-Said, 'Territorial Behaviour and the Built Environment: The Case of Arab-Muslim Towns, Saudi Arabia' (Unpublished PhD Thesis, University of Glasgow, Glasgow, 1992), p. 217.

12   Ibid., p. 225. The original settlement was described by the Ministry of Municipal and Rural Affairs (MOMRA) in 1981 thus: 'The dwelling unit and clusters were added onto or joined to one another according to needs of the inhabitants. Neither the open space nor circulation pattern was predetermined. They resulted from the accidental disposition of dwelling units and the definition of family territorial holdings.'

13   Ibid., p. 234.

14   Ibid. In the 1960s Dammam municipality had the power to apply Aramco's desired building regulations. However, this was applied only for the Aramco neighborhoods. Al-Said said, 'even though Dammam municipality has complete control over its streets and building regulations, the neighbourhood has only been affected by the creation of a major street … in the north, and the winding of the south street'.

15   This phenomenon is found in most Arab countries which tried to achieve modernity rapidly. Lerner mentioned this issue, saying: 'what happened in the West over centuries, some Middle Eastern now seek to accomplish in years.' See: Daniel Lerner & and Lucille W. Pevsner, *The Passing of Traditional Society: Modernizing the Middle East* (Glencoe, NY: Free Press, 1958), p. 47. This rapid change, coupled with a lack of local design and construction firms, served to accelerate the gap between traditional culture and the new westernized culture being introduced in the Saudi domestic environment.

16   A.B. Jarbawi, 'Modernism and Secularism in the Arab Middle East' (Unpublished PhD Thesis, University of Cincinnati, Cincinnati, OH, 1981), p. 21.

17   In an interview with Dr. Said Farsi (the former mayor of Jeddah) in the Saudi newspaper Al-Madina on 3 August 1997, he indicated that 'the real modern planning in Jeddah and other Saudi cities was started in 1958. This was with the co-operation with … the United Nations, which sent Dr. Sayed Karim who later recommended creating the first office for city planning. The first resident expert in this office was Dr. Abdulrahman Makhloof between 1959 and 1963.'

18   These Saudi building regulations were as follows: 1) Prior to the issuance of building permits, confirmation must be made of the existence of concrete posts; 2) Plots are to be sold according to their drawn and established boundaries, and should be strictly prohibited from further subdivision; 3) Height should not exceed eight metres, except with the approval of the concerned authority; 4) A built-up area generally should not exceed sixty percent of the land area, including attachments; 5) Front setbacks should be equal to one-fifth of the width of the road and should not exceed six metres; 6) Side and rear setbacks should not be less than two metres and projections should not be permitted within this area; 7) Building on plots of land specified for utilities and general services should only be permitted for the same purpose; 8) Approval of the plan does not mean confirmation of ownership limits [boundaries] and the municipality should check the legal deed on the actual site; 9) The owner should execute the whole approved plan on the land by putting concrete posts for each plot of land prior to its disposal either by selling or building. See: Al-Hathloul, 'Tradition, Continuity and Change', pp. 205–206; Al-Said, 'Territorial Behaviour and the Built Environment', 1992, p. 257.

19   Al-Said, 'Territorial Behaviour and the Built Environment', pp. 258–259.

20   Al-Hathloul & Anis-ur-Rahmaam, 'The Evolution of Urban and Regional Planning in Saudi Arabia', pp. 208–211. This can be seen from the master-plans that were launched in all regions in Saudi Arabia from 1968–1978, as follows: Western Region by Robert Matthew, Johnson-Marshall & Partners in 1973; Central and Northern regions by Doxiadis and Ekistics, completed in 1975; Eastern Region by Candilis Metra International Consultants (France) in 1975–1976; Southern Region by Kenzo Tange & UTREC in 1977–1978.

21   Al-Hathloul, 'Tradition, Continuity and Change', p. 174.

22   The first relevant regulation, the Municipalities Statute, was issued by the government in 1937 under the Royal Order No. 8723, Rajab 1357H. This order defined the role of the municipality in supervising the city, including construction. This statute was followed by another one called 'Roads and Building Statute' in 1941. See: Al-Hathloul & Mohamed Anis-ur-Rahmaam, 'The Evolution of Urban and Regional Planning in Saudi Arabia', p. 206.

23   Al-Said, 'Territorial Behaviour and the Built Environment', p. 257.

24   Shirreff, 'Saudi Arabia', pp. 315–338; A.J. Al-Saati, 'Housing Finance and Residents' Satisfaction: The Case of Real Estate Development Fund (REDF)', *Open House International*, vol. 1, no. 2 (1989): 33. See also, Tarik M. Al-Soliman, 'Societal Values and their Effect on the Built Environment in Saudi Arabia: A Recent Account', *Journal of Architectural and Planning Research*, vol. 8, no. 3 (Autumn 1991): 235–255. The Real Estate Development Fund (REDF) was established in 1975 to provide people with interest-free loans to build new houses. For example, between 1974 and 1987 more than 440,000 new homes were constructed in different Saudi cities as a result of government loans.

25   Al-Hathloul, 'Tradition, Continuity and Change', p. 171.

26   Al-Saati, 'Housing Finance and Resident's Satisfaction', pp. 33–41; Saleh Al-Hathloul & Edadan, N., 'Housing Stock Management Issues in the Kingdom of Saudi Arabia', *Housing Studies*, vol. 7, no. 4 (1992): 268–279; Tawfiq M. Abu-Ghazzeh, 'Vernacular Architecture Education in the Islamic Society of Saudi Arabia: Towards the Development of an Authentic Contemporary Built Environment', *Habitat International*, vol. 21, no. 2 (June 1997): 229–253.

27   Thomas W. Shea, 'Measuring the Changing Family Consumption Patterns of Aramco's Saudi Arab Employees – 1962 and 1968', in Derek Hopwood (ed.), *The Arabian Peninsula: Society and Politics* (London: George Allen & Unwin, 1972), p. 249.

28   It was commonplace, for instance, for British visitors to talk about the contradictory faces of Riyadh in the 1960's, with one recalling being told by his Saudi friends: 'It's becoming a city of two different worlds'.

29   Yousef M. Fadan, 'The Development of Contemporary Housing in Saudi Arabia (1950–1983)' (Unpublished PhD Thesis, MIT, Cambridge, MA, 1983), p. 74.

30   The appearance of such a class, however, conflicted with the egalitarian characteristics of traditional Saudi society, where rich and poor lived closed to each other. This increased the conflict between old and new, and the issue of identity appeared as a social problem, especially with the acceleration towards change in the following years.

31   J.J. Boon, 'The Modern Saudi Villa: Its Cause and Effect', *American Journal for Science and Engineering*, vol. 7, no. 2 (1982): 132–143.

32   Ibid., p. 140.

33   H.S. Jomah, 'The Traditional Process of Producing a House in Arabia during the 18th and 19th Centuries: A Case of Hedjaz' (Unpublished PhD Thesis, University of Edinburgh, Edinburgh, 1992), pp. 327–328.

34   Ibid., p. 328.

35   Irwin Altman & Mary Gauvain, 'A Cross-Cultural and Dialectic Analysis of Homes', in Lynn S. Liben et al. (eds), *Spatial Representation and Behavior A Cross the Life Span: Theory and Application* (New York: Academic Press, 1981), pp. 283–320.

36   Ibid., p. 296. The authors state that 'the uniqueness and identity of a family is often reflected in the construction of individual homes', and then add that 'a family's identity is often symbolized by the number and variety of rooms in its home'.

37   Witold Rybczynski, *Home: A Short History of an Idea* (Harmondsworth: Penguin Books, 1986), p. 9.

38   Mashary Al-Naim, 'The Home Environment in Saudi Arabia and Gulf States – (Vol. 1) Growth of Identity Crises and Origin of Identity + (Vol. 2) The Dilemma of Cultural Resistance, Identity in Transition', *CRiSSMA Working Paper no. 7* (Milan: Pubblicazioni dell'I.S.U. Universita Cattolica, 2006).

39   Mashary Al-Naim, 'Political Influences and Paradigm Shifts in The Contemporary Arab Cities: Questioning the Identity of Urban Form', *CRiSSMA Working Paper no. 7* (Milan: Pubblicazioni dell'I.S.U. Universita Cattolica, 2005).

1   Burj Khalifa in Dubai by SOM Architects (2004–2010)

2　Aerial view of the new blocks and landscaping around the Burj Khalifa in Dubai

3   Ghani Palace Hotel (2002) by Saleh Al Mutawa in Kuwait City

4   National Assembly Building (1978–1982) by Jorn Utzon in Kuwait City

5   General view of the city of Dammam, Saudi Arabia

6   Luxury villa-type dwelling in Dammam, Saudi Arabia

7   Renovation of Manama Souk

8   Religious festivities in Manama, Bahrain, on the evening of the Day of Ashura

5

Manama, Bahrain

Ali A. Alraouf

Bahrain, a small island archipelago located in the heart of the Gulf, is often described as one of the most developed economies in the region. Along with Dubai, it certainly offers the only model as yet for post-oil economics amongst the Arab oil-producing states. With its oil resources about to dry up, Bahrain realised that it needed to invest in other economical activities to maintain and develop its progress. During the last decade, therefore, Bahrain has started to take major steps towards economic diversification, primarily by addressing the financial and tourist sectors. To emphasize the new reality of the Bahraini economy, and to highlight its altered identity as a post-oil country within the Gulf region, the Ministry of Oil was eradicated at the end of 2005. The search for a new identity for Bahrain and its capital city, Manama, has swiftly encouraged new models of development based on providing hybrid urban spaces and iconic developments.

In this chapter, I will narrate the story of an individual city, Manama, in relation to local, regional and international influences. I will critically examine the major transformation that Manama has witnessed from being a small town based on pearl-diving and maritime trade to a city which is now trying to use large-scale urban projects and iconic buildings to become a global player – all with the aim of creating an international hub that will attract tourists, business visitors and investors. Ironically, Manama's past relationship with pearl-diving appears to be endless, given that all of its newly constructed iconic projects are related to pearls – either as a morphological reference, or as an attractive commercial name that invokes history to facilitate marketing. With this type and volume of projects, Manama, like other Gulf cities in the vein of Doha, Abu Dhabi and Dubai, is undeniably one of the key centres for unprecedented levels of development in the Middle East. One ought to note, however, that it is much smaller than these other Arabic Gulf cities: Manama's estimated population is currently around 330,000 citizens in its wider metropolitan area.

The chapter sheds light on a new emerging form of urbanisation resulting from global influences interacting within the Gulf context. Hybrid urbanism will be discussed as a major form of development which is clearly present during the last five years in globalising Gulf cities including Manama. Hybridity, as a significant result of cultural interchange and diversity, is one of the primary characteristics of global and post-global societies. I will argue that the general transformation of Bahrain's urban identity – and that of Manama in particular – into hybrid entities, is already having a huge impact on development, imagery and social structure. The chapter will thus investigate and evaluate the impact of globalization, hybridity, and post-oil economics on the production of actual places in Manama. This topic will be studied from two perspectives: first, there will be a historical review and interpretation of the emergence of architectural and urban hybridity in Bahrain; second, there will be a closer investigation and assessment of the workings of architectural hybridity within Manama's contemporary urbanism.

BACKGROUND TO GULF CITIES

Major cities in the Gulf region have for decades been experiencing rapid changes and transformations in their social, economic, environmental and physical structures. One of the most unique features about Gulf cities is their demographic structure. The ratio between the local and expatriate population is reaching phenomenal percentages. For instance, in the case of Bahrain, local citizens today represent only 50 per cent of the total population. An even more radical example can of course be seen in Dubai, where locals form just over 15 per cent of the population.[1] What is important about these figures is that it shows the clear presence of hybrid identities within most contemporary Gulf cities. Due to economic reasons, those expatriates are often stay more or less permanently, and in the process they dwell, interact with, influence and become influenced by their surroundings. Demographic trends of the local and expatriate populations, which can be seen as 'internal' factors of a city, determine the rate of growth of their relative sizes and the degree of spatial differentiation or integration; whereas 'external' factors, mainly globalization and the shift towards hybridity, have major effects on the changing economics and lifestyles of Middle East countries. Special attention thus needs to be paid to how urban space in Manama can be shaped and dimensioned to satisfy the new expectations and needs of its diverse inhabitants, who while living in the same city environment, exhibit significant cultural and socio-economic variations.

Debates around this issue rely on our ability to understand social dynamism and what people think about their domestic environments – in other words, how they organize themselves and why. How do traditions work in society? How and why do people create new traditions? It seems evident that every society has its own continuous traditions; they may change and take on different forms, but their existence is essential for that society to survive. Citizens in Gulf cities have long tried to maintain continuity through the strong impact of their main religion, Islam. These traditions can be linked with what Rapaport calls the 'cultural core'.[2] By using this term, he differentiated the idea of essential cultural values from the more 'peripheral' values which are modified to suit changes in life circumstances.

The real challenge for contemporary Gulf cities seems to emerge from their desire to develop in a global world, with a growing tendency towards openness and transparency. Therefore, religion might now be seen as part of a Gulf city's identity but it is not the sole one. Beside religious factors, social structure in Bahrain has long been shaped by the power and hierarchy of tribes, and the cosmopolitanism of its demographic structure.[3] Today, the right of citizenship is overriding religious beliefs and tribal allegiances in the new hybridised Gulf condition.

HYBRIDITY DISCOURSE AND THE BUILT ENVIRONMENT

The contributors to the 2001 book on *Hybrid Urbanism* set out to revise our understanding of city building and identity formation.[4] Their concept of 'hybridity' was borrowed from post-colonial theory to challenge both essentialist and multicultural explanations of these intertwined processes.[5] According to this view, built environments and the social meanings they convey are neither the products of individual cultures nor the creations of discrete groups. Rather, they are syncretic, the result of a constant interplay of cultures and traditions. Yet, as Alsayyad rightly states, hybrid groups of people do not always create hybrid places, and hybrid places do not always accommodate hybrid groups of people.[6] This argument will be used to examine the status of the newly introduced concept/process of hybrid urbanism in Manama and Bahrain in general. The hypothesis will be that due to increased openness, the desire for a more diversified economic base, and existence of multicultural groups of people, hybrid places can be created. It will also be argued that historically, cosmopolitan nature of a place or a city like Manama might facilitate the process of hybridity.

City building has often been portrayed as the self-conscious efforts of a few powerful people seeking to create distinctive and authentic urban visions. Some participants in the process in places like the Middle East might have in the past been colonialists or western authorities, while others were locals, but almost all belonged to elites who could operate within a global network of policymakers, architects and planners. This interpretation seems especially true of the modern era, although some researchers suggest that global interaction was shaping cities as early as the thirteenth century.[7] Straightforward accounts of colonial dominance and indigenous resistance give way here to analyses suggesting that even in the inequitable power relationships created by Western imperialism, urban forms grew from combinations of cultures rather than the simple imposition of European ideas. In Celik's view culture was a crucial element in power structures in the colonial condition, according to Celik.[8] Architecture and urbanism have an obvious advantage over other cultural formations in shedding such direct light on social relations and power structures. Additionally, many scholars suggest that understanding urban history needs to be intertwined with the study of urban processes that embody the intricate interaction of social, economic, political, technical, cultural, and artistic forces which bring about the urban form and give dynamism to the city over time.[9]

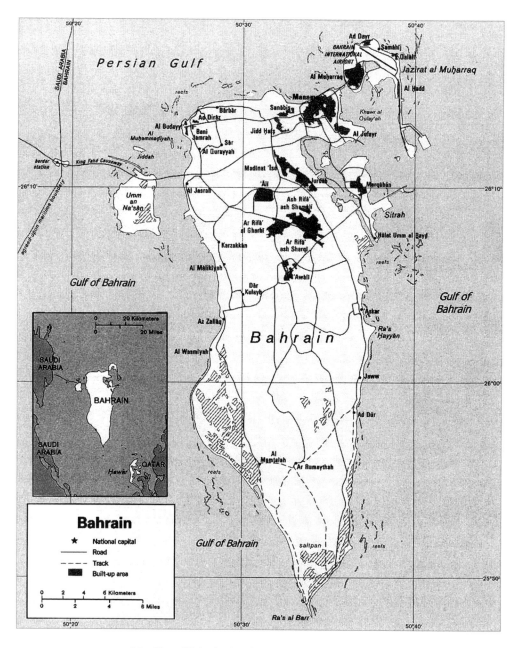

5.1   Map of Bahrain showing its contextual relationship

More importantly, as argued by Bhabha, the colonial relationship is not symmetrically antagonistic, due to the ambivalent positioning of the colonizer and the colonized.[10] Ambivalence is connected to the presence of 'hybridity' in which the other's original identity is rewritten, but also transformed through misreadings and incongruities, resulting in something quite different. Such a process can be seen in Manama during the last decade as it has developed at significant pace into a cosmopolitan global center. Its reputation as a unique and vital trading city supports its effort to retain a regional importance and aspire to global importance. Historically, all the Bahraini cities seem peculiar: heterogeneous, hyperactive and with great deal of commercial exchange and maritime trading. This back-story has enabled Manama to go through a smooth process of transformation from a old trading city to a modern hybrid one. As Katodrytis has argued in terms of Dubai, hybrid cities demonstrate in their apparent lack of identity a complex urbanism based on an invisible infrastructure: a fluid and non-hierarchical system of activities, goods and participants. More than just a static collection of buildings, these cities can be described as a piling up of activities that change more quickly than the planning process can respond to. Katodrytis rightly states that existing buildings seem unable to sustain this dynamic, complex and fluid 'urban condition', one which is hybrid, synthetic and post-modern.[11]

A more accurate description of Bahraini urbanism can thus be generated from the fact that it is a city state in terms of urban setting. In other words, because of Bahrain's nature as an island of very limited area, there is major difficulty in any attempt to separate the country from the city. Hence, reading Manama's story actually gives a fair reading of the driving forces for all of Bahrain's urbanism. In the next section, I will try to shed some light on Bahrain's economic, cultural, social, geographical and environmental character so as to offer a deeper understanding of Manama, and given that both entities interact, overlap and intertwine continuously.

CONTEXTUAL UNDERSTANDING OF BAHRAIN

Bahrain consists of a group of 33 islands with a total land area of about 700 km^2. The unique relation between Bahrain and the sea established its economic development, with its two main cities, Manama and Muharraq, originating as primitive fishermen's settlements on the Gulf coastline. Historically, the major factors which shaped Manama were pearl fishing and trading. Bahrain was also famous for building traditional wooden boats used mainly for pearl-diving, fishing and trading. Some historical documents suggest that by the beginning of the 20th century, Oman and Qatar had purchased more than 100 fishing boats from Bahrain. The port of Manama was then so vibrant that it had over 100 trading and fishing ships entering and leaving on a daily basis.[12]

Looking more closely at Manama, there is a lot of evidence which shows the importance of the Gulf to the life of the city, its local community and its urban morphology. The urban structure of the road network is marked by the orientation of the main roads towards the Gulf. The old port that was once the main gate to

5.2 Distinctive urban and architectural features of traditional Bahraini settlements

the city, called Bab-al-Bahrain (Bahrain Gate), was a commercial hub that extended up to the main market. The city in its early stages therefore extended along the coast in a north-east/south-west direction, having a long frontage onto the coast that was then regularly interrupted by a series of lanes leading inland.[13]

From an environmental perspective, Manama, like most of Bahrain, is located in a hot humid climate. This climatic condition is largely responsible for its urban morphology and architectural forms. Natural ventilation is a major challenge since it is so important in buildings to try to keep out humidity. A unique street pattern can thus be noticed clearly in Manama's spatial order. As is also observed of many traditional cities in the Middle East, the requirement for shading from the sun was achieved by having narrow winding streets.[14] The tight urban pattern gives Manama's old core its distinguishing character. In the case of wide roads, the market, communal spaces were shaded by hanging out traditional clothes. In response to the climate, the city also relied on two housing typologies. In earlier times, houses were made of very light framed structures consisting of mat huts with a sloping roof, known locally as *barasti*. The second typology used masonry load-bearing walls and relied on local building local expertise. Other techniques were also imported from surrounding Gulf countries to enhance the environmental performance of dwellings. For example, ventilation was improved through wind towers, locally known as *badjir*, which originated in Iranian traditional settlements.

Bahrain's maritime location therefore played a crucial role in shaping its history, politics and social structure. Politically, it has long been a strategic centre between the two Islamic entities – the Arabs and the Persians, respectively the Sunni and the Shi'a Muslims – which today are regionally crystallized in the two regional powers of Saudi Arabia and Iran. Bahrain was thus a transit point between Arabia and the Persian and Indian sub-continents in many senses.[15] This explains its well-established cosmopolitan demographic formed mainly of Arabs, Persians and Indians.[16]

While the city of Muharraq, which sits on a smaller island just to the north-east, was considered to be Bahrain's political centre up to the late-18th century, Manama retained its purpose as the locus for foreign occupation and a focal point for regional and international trading networks. British colonial interests in Bahrain were mainly economic, with Manama acting as the base for British commercial operations in the archipelago. Only after the agreements of 1881 and 1892, when

Bahrain became a *de facto* British protectorate, did British interference in the affairs of the islands increase dramatically. As a result, Manama became the stage for a power struggle between the Al-Khalifa rulers and the British colonists.[17] This was a significant moment in the city's history: while there had been earlier fishing settlements on the northern coast of Bahrain for centuries (references to what became Manama date back at least to the 14th century), it had been the advent of the Al-Khalifa dynasty in 1783 that transformed it into a proper urban centre. Historical sources duly note that the twin cities of Manama and Muharraq were founded soon after 1780.[18] British interests thus challenged the existing power order; however, the Al-Khalifa rulers managed to survive and retain their power to the present day.

Once established as a key trading, fishing and pearl-diving centre, there were no natural barriers to Manama's expansion due to its flat topography. Its only limits were the presence of the Gulf to the north, as well as some cemeteries surrounding the city core. Paradoxically, over the last decade, not even the Gulf was considered an obstacle to expansion given an organized and rapid process of land reclamation. The Bahrain Financial Harbour, begun in 2004, is the most important project in Manama constructed completely on reclaimed land; its second and third phases are intended to add even more land to the total area of the city. Similar projects, including man-made islands of Durrat Al Bahrain and Bahrain Bay, demonstrate the tendency to use land reclamation to accommodate iconic mega-projects.

URBAN TRANSFORMATIONS IN MANAMA

As mentioned, Manama was truly established by the end of 18th century, directly after the Al-Khalifa ruling family had achieved political stability. From 1818 to 1905, the city grew from a small village of just 8,000 people to a sizeable town of 25,000. Its role as a port city within the Gulf region made it a hub for transnational communities, most of which are now represented to different extents in the social fabric. The immigration of labourers, in search of a better life, continually shaped Manama's population by making it be characterized by cosmopolitanism.[19] Manama was also unique because it became a regional capital created by the British following the signing of the 1892 Protectorate Treaty. As a result, the city became the headquarters for British power, and was from where the whole Gulf region was managed and controlled. In terms of religion, the co-existence of the two main Islamic sects, Sunni and Shi'a, is part of the social mosaic that makes up the city.[20] Both sects are represented by distinctive groups organised around large families: some are local Bahrainis, some are Persians, and some are Arab Bedouins. They once co-existed in Manama with other non-Muslim entities such as Oriental Christians, Indians of various sects, and Jews. Such a rich tapestry was further enhanced by the arrival of other ethnic communities, initially as a consequence of economic prosperity, and later due to geopolitical factors which characterized the colonial period.[21]

5.3 Aerial photograph showing the contrast of Manama's
old urban fabric to newer modern planning

5.4 Details of Manama's traditional architectural vocabulary

As in other Middle Eastern cities, Bahrain's traditional urban form was the product of harmonious interaction between cultural norms and climatic conditions to produce effective housing clusters that used standard architectural elements and simple local construction techniques. The guiding principle was 'Form follows Family', according to Yarwood.[22] Following the discovery of oil in Bahrain in 1930, however, it is noticeable that the traditional urban structure started slowly to change from a compact irregular organic form to a modern grid system. From 1930 until the 1960s, urban changes in cities like Manama were the result of a massive influx of foreign labour, the introduction of town-planning principles by the British colonial power, and the pursuit of a modernisation process. In 1934, the new city of Awali was built, and thereafter many modern areas adopted the 'Form follows Function' doctrine, sprouting out especially around traditional areas in Manama and Muharraq. In order for Manama to modernise, new functions were added to the city form: wide roads, institutional buildings, housing blocks and oil industry facilities became the new elements in this transformation. In the more traditional areas, there was also a shift of local communities to newer housing areas due to many factors: dilapidated traditional areas offered cheaper accommodation for foreign labourers, uncoordinated building activity and the absence of a comprehensive conservation strategy led to the loss of urban homogeneity in traditional areas, plus there was a widespread lack of appreciation of the value of traditional dwellings opposed to modern housing projects.[23]

Even though oil was first discovered in Bahrain during the 1930s, its full scale commercial production started around 1950, following the disruption of the Second World War. At this point the British colonists allowed masses of foreign

5.5   The old and the new in Manama, showing the distinctive Bahrain World Trade Centre (BWTC) and the reclaimed land for the Northern City

workers to come into Bahrain to support the new industry. This flow of poorer labourers from India, Pakistan, Bangladesh, Philippines, Thailand and other parts of the Asian continent contributed substantially to new social structures. Large urban extensions outside the boundaries of Manama were established to accommodate these new communities of expatriates.[24] Already by 1954, the old centre by Manama had become a small nucleus surrounded by vast modern quarters. Ever since then, a dual image between the old and the new, the past and the present, tradition and modernity has been established as a key element of Bahraini urbanism.

> The … [hitherto] Oasis turned into a city of glass, iron and stone, and hordes of adventurers and entrepreneurs swarmed in. Thus patterns of behaviour, relationships and interests very different from the existing ones began to form. In the midst of all this mutation, the indigenous inhabitants were unable to adjust to the new fast rhythm and the new relationships, and in their search for a new identity they became distorted.[25]

Two key events in the history of Bahrain coincide perfectly and helped dramatically in its modernization process: these were Bahrain's independence from British occupation in 1971, and then the economic boom in the Gulf region created by the 'Oil Crisis' of the mid-1970s.[26] Many Arab researchers have argued that the subsequent benefits were manifested in the western cultural models imported to the Gulf countries, not least in terms of the built environment.[27] After all, colonization had long been a crucial force in shaping the urban scene in major cities in Arab countries. In the case of Bahrain, and cities like Manama, the British had exercised extensive control from 1820 up to 1971. Following independence, dramatic changes took place in political, economic, social and cultural spheres.

Urban changes in Manama had started to accelerate in the 1960s, even before independence, due to population growth and the pressure for modernisation. The Isa Town was built in 1963, followed later by Hamad Town in 1982. Both areas were built based on the western planning philosophy of the grid-iron system and zoned land use, and were implemented in favourably prosperous economic conditions. Indeed, the oil boom of the 1970s was to have a dramatic social and economical impact on Manama's local community. The city witnessed a rapid outwards migration of local inhabitants to newer settlements as an indication of economic prosperity and the move towards modernization.[28] Living in the old core of Manama became perceived as an indication of poverty and backwardness. Subsequently, the new edges of Manama's old core gradually turned into an administrative and business centre. More dramatically, low-income expatriate groups transformed the older districts by turning traditional houses into ever-denser residential quarters to accommodate the rapid increase in labourers working in different development projects around the city.

During the mid-1980s, however, there arose a strong regionalist movement calling for a rethinking of the western models of urban planning and architecture implanted into Bahrain and other Gulf countries. According to Mortada, there were two major reasons for this 'awakening'.[29] The first was the realization of the socio-cultural inappropriateness of western models. The second factor was more related

to the environmental sustainability movement that started in western countries around the mid-1970s. We might also add to this the emergence of Arabic regionalism that demanded design and planning ideas drawn from traditional local cultures. It was trend celebrated by the Aga Khan Trust's establishment in 1977 of the most prestigious and generous architectural award in the world to encourage local, regional and international designers to create architecture that improves the physical environment of Muslim people, and which recognises more distinctive Middle Eastern models of architecture and planning.

5.6   Bab Al-Bahrain Mosque as a representation of Islamic regionalism in a modernizing city

The invitation of influential regional architects like Mohamed Makiyah and Abdel Wahid Al-Wakil, both recipients of the Aga Khan Award, to design in Bahrain during this period was a clear manifestation of this regionalist movement. Both successfully managed to design two of the most important landmarks of Bahrain at that time: the main gateway into Isa Town and the Bab Al-Bahrain mosque respectively. Their influence was echoed in a variety of institutional buildings, hotels and new dwellings for local people around the outskirts of Manama. In these designs, the interpretations of Islamic regional architecture reached far greater levels of understanding and depth.

Later still, the last decade of the 20th century is so crucial to understanding Manama's urbanization, for that was the period when globalising influences started to reach the Middle East.[30] It is of course necessary to question if there is evidence of a new spatial order resulting from globalization, and whether this influences a Middle Eastern city like Manama. The impact of globalization on cities in developed and developing countries has been a focus for numerous commentators.[31] They

5.7   Aerial photo showing Bab-Al-Bahrain, Bahrain Financial Harbour and the renovated Manama Souk

all agreed on the main causes such as capital flow, labour markets, information flow, management and spatial organization. One can conclude from this a simple definition that a city is globalised if it has the ability to capture economic flows through linkage-based strategies and connectivities within the overall morphology of the global urban system. Since the 1990s, Bahrain's urban development indeed entered a new phase of globalisation with the encouragement of external investment, trade and tourism, and the resulting growth in real-estate projects. Urban form now started to be influenced by a new slogan, 'Form follows Finance'.[32] From the point of view of urban space, Manama's historical core witnessed a tangible spread of new hotels along its waterfront edge. In addition, institutional and financial buildings continue to be constructed around the urban peripheries and along main roads into the city.

MANAMA'S PREPARATIONS FOR A POST-OIL WORLD

As mentioned earlier, in Bahrain's case the diversification into the financial and tourist sectors was more urgent than for its Gulf neighbours: it had been the first

Gulf country to discover oil resources but also the first to encounter their depletion. Manama entered the post-oil paradigm by emphasizing its new role as a global financial hub for the region, especially in terms of banking. Manama is indeed one of the oldest banking centres in the Gulf and has over 350 financial institutions today.[33] Due to a favourable new free-trade agreement with the USA, Bahrain became even more open to foreign commerce. All these factors have rejuvenated its economic market, and there countless commercial, financial and other real-estate projects in the pipeline in Manama. More importantly, a fundamental focus on tourism as an economic pillar based on Bahrain's unique and diverse history has been intensely developed over the last five years or so.

Tourism is a major international industry, with many countries all over the world now relying on the income it produces. The demands of tourism can however contribute to the destruction of the natural and cultural environment upon which it depends. It is essential, as Pineda and Brebbia argue, to find ways to protect these environments for future generations.[34] Therefore there is a need to explore issues linked to the environmental, social and economic sustainability of tourism alongside governance mechanisms needed to support sustainable tourism. I would suggest that a struggle to achieve sustainable and cultural tourism is absolutely crucial in a locality rooted in authentic traditions. A key component of any sustainable tourism strategy lies in its ability to incorporate local communities, and also important is the role of other communities surrounding the touristic sites. In any cosmopolitan city, such as Manama, the presence of different immigrant ethnic groups is inevitable. Hence, cultural diversity and all its manifestations need to be transformed into

5.8   Manama's old core being 'invaded' by expatriate communities imposing their cultural references and hybrid lifestyles

vehicles for socio-economic development to the advantage of both immigrants and the city at large, as Rath argues.[35] In the context of Middle Eastern cities, according to Daher, the discourse of tourism should be linked to issues like cultural heritage and identity construction, national and global economics, and the development of local communities.[36] This analysis implies that issues like national identity, authenticity, representation of cultures and regions, and community and tourism development are of vital importance to understanding what role tourism can play in the economic development of Middle Eastern cities like Manama.

Here it is worth sketching the forces which are reshaping today's tourism industry in the light of issues related to identity, heritage and religious/ethnic festivities. Touristic practices in relation to forms of traditional and contemporary religious festivity are crucial, since the relation between the place and the event adds another dimension to the richness of the traveller's experience. Rath

5.9   Renovation of Manama Souk opposite to Bab Al-Bahrain Mosque and the waterfront

5.10   Manama's emerging urbanity of vertical towers, shopping malls and financial centres

in particular is interested in the interrelationship between tourism, migration, ethnic diversity and place.[37] In Manama, a fascinating example of touristic development is found on the opposite side of Bab Al-Bahrain, in the renovated Manama Souk (see Plate 7). This *souk* is located within the old city core and is considered as Bahrain's oldest. With its traditional architecture of narrow roads and little shops, the project cost around US$ 90 million when finished in late-2009. The souk has since become a must-see tourist experience where one can buy all kinds of spices, fabrics, handicrafts, souvenirs, dried fruits, nuts, and other traditional goods. The crowd as well as the traders in Manama Souk consists of Bahrainis as well as expatriates from India, Pakistan, Bangladesh, and neighbouring Gulf countries. As the architects, Gulf House Engineering, proclaimed:

> We seek continuity, sustainability and balance through our culture and architectural heritage, in such a symbolic, traditional, environmental and homogenous district. The design is comprehensive as micro-scale architectural language complements macro-urban design. We preserve identity and respect the alphabet of the architectural vocabulary of the region.[38]

This revealing quote from the project report reflects the social, cultural, environmental and economic agenda of the developers, as substantiated by a series of project objectives. Two of these objectives deserve to be spelled out. The first is of attracting tourists and other expatriates to visit the area by providing activities, shops, and urban infill projects to meet their needs, and provide an experience worth travelling for. The second objective is the importance of providing a theme for the Manama Souk in terms of rehabilitating buildings and creating public spaces and other facilities. According to the project master-plan, the area is divided into zones such as the 'cloth zone', 'gold souk', 'spice souk', and even an area called 'Little India'! None of the goals mentioned in the report, however, refer to the local community, older shopkeepers, or the presence of diverse ethnic groups. But it is this unique tapestry which gives the urban area its character and helps to construct its hybrid identity.[39] As the project manager stated:

> Manama Souk renovation will positively contribute in boosting commercial activities and increase number of visitors and tourists coming to the area dramatically ... The objective of the project is to preserve the unique heritage and traditional character of the souk and activate its touristic and cultural roles which were endangered due to unplanned increase in surrounding high-rise buildings.[40]

Paradoxically, the renovated vision for the *souk* stresses the ideals of continuity, sustainability and balance. Preserving the area's identity was limited to using architectural vocabulary only from the Gulf region, without considering how this will fit in with, say, 'Little India'. Here in Manama Souk, a clear example of Eco's 'authentic fake' has been constructed.[41] Real sources of authenticity have been neglected in favour of the fakeness of a questionable imported architectural vocabulary. Ahmad Bucheery, the local Bahraini architect who works for Gulf House Engineering, and who was the figure commissioned to design the renovated *souk*, earned his reputation as an architectural traditionalist after designing a famous hotel along the old link connecting Muharraq to Manama. In that scheme, Bucheery used all architectural vocabulary inherited in traditional Gulf architecture including wind-catchers to impress the hotel's guests and associated visitors. In an essay on 'Contemporary Architecture in Bahrain', he divides the development of Bahraini architecture into five stages: the traditional; the transitional period; the modern; the post-modern; and finally, identity revivalism.[42] Surprisingly, Bucheery concluded his essay with a position that rejects copying from the past, and instead preaches innovation and creativity:

> We, in Gulf House Engineering, have attempted through the various projects to go beyond the simple copying of the past through innovation, interpretation, and reflection. We are trying to balance between tradition and modern, simultaneously "localizing" international ideas, materials and aspirations to suit local needs. We hope that the new millennium will bring architectural achievements that truly reflect the identity of the Bahraini people and their local architecture.[43]

Another missing dimension in the redevelopment of the Bab Al-Bahrain/ Manama Souk area, and which contributes to its fakeness, is the absence of festivities, especially religious ones. Being in the centre of old Manama, it sits on several festival routes, but the multi-faceted relationship between tourism and festivals was simply not incorporated into the new development of the Bab Al-Bahrain/Manama Souk. It is a real loss, since the religious events and ceremonial processions performed by Shi'a groups for the anniversary of Imam Hussain (the martyred grandson of the Prophet Mohammed) sees the use of urban space and street furniture change dramatically. The ceremony extends for ten days and reaches its climax on the night of the tenth day, which is called the Day of Ashura (see Plate 8). Tens of thousands of people poured towards the streets and alleys of Manama either to participate or simply to see the events. Inspired by the 'Arab Spring' revolts in Tunisia and Egypt, crowds of up to 150,000 mainly Shi'a Bahrainins demonstrated in the heart of Manama during February and March 2011. Their replica of Cairo's Tahrir Square was Pearl Square. The protest wave was suppressed by heavy army intervention supported by military forces brought in from Saudi Arabia and the United Arab of Emirates, causing many fatalities. To eliminate any further mass protest or any occupation of main public spaces, the Bahraini authorities stormed Pearl Square. Protesters were evacuated and then the whole square including its central landmark sculpture – symbolizing Gulf Cooperation Council unity – was razed to the ground. These events however only brought further to the surface the importance of a need for just coexistence in Manama and Bahrain.

Another critical dimension affecting not only Manama but literally every single city in the Middle East is the impact of Dubai, or more specifically what is often described as 'Dubaification' or 'Dubaization'.[44] As is well known, the contemporary urban scene in Dubai is characterized by an infusion of new privately-owned building types: shopping malls, gated housing communities, theme parks, and headquarters of multinational corporations.

5.11   Spectators waiting for the main procession on the Day of Ashura

5.12   Religious festivities change Manama's urbanism radically
especially in the evening of the Day of Ashura

5.13   Dubai's coastline showing the built and proposed iconic development islands of 'The Palm 1, 2 & 3' and 'The World'

Dubai's leaders, also realising the realities of oil depletion, have constructed an unprecedented model of development based on economic diversification and a reliance on services industries, not least tourism.

All along the beaches stretching away from Dubai's famed creek, armies of overseas construction workers are once again racing to complete giant housing complexes which will permanently change the lie of the land. To visualize the scale of development, the case of Al Nakheel Properties offers an interesting example. This one developer has designed a series of residential environments whose opulence rivals anything in southern California or Florida's 'Gold Coast'.[45] In one development known as 'The Palm', three man-made palm-tree-shaped islands were created for expensive condominiums and yacht basins. It is promoted as the 'Eighth Wonder of the World', in part because, like the Great Wall of China, it can (just about) be seen from outer space. Al Nakheel was so pleased with the result that it went on to build 'The World', a collection of 300 man-made islands shaped like a map of the continents.

Most of the Arab cities aspiring to world status have been competing to imitate Dubai in the unprecedented effort to build the tallest and the largest-ever architectural and urban statements. A growing number of projects around the Gulf show the severity of this competition: examples include Abu Dhabi's Sorouh project, Bahrain's Financial Harbour, Qatar's Pearl Development, Oman's Blue City and Riyadh's Desert Islands. More importantly, it represents the dramatic influence of Dubai's icons on the developmental strategies of these cities, hence the term 'Dubaization'. Elsheshtawy argues that the development of Dubai as a global

5.14   The 'Palm 1' project is already a major manifestation of Dubai's new urban brand

centre remains unique, in that it now serves as a 'potential model for other cities in the region'.[46] However, Dubai as a model of urban development for contemporary Arab cities is entirely lacking, since it is based primarily on images and icons rather than sustainable concepts and strategies. For today's Arab cities which imitate Dubai the result from this process is the failure to consider sustainability in development planning, as well as limited interpretation of what globalization might mean and the resulting degradation of a sense of locality.

Dubai's new urban brand not only creates a developmental model to be followed by Gulf and Arab cities, but it also promotes the role of Dubai-based development companies to extend these vast projects outside their home city. Dubai International Properties unveiled plans to build the Salam Beach Resort and Spa in Bahrain, located on the south-west coast of the main island, and completed in mid-2009. The announcement of this project in Bahrain came soon after their vast projects in Qatar,

5.15   Bahrain Financial Harbour (BFH) emerging close to Manama's old traditional core

Oman, Morocco and Turkey, making Dubai International Properties one of the fastest growing real-estate developers in the region.

It is also a process which is being taken up vigorously in Manama itself. Evan just a decade ago, the skyline of Manama was dominated by the 29-storey tower of the National Bank of Bahrain. Since then, however, a newly introduced sense of verticality has gradually changed the image of the city (as well as the rest of Bahrain). It marks the beginning of a new era of iconic development. Manama, like many other Arab cities, has therefore subscribed to the 'Dubaization' process. This was clearly prompted by the need to respond to Dubai, which due to its unprecedented growth and unmatched desire to become a unique, global-scale model had also aggressively captured the hitherto role of Bahrain as the mixing point and the financial, commercial, recreational hub of the Gulf region. Hence in responding to Dubai's challenge, Bahrain has been forced to develop a new rhythm of urban development, with iconic towers and an increasing number of shopping malls becoming today the visible signs and symbols of globalisation.[47]

Bahrain is now basking in the glory of its financial might and throwing it doors open to international visitors with a flurry of cutting-edge business landmarks and boutique hotels. On one hand are the multi-functional skyscrapers which now characterize the waterfront: projects like Bahrain's Financial Harbour, Bahrain World Trade Center and Bahrain Bay are good examples of a new vertical dimension added to Manama's image. Secondly, there is a spread of man-made fantasy islands to promote exclusive lifestyles (see Plate 9). Mega-developments

5.16   The fast-changing Manama waterfront and with the iconic
BWTC and BFH towers dominating its skyline

5.17   Manama's reclaimed north shoreline, adding new urban centres
such the Northern City and Al Seef commercial area

5.18   Durrat Al Bahrain, a new iconic resort development on the south-eastern coast of the main island

like Durrat Al Bahrain, Amwaj Islands and Lulu Islands are representations of this category. Durrat Al Bahrain (Bahrain's Pearl), a 20 km² area of desert and sea, will be one-and-a half-times larger than downtown Manama. Originally scheduled for completion in late-2010, at full capacity it is intended accommodate more than 30,000 permanent residents in addition to some 4,000 visitors a day on its fifteen crescent- or fish-shaped islands. Obviously, the global financial crisis and the recent 2011 revolt in Bahrain have delayed the completion of the project, and indeed affected the pace of development in Manama as a whole.

Table 5.1   Urban development in Manama and Bahrain – main paradigms and transformations[48]

Timeframe	Patterns of Urban Development	Governing principle
Before 1930s	Traditional urban fabric with Islamic and regional references; the architectural language is generated from traditional settlements locally and regionally.	'Form follows Family'
1930s–1960s	The first impact of modernization; a gradual deterioration of traditional areas and the spread of modern urban settlements.	'Form follows Function'
1970s–1990	Regionalism and oil boom impact; massive government building programme of new cities and other settlements	'Form follows Identity'
1990s	Globalization; continued government involvement in urban projects, and the emergence of land-trading and the real-estate market	'Form follows Finance'
2000s	Post-oil economy, typified by tourism and iconic development.	'Form follows Icons'

Source: Ali A. Alraouf

5.19 Continuous
land reclamation
is changing
Manama's urban
morphology at an
unprecedented
pace, here
showing the
northern coastline
from the BFH
Tower to the Al
Seef district in
the distance

HYBRID URBANISM IN CONTEMPORARY BAHRAIN

The issues discussed in this chapter lead inevitably to questions about developments following Bahrain's independence as well as its contemporary situation as a globalising country. Bahrain is witnessing dramatic changes in land use and spatial organization generated by the accumulation of successive economic shifts. It passed from pearl-diving, fishing and maritime trade to an oil-based economy in the early-1930s, and more recently has entered the globalised economy through the promotion of the financial and tourist sectors. Likewise, a new type of urbanism emerged. Yet this reality has nothing to do with traditional or modernist dogmas: it is a spontaneous condition, driven by an instinct for survival, utility, money and fantasy. In an act of self-stylization, Bahrain is a raw experiment in the context of 'hybridization', where any proposed structure is ultimately measured by its ability to thrive in new and unpredictable conditions.

It seems that Bahrain is smoothly entering the new paradigm of a post-oil economy, which makes hybrid urbanism an unavoidable process. The challenge for Manama, as indeed for other Gulf cities, is not how to stop hybridity but how to integrate it into a more holistic process of sustainability. Sustainability emphasizes the integrated nature of human activities and therefore the importance of comprehensive planning which is coordinated between groups. Planning for sustainability implies creating liveable, equitable and ecologically-minded communities. Wheeler has stressed that the concept of sustainability has to be extended all the way from the planning level to the individual building site.[49]

While the architecture for the rehabilitation of the Manama Souk is to a great extent a fake representation of the past, the event of the Day of Ashura and its sacred power to collect thousands of people together is the most authentic dimension of this part of the old city. All new developments should focus on the event as the generator of the spatial and social spirit of the local context. As Frenchman argues convincingly, the making of good event-places represents far more than successful urban design. It becomes a powerful means of city building because it creates both social and physical capital, and as such contributes to the local economy.[50]

We must not forget that all of the Arab Gulf countries have been fortunate. They are oil-and-gas rich states, and although reserves are dwindling, prices are going down, and other energy alternatives are emerging, they are still able to use oil and gas revenues to develop projects to diversify their economies.[51] The grand plan for most of the Gulf economies is that in future they will become knowledge-based, which means that the services sector will be ever more important. Manama is moving with giant steps in this direction by using its financial resources and historical reputation as the Gulf's original financial centre. It needs however to add an ecological dimension to its thinking, and in that regard, here a useful definition given at the Sustainable City Conference in Rio de Janeiro in 2000:

> The concept of sustainability as applied to a city is the ability of the urban area and its region to continue to function at levels of quality of life desired by the community, without restricting the options available to the present and future generations and without causing adverse impacts inside and outside the urban boundary.[52]

Another important conclusion lies in acknowledging the contemporary challenge for globalised cities to maintain their ability to be different, avoiding physical homogenization. The argument is more severe in the case of Gulf cities given the magnitude of Dubai's impact (even if the current global financial crisis has shown to all just how much Dubai's economy is suffering from speculation and inflated real estate profits). All cities have historically been key contributors to personal and local identity. In the era of globalization, urban difference can also be a guarantor of social and political differences. As Sorkin argues, the crucial question is what are the sources of fresh and authentic difference within the spreading ocean of global uniformity.[53] He suggests three sources; the environmental *genius loci*, the model of the city as an autonomous environmental, political and economic entity, and the role of artistic invention in creating genuine and meaningful differences within urban patterns.

In the light of this chapter, we clearly need to keep up a continuous interpretation of relationship between Bahrain's post-oil economy and the development process in cities like Manama. This will involve examining the effects of the phenomenon of globalization on urban spaces in Bahrain's cities, whether in analyzing iconic developments for their social, cultural and environmental consequences, or the spatial impact of hybrid urbanism and the globalisation paradigm on architectural and urban spaces. From this we then need to suggest concepts, strategies and processes to incorporate a more sustainable approach to community development in the kingdom of Bahrain. It is clear that our future cities need to be sustainable; this is no longer a choice, it is an urgent demand for the coming generations. Cities in the Gulf region, in approaching the post-oil economy era with confidence, can show that they can be hybrid, globalized and sustainable.

NOTES

1   The recent global financial crisis has highlighted the negative consequences of such a demographic structure. See: Lucia Dore, 'Innovation and entrepreneurship critical to Middle East economies', 17 March 2006, *Khaleej Times* website, http://www.khaleejtimes.com/DisplayArticle.asp?xfile=data/business/2006/March/business_March333.xml&section=business&col (accessed on 24 September 2010).

2   Amos Rapaport, 'Culture and Built Form – A Reconsideration', in David G. Saile (ed.), *Architecture in Cultural Change: Essays in Built Form and Culture Research* (Lawrence, KS: University of Kansas, 1986), pp. 157–175.

3   Nelida Fuccaro, *Urban History of Bahrain* (Bahrain: Excess University, 1999); Nelida Fuccaro, 'Islam and Urban Space: Ma'tams in Bahrain before Oil', *Newsletter of the Institute for the Study of Islam in the Modern World* (July 1999), p. 12; Nelida Fuccaro, 'Understanding the Urban History of Bahrain', *Journal for Critical Studies of the Middle East*, vol. 17, no. 2 (2000): 49–81.

4   Nezar Alsayyad (ed.), *Hybrid Urbanism: On Identity Discourse and the Built Environment* (New York/London: Praeger, 2001).

5   Edward Said, *Culture and Imperialism* (New York: Alfred A. Knopf, 2003).

6   Nezar Alsayyad, 'Hybrid Culture/Hybrid Urbanism: Pandora's Box of the "Third Place"', in Alsayyad, *Hybrid Urbanism*.

7   Thomas R. Gensheimer, '*Cross-Cultural Currents: Swahili Urbanism in the Late Middle Ages*', in ibid.

8   Zeynep Celik, *Urban Forms and Colonial Confrontations* (Berkeley, CA: University of California Press, 1997).

9   Janet Abu-Lughod, 'On the Remaking of History: How to Reinvent the Past', in Barbara Kruger & Phil Mariani (eds), *Remaking History* (Seattle, WA: Bay Press, 1989), pp. 111–129; Henri Lefebvre, *The Production of Space* (Oxford: Basil Blackwell, 1974/91).

10 Homi K. Bhabha, 'The Other Question: Difference, Discrimination and the Discourse of Colonialism', in Russell Ferguson et al. (eds), *Out There: Marginalization and Contemporary Culture* (Cambridge, MA: The MIT Press, 1990), pp. 71–87.

11 George Katodrytis, various design projects and written texts on 'Hybrid Urbanism and Constructed Identity', 2004.

12 John Gordon Lorimer, *Gazetteer of the Persian Gulf – Oman and Central Arabia* (2 vols, Cambridge: Cambridge Archive Editions, 1908–15/86).

13 Fuad Khuri, *Tribe and State in Bahrain: The Transformation of Social and Political Authority in an Arab State* (Chicago, IL/London: University of Chicago Press, 1980).

14   Besim S. Hakim, *Arabic-Islamic Cities: Building and Planning Principles* (London/New York: Kegan Paul International, 1986).

15   Mahdi Abdalla Al-Tajir, *Bahrain 1920–1945* (London/New York/Sydney: Croom Helm, 1987); James Belgrave, *A Brief Survey of the History of the Bahrain Islands* (London: Journal of the Royal Central Asian Society, 1952).

16   John R. Yarwood, 'Al-Muharraq: Architecture, Urbanism, and Society in an Historic Arabian Town' (Unpublished PhD Thesis, University of Sheffield, Sheffield, 1988).

17   Mohammed G. Rumaihi, *Bahrain: Social and Political Change since the First World War* (London: Bowker, in association with Centre for Middle Eastern and Islamic Studies of the University of Durham, 1976).

18   Tariq Wali, *Al-Muharraq 1783–1971* (Bahrain: Gulf Panorama, 1990). See also Fuccaro, 'Understanding the Urban History of Bahrain', pp. 57–59, 65–72.

19   Nelida Fuccaro, 'Mapping the Transnational Community: Persians and the Space of the City in Bahrain 1869–1937', in Madawi Al-Rasheed (ed.), *Transnational Connections in the Arab Gulf* (London: Routledge, 2005), pp. 39–57.

20   Fuad I. Khuri, *Tribe and State in Bahrain* (Chicago, IL/London: University of Chicago Press, 1980).

21   Fuccaro, 'Mapping the Transnational Community'.

22   Yarwood, 'Al-Muharraq'.

23   Souheil El-Masri & Fa'eq Mandeel, 'Urban Planning Institutions in Bahrain', *8th Sharjah Urban Planning Symposium Proceedings* (Sharjah: SUPS, 2005), pp. 214–227.

24   Fa'eq Mandeel, 'Planning Regulations for the Traditional Arab-Islamic built Environment in Bahrain' (Unpublished MPhil Thesis, University of Newcastle, Newcastle, 1992).

25   Quote from Abdul Rahman Munif in Rasheed El Enany, 'Cities of Salt: A Literary View of the Theme of Oil and Change in the Gulf', in Ian Richard Netton (ed.), *Arabia and the Gulf: From Traditional Society to Modern States* (London: Croom Helm, 1986), p. 216.

26   Shirley R. Taylor, 'Some Aspects of Social Change and Modernization', in Jeffery B. Nugent & Theodore H. Thomas (eds), *Bahrain and the Gulf* (London: Croom Helm, 1985).

27   Jamel Akbar, *Crisis in the Built Environment: The Case of the Muslim City* (Singapore: Concept Media, 1988); Saleh Al-Hathloul, 'Tradition, Continuity and Change in the Physical Environment: The Arab-Muslim City' (Unpublished PhD Dissertation, MIT, Cambridge, MA, 1981).

28   Curtis E. Larsen, *Life and Land Use on the Bahrain Islands* (Chicago, IL: University of Chicago Press, 1983).

29   Hisham Mortada, *Traditional Islamic Principles of Built Environment* (London: Routledge Curzon, 2003).

30   Stefano Bianca, *Urban Form in the Arab Worlds: Past and Present* (London: Thames & Hudson, 2000); Gerald H. Blake & Richard I. Lawless, *The Changing Middle Eastern City* (London: Croom Helm, 1980).

31   Saskia Sassen, *Global Networks, Linked Cities* (London/New York: Routledge, 2002); Manuel Castells, *The Rise of The Network Society* (Oxford: Basil Blackwell, 1996).

32   Carol Willis, *Form Follows Finance: Skyscrapers and Skylines in New York and Chicago* (New York: Princeton Architectural Press, 1995).

33   Methil Renuka, 'Money Talks', *Business Traveler: Middle East* (July/August 2007): 18–22.

34   Francisco D. Pineda & Carlos A. Brebbia (eds), *Sustainable Tourism II* (Southampton: WIT Press, 2006).

35   Jan Rath, *Tourism, Ethnic Diversity and the City* (London: Routledge, 2006).

36   Rami Daher, *Tourism in the Middle East: Continuity, Change, and Transformation* (Bristol: Channel View Publication, 2007).

37   Rath, *Tourism, Ethnic Diversity and the City*.

38   Quoted in the 'Bab Al-Bahrain Area Development Design Report' by Gulf House Engineering for the Ministry of Municipalities and Agriculture Affairs, Bahrain (2006).

39   This debate around architecture, urbanism and identity is the main concern of numerous researchers. See, for instance: Cliff Hague & Paul Jenkins (eds), *Place Identity, Participation and Planning* (London: Routledge, 2004); Anthony D. King, *Spaces of Global Culture: Architecture, Urbanism, Identity* (London/New York: Routledge, 2004); Liane Lefaivre & Alexander Tzonis, *Architecture and Identity in a Globalized World*, Architecture in Focus Series (London: Prestel, 2003); William Neil, *Urban Planning and Cultural Identity* (London: Routledge, 2003).

40   Mohammed Al-Makdadi, Project Manager for the Manama Souk, as quoted in *Gulf News*, 26 February 2008, p. 13.

41   Umberto Eco, *Faith in Fakes: Travels in Hyperreality* (New York: Vintage, 1986).

42   Ahmed Bucheery, 'Contemporary Architecture in Bahrain', in Jamal Abed (ed.), *Architecture Re-introduced: New Projects in Societies in Change* (Geneva: Aga Khan Award for Architecture, 2004), pp. 62–69.

43   Ibid., p. 69.

44   Ali A. Alraouf, 'Dubaization vs. Glocalization: Territorial Outlook of Arab/Gulf Cities Transformed', paper presented to 9th Sharjah Urban Planning Symposium, Sharjah, UAE, 2–4 April 2006.

45   For a more detailed review of the real-estate boom in Dubai, see 'Arab Property: Boom Time' (special issue), *The Middle East Journal*, no. 395 (2005): 34–39.

46   Yasser Elsheshtawy (ed.), *Planning Middle Eastern Cities: An Urban Kaleidoscope* (London: Routledge, 2004), p. 17.

47   Souheil El-Masri, 'Towards Intelligent Urban Sustainability: Reviews of Initiatives & Future Prospects in Bahrain', paper presented to 6th Sharjah Urban Planning Symposium, 6–8 April 2003, Sharjah.

48   The table was developed as a result of findings in Yarwood, 'Al-Muharraq' and in El Masri & Mandeel, 'Urban Planning Institutions in Bahrain'.

49   Stephen M. Wheeler, *Planning for Sustainability* (London: Routledge, 2004).

50   Dennis Frenchman, 'Event-Places in North America: City Meaning and Making', *Places*, vol. 16, no. 3 (2004): 36–49. In this essay, Frenchman stresses that the popularity of event-places in the North American context has to do with a search for meaning in American public life and a yearning for community.

51   See the GCC hospitality report in *Gulf Business* (May 2007): 86–89. Here Guy Wilkinson sheds some light on the fact that the hotel projects in the pipeline and those under execution are countless, and he questions whether the market is open to that need. He states that the average rate of increase of hotel chains and rooms has been close to 60 per cent each year for the last five years.

52   Guy Battle & Christopher McCarthy, *Sustainable Ecosystems and the Built Environment* (London: Wiley-Academy, 2001), pp. 88, 91, 96.

53   Michael Sorkin, 'Difference in the Global City', abstract in special conference issue of *Traditional Dwellings and Settlements Review*, vol. 16, no. 1 (Fall 2004).

6

Doha, Qatar

Robert Adam

Modern Doha, capital of the small but fabulously wealthy Gulf state of Qatar, is built on the very substance that made modernity possible: oil. The city is a mirror of the economy that created it. Expansion began as the world moved from Empire to free trade and exploded into free market globalised western-style modernity. The impact of global capital is not, however, the same wherever it falls and Doha has translated its meteoric projection into modernity in its own particular way.

First impressions, nonetheless, seem to confirm the view that globalisation produces identical products wherever you go. On the way from the international airport (already bursting at the seams with its bigger and better replacement under construction next door), you pass by suburban houses on the American model and quickly reach a centre dominated by international style buildings. As you take the Corniche Road, a six-lane motorway curving round the bay, you pass by modernist cultural and government buildings and look over at West Bay, a forest of glass-walled and wonderfully shaped offices, apartment buildings and hotels. When you reach your internationally-branded hotel all is either reassuringly or disturbingly familiar, depending on your point of view.

Above all, you are aware of the sheer newness of it all. But there must be a story beyond the glitz and the signs of relentless construction. As so much of the city is so clearly modern, the condition and culture of the people in the recent past will have had a major influence on what we see now. We need to start by looking at how it all came about.

BACKGROUND TO DOHA

Qatar is a north-pointing finger of desert sticking out into the Gulf of Arabia or Persia, measuring some 11,500 km sq. It lies at only 13 m above sea level. Narrower at its base, it is a distinct geographic entity. Historically, it fell under the influence or control of different Empires: Persia, Portugal, Turkey and finally Britain. It was recognised internationally as a distinct political entity led by the Al Thani sheikhs in 1868. It was occupied by the Ottoman Empire in 1872 but, following a successful armed revolt, they finally left during the First World War. In 1916, Sheikh Abdulla bin Jassim Al Thani signed a protection treaty with Britain that guaranteed Qatar's defence from the sea and support in the event of land attack.

At that time, Qatar was poor with no significant agriculture or major sources of water. A few small towns around the coast were supported by fishing and pearl fishing was its major source of foreign income. The principal town and home of the ruling family was Al Bida, founded in 1825, which became known as ad-Dawha ('the big tree') or Doha. The demography of Qatar was a mix of settled seaboard Arabs and traders of Persian and Arabic origin in the coastal towns and nomadic Bedouins inland. The total estimated population was about 15,000 in 1920. Even this small population was driven to poverty, starvation and emigration when the Japanese developed cultured pearls in the 1920s and the impact of the 'Great Depression' from the USA crippled the small cash economy. This was the first major global event of many to affect Qatar.

Later global economic developments were much more benign. Worldwide demand for oil increased and the Middle East was identified as a major source. In 1934 Britain entered into a treaty granting further protection in return for granting a concession to the Anglo-Persian Oil Company. Oil was discovered in 1939 but exploitation was delayed until after the Second World War. In 1949, oil exports and payments for offshore rights began, as did the transformation of Qatar. This coincided with the elderly ruler abdicating the previous year in favour of his eldest son, Sheikh Ali Bin Abdullah Al Thani, who duly became Emir of Qatar (1948–1960).

Under a 1952 agreement with Shell, Qatar took 50 per cent of all oil revenues. This dramatic increase in wealth, along with social change and unrest in the Arab world following the Suez War in 1956, led to domestic unrest and pressure on the Al Thani family. Relying on British support, an embryonic government bureaucracy (staffed by foreigners) and a police force were created. In the 1950s, modern facilities were gradually introduced into Doha, including the first hospital, school, air-strip and telephone exchange. In 1960 huge offshore oil reserves were discovered and, under pressure to distribute the country's new-found wealth outside his immediate family, Sheikh Ali bin Abdullah Al Thani abdicated in favour of his eldest son, Sheikh Ahmad bin Ali Al Thani (1960–1972). Limited reforms were introduced, including the provision of land for poorer Qataris.

In 1971, as Britain's global power and wealth declined, it concluded its withdrawal from military commitments east of Suez, so ending the imperial era in the region. In the same year, Qatar withdrew from the formation of what would later become the United Arab Emirates, becoming instead a sovereign independent Arab Islamic state. At the time of its independence in September 1971 the population of Qatar had risen to over 100,000. The following year, Sheikh Ahmad bin Ali Al Thani was deposed by his cousin, Sheikh Khalifa bin Hamad Al Thani (1972–1995), who consolidated his family's position in the governance of the new state while introducing social programmes, including public health, education and pensions. During the 1973 global oil crisis Qatar created the Qatar General Petroleum Corporation and by 1977 it had nationalised all oil production. In a few years, from a dependent state and a colonial protectorate, Qatar had suddenly become enormously wealthy; by 1975 it had risen to enjoy the second highest GDP-per-capita in the world. Its last major political upheaval came in 1995 when Sheikh Hamad bin Khalifa Al Thani deposed his father while the latter was on holiday; Sheik Hamad then abdicated for his son in 2013.

This brief outline maps the beginnings of Qatar as a modern oil-dependent Arab country and of the rapid growth and development of its main city, Doha. As one Qatari told me when I visited, 'we have fast-forwarded a whole century'. But while a fully modern city has indeed grown up in a period of 40 years, the collective memory of extreme poverty and an insecure tribal past remain as real factors in the social, political and psychological life of Qatar. Another Qatari, from one of the major families, pointed out that his grandfather always went to bed with a loaded shotgun. This rapid history, from starvation to unimagined wealth within living memory, is essential for an understanding of the political reality behind the new institutions, the identity of the people, the pervasive Anglo-Saxon influence (first British and then American), and the interface between a tribal desert culture and global modernity. All of these things have and continue to leave their permanent mark on the city of Doha, which is home to 80 per cent of Qatar's population.

From the time of the first Qatari oil revenues in the late-1940s to independence in 1971, the town of Doha expanded accordingly. By recent standards, the earlier expansion was modest but it established a pattern of development that would be repeated in the following decades.

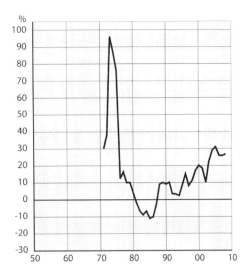

6.1   Gross Domestic Product of Qatar, Percentage year-on-year rise averaged over three years
Source: Author (figures taken from nationmaster.com)

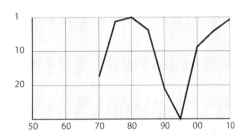

6.2   GDP per capita, world rankings for Qatar
Source: Author (figures taken from nationmaster.com)

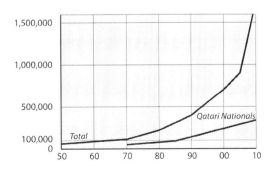

6.3   Qatar's population growth (Doha is approximately 80 per cent)
Source: Author (figures taken from Qatar Statistics Authority)

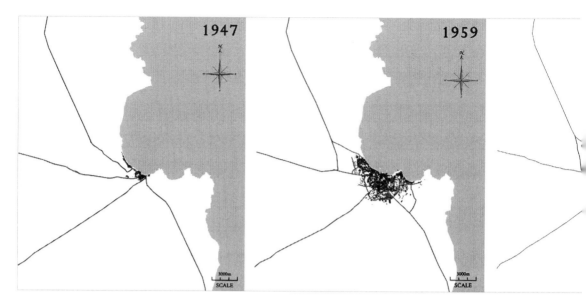

6.4   City growth in Doha from 1947 to present

The first major land reclamation project began in the early-1950s, moving the waterfront in the city centre out by 100 m and creating a series of new urban blocks. This was followed by the Corniche Road in the early-1960s, following the direction of the most recent urban expansion and running in front of long-established water-frontage merchant's houses. The loss of waterfront rights could be justified by the insanitary conditions that had developed in the shallow waters along the water's edge. The Corniche Road remains today as one of the defining features of the city.

Both the city's new waterfront and the Corniche Road were constructed by building the roads in the sea and then backfilling the space behind them, creating new real estate. This delivered high-value, state-owned land for building that was free from claims of historic land rights. Government House was built on the city centre reclamation and some ministries and government buildings were constructed on new land behind the Corniche Road. Land reclamation became, and continues to be, a key strategy in Doha for the creation of new high-status city districts.

Roads were also generally modernised. In accordance with the prevailing British typology, a number of by-passes or ring roads were constructed. These were named, successively and prosaically, 'A Ring Road' and 'B Ring Road' and so on. The A Ring Road joined the two ancient routes branching out to Saudi Arabia and the centre of the peninsula, and encompassed much of the 1950s town. The B Ring Road contained the 1960s urban expansion. By 1970, the C Ring Road was already under construction to contain further sporadic growth.

A new civic centre was created to the west of the old town in the 1950s. The Grand Mosque and Diwan al Amiri, or Royal Palace, were built around a ceremonial square centred on a landmark clock tower. Otherwise the architecture of the growing town was of no particular type or standard, often being on an ad-hoc

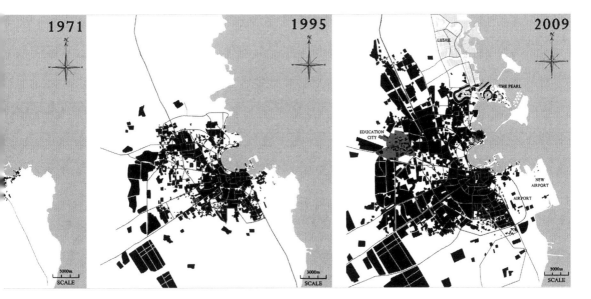

basis by Egyptian or Indian draftsmen. Low-rise concrete apartments and shops were mixed with traditional houses sited along and between the new roads. Much of this remains as a dense, active and lively urban area but in a poor state of repair, with no resident Qataris living there; instead, these dwellings are let out to expatriate workers. The old houses that do survive are not held in high regard and, in discussion, many Qataris described some of the older parts of the town as slums suitable only for demolition. Today, whole inner urban blocks are being bought up by the government for comprehensive redevelopment.

As Qataris became wealthier they sold, redeveloped or let out their traditional courtyard houses in the centre, preferring to move to new villas beyond the built-

6.5   Outer area of Doha showing traditional homes mixed with ad-hoc 1960s and 1970s developments

up area. Older houses represented for many the poverty they had just left behind and so there was a demand for new villas modelled on luxurious foreign designs. The use of standard American and North European suburban house types, with the dwelling placed in the centre of a plot, was also dictated by the introduction of boundary set-back regulations. Still in force today, these regulations made the construction of new houses in the Qatari tradition, with rooms built around the perimeter of walled courtyards, impossible. Villas and residential compounds for foreign workers were also built on open desert land outside the town in a haphazard fashion, setting the pattern for the later development of what has become a huge suburban hinterland.

THE REPLANNING OF DOHA

6.6   Masterplan for Doha by Llewelyn-Davies (1972)

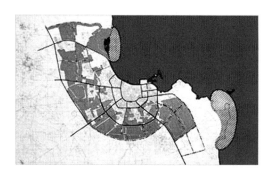

Alongside the creation of the independent sovereign state of Qatar, the capital was re-planned. In 1972 the well-known British urban designers, Llewelyn-Davies, were called in to study the possibilities for future expansion. Their plan built upon the ring road system, as well as on the presence of Corniche Road, adding a further D Ring Road to the network. They also created a loose grid stretching behind the Corniche Road and south towards the airport to allow for future structured growth. Llewelyn-Davies also proposed some further land reclamation work to the east and to the north to 'tidy up' the coastline.

Shortly afterwards in 1975, the then Emir of Qatar called in the, now largely forgotten, Los Angeles star architect William Pereira as an advisor. He proposed a much larger area of land reclamation to the north – this is now called West Bay – which turned the straight northern coastline around to form a new bay, and also creating a destination for the Corniche Road. This project has had a major impact on the town and was intended to be a model development area. It included a Diplomatic District on the new shoreline along with one of Pereira's trademark concrete pyramids as a Sheraton Hotel on the new promontory. This hotel was to be both a landmark viewed across the bay from the old town and a symbol of modernity. The Sheraton Hotel became part of a grand urban scheme which included a projected (but never executed) water spout on a new island in the bay and an axial boulevard, Grand Hamad Street, which was duly cut through the souks to focus on a pier-end lighthouse and the Sheraton Pyramid. Grand Hamad Street, now lined with modern bank buildings and featuring a crossed-scimitar ceremonial gate, remains as an uncomfortable insertion into the small-scale streets and alleys of the old town.

6.7   Plan of central Doha showing key elements

6.8   Sheraton Hotel by William Perreira Architects (1983), with West Bay behind and to the right

6.9   The formal civic gesture of Grand Hammad Street and its line of banks

RESHAPING DOHA

By the mid-1980s Doha had become a fully-functioning capital with new ministry buildings, National Theatre, National Museum and National Bank. By 1985 the population had tripled from its 1970 level to 320,000 people. After nearly two decades of world-class wealth, however, in the mid-1980s the global economic tide was turning. By 1986, oil prices had dropped to nearly one quarter of their 1980 price, and, along with other OPEC countries, Qatar's rapid financial growth stalled. GDP remained static or slightly dropped for twelve years from 1982, and expenditure was cut on public projects such as building works in Doha.

As noted before, in 1995 the Emir, Sheikh Khalifa bin Hamad Al Thani, was deposed suddenly by his Sandhurst-and-Cambridge-educated son, Sheikh Hamad. The following year the economy received a substantial boost as Qatar began to ship Liquefied Natural Gas (LNG) to Japan. Natural gas had been discovered in 1971 and Qatar's gas fields were found to constitute the world's largest single gas reservoir. Today, Qatar holds the world's third largest reserves, and at present levels of extraction there are 200 years of supply left. In 1995, as a result, Qatar's GDP began upon a steady rise that continues to this day.

The accession of Sheikh Hamad bin Kahlifa Al Thani therefore corresponds to the start of the new global age. In 1993 the Russian and Indian markets were liberalised and in 1994 China reformed its exchange and trade laws. Sheikh Hamad, aware of the emerging changes in the world order, set in motion what can only be called a revolution in the social and political order of Qatar. In his words, as quoted in the *New Yorker* on 20th November 2000: 'We have simply got to modernise ourselves. We're living in a modern age ... You cannot isolate yourself in today's world.'

The steps taken to modernise Qatar in the last ten years are impressive. The Ministry of Information was disbanded and censorship abolished. Women were given the right to vote and stand for office. A 'Qatar Permanent Constitution' was approved by referendum in 2003 which, amongst other principles stipulates that there will be 'no discrimination on account of sex, origin, language or religion' and establishes an elected legislative Advisory Council. The Emir's second of three wives, Sheikha Mozah, has been taken a high profile in the promotion of women's rights and in the advancement of education generally. On the world stage, Qatar hosted the 'Doha Round' of the World Trade Organization in 2001 and the 15th Asian Games in 2006. Qatar will hold the 2022 World Cup tournament. The global significance of the Emir's support for Al-Jazeera, the only uncensored Arab satellite television news channel, and based in Doha, cannot be underestimated.

The city of Doha today has grown to a population of an estimated 1,450,000 in 2011 living in its metropolitan territory. As noted, only 20 per cent of its citizens are Qataris. The current dramatic growth in the city will be as much an expression of the changes of the last 15 years as the legacy of the preceding decades. As I was told by the Manager of the Urban Development Department within the Urban Planning and Development Authority: 'When Emir Sheikh Hamad was directly modernising the country economically, socially and politically he took great interest in urban and architectural issues.'

CULTURAL IDENTITY IN DOHA

From the first days of its oil revenue, Qatar has seen the rapid introduction of wealth and modernity into a traditional society largely based on a marginal economy. Unlike Europe and North America, there has been no philosophical 'Enlightenment', no trial-and-error development of civil institutions, and no cultural or political evolution in parallel with the growth of an industrial and consumer society. The introduction of the apparatus of modernity includes its undeclared history, which can create tensions and conflicts.

As communications increase and international capital is liberalised, those concerned with the support and supply of the industrialised and consumerist society are drawn into its net. This form of modernity began in the North Atlantic nations and its later manifestations bear their stamp. The phenomenon is called globalisation and where it impacts on previously unaffected societies it sets in motion a dialogue between the global and the local or the modern and the traditional. This is a worldwide process but its manifestations are always local. The combination of rapid change and huge wealth in Qatar throw this dialogue into sharp focus.

The development of Doha is bound to give expression to the friction between the global and local, but this may not be immediately evident to the visitor. While by far the larger portion of the current population comes from elsewhere (in a short visit I met people from other Arab countries, Lebanon, India, Philippines, Nigeria, Australia, Canada, USA, Japan, and Russia), I was told more than once that expatriates feel that 'you're always a foreigner here', and naturalisation is not an option. The city belongs to the minority native Qatari population and so the way they identify with their rapidly changing capital city is relevant.

In discussion with Qataris about their personal identity, the response I got was consistent. Identity was about the family, the tribe and lineage. The nation was occasionally mentioned but so was the larger Gulf Arab community. Even when pressed on the role or place of Doha as a city, it did not have any significance in the individual's perception of themselves in their society. Comments included phrases such as 'the identity of the Qatari is inside himself, not the exterior', and 'there probably never was a Qatari identity and if there was it was never linked to the physical aspects of the place', and 'when you come home from abroad you look for the manners of the people, not so much the place'.

At the same time there is in Qatar a consciousness of the need to maintain or create a physical identity and of the dangers of outside influence. The Curator of the National Museum said: 'We have a tangible heritage in Qatar, our archaeology and our history, but we are in danger of submerging the old city.' One Qatari told me that there is a 'tension between traditional and modern design, we are now moving to a change in the culture and custom of Qatar from heritage to modern', and another that 'the foreigners we choose are not the right ones'. A young Qatari woman stated that 'we are copying international things but trying our best to maintain our identity'. And yet another told me that 'in reality we don't have much physical heritage'. However, Ibrahim Al Jaidah, a leading architect in the city, said more optimistically: 'I dream that we can turn this identity into something of our own'.

6.10   West Bay, with its cluster of international-style skyscrapers built round a shopping mall

RECENT DEVELOPMENT ACTIVITY IN DOHA

The most obvious expression of the new global North Atlantic modernity is West Bay. In the early-1990s, on the land behind the landmark Sheraton Hotel, Sheikh Hamad, in the words of the Manager of Urban Development, 'decided to change the masterplan so we can have a modern city'; he duly abolished the previous height limit of ground-floor-plus-ten storeys. The outcome is a group of high-rise buildings, centred on the other global type – a huge shopping mall. This totally eclipsed the landmark status of Pereira's Sheraton hotel. The start-up stimulus for this ongoing commercial development was provided by a take-up of office space by government departments. Most of the designs are the standard global glass-walled tower, some extravagantly modelled and some by star architects. Currently suspended due to concerns it might interfere with traffic at Doha International Airport, but apparently soon enough to join them is a very tall and super-slim 550 m tower (with a design seemingly re-cycled from the failed Grollo Tower in Melbourne, Australia) by Qatari Diar, the state development company. It would be only second in height to the Burj Khalifa. This will act as a landmark for a huge convention centre, reinforcing

6.11   Attempts to build a distinctive Arab (if not Qatari) style of glass high-rise in West Bay

6.12　The Barzan Tower at the entrance to West Bay from the Corniche shows the dilemma of creating a global-local or modern-traditional fusion

6.13   Strip mall
in the suburbs
of Doha

Doha's aspirations to become a high-status international conference venue. On closer examination, however, amongst the shiny towers are clear attempts to introduce a regional design type, mostly similar to American post-modernist towers but with Arabian detailing. Some, such as a version of Jean Nouvel's Barcelona tower now under construction, add abstracted Arabian details to familiar high-modernist types. On the entry to this area from the Corniche is the Barzan Tower with its traditional base and glass-walled top – a surprisingly eloquent expression of the unresolved global-to-local dilemma.

At the other end of the scale, the city is surrounded by vast suburbs of villas and gated 'compounds' complete with roadside strip malls, like the worst American suburban sprawl. The villas are often those of an American suburban type with illiterate versions of something vaguely traditional from the region or classical Europe. But quite unlike the North Atlantic suburb, these villas are all surrounded by high walls. While Qataris were keen to exchange their small courtyard houses for villas, they would not sacrifice their culturally-rooted standards of family privacy. In between these walled enclosures there are large and small areas of undeveloped land, dusty and seemingly uncared for. While the narrow lanes or *sikkats* between the old houses had been looked after by adjacent properties, this tradition clearly did not carry through to the wide residual spaces in the new suburbs, with unfortunate consequences.

Out in the suburbs are two quite different but explicit representations of North-Atlantic culture: the Villagio Shopping Mall and Education City. The popular and huge American-style Villagio Mall is made up of a half-digested pastiche themed on renaissance Italy, and is incongruously attached to the modernist 'Aspire Tower' built for the 2006 Asian Games. In the midst of a large car park, the Villagio Mall has a cartoon collection of bits and pieces from Italian cities disguising the blank outside walls and a Disney-style interior of what is meant to pass for Italian street facades under a painted cloudy blue sky. In the centre is a canal, complete with gondolas, and at one end a skating rink open to the mall.

6.14   Post-modern suburban houses behind high walls with uncared for residual space

6.15   'Aspire Tower' for 2006 Asian Games, now with link to Villagio Mall

6.16   Villagio Mall with its Italianising details making a vast suburban mall

6.17   Interior of Villagio Mall with its painted sky ceiling and imitation Italian street

At the opposite intellectual extreme but still culturally contiguous is Education City, a campus of outposts almost exclusively from American universities brought together by the Qatar Foundation, chaired by Sheika Mozah. Cornell University, Carnegie Mellon University, Georgetown University, Texas A&M University, Virginia Commonwealth University and Northwest University are represented. While the institutions are generally American, the list of architects reads likes a global *Who's Who* of the profession: Pelli, Koolhaas, HOK, Atkins, Legorreta and others. The key buildings are by Arata Isosaki including one of the most extraordinary attempts at synthesising international modernism and Qatari identity, the Education Convention Centre. This is a big dumb glass box fronted by a vast ground-to-eaves representation of the trunk of the Sida Tree (the logo of the Qatar Foundation and the symbol of the knowledge of the Divine from the Koran).

In Doha's city centre, the struggle to navigate between Qatari identity and global modernity is more complex. Government buildings are often just low-rise variants of the universal glass box but two major buildings stand as visible symbols, not so much of local identity as of a wider global mission – in the words of a local Qatari cultural institution – 'to diffuse the culture, ethical values and principles of Islam to mankind'.

6.18 Education City campus with various US university outposts

6.19 Education City Convention Centre by Arata Isozaki; the concrete structure imitates the Sida Tree, symbol of the Qatar Foundation

6.20 Museum of Islamic Art (2008) by I.M. Pei

The Museum of Islamic Art was opened with great fanfare in late-2008. It sits on its own man-made island and is approached down a grand avenue from the city centre. Its nonagenarian American star architect, I.M. Pei, said he was looking for 'the essence of Islamic architecture' and found it in the 13th-century fountain pavilion added to the 9th-century Mosque of Ahmad Ibn Tulun in Cairo. Pei drew on 'an almost Cubist expression of geometric progression from the octagon to the square and the square to the circle', and a 'severe and simple' Islamic tradition that he feels has a satisfactory affinity with the abstract principles of international Modernism. His building is, however, much more than a display of its fabulous collection and must be seen in relation to the objectives of a nearby institution, the Qatar Centre for the Presentation of Islam, or *Fanar* (the beacon), which also opened in 2008. This proselytising organisation is housed in a prominent building at the end of the Grand Hamad Street, designed by a little-known Egyptian architect, Husam Al-Ahmadi. It uses more literal traditional Islamic decoration and has at its centre a tall spiral landmark minaret said to be derived from the famous 9th-century minaret in Samarra, Iraq – but it is in fact closer to a 13th-century Egyptian version found in the same Ibn Tulun Mosque that inspired I.M. Pei, symbolically (but possibly fortuitously) reinforcing the relationship between the underlying agenda for both of these buildings.

While these landmark structures look to worldwide Islam in mission and design, two other urban projects in central Doha represent quite different approaches to maintaining a local built identity in a city with a minimal built heritage.

6.21   Qatar Centre for the Preservation of Islam (2008) by Husan Al-Ahmadi

The Souk Waqif is locally famous as a complete recreation of the original historic *souk* alongside the old waterway, or *wadi*, which led down to the port. The project was initiated in 2004 by Sheikh Hamad out of a concern that all evidence of the old town would be lost. Instead of a restoration, the *souk* is in fact a complete reconstruction of its pre-1950s state based on evidence from what remained, as well as photographic records, personal recollection and a fair bit of imagination – all put together by the Ohio-educated Qatari architect, Mohammed Ali Abdullah. The result has the basic form and appearance of an old *souk* but the character of something new: surrounded by car parking, all of the same age, and all of the same deliberately coarse cement render with ubiquitous projecting mangrove poles. In discussion with locals, reactions varied from enthusiasm to sadness, but a young woman was typically more concerned with the way of life of the people than the architecture, telling me: 'The old *souk* may not be real buildings but the way people use it, the opening and closing of the shops, the patterns of use are all the same.'

6.22   Souk Waqif, a complete recreation of the old souk on the same site

Taking a different direction, the Qatar Foundation purchased an adjacent urban district and commissioned the American international urban planners and landscape architects, EDAW (since subsumed within the giant global practice, AECOM), along with the British multi-disciplinary

6.23   Typical street in the outer section of the old town which is to be demolished for the Msheireb project

firm Arup, to completely re-plan the area based on an almost total demolition of the largely mid-20th century small shops, businesses and apartments. The tidied-up comprehensive redevelopment, called the Msheireb project, is based on a tight pattern of traditional narrow *sikkats* and courtyard urban blocks, retaining only a few old houses and the routes of two historic streets (see Plate 10). It is hoped that a smarter and cleaner precinct will encourage Qataris to re-inhabit the city centre. A design competition for the three key government buildings and the design coding of the future development was won by the established UK firm, Allies and Morrison. At this early stage, while the street planning follows the now widely-accepted principles of traditional urban design by drawing on local precedents, anything local in the architecture seems to be so abstracted that the European and even London origin of the architects shines through. This huge scheme, being built in five phases and covering 31 hectares, is currently scheduled for completion in 2016.

Moving from literal re-creation in Souk Wafiq to modern contextual abstraction in the Msheireb project is but the next stage in the 50-year struggle to find a balance

6.24 The Msheireb project by AECOM/Arup/Allies and Morrison

6.25 'The Pearl' development on the northern edge of the city

Lusail Development Masterplan

0   1 KM

6.26   Lusail district planned for the north of Doha

between the powerful culture of globalised architecture and urbanism and fragile local traditions. The success or otherwise of the creation of a Qatari character in the Msheireb project will not be evident for some years to come. It might, nonetheless, stand up well against other ongoing projects.

To the north, a large new resort-style waterfront development called 'The Pearl' is under construction for 50,000 inhabitants. Advertised with illustrations of Venice and an attractive girl in a *hijab*, the only relationship with Venice is the presence of water. Instead, the standardised designs are decorated with Arabian details. Occupation has already started, with anticipated completion for the scheme in 2015. Beyond this, 35 square kilometres has already been prepared by Qatari Diar to make way for Lusail, a new urban area with a projected population of 445,000. Its models and illustrations show the by now familiar huge glass towers and separate areas for villas and shopping with localised details added to American building types. The promotional literature speaks of 'distinctive features that celebrate traditional Qatari and Islamic architecture in a striking, contemporary way', thereby unwittingly capturing the very dilemma that underlies all development in Doha since the early-1950s.

With relaxed land ownership rules, the marketing of these new urban areas is being directed to foreign as well as local purchasers, and consequently progress has been slowed by the global recession. Rents in Doha generally were down by 35 per cent in 2009 due to declining demand. The second highest GDP per capita in the world, and generous financial support for Qataris from the national budget, however, means that this will probably only be a temporary slowdown, largely affecting expatriates. I certainly heard little concern from locals about any long-term impact of the current global recession, and indeed rents have already started to rally.

Sustainability, however, is only just emerging as an issue in Doha. In 2009 saw the launch of the Qatar Green Building Council, coupled with calls to abandon glass towers and, in the phrase used by Issa Al Malahni in *The Peninsula* newspaper on 19th March 2009, to 'go back to the DNA of [Qatar's] ancient building designs'. Given the scale of historic Qatari building and the scale of development in the last twenty years, this would require a seismic transformation and there seems to be no sign of any reining back of the cult of star architects or grandiose urban gestures. Low densities and glazed high-rise buildings are envisaged for Lusail for many years to come. A new public transport system is planned by the German firm PTV to counteract the almost totally car-based transport of the city. But with petrol at around $0.25 (15 pence) a litre, plus huge and sprawling suburbs and the ubiquity of four-wheel-drive vehicles, any public transport system in Doha would most likely be used predominantly by the poorer expatriate population. With summer temperatures at 45°C, life in Qatar is made tolerable for all sectors of the population by air-conditioning in buildings and vehicles, so much so that in 2004 the UN ranked the country as the highest-per-capita carbon emitter. The reality of environmental sustainability will take a long time to catch up with the rhetoric in Doha (if it ever does).

FUTURE PROSPECTS FOR DOHA

As Qatar looks to the future, how will Doha change? In 2005 the Urban Planning and Development Authority launched an invited competition for a new national masterplan to take the country through to 2025. This was won by a Japanese firm, Oriental Consultants, who in September 2010 presented their Qatar National Master Plan, which sets out a vision to make Doha the 'most liveable' city in the Persian Gulf region. It remains to be seen if this plan fares better than the still-current 1994 plan (also intended to last for 25 years) by the American firm, Louis Berger, which set up zoning standards, development policies and design guidelines as well as a planning council to administer the plan. I was told that because 'unexpected political and economic changes' overtook that plan for Doha, only 50 per cent of its proposals have survived. Whatever formal systems and orderly processes are set up by foreign firms, familiar with committee-based regulatory systems, these are always vulnerable to revision through the long-established family and hierarchical patronage (or *majlis*) system exclusive to the Qatari community. Also of critical importance is the make-up of Doha's population, with the sharp divide between native Qataris and the large workforce drawn from overseas countries. As noted before, Qataris today constitute around 20 per cent of the overall population, a proportion equalled also by other Arabic residents, Indians and Pakistanis; the remaining 20 per cent consist of Iranians or other nationalities. There is also a striking gender imbalance, with males being around 80 per cent of the population of Qatar due to the massive influx of non-permanent immigrant workers; this latter group also totally skews the age distribution of the population, since most are males from their 20s–40s who have come to seek work in Doha.

In the Msheireb project, the introduction of traditional urbanism may herald the start of a move from big-scale anonymous urban design to closer-knit vernacular planning. Much will depend on whether Oriental Consultants are genuinely in tune with this new direction in urbanism. The global-to-local or modern-to-traditional architectural dialogue, however, shows no sign of resolution. There are regular official statements aspiring to a combination of modernity and tradition which fail to recognise that imported and globalised North Atlantic architectural modernity was developed precisely as an antithesis to tradition. Most American and European architects who are now building in Doha would never combine these concepts for designs in their home countries. As architecture inevitably reflects social, political and economic developments, if there is to be a change there it is here that we should look for the future. The direction of change in Qatari society is defined by the new Permanent Constitution. This must be seen, complete with its democratic underpinning, not as a westernising reform but rather as a modernising and formalising of traditional Muslim and Arab governance. Alongside the new constitution is a policy for the 'Qatarization' of society – in other words, the re-assertion of Qatari institutional leadership. If Qataris can use their (often foreign) education as a springboard for a rediscovery of their cultural heritage, instead of a mimicry of global culture, then a quite different and unique kind of architectural modernisation can take place that develops those built traditions that help to define Qatari culture.

7

Abu Dhabi, UAE

Olivia Duncan and Sonny Tomic

The land where the United Arab Emirates lies today is in a geographical location which contributes to its high temperatures, its challenging desert climate, as well as its inhospitable and desolate terrain. At the same time, the very same location provides for abundant petroleum and natural gas reservoirs which have been blessing the country – and more specifically, in relation to the UAE's capital city of Abu Dhabi, with the means to provide for a better future for its people and future generations. A society burdened by such a harsh climate and sterile land developed sophisticated survival skills through ephemeral architecture and its connection to the water. The nomadic nature of the Bedouins, and the need to deal with the extreme heat and high humidity levels, informed a specific quality of shelter, one that needs to deal with controlling the micro-climate while serving the community's needs. 'In less than one lifetime, the Gulf has transformed from one of the most disengaged parts of the world to a strategic fracture point of globalization in a regional context.'[1]

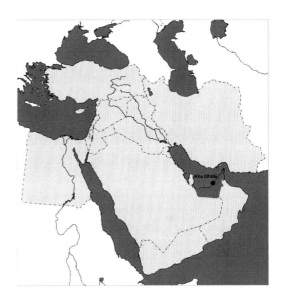

7.1 Map of Abu Dhabi in context of the Persian Gulf

Abu Dhabi is becoming a fascinating amalgam of thresholds. Successive tensions between its historic, economic, political, cultural, social and technological thresholds in the last 50 years have created the ever-evolving experience of the contemporary Abu Dhabi. This evolution was carefully shaped by inspired political leadership who channeled large sums of investment into culture and building infrastructure, while also embracing globalization as a means to modify cultural traditions in a non-threatening way, and sharing the newly found wealth with the native society.

Informal coastal settlements and traditional Gulf architecture, composed of vernacular use of temporary available materials, were unable to provide for the new demands of a modernizing city – and currently a globalizing city. A fascination for progress and development in such a barren land is not only understandable, but also predictable. This dramatic shift affected Abu Dhabi's urban design and architecture in many ways. This is clearly represented in the introduction of a rigid street grid with oversized boulevards and superblocks and the imported Modernist approach to urban development which demanded building designs that carried 'Brutalist' characteristics, expressed as modest-sized concrete blocks. The 1980s and 1990s brought Islamic ornamentation to the concrete boxes as well as into the more recent glass curtain facades. The first decade of the 21st century embraced gargantuan architectural and urban scale in Abu Dhabi, introducing the currently accepted 'hyper-modernism' direction into built form in the city.

This chapter investigates the particularities and ways in which these dynamic inter-relationships, which can be seen as urban 'thresholds', have impacted upon Abu Dhabi's physical evolution. Particular interest will be shown in discovering how forces of globalism influenced changes in the traditional delineation of social space, the private *versus* the public, and the introduction of pseudo-traditional Islamic principles in urban design and architecture.

HISTORICAL BACKGROUND

The bleakness of the land compelled local Bedouin tribesmen to explore the sea and its resources. Western descriptions both from the early- and late-20th century evoked the natural setting in which settlers had to deal with in the region. One wrote: 'The coast of the Arabian [Persian] Gulf presents remarkable peculiarity in possessing from one end to the other a series of creeks, lagoons and backwaters without which its barren and desolate terrain would barely have been habitable.'[2] Abu Dhabi Island served essentially as an ephemeral site for shelter, supporting the fishing and pearl-diving activities performed by nomadic people travelling from the mainland: 'For centuries they had to fight against the privations of a land that barely provided the means of subsistence, and their lives revolved around the presence or absence of water.'[3] Then, according to Bedouin tradition, one tribe's leader happened to find a fresh-water spring after crossing over to the island to hunt a particular gazelle. It seems that the gazelle stood on the very spring of fresh water which was to become the basis of the settlement. This availability of water attracted other nomadic people, and it is believed that the first proper settlement of Abu Dhabi dates back to 1761; at that point, it consisted of 20 *barasti* huts built of palm fronds on timber frames. Sheikh Dhiyab bin Isa led his people from their home in Liwa to this area, which became known as Abu Dhabi, meaning 'father of gazelle'.[4]

Historical evidence about the early settlement of Abu Dhabi Island was most likely kept alive by oral traditions and legends among the local population. As is described by the Centre for Documentation and Research, Sheikh Dhiyab founded the coastal settlement but he himself remained in the area between the island and the inland oases of Liwa and Buraimi, leading the Al Bu Falah section of the Beni Yas tribe.[5] According to Trench, the earliest inhabitants of the Abu Dhabi settlement relied almost entirely on fishing and pearl diving as there were no traces of ordinary crop cultivation and very few date palms. He also suggests that even after the arrival of foreign presence due to European colonial intervention in the Gulf region, development was uncommon: '… the anchorage for large vessels is totally unsheltered and lies more than two miles from the shore.'[6]

The need for each Bedouin tribe to control and cater for its own water supply and livestock perpetuated the erection of watchtowers and forts: 'It is presumed that the round tower [Qasr al Hosn] which still exists today, is probably the remnant of the earliest-known structure built by the Al Bu Falah Sheikh during the first settlement of Abu Dhabi.'[7] Within a couple of years after being founded, the settlement of Abu Dhabi had expanded to 400 *barastis*, and its population continued to increase thereafter. The watchtower of Qasr al Hosn was most likely erected at the end of the 18th century, this also being period in which the Beni Yas tribe recognised Abu Dhabi Island as its capital. During its early days, the fort stood 'among a few crumbling houses built of coral and a hundred or so palm frond huts'. Abu Dhabi was described by one contemporary English commentator as:

> A coastal town of about 6,000 inhabitants. There is a fort, and the houses are
> mostly built of date matting though some are of masonry. There is a small
> bazaar, and a poor anchorage. The water supply is from pits and wells, and is
> not very good. The supplies are particularly nil. There is usually no cultivation,
> and there are very few dates. Small quantities of cloth, rice, coffee and sugar are
> imported. There are about 750 camels and 65 horses.[8]

Throughout the 19th century, the Bedouin desert tribe continuously enjoyed access to the rich pearl beds of the Gulf coast, which helped the further evolution of Abu Dhabi as an emerging coastal town. Parallel to this flourishing of the city was of course the British presence. Britain had an imperial interest in India and it was also in her interest to protect the maritime area of the Gulf region and peace was necessary for business. As is highlighted by Muhammad Abdullah, 'Abu Dhabi's economic interests laid mainly in the date groves at Liwa and in the pearl fisheries around Dalma Island, far from the navigation channel of the Gulf, therefore the Beni Yas had no conflict with the British at sea.'[9] The tiny sheikhdoms sparsely inhabited the southern shores of the Gulf Coast and for a long time were known as the 'Trucial States' due to the maritime truce drawn up between these tribes and the British Empire in the late-19th century. It was an arrangement that helped the city to prosper:

> Abu Dhabi developed around the Qasr al Hosn and local construction material
> was used to build the surrounding housing areas. Ihilati and Ibarastii were the
> typical architectural styles used to build the dwellings which consisted of local

materials such as clay, coral, sandstone, sea stone, palm trees and wooden pillars connected together with ropes.[10]

Later on, Abu Dhabi's pearl trade was devastated by the marketing of Japanese cultured pearls at a fraction of the cost of Gulf pearls. This situation, combined with the worldwide economic depression of the 1930s, had a disastrous effect on the town's commerce.[11] However, a dramatic turnaround for Abu Dhabi soon came with the discovery of a more precious resource: petroleum. 'The discovery of oil and the signing of concession agreements initiated a process that would transform what was in essence a provincial backwater, a collection of mud huts, into a recognisable urban entity.'[12]

In 1953, Abu Dhabi Marine Areas Ltd obtained offshore oil concessions, resulting in substantial royalty payments. Following Abu Dhabi's first oil exports in 1962, Sheikh Shakhbout – who was then the leader of the tribes in the local area – started developing social conditions in a progressive manner. A municipal department was established in Abu Dhabi with the responsibility for improving living conditions and ensuring provision of drinkable water supplies and accessible public health services. In the same year, Halcrow & Company (a well-known British consultancy firm, today known as Halcrow Group) was commissioned to produce a master-plan for the city's urban transformation. As described by Yasser Elsheshtawy, this master-plan included a series of north-facing buildings, a new road network, and the provision to raise the existing ground level through dredging and land reclamation.[13] The plan also proposed the demolition of all existing buildings except for Qasr al Hosn, two water distillation plants, a few schools, and a power station.[14] Nonetheless, despite these ambitious large-scale proposals, it was also evident that Sheikh Shakhbout was resistant to the idea of Abu Dhabi becoming a modern state, as he was still in favour of preserving a traditional lifestyle. He refused, for example, 'to generate electricity, with the exception of the palace which was lit using a portable electrical generator.'[15]

In contrast to Sheikh Shakhbout's reluctance to transform the island town into a dynamic modern metropolis, the accession to power of Sheikh Zayed bin Sultan Al Nahyan in 1966 altered and improved the urban development process. His leadership also brought political tranquillity and pride to the new nation to-be: 'Sheikh Zayed's known achievements in Abu Dhabi, his generosity to the other emirates, together with his outstanding personal qualities, made him a popular figure and an obvious leader.'[16] Mohammed Al-Fahim further described the leader: 'Sheikh Zayed's name was known by everyone, his reputation as a fair and generous man was equally widespread. He was a fiercely patriotic man who loved his country and its people above all else.'[17] In addition, 'Sheikh Zayed strongly believed that the revenues that were being generated as a result of the oil royalties should be used to develop Abu Dhabi and to assist the native population.'[18]

In 1968, during this period of internal political transition and the rapid development of the city, the Gulf States experienced the withdrawal of the

British presence due to the latter's economic pressures back home.[19] As was pointed out, 'British withdrawal from the Trucial States meant the latter would be left without the umbrella of protection that had guarded the coastal area against external aggressors since 1892.'[20] Concerned about possible conflicts with neighbouring countries, Sheikh Zayed was convinced of the advantages of pursuing the unification of the surrounding sheikdoms, although he had to overcome natural resistance and scepticism from the other ruling sheikhs. Ultimately, in 1971, the formation of the political union known as the United Arab Emirates was achieved – made possible by Sheikh Zayed's vision of a unified country, as well as encouragement from Britain. The city of Abu Dhabi, now established as the capital of the UAE, expanded within its isosceles-triangle-shaped island situated just off the coast at 24° north, 54° east. The city's urban palette continued to extend towards the mainland and onto surrounding islands, the latter consisting usually of geometrically-shaped pieces of land reclaimed from the sea. Today the Abu Dhabi Emirate is the largest of the seven Emirate states, since it includes Abu Dhabi Island and numerous smaller islands nearby along with regions to the west and east on the mainland: altogether it constitutes 87 per cent of the UAE's total land area.[21]

Concomitantly, Abu Dhabi underwent major urban change, with local inhabitants being asked to move from their traditional housing into newly

7.2   Sheikh Zayed poster in Abu Dhabi central business district (CBD)

7.3   Abu
Dhabi Island

constructed homes. Buildings from the early days of the settlement were demolished, as had been recommended by the initial Halcrow plan, and the city was re-zoned yielding to modernity. Government compensation was given to those families who had to be relocated, and the sum each family was paid to abandon its old dwelling was sufficient to build a new abode as well as set up businesses with the remaining funds.[22] Al-Fahim describes his childhood in the city at that time:

> In five years the metamorphosis of Abu Dhabi occurred at lightning speed ...
> While it took most countries decades to develop communications and
> transportation systems for example, we did so in a very short time. We had
> electricity by 1967, phones in 1972. Wherever we turned to, something was under
> construction – government buildings, homes, roads, telephone lines.[23]

Around the same time, the Egyptian engineer Abdul Rahman Makhlouf was invited by Sheikh Zayed to continue the plan proposed by Halcrow & Company. To achieve this goal, Makhlouf was appointed as Director of the Town Planning Department of the Abu Dhabi Emirate from 1968–1976, making him responsible for the planning of both Abu Dhabi and Al Ain. His scope included deciding on the locations of key buildings, marketplaces, and the infrastructure for the city.[24] Makhlouf also introduced the concept of the 'national house', which aimed to aid the Bedouin citizens adapt to urban life. As described by Elsheshtawy, 'the

house consisted of a large one-storey structure of concrete blocks with open and closed spaces suited to the Bedouin traditions. Each had two bedrooms, a kitchen, bathroom, garden, courtyard and other open spaces and a wall to hide the women's quarters.'[25] There was also a particular concern to build new mosques and markets (*souqs*) located at walking distance from the major residential clusters.

7.4   Continuous refurbishing of street layouts in Abu Dhabi

The logic behind the city's planning in this period, which is still recognisable today, demonstrated a strong reliance on imported western modernist planning principles. Wide grid-pattern streets with their emphasis on vehicle connectivity, an orientation towards methodical building processes, and the use of high-density tower blocks were some manifestations of what was believed to be the solution for Abu Dhabi's urban development. However, this new need to maximize accessibility for motor vehicles undermined the original organic way of travelling around the island. The human-scale yielded to vehicle-scale, and informal narrower alleys gave way to broad roads: 'While the streets in the traditional patterns reflected residents needs such as climatic comfort, privacy and security, the streets in the modern patterns disregard these aspects.' As the city's population increased, rising building heights became not only a design choice but also an urban design necessity. The need to accommodate commercial and trading activities as well as housing needs pushed building density up. Alongside this new architectural solution for a modern Bedouin city in Abu Dhabi, with its imported greenery and technological infrastructure, came air-conditioning systems. This also altered the way in which people conducted their lives and had a large impact in encouraging tourism.[26]

7.5   Average building height in Abu Dhabi's CBD

7.6   Canyon-effect produced by the typical building threshold in CBD

In order for the city to expand according to its leader's vision, and meet the demand for developable sites, the 1970s and 1980s brought extensive land reclamation for waterfront development. This increased the size of the island from its original 60 km^2 to 94 km^2 by 1994, making it 50 per cent larger. Abu Dhabi's population also grew exponentially: in 1966 it had been only 17,000 people, but this then soared to 70,000 in 1972, following the country's unification. 'A remarkable increase mostly attributed to immigrants', is how this population boom has been summed up.[27] Following this period, and more particularly throughout the 1990s, the Khalifa Committee (named after Sheikh's Zayed's son, the current ruler of Abu Dhabi and the UAE) became responsible for building a large percentage of the city, and providing also for housing needs. Its aim was to densify development: 'The current urban form of the city was strongly influenced by this policy since plots handed out were small, resulting in the construction of towers which are particularly evident in the city's centre. Some 95 per cent of plots in Abu Dhabi range between approximately 25m × 15m to 30m × 30m, and were occupied by multi-storey buildings with an average height of twenty storeys.'[28] This particular building endeavour, however, has produced a rather repetitive canyon-like urban character, with an intensive repetition of high-rise towers close to each other (see Plate 11).

In anticipation of reaching even more advanced achievements in the early-21st century, and continuing urban progress and development, the Emirate's Executive Council decided to prepare a further master-plan for Abu Dhabi. Hence in 1988, the Abu Dhabi Town Planning Department – in collaboration with UNDP and various international consultants – came up with the Abu Dhabi Comprehensive Development Master Plan.[29] While planning for the future, the government also used this to inform people about the new levels of acceptable and unacceptable urban lifestyle. For instances, it stipulated that Bedouin families who tethered

7.7   The coastline
of Abu Dhabi seen
from on high

camels and other animals outside their residences were now forbidden to do so. The planning agency in charge justified the new measures: 'The decision aims at preserving the urban outlook of the city, where under the current modernization programme, gardens are springing up everywhere, including residential areas.'[30] Thus, traditional customs were deemed as not in accordance with the implementation of 'disciplined' housing compounds and modern high-rise areas, such as where the foreigners live. Another key aspect of the new Abu Dhabi was the introduction of western building materials, such as concrete, steel and glass. Such construction materials made the raising of floor levels feasible, but relied heavily on centralised air-conditioning systems which introduced an entirely different relationship of people to their environment. Another undesirable result was the visual impact of air-conditioning units, as well as, more recently, the satellite dishes which continuously riddle the city's facades and rooflines.

In the analysis of John Fox, the effects of globalization were, and still are, rendered differently in the Gulf region compared to other parts of the world. Hence, despite the continuous external forces being introduced into social and economic life in the Abu Dhabi Emirate, the nation's strong traditional familial structure has 'developed receptive ways of synchronizing localism with globalism within the area … the traditional social structure persists to direct the changes, and serves to filter what is acceptable – working as a sort of indigenous conservatism.'[31] But within the Gulf, however, there are also significant disparities between the evolution of even nearby cities. When compared to Dubai's rapid urbanising phenomenon, Abu Dhabi has taken a more conservative approach to its urban expansion. While

7.8   Pseudo-traditional architecture in Abu Dhabi

7.9   *Dhow* boat with Abu Dhabi skyline behind

7.10   Grand
Mosque (Sheikh
Zayed Mosque), in
Abu Dhabi, UAE

the 'louder' Dubai has developed an economy based on international commerce,
opening its city to a more intensified urban and architectural resolution driven
by other countries, Abu Dhabi (backed by Sheikh Zayed's vision) stands closer to
Arab-Gulf traditions, with an added tolerance and interest in modernization, and
the cultural infusion of new kinds of people, ideas and technologies.

> *Religion is embedded in most social relationships in the Gulf, including the
> practice of capitalism. Only a small part of Gulf society sees capitalism as
> antithetical to the strong community values of Islam and have spawned anti-
> globalism political movements. The leadership constantly strives to show how
> tolerant Islam is as a religion so that globalization development may contribute
> bereft of indigenous reactions.*[32]

In addition, Abu Dhabi has taken a strategic decision to emerge as a major
international quality tourist destination. Large projects such as the Grand Mosque
showcase the city's desire to portray bold architecture that reflects the country's
Islamic religion, while at the same time symbolising the desirable institutional
power for both the royal family and ordinary UAE nationals (see Plate 12).

THE GLOBAL 'INSTANT' CITY

The phenomenon of globalization, and its origins, is not necessarily of the 20th
century, and indeed the concept of being 'global' seems to be constantly mutating.
Back in 2000, Clark and colleagues explained the concept as being:

… the process of creating network of connections among entities at multi-continental distances, mediated through a variety of flows including people, information and ideas, capital and goods. Hence, globalization is conceptualized as a process that erodes national boundaries, integrates national economies, cultures, technologies and governance and produces complex relations of mutual interdependence.[33]

For the purpose of this essay, the concept of globalization is recognised as a multi-dimensional global event; it is a phenomenon that is experienced across the world and is 'being driven by a combination of economic, technological, socio-cultural, political and biological factors.'[34]

Hence the presence of immigrants from skilled or unskilled background increased proportionally to the amount of new development that took place, and is still happening, in Abu Dhabi. Along with the new forms of architecture and the modern lifestyles freshly imposed on its people, new social dynamics have arisen from the introduction of 'strangers' who were vital to deliver the leader's vision: 'Oil-generated growth has literally demolished mud-walled small seaports and villages. In less than fifty years Abu Dhabi has transformed into a commercial capital with its sprawling suburbs integrated within the global economy and culture.'[35] The advent of the 21st century has brought even further transformation. Hundreds of low-rise buildings from the early-1970s are currently being demolished and replaced by high-rise blocks. There are also strong moves to improve the landscaping. According to the Abu Dhabi Municipality, the city has, since its inception, undergone an extensive forestation process including the planting of parks and tree-lined boulevards with evergreens and literally millions of palm trees.[36] Certainly, the municipal statistics from 2003 reveal that there were then about 80 million trees in Abu Dhabi.

7.11 Continuous demolition in Abu Dhabi

Despite the current prolonged global economic recession, Abu Dhabi continues to move ahead with high expectations; its current total value of announced projects is close to the AE Dirham1,835 billion (US$ 77 billion) mark.[37] According to the Abu Dhabi Emirate's yearbook in 2009, its status as an emerging market is highlighted by the large investment being poured into real estate, tourism and leisure. Developments such as Masdar City, Capital District, Saadiyat Island, Yas Island, Al Suwwah Island, Al Reem Island and Al Raha Beach represent Abu Dhabi's ambition to become a capital not only for its country, but also for culture, education and research within the Gulf as a whole. The city is setting new standards in building, urban planning, design and cultural development. In 2007, therefore, Abu Dhabi's government announced a modified master-plan, an urban structure framework for the city during its rapid urban evolution, which would showcase its vision as a world-class leader in creating an innovative and sustainable Arab capital city. Thus the 'Plan Abu Dhabi 2030' delineates the official framework for substantial development across the entire Abu Dhabi metropolitan area, providing the vision for all aspiring projects.[38] There are five central principles which inform the plan's ideas and policies, but the imperative goal is for Abu Dhabi to be 'a contemporary expression of an Arab city', with its inhabitants thriving in the supportive and healthy community which Abu Dhabi will ultimately become. In addition, another key element lies in the importance for Abu Dhabi to continue to practice measured growth as part of a sustainable economy, with the master-plan recognising the significance of environmental sustainability and the need to respect the city's sensitive coastal and desert ecologies.

The 'Plan Abu Dhabi 2030' addresses concerns for a more coherent matching of built form with social and functional needs. Abu Dhabi has a particularly unique real-estate allocation system in which land ownership is granted exclusively to every male head of an Emirati family. As a result of this process, it becomes imperative to provide adequate housing for the evolving needs of Emirati families, and to reduce the waiting time for receiving government sponsored dwellings by increasing their availability. Hence the plan offers guidelines for building blocks designed around specific needs of UAE nationals:

> These include the fareej – modelled on a set of villas around a central courtyard, reflecting an extended Emirati family structure – as well as island and desert eco-villages. The villages are based on traditional Emirati ways of life, and the aim is to ensure these environments are provided across the emirate in a way that reflects local customs. Sustainability initiatives such as solar and wind power will also make these communities more self-reliant in the future.[39]

EMPIRICAL DATA ABOUT ABU DHABI

Taken altogether, the UAE's population increased by 74.8 per cent from 1995–2005, with the Ministry of Economics predicting this figure would reach a total of 5.06 million people by the end of 2009. The discrepancy between nationals and non-nationals, however, is extremely noticeable: 'a breakdown of the 2007 figures indicates that there were 864,000 UAE nationals and 3.62 million expatriates in the country.'[40] Within the UAE, Abu Dhabi was the most populous state in late-2007, with 1.493 million people. However, the population in the Abu Dhabi Emirate when divided by gender at this date was 982,000 males and 511,000 females, the difference being because of the high numbers of male immigrant workers. There are also very sharp economic divisions. According to the Department of Economic Development, the average monthly income of Emirati households in Abu Dhabi in 2008 was Dh47,066 (12,815 USD), but the average monthly income in the same year for expatriate households – mostly overseas labourers – was Dh15,000 (4,084 USD).[41] This social division is even greater when one realises that the Emirate's per-capita income surged from around Dh76,600 (20,856 USD) in 2006 to Dh162,000 (44,107 USD) in 2007, with the overall gross domestic product increasing from Dh624 billion to Dh729 billion in the same period.[42] The key areas influencing this rapid economic growth were – from the UAE Central Bank's statistics – the astonishing boom in the construction sector (25.6 per cent rise) along with significant growth in manufacturing and industry (19.8 per cent); real estate (16.9 per cent); finance (11.5 per cent); transportation and communications (8.3 per cent), and tourism, which continued its steady growth by growing by 6.4 per cent in terms of trade volume. Exact and up-to-date data is hard to obtain, but certainly recent statistics suggest that these demographic and economic trends still hold true for Abu Dhabi. In estimates from mid-2009, the city had around 970,000 citizens, some 60 per cent of the Emirate's population, with two-thirds of them being male. Emiratis continue to comprise just 20 per cent of Abu Dhabi's populace.[43]

7.12 Threshold matrix – Layer 01

ANALYSIS – THRESHOLD MATRIX

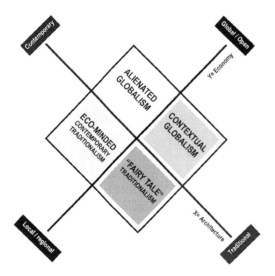

The impact of globalization in the contemporary Abu Dhabi built environment can be analysed through the lenses of issues of privacy, physical walls and the notion of gate. In order to do so, tangible and intangible thresholds in the city can be categorized into the tangible physical urban design (such as gated communities) and architecture (gated villas and high-rise towers); as well as the intangible notions of exclusion by the presence of walls and gates.

The proposed 3D-threshold matrix analyses Abu Dhabi's current urban design and architecture. This matrix consists of a model with three axes (x, y, z) which consequently form eight planes that can be juxtaposed in either two and/or three dimensions. The data analysis was limited to the following three parameters: architectural expression (whether contemporary or traditional); economy (global or local/ regional); and Arabic cultural traditions/interfaces (such as open/inclusive and. closed/exclusive). The investigations produced four typical strands within Abu Dhabi's current urban realm. They consist of: 'alienated hyper-modernism', 'contextual globalism', 'fairy-tale traditionalism' and 'eco-minded contemporary traditionalism'. By following the global side on the economy 'Y' axis (as in societies open to external influences) and the architecture side on the 'X' axis (contemporary or traditional) on the first layer of the matrix, we were able to trace an apparent pattern of current and future architectural trends which respond to two major attitudes towards globalism. The findings were then further elaborated:

1   Alienated hyper-modernism (mid-2000s to date)

This concept is characterized by a hyper-dense master-plan with building heights ranging from 40–80 storeys. Its street pattern tends to be of a previously modified grid, catering for motor vehicles, with a resulting disconnected public realm. As a consequence, the scale of buildings and their podiums façade treatment (for multi-storey parking garages) do not contribute towards an enjoyable pedestrian realm. In most cases, the individual structures have fully or partially controlled access to their own amenities/ park areas, and/or stretch of waterfront. The Abu Dhabi Urban Planning Council currently addresses issues caused by this type of design proposal with the aim to safeguard quality urban space for public use, ensure urban connectivity across the city and influence the quality of the city's public realm.

Most of the proposed buildings which fall under this sub-category consist of reinforced-concrete structural frames clad with glazed curtain wall. In the context of Abu Dhabi, this architectural solution does not consider basic principles of building massing or vertical/horizontal articulation. The harsh microclimate and building physics (i.e. high sun exposure, sand accumulation, extreme temperature fluctuations, and the need for energy preservation) tend to challenge any architectural proposition. In addition, this kind of hyper-modern architecture tends to ignore its context, particularly at ground level, and as a result, it creates human isolation and denies a desirable human scale within the city's public realm. Arabic motifs are rarely incorporated into the design process, and when Arabic identity is addressed, it is usually expressed through a simplistic interpretation of the *mashrabiya* form.

Occasionally, there are more complex, sophisticated and innovative architectural elements that do not necessarily contribute to an inclusive pedestrian urban experience but its geometries and avant-garde design demands a certain level of recognition. Examples of buildings at this end of hyper-modern typology include the proposed works by Jean Nouvel and Norman Foster for emerging developments on Saadiyat Island. Another example is the recently built tower for the Abu Dhabi National Exhibition Centre (ADNEC).

7.13 Contextual
globalisation
in Abu Dhabi

2   Contextual globalism (mid-1980s to mid-2000s)

At a master-plan level, this sub-category is characterized by mid-to-high density buildings with a maximum height of 25 storeys. The street grid is likely to be tight, as in the case for the superblocks in Abu Dhabi's central business district. The urban design patterns are clearly modernist, more specifically of the 'tower in the park' typology. These typologies are usually based on three layers of developments: higher individual towers forming a perimeter block, mid-height towers that create the first row of inner blocks, and then two-storey villas or four-storey multi-complexes that fill the core of the block. The street patterns are disjointed, typically confusing, and seemingly every inch of public space is populated by parking lots. An absence of a coherent pedestrian realm and severe challenges to accessibility are distinctive of this typology.

Architecturally, the building lines are clear, and façades present minimal articulation. The use of glass curtain walls tends to be pervasive, with superficial application of generic ornamentation without proper referencing of Arabic arts-and-crafts traditions. The late-1990s and early-2000s brought a few sophisticated examples whereby modernism was balanced with strong references to regional Arabic architecture. This typology is particularly represented in Abu Dhabi's central business district, but can also be seen in newer suburban neighbourhoods. In some of the latter, cultural and environmental sensitive housing proposals of contemporary courtyard housing have the opportunity to add positively to the not successful aspects of this typology.

The previously discussed subcategories refer to a global scale. The 'Y' axis, which covers the local/regional mode showcase the emergence of two different trends:

3   Fairy-tale traditionalism (1990s to date)

This typology is the result of two influential forces: firstly, reluctant clients who wish to deny the embracing of global modernism, and are typically inclined towards the popular expression of regional architectural features; and secondly, the lack of professionalism and quality control present in the architectural and engineering field available in Abu Dhabi. The professional body that is responsible for delivering meaningful architecture in Abu Dhabi has not

7.14   Fairy-tale contextualism

7.15   Some more fairy-tale contextualism in Abu Dhabi's CBD

been diligent and is partially responsible for the widespread of architectural work favoring superficial Arabic geometric form. In this sub-category, the buildings showcase an inaccurate and artificial localized style, if not indeed a kitsch version of refined traditional Arabic architecture. Therefore, the kind of building produced does not in any sense represent the original aspirations of Arabic architecture. This typology has now spread all over Abu Dhabi in the form of typical villa housing or other more exuberant building typologies such as hotels. The Emirates Palace Hotel can be seen as a high-end, slightly more crafted expression of this fairy tale tendency.

4   Eco-minded contemporary traditionalism (current)

This last sub-category represents a critical and intriguing new threshold within the urban evolution of Abu Dhabi. It reflects the elevated confidence of visionary leadership and evolving strategic planning of Abu Dhabi's government, which is committed to incorporating sustainable practices in its city-making process. This increased awareness prioritizes an interest in traditional and compact urban Arabic relationships (such as pedestrian-oriented streets), a contemporary interpretation of the principle of *fareej* (as a social urban component, with each neighbourhood acting as a playground for the traditional Emirati extended family), and finally a revival of courtyard housing concepts (including privacy, contemplation and safety).

In conjunction, this sub-category is being driven by microclimatic issues, involving the basic elements of survival in such a harsh desert climate, and the growing global issue of energy availability. It is well known that methods of energy conservation and on-site energy production are currently being addressed by many countries across the globe. An emphasis on public transport and human-scale urbanism are also being brought to the forefront of this typology. Its architectural components tend to accentuates both modernity and tradition through a contemporary reinterpretation of Arabic architectural forms and elements. At the same time, such commitment to sustainable development provides a functional solution to the sustainability agenda, and this trend is well represented by the construction of Masdar City.

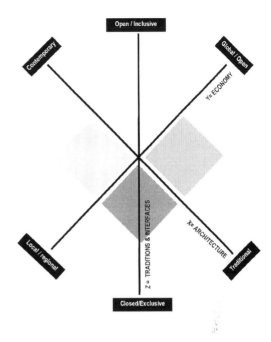

7.16 Threshold matrix – Layer 02

After identifying these four trends, the analysis continued to the 'Z' axis, which deals with Arabic cultural traditions/interfaces. The prime interest lies in investigating the extent of its influence on the urban and architectural scales of Abu Dhabi after over 40 years of global exposure. The subject of 'threshold', as an interface between the private and public realms, is of fundamental cultural and spiritual importance to the Emirati population, as well as to the other present nationalities who are Muslims. There are important social,

7.17 Interface 1

7.18   Interface 2

spiritual, psychological, cultural and physical/architectural interpretations of the meanings of 'wall' and 'gate' within Arabic culture. As Anwarul Islam and Naval Al-Sanafi note: 'Invasion of domestic privacy in Islam is discouraged by a formidable system of religious, legal and social prohibition so that the house entrance – the vulnerable threshold between the household and the public – is accorded particular symbolic importance.'[44]

The notion of privacy is present in Abu Dhabi within its: urban design (neighbourhood, urban block) and its architecture (outer wall, the gate/entry point, and inner building wall). The importance of this classification lies in the fact that traditional Arabic houses were designed with limited exposure to the outer 'world', as the houses were opened towards an internal courtyard instead of a public street. Dwellings were window-less, or had a limited number of carefully sized and specifically located apertures which served other functions. Rapid globalization, however, introduced dramatic changes in social life and architectural morphology in the Gulf region, as Yassine Bada explains:

> In both types of transformations, windows appear on the external facades, which were originally windowless. These windows are not only used for their prime role of lighting and ventilation, but are also a medium for people to appear on the social scene as modern and progressive. Windows are often the first sign of the beginning of individualization and reorientation of the house to the public space, and a symbol of rejection of deep-rooted cultural/religious imperatives. It is also the result of a new urban organization where the houses are not clustered in the traditional way.[45]

Hence the notions of interface between private and public realms are much more complex nowadays in cities such as Abu Dhabi, and as such these thresholds vary greatly in scale and morphology, to an extent that would have been difficult in earlier generations.

7.19   Corniche panorama in Abu Dhabi

7.20   Aerial view of Masdar City on the edge of Abu Dhabi

Table 7.1 Classification of design approaches and building features in Abu Dhabi

#	Urban Design/ Architectural Trend	Traditional Response To Interface	Neighbourhood/ Urban Block	Individual Plot/ Building		
				WALL	BUILDING GATE/ENTRY POINT	BUILDING FACADE
0	Traditional dwelling	Blank walls	Fareej (visually controlled, free access)	Yes, opaque	Yes, opaque	Blank (inward orientation to courtyard)
1	Alienated globalism	Blank walls at street level with multi-storey garage podiums	Exclusive/gated community with controlled access	No wall or transparent wall	Strictly controlled access	Curtain wall, opaque
2	Contextual globalism	Limited number of interfaces (blank walls or interaction at street level with retail or service outlets)	Open (high-rise) Gated (if townhouse/villa typology)	No outer wall (high-rise); Outer wall (townhouse/ villa)	Controlled or free access (high-rise or townhouses/ villas)	Curtain wall, opaque, or limited balconies with screens
3	Fairy-tale traditionalism	Blank walls	Exclusive/gated (private palaces) Controlled access (e.g. hotels)	Opaque or semi-transparent wall	Strictly controlled access	Opaque windows or curtain wall, stone wall, balconies with screens
4	Eco-minded contemporary traditionalism	Variety of interface typologies (private, semi-private, public; interactive at ground level with retail or service outlets)	Open	No wall or courtyard wall	No control or else strictly controlled access	Opaque windows or curtain wall, stone wall, balconies with screens

Source: Olivia Duncan and Sonny Tomic

CONCLUSION

Abu Dhabi's urban evolution timeline has been compressed since its inception and it continues to be challenged by a harsh climate and ever-insistent globalising forces. Political, economic, social and cultural factors have contributed to Abu Dhabi's cautious, but informed, urban leadership in all those aspects. A wise conservativism has ensured the continuity of a strong national identity while also reinforcing the image of the city as the capital of a progressive Arabic society. Urban planning and architecture played important roles throughout this story. As a result of the continuous state of change, and an aspiration for improvement, Abu Dhabi embraced several 'foreign' design proposals which were – over time – counterpoised and blended with more local/regional Arabic design considerations. This fusion of avant-garde international modernism with Arabic traditionalism has produced a profound change in attitudes towards housing and public realm design, in particular in regard to the issue of privacy levels. Our analysis demonstrates that despite what appear to be dramatic shifts in formal planning and architectural paradigms, resulting in the creation of new building forms and thresholds, Abu Dhabi's society continues to find ways to adjust to these contemporary demands while celebrating Arabic-Emirati culture. Under its visionary political leadership, and a maturing approach to planning and architecture, Abu Dhabi is on the brink of truly becoming a leader in the creation of sustainable living urban environments, through initiatives such as Masdar City. In many respects, Masdar's low-energy vision synthesizes internationally-available technologies with a deep understanding of local climate and local Emirati wisdom; and as such, it symbolizes Abu Dhabi's newest threshold into the future.

NOTES

1   John Fox, Nada Mourtaba-Sabba & Mohammed Al-Murtawa (eds), *Globalization and the Gulf* (London/New York: Routledge, 2006).

2   Samuel B. Miles, *The Countries and Tribes of the Persian Gulf* (London: Ithaca Press, 1919), p. 443.

3   Jayanti Maitra & Afra Al-Hajji, *Qasr Al Hosn: The History of the Rulers of Abu Dhabi, 1793–1966* (Abu Dhabi: Centre for Documentation and Research, 2001), p. 4.

4   A. de Lacy Rush (ed.), *Ruling families of Arabia* (Vol. 1, UAE: Archive Editions, 1991), p. xix.

5   Maitra & Al-Hajji, *Qasr Al Hosn*, p. 9.

6   Richard Trench, *Arab Gulf Cities* (Slough: Archive Editions, 1994), p. 132.

7   Maitra & Al-Hajji, *Qasr Al Hosn*, p. 1.

8   Ibid., p. 47.

9   Muhammad M. Abdullah, *The United Arab Emirates, a Modern History* (London: Croom Helm, 1978), p. 96.

10   Abu Dhabi Municipality & Town Planning Department, *Abu Dhabi, Dana of Gulf, Planning and Urban Development Studies and Research Centre* (UAE: Abu Dhabi Municipality, 2003), p. 22.

11   Maitra & Al-Hajji, *Qasr Al Hosn*, p. 12.

12   Yasser Elsheshtawy (ed.), *The Evolving Arab City: Tradition, Modernity and Urban Development* (London/New York: Routledge, 2008), p. 265.

13   Ibid., p. 266.

14   Abu Dhabi Municipality & Town Planning Department, *Abu Dhabi*.

15   Elsheshtawy, *The Evolving Arab City*, pp. 264–267.

16   Abdullah, *The United Arab Emirates*, p. 140.

17   Mohammed Al-Fahim, *From Rags to Riches: A story of Abu Dhabi* (UAE: Makarem Trading and Real Estate, 2007), p. 130.

18   Ibid., p. 133.

19   Abdullah, *The United Arab Emirates*, p. 323.

20   Al-Fahim, *From Rags to Riches*, p. 148.

21   Abu Dhabi Municipality & Town Planning Department, *Abu Dhabi*.

22   Al-Fahim, *From Rags to Riches*, p. 140.

23   Ibid., p. 137.

24   'The master planner of Abu Dhabi, Al Ain', March 2007, *Khaleej Times* website, http://www.khaleejtimes.com/DisplayArticleNew.asp?section=theuae&xfile=data/theuae/2007/march/theuae_march284.xml (accessed 31 August 2009).

25   Al-Fahim, *From Rags to Riches*, p. 269.

26   Ann Coles & Peter Jackson, *Windtower* (UAE: Stacey International, 2007), p. 4.

27   Fred Halliday, *Arabia without Sultans* (London: Saqi Books, 2002).

28   Elsheshtawy, *The Evolving Arab City*, p. 272.

29   Abu Dhabi Municipality & Town Planning Department, *Abu Dhabi*, p. 55.

30   Fox, Mourtaba-Sabba & Al-Murtawa, *Globalization and the Gulf*, p. 211.

31   Ibid., p. 9.

32   Ibid.

33   Quoted in Axel Dreher, 'Does Globalization Affect Growth? Evidence from a new Index of Globalization', *Applied Economics*, vol. 38, no. 10 (2009): 1091–1110 (accessible at http://globalization.kof.ethz.ch/static/pdf/rankings_2009.pdf).

34   Sheila L. Croucher, *Globalization and Belonging: The Politics of Identity in a Changing World* (Lanham, MD: Rowman & Littlefield, 2004), p. 10.

35   Fox, Mourtaba-Sabba & Al-Murtawa, *Globalization and the Gulf*, p. 247.

36   Abu Dhabi Municipality & Town Planning Department, *Abu Dhabi*, p. 41.

37   Peter Vine (ed.), *United Arab Emirates Yearbook 2009* (London: Trident Press, 2009), p. 146.

38   Abu Dhabi Urban Planning Council, *Plan Abu Dhabi 2030, Urban Structure Framework Plan* (Abu Dhabi: UPC, 2007), pp. 15–16.

39   Vine, *United Arab Emirates Yearbook 2009*, p. 150.

40   Ibid., p. 206.

41   'Average Emirati household income in Abu Dhabi is Dh47,066', *Gulf News* website, http://archive.gulfnews.com/business/General/10329531.html (accessed 12th August 2009).

42   Vine, *United Arab Emirates Yearbook 2009*, pp. 57–58, 206.

43   'Abu Dhabi has over 1.2 million expatriate residents', Emirate 24/7 website, 26 September 2010, http://www.emirates247.com/news/emirates/abu-dhabi-has-over-1-2-million-expatriate-residents-2010-09-26-1.295398 (accessed 23 November 2012). Similar, yet slightly different, figures are given in CIA, 'The World Factbook – Middle East: United Arab Emirates', https://www.cia.gov/library/publications/the-world-factbook/geos/ae.html (accessed 23 November 2012).

44   Brian Edwards, Magda Sibley, Mohamad Hakmi & Peter Land (eds), *Courtyard Housing: Past, Present and Future* (Abingdon: Taylor and Francis, 2005), p. 91.

45   Ibid., p. 215.

8

Dubai, UAE

Kevin Mitchell

In less than a century, the city of Dubai has grown from a small coastal village to one of the largest urban areas in the Gulf. According to Government of Dubai statistics published in 2009 the Emirate had a population of approximately 1,770,000 people, with over 75 per cent (1,370,000) of residents being male.[1] The gender imbalance results from the fact that many expatriate members of the male-dominated labour force do not earn the minimum salary necessary to obtain residence permits for their families, which was AE Dirham 10,000 (US$ 2,700) per month in late-2009.[2] Data gathered by the Dubai Statistics Center in 2009 indicates that the majority of the Emirate's expatriate males were employed in construction (48 per cent) and trading and repair services (12 per cent), while the majority of female expatriates were employed by families to perform household duties (34 per cent).[3] Low wages among a significant part of the expatriate population has contributed to the extraordinary economic growth that supported expansion of the built environment during the first decade of the 21st century.

From the mid-1990s onwards, press releases heralded ever-larger projects presented through lifelike renderings that promised soft light, sea views and serenity. These renderings were necessary for indicating what a building was intended to become, but more importantly they represented the potential for exceptional returns in a real-estate market fuelled by off-plan sales and purchasing with the aim of reselling prior to the project even being completed. Man-made islands created a new coastline and almost instantly increased the supply of waterfront property. The developers of the Palm Jumeirah Island claim that this project alone expanded Dubai's waterfront by 100 per cent, with the addition of 78 km of coastline. An extra 70 km could be provided by the aptly titled Waterfront scheme, which was purportedly designed for 1.5 million inhabitants. While it is unclear how the current global financial crisis will ultimately affect the project, the Waterfront's developers have claimed that it 'is on track to becoming the exemplar sustainable city founded on resource efficiency, social equity, and economic prosperity.' Perhaps anticipating criticisms of this project, the developer's statement succinctly addressed some of the negative effects of Dubai's rapid growth while maintaining

8.1 Male-dominated urban space in Dubai

8.2 Palm Jumeirah Island

the promise of economic prosperity that could potentially attract 1.5 million people to live in the proposed scheme. This chapter takes the claims made by the Waterfront's developers as a point of departure to discuss the complex interplay between political structure, economic conditions and architecture in Dubai. After providing a brief overview of the governance structure of the Dubai Emirate, I will consider how these political and economic forces have contributed to shaping the built environment, focussing specifically on challenges to sustainability-related measures and the complex issue of 'identity'.

GOVERNANCE STRUCTURE AND THE FOUNDATIONS FOR PROSPERITY

Dubai's system of governance is autocratic; however, scholars often point to the neo-patrimonial aspects of the system that result in a hybrid web of bureaucratic state structures that are intermeshed with the patronage networks. Gero Erdmann and Ulf Engel have described neo-patrimonialism as:

> … a mix of two types of political domination. It is a conjunction of patrimonial and legal-rational bureaucratic domination. The exercise of power in neopatrimonial regimes is erratic and incalculable, as opposed to the calculable and embedded exercise of power in universal rules (or, in Weber's terms, abstrakter Regelhaftigkeit). Public norms under neopatrimonialism are formal and rational, but their social practice is often personal and informal. Finally, neopatrimonialism corresponds with authoritarian politics and a rent-seeking culture, whereas legal-rational domination relates to democracy and a market economy.[4]

Another important aspect of Dubai's governance structure is the complex relationship between the public and private sectors. Martin Hvidt has addressed this in an analysis of the public/private ties as manifest in the autocratic and neo-patrimonial setting of Dubai. In autocratic and neo-patrimonial systems, the decision-making process remains centred on the ruler. But, because power must be legitimated, it results in what has been termed a 'soft' autocracy. Within democratic governance structures, the private sector relies on formal channels of interaction through state bureaucracies, whereas in autocratic and neo-patrimonial systems, the ruler is the sole decision-maker and exerts a significant influence over the private sector through patronage networks. However, in spite of the fact that the private sector does not have a formal means of participating in governance, it is not necessarily excluded from decision-making and influencing policy formulation. In the case of Dubai, Hvidt maintains that:

> … the more the development strategy relies on the activities of the private sector, the more influence the actors of this sector will have in relation to policy formulation and decision-making. Furthermore, and as a corollary to this, it is assumed that the greater economic power of the private sector in relation to the ruler (the ruler – merchant power balance) the more influence the private sector will have in regard to decision-making.[5]

8.3   *Dhows* along
the Dubai Creek

During the latter half of the 20thcentury a number of Gulf States depended on oil revenues to increase their prosperity. In contrast, Dubai's relatively limited natural resources required that the Emirate concentrate on exploiting its established position within an interdependent trade network that extended across the Gulf region and beyond. Throughout the rise and decline of the pearl-diving industry and the increasing dependence on trading activity, Dubai relied heavily on foreign merchants. Michael Herb argues:

> The merchants did not translate their economic power into institutions through which they could exert political control over the state. The merchants ... did not have a parliament through which they could bargain with rulers over the raising and spending of taxes. Instead rulers levied the taxes and deputed their bodyguards to collect them; the merchants most effective tactic against the rulers' exactions was that of capital anywhere–the threat of flight. Merchant bargaining power lay in the mobility of their trade (and of pearling) which allowed them to flee to a different shaykhdom if the rulers' exactions grew too heavy. The position of a ruler, at least in the smaller Gulf state shaykhdoms, could not easily withstand a wholesale alienation of the merchant community, and rulers in any case had an interest in the prosperity of the merchant class.[6]

Strategic measures such as abolishing import and export tariffs to create a duty-free port during the early part of the 20th century, dredging the creek at the beginning of the 1960s to accommodate larger trading vessels, and the construction of container ports from the late-1960s onwards have made Dubai a primary hub for regional and global trade activity. Measures taken throughout the 20th century formed the foundation for diversification that ultimately contributed to attracting the significant foreign direct investment (FDI) to support the rapid expansion of the built environment during the ten-year period from 1998 to 2008.

Data compiled by the Dubai Statistics Center indicates that FDI in Dubai totalled AED 42.5 billion (approximately US$ 11.6 billion) in 2006, which represented a 13.4 per cent increase over 2005.[7] The sectors benefitting most were construction and financial intermediation/insurance (each accounting for approximately 35 per cent of the total FDI in 2006). European and non-Arab Asian countries combined were responsible for the largest share of FDI in Dubai in 2005 (82.7 per cent) and 2006 (86.2 per cent). And according to a report from the fDi Intelligence division of the *Financial Times*, 'Dubai became the top destination city by number of FDI projects and capital investment, growing by an impressive 59 per cent and 122 per cent, respectively, between 2007 and 2008 and racing past Shanghai and London to take the top spot.'[8]

While the impressive inflow of foreign direct investment into Dubai resulted in rapid economic development and funded projects that may serve the city well in the future, the built environment has suffered from the lack of planning control and a narrow focus on short-term returns derived from real-estate investment. At the height of the speculative frenzy that drove development in Dubai, investors bought and sold off-plan projects at an alarming rate, pushing prices to levels considerably higher than the initial cost of the property. Although those attracted by immediate gain were keen to believe claims that Dubai was immune to boom-and-bust cycles, the global financial crisis from late-2008 proved otherwise. By late-August 2009, *The Wall Street Journal* reported that a number of distressed funds were preparing to purchase Dubai real-estate after values dropped 50 per cent in less than twelve months.[9] In spite of this significant drop in values there has not yet been a rush of new potential buyers willing to invest in Dubai property; however, analysts suggest that if concrete actions are taken to improve transparency following the 2008 collapse, then capital may once again settle in Dubai due to its liberal economic policies and the progress made in providing public infrastructure and an urban rail system.

8.4   Dubai Metro

8.5   Park and commercial buildings near Dubai Creek

Autocratic rule, neo-patrimonial tendencies, and the intense reliance on the private sector have presented challenges, but these conditions have also contributed to Dubai's success. Maintaining the delicate balance between public authorities and the private sector, and ensuring that FDI flows in (instead of out) to support growth in the Emirate, are strategies that influence decision-making, policy formulation and, as discussed later, the design and construction of the built environment.

CHALLENGES TO SUSTAINABILITY IN DUBAI

The desire to project an image of a 'modern' city complete with shimmering glass facades and grass-filled parks has significantly impacted the natural environment in Dubai. The 'Living Planet Reports' of the World Wide Fund for Nature (WWF) have focused attention on the excessive use of resources in the UAE as a whole. According to reports issued since 2004, the ecological footprint for the country continues to remain the highest per capita in the world. Industry estimates indicate that 75–85 per cent of the total power generated during the summer season in the Gulf is used for air-conditioning, and cooling can cost as much as one-third of the total cost of the building over the lifetime of the structure. There has, however, been increasing recognition of the ecological challenges associated with architecture and planning in an environment characterized by intense climatic conditions and a scarcity of fresh water. The UAE Ministry of Environment & Water and the Environment Agency of Abu Dhabi revealed plans to address excessive consumption through the *UAE Ecological Footprint Initiative*, announced in conjunction with the publication of the Living Planet Report 2010.

In 2007 a resolution decreed that all residential and commercial buildings in Dubai must comply with a set of 'green building' specifications that would be effective from January 2008. No legislation had been enacted by the beginning of 2008, and in mid-August that year the Dubai Municipality held a conference in which it announced that along with the Dubai Electricity and Water Authority (DEWA) it would be developing an integrated 'green building' system for the city. But no regulations had appeared by the end of 2008, and on 24th January 2009 an article reported that these proposed 'green building' regulations would not be unveiled 'for some time'.[10] The article claimed that the delays could potentially be attributed to the global financial crisis and the resultant economic difficulties being faced by Dubai property developers.

The delays in developing comprehensive legislation that would result in sustainable approaches to building design and construction illustrate the complex nature of public/private relations in Dubai. While the governmental decree mentioned above recognizes that the long-term environmental impact of present practices cannot be sustained, the stringent measures necessary to regulate the building industry would almost certainly adversely affect short-term profit margins, and thus may jeopardize a reputation built upon neo-liberal economic policies and *laissez-faire* capitalism. Dubai's reliance on FDI to fund its real estate and construction projects ultimately empowers the private sector, and results in concessions that negatively affect the built environment. Michael Herb has pointed out that the early-20th century merchants in the southern Gulf possessed bargaining power resulting from their ability to transfer their operations to a different sheikhdom if the rulers' demands were deemed to be unfair. However, in the early-21st century, capital is infinitely more mobile, and advanced communication technology ensures that funds can be easily transferred across the globe in minutes. In neo-patrimonial systems this mobility of capital has significant consequences that fundamentally affect the power balance between public and private entities and, because of the influence that can be exerted on aspects such as the development of sustainability measures, it ultimately shapes the built environment.

Dubai's authorities have announced a series of initiatives to reduce energy and water usage, including the introduction of a revised tariff structure known as the 'slab system' in March 2008. This system charges users for electricity and water using a sliding scale: the greater the consumption, the higher the tariff. According to news reports, those who failed to implement energy- and water-saving measures after the first year would have seen cost increases of up to 66 per cent.[11] In spite of this, DEWA reported a rise in peak demand from 4,736 MW in 2007 to 5,287 MW in 2008.[12] Perhaps this was due to the fact that the tariff affected only those with high consumption levels, and the system had been structured to ensure that approximately 80 per cent of consumers would not be subject to increased costs. In addition, the homes or farms owned by UAE citizens were exempted from the 'slab system'.[13]

Although these preliminary measures have been taken, energy costs remain low and there is little incentive for fundamental change in building design and construction. While one may argue that *laissez-faire* economic policies and ecological sustainability are not mutually exclusive, the current situation in Dubai indicates that direct intervention may be required to balance the desire for profit with the urgent need to reduce the consumption of resources and environmental degradation. Long-term sustainability will depend on comprehensive measures and widespread implementation. The cases of the 'green building' legislation and the 'slab system' illustrate the impediments associated with implementing stringent sustainability measures within a neo-patrimonial system. In both cases the concessions made to private sector interests and the expatriate community ensured that the costs of doing business remain low, which encourages existing investment to remain and attracts new FDI. Additionally, measures like excluding the residential or farm properties of UAE citizens from the slab system seek to establish political legitimacy through benefactions that bestow favour upon citizens. Architects and planners may possess the knowledge to address issues related to sustainability, but design strategies and construction technology may prove less important than political solutions that seek to balance private interests and the 'public good'.

THE IDENTITY DEBATE

It is difficult to specifically define what is meant by 'identity'. Marxist conceptions of class consciousness, Émile Durkheim's notion of collective consciousness, and Ferdinand Tönnies' category of *Gemeinschaft* have provided the foundations for thinking about collective identity, focusing on what are believed to be 'essential' characteristics of a unified social experience that binds individuals together through commonalities. While Durkheim's work concentrated on the cultural construction of reality, later social constructionist approaches have rejected any essentializing tendencies, maintaining instead that those aspects that characterize a collective group are socially constructed through the interaction and agreement of individuals. Post-structuralist thinkers have insisted on the relative nature of the notion of identity, emphasizing its multiple, shifting, and fragmented character, and arguing that processes of identity formation are ambiguous and unstable.

8.6   Urban space near to the Dubai Mall

The question of identity in the built environment is equally complex, although it is often reduced to issues related to the visual appearance of a building or urban area. Some argue that new urban areas in Dubai cannot be distinguished from those found in other rapidly developing cities throughout the world. In an essay entitled 'In What Style Should Dubai Build?', I considered how the speed, scale and variety of architectural production induced anxiety of the sort that had motivated the 19th-century German architect, Heinrich Hübsch, to pose the question *In What Style Should We Build?*[14] Answering Hübsch's question within the context of Dubai presents challenges, however, because it involves the use of 'we', implying communality and the potential for consensus regarding a singular 'style' of buildings that would reflect and respond to the diverse population in the Emirate. Although the marketing material produced by Dubai-based developers often claim the creation of 'communities', it is questionable whether shared norms and values will emerge and lead to the development of public institutions within an autocratic system (see Plate 13).

Currently, UAE citizens comprise less than 20 per cent of the population of Dubai, and some projections made prior to the current global financial crisis indicated that the proportion could shrink to 5 per cent. The tensions resulting from an increasing expatriate population are summarized in a quote that appeared in a 2007 *Gulf News* article: 'The issue is we are losing our identity. The national identity is about to get lost because of foreigners … If we focus on westernization we will lose everything.'[15] In presumably a response to the growing concern among Emiratis over this issue, the UAE Ministry of Culture, Youth and Community Development organized a 'National Identity' conference in April 2008 to consider the consequences of the demographic imbalance between citizens and what is an extremely diverse expatriate population. And in a debate regarding appropriate dress within Dubai's shopping malls, a UAE citizen was quoted in the *Gulf News* as saying: 'I don't want to generalise and say that all expats behave in that inappropriate way. However, certainly many expats who come to our country are either not aware of our cultural norms or are just not respectful of them and choose to behave any way they want to.'[16] An expatriate from a neighbouring country presented an alternative viewpoint: 'I love Dubai and I like its style. But the way I dress is completely a personal matter and I don't allow anybody to educate me on what to wear and what not to wear.'[17] While the few individuals interviewed for the *Gulf News* article may not necessarily be representative of the opinions and attitudes of the larger population, the views expressed are indicative of the tensions that exist.

The fact that a shopping mall happens to be the site within which tensions between Dubai's diverse populations become manifest warrants further consideration. Dubai's larger shopping malls are typologically equivalent to those of a similar scale found elsewhere throughout the world. Hypermarkets from Europe and Asia, jewellery stores selling Swiss watches, electronics stores offering the latest in mobile phones, and food courts with restaurants serving everything from *fatoosh* to French fries reveal the increasing standardization of global consumption patterns. The architecture of the Dubai shopping malls provides little more than superficial nods to the context; however, by observing the variety of clothing

8.7   Mall of
the Emirates

worn by shoppers, one can perhaps deduce that they are in one of the Gulf states where those who outwardly express a sense of modesty mingle among others who appear to be dressed for a day at the beach. In the case of recommended dress codes for shoppers, the privatized space of the mall becomes the site within which the public can test the limits of tolerance and contest context-specific norms.

Maintaining a balance between a relatively small group of Emirati citizens, a large expatriate work force, and transient tourists compounds the difficulties associated with defining the role of identity. In addition, the right of residency in Dubai is based on employability and the right to work (and therefore the right to remain in the country), and is not extended to expatriates past the age of 70 years old.[18] Although developers have marketed residential projects based on the fact that a life-long visa would come with a freehold purchase, in mid-2008 the Dubai Real Estate Regulatory Agency stated unequivocally: 'There is no direct link between property ownership and residence visas. Developers should not lure investors to property sector with a promise of residence visa.'[19] And in 2009 the Dubai Naturalisation and Residency Department issued a statement saying that residents who own property in the UAE but are not employed there will be required to leave the country every six months, and their visa would then be renewed as they re-entered Dubai at the airport.[20] This legislation was later revised and is now assumed to allow a three-year residency visa for those owning property with a value of at least AE Dirham 1 million. The lack of clarity and consistency and the legal constraints on establishing long-term residency will continue to have an effect on the built environment. Although the present financial crisis may curb off-plan sales and lead to legislation that restricts the practice of buying and selling before completion, architects will continue to face the challenges associated with designing for a population that is both extremely diverse and largely transient.

8.8   Typical suburban villas in Dubai

Faced with such uncertainty, many architects have imported pre-existing models from elsewhere, or resorted to reproducing 'traditional' architecture, or concentrated on developing an iconic formal language. Perhaps the most ubiquitous case of imported models has been the transplantation of North American suburban settlement patterns, resulting in houses designed as detached free-standing dwellings located in the centre of relatively large plots of land. George Shiber described a situation in Kuwait in the 1960s, which has since been repeated in residential neighbourhoods throughout Dubai as well:

> … the modern house or "villa" plunked on a uniform and non-descript plot which, with several hundred similar plots constitute the inorganic and uneconomic new neighborhoods of Kuwait, is often a caricature house in a caricature setting obeying a caricature philosophy of architecture and urban form that could have only emanated from caricature architectural concepts. The house sits clumsily in its plot exposed on all four sides to the elements, with a garden that is no garden at all for it consists of the "corridor" set-backs from every boundary of the lot.[21]

The Madinat Jumeirah hotel resort and mall represents one of the prime examples of reproducing what is believed to be the past (see Plate 14). The resort complex is described by its owners as 'a magnificent tribute to Dubai's heritage and is styled to resemble an ancient Arabian citadel'. It is unclear which particular 'Arabian citadels' informed the design of the complex, and there is little beyond the façade treatment and non-functional wind towers that makes reference to 'Dubai's heritage'. The following statement made by the architects reveals that the basis for their design was not necessarily actual architecture from the past, but the result of imagining what might have been:

> What if in ancient UAE or ancient Oman they had the money we have now and the technology we have now? What would they have built? That's how we

8.9   Madinat
Jumeirah hotel
resort and mall

*came up with Madinat Jumeirah. We built what they might have built with the
resources available to us.*[22]

The interpretative freedom that is evident in the admission that the designers
'built what they might have built with the resources available to us' reveals the
wholesale negation of the complex relation between time and place. Although
it was perhaps unintended, the statement also presupposes that architecture is
reducible to stable stylistic tendencies and determined by money and technology.

While developments like the Madinat Jumeirah have been constructed as an
assemblage of iconic elements derived from an imagined past, others have treated
buildings as singular iconic statements. A survey of 20th-century architecture in
Dubai certainly reveals a steady progression toward the iconic.[23] This has had a
significant effect on the built environment, and has resulted in an emphasis on the
image of singular buildings. Projects like the Palm Jumeirah and The World islands
are massive manifestations of the iconic at an urban scale. The speculation that
supports growth in the real-estate and construction industries demands investors
and their money, which, in turn, requires visually arresting icons that attract
attention. In Dubai and neighbouring Emirates, many real-estate transactions were
based on little more than visual representations in sales brochures and elaborate
models. The material reality has been less important than the reality constructed
by photorealistic images; the craft of making – often absent in the final building
itself – was replaced by the artifice of well-trained CAD technicians.[24]

While the speculative real-estate market supports economic growth in Dubai, it
also raises questions of a political nature as the aim is to sell residential buildings
that owners will ultimately expect to inhabit. Statistics provided by Dubai's Real
Estate Regulatory Agency indicate that, since 1973, Indian nationals have been
the largest group of expatriates involved in land transactions in Dubai (AED 18.7

8.10 'Cityscape Dubai' real-estate and development trade fair

8.11 Residential development along Jumeirah Beach

billion); they has been followed by citizens of the United Kingdom (AED 17.3 billion), Pakistan (AED 10.4 billion), Iran (AED 8.4 billion), Saudi Arabia (AED 7.8 billion) and the Russian Federation (AED 5.5 billion).[25] At least prior to the start of the financial crisis in late-2008, the majority of buyers were foreign investors – some companies saw this as a positive advantage, and liberally interpreted the statistics to market their properties. One company wrote:

> In Dubai the majority of the population herald from abroad, up to 94 per cent of the entire population are expatriates and the number of those coming to the emirate grows substantially on a weekly basis as up to 20 new companies establish themselves in the emirate each week. This trend is projected to continue for at least the next five years as the remaining planned 7 free trade zones move from the planning stages into realisation and more opportunity is created in Dubai for international companies from around the world.[26]

If one maintains that the built environment should respond to and reflect its inhabitants, then the situation in Dubai presents complex challenges. Ultimately, Emirati citizens who form part of a shrinking minority, and the expatriate population comprising the majority, may have substantially different needs and competing interests. Diversity within the citizen population and among the various expatriate groups further compounds the challenges. To say that architecture and planning should serve all groups could result in universalizing tendencies that may deny the cultural differences present within the heterogeneous population, and which has enriched and made substantial contributions to the growth of Dubai. And, as the debate regarding appropriate dress within Dubai's shopping malls proves, the negation of difference would certainly prove problematic. Attracting FDI after the current global recession will require that vaguely defined property ownership legislation be clarified. Stable and more inclusive residency policies may foster a sense of belonging and encourage the substantial expatriate population to identify with, and contribute to, improving the built environment. However, as is indicated by the long delays and contradictory messages that have characterized the process of developing clear rules on such issues, the desire to attract investment is tempered by the need to address the concerns of the Emirati citizen by imposing restrictive visa regulations for expatriates who purchase property. But if non-citizens do not view Dubai as home, it is likely that buildings will continue to be treated as mere commodities to be considered as investments with no value beyond the market price.

CONCLUDING REMARKS

According to the *Dubai Strategic Plan 2015*, development will be guided by the adoption of free-market economic principles and the following initiatives: a unique relationship and partnership with the private sector; the protection of the national identity, culture and way of life; an openness to the world while maintaining uniqueness; providing a world-class infrastructure to suit the requirements of all users; and preserving the environment in line with international standards.[27]

8.12
International City
development

Reflecting some of the neo-patrimonial aspects of Dubai's governance structure, the initiatives also reveal some of the inherent challenges that the Emirate faces. Balancing free-market principles and the informal power of the private sector with protecting 'national identity' and preserving the environment may prove incredibly difficult, even within an autocratic system. As discussed above, the specific political and economic forces that have developed and transformed over time continue to condition Dubai's built environment. Trading activity and the Emirate's increasing reliance on merchants during the 20th century resulted in private sector influence on policy formulation and decision-making. And this influence seems to have increased with the efforts to attract FDI, and the measures now being taken to ensure that investors remain confident in Dubai's ability to manage the substantial debt that was amassed to fund its decade-long building boom.

8.13   Burj Al Aarb

Until late-2008, these rapid inflows of FDI were hastily converted into new urban quarters and iconic architectural statements. Announcements of cancelled projects were quickly followed by statements claiming that a respite from the rush to build would result in more considered approaches to the built environment. Nevertheless, as the case of sustainability legislation discussed above indicates, the influence of the private sector and the necessity to ensure that capital does not flow outward may hinder efforts to implement measures that would improve the quality of design and construction. Now that Dubai's economy and building activity has begun to pick up again after the financial crash that

8.14   Burj Dubai and Business Bay development

started in 2008, these urban tensions may resurface. Estimates suggest that Dubai's population has continued to rise, such that it is now probably around 1,900,000, and with the same demographic features noted earlier.

Critics that hastily conclude that 'Dubai has no identity!' also tend toward superficial pronouncements that focus solely on instances of iconic form-making and the isolated enclaves resulting from an emphasis on large-scale projects such as the offshore islands. Dubai's built environment in fact grows out of the tensions resulting from embracing free-market principles, balancing the demands of a minority Emirati population while attracting foreign investment (as well as a foreign labour force to translate this finance into buildings, goods and services), and managing a web of bureaucratic structures intermeshed with patronage networks. These tensions make Dubai what it is, and they will continue playing a role in determining what it will become.

ACKNOWLEDGMENTS

Sara Kasa made significant contributions to this essay through editorial comments and research assistance.

NOTES

1   Dubai Statistics Center, *Dubai in Figures 2009* (Dubai: Government of Dubai, 2009), p. 4.

2   Abdullah Rasheed, 'Salary norm for family visas to be revised', *Gulf News* website, http://www.archive.gulfnews.com/nation/Immigration_and_Visas/10327894.html (accessed 1 July 2009).

3   Dubai Statistics Center, 'Employed (15 Years and Over) by Nationality, Sex and Economic Activity – Emirate of Dubai (2009)', Table (02-05), http://www.dsc.gov.ae/Reports/DSC_LFS_2009_02_05.pdf (accessed 15 September 2011).

4   Gero Erdmann & Ulf Engel, 'Neopatrimonialism Revisited – Beyond a Catch-All Concept', GIGA-WP-16/2006, *German Institute of Global and Area Studies (GIGA) Working Papers Series*, Hamburg (2006), p. 31.

5   Martin Hvidt, 'Governance in Dubai: The Emergence of Political and Economic Ties between the Public and Private Sector', *Centre for Contemporary Middle East Studies Working Paper No. 6*, Centre for Contemporary Middle East Studies, University of Southern Denmark (June 2006), p. 5.

6   Michael Herb, *All in the Family: Absolutism, Revolution, and Democracy in the Middle Eastern Monarchies* (Albany, NY: State University of New York Press, 1999), pp. 57–58.

7   Dubai Statistics Center, 'Bulletin: Foreign Direct Investment – Dubai Emirate 2007' (Dubai: Government of Dubai, 2007), p. 1.

8   '"Asian Attraction", The Shape of Things to Come: The FDI Outlook for 2009 and Performance Analysis for 2008', *Financial Times fDi Intelligence Report* (April/May 2009), p. 9.

9   Stefania Bianchi, 'Funds Prowl Dubai Properties Investors' Interest After Price Tumble Could Revive Market', *The Wall Street Journal* website, 12 August 2009, http://online.wsj.com (accessed 12 August 2009).

10   Jamie Stewart, 'DM Delays Green Regulations to Aid Troubled Developers', Arabian Business.com website, http://www.arabianbusiness.com/544381-dm-delays-green-regulations-to-aid-troubled-developers (accessed 28 January 2009).

11   Roxane McMeeken, 'Soaring electricity costs hit Dubai', *Building* website, http://www.building.co.uk/story.asp?storycode=3135161 (accessed 5 March 2009).

12   Dubai Electricity and Water Authority (DEWA), http://www.dewa.gov.ae/aboutus/electStats2008.aspx (accessed 10 August 2009).

13   'DEWA Restructures Tariff for More Responsible Electricity and Water Consumption', Eye of Dubai website, http://www.eyeofdubai.com/v1/news/newsdetail-18501.htm (accessed 25 February 2008).

14   Kevin Mitchell, 'In What Style Should Dubai Build?', in Elisabeth Blum & Peter Neitzke (eds), *Dubai: Stadt aus dem Nichts* (Basel: Birkhauser, 2009), pp. 130–140.

15   Reema Saffarini, 'How does my City Grow?', *Gulf News* website, http://archive.gulfnews.com/articles/07/06/16/10132864.html (accessed 12 September 2009).

16   Fatma Salem, 'Dubai malls join anti-indecency campaign', 8 August 2009, *Gulf News* website http://www.gulfnews.com/nation/Society/10338386.html (accessed 8 August 2009).

17   Ibid.

18   Procedure Manual for Ministry of Labour United Arab Emirates, Version 2.6B, MENA Business Services.

19   Bassma Al Jandaly, 'No automatic residency for property buyers in Dubai', *Gulf News* website http://www.gulfnews.com/business/Real_Estate_Property/10223351.html (accessed 25 June 2008).

20   Martin Corucher, 'UAE property owners must exit to renew visa', *KhaleejTimes*, 4 August 2009.

21   Saba George Shiber, *The Kuwait Urbanization: Being an urbanistic case-study of developing country* (Kuwait: Kuwait Government Printing Office, 1964), pp. 287–288.

22   'Brand New Old', *Identity* (July/August 2004), p. 86.

23   Kevin Mitchell, 'From the intimate to the iconic: Architecture in Dubai from 1967 to 1997', in George Katodrytis (ed.), *Dubai: Growing through Architecture* (London: Thames & Hudson, in press).

24   Kevin Mitchell, 'Speculations on the Future Promise of Architecture in Dubai', in Ahmed Kanna (ed.), *The Superlative City: Dubai and the Urban Condition in the Early Twenty-First Century* (Cambridge, MA: Harvard University Press, 2013), pp. 149–166.

25   Real Estate Regulatory website, http://www.rpdubai.com (accessed 9 September 2009).

26   Clifton website, http://www.clifton-dubai.com/working_in_dubai.html (accessed 2 July 2008).

27   Government of Dubai, *Dubai Strategic Plan 2015*, http://egov.dubai.ae/opt/CMSContent/Active/CORP/en/Documents/DSPE.pdf (accessed 1 August 2009).

9   In Manama, Bahrain, continuous land reclamation is changing the urban morphology at an unprecedented pace, here showing the northern coastline from the BFH Tower to the Al Seef district in the distance

10   The Msheireb project in Doha, Qatar, by AECOM/Arup/Allies and Morrison

11   The coastline of Abu Dhabi, UAE, as seen from on high

12   Grand Mosque (Sheikh Zayed Mosque) in Abu Dhabi, UAE

13 'Cityscape Dubai' real-estate and development trade fair

14   Wind-tower motifs at the Madinat Jumeirah in Dubai, UAE, with the Burj Al Arab Hotel beyond

15 'Chinese' section of the Ibn Battuta Mall in Dubai, UAE

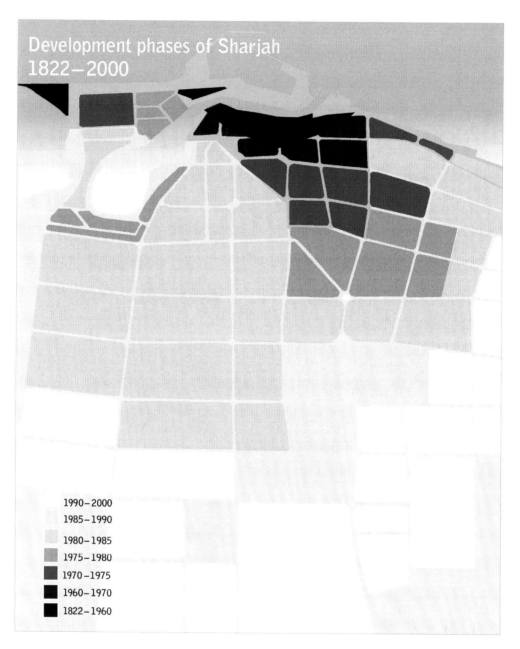

Development phases of Sharjah
1822–2000

1990–2000
1985–1990
1980–1985
1975–1980
1970–1975
1960–1970
1822–1960

16   Development phases of Sharjah, UAE, from 1822–2000

9

Shopping Malls in Dubai

Nicholas Jewell

While Dubai's mercantile origins occupy a longer timeline and different physical landscape to today's modern metropolis, this essay focuses on the compressed historical-spatial dialectic that has imprinted Dubai within the collective global consciousness. Chronologically, the infrastructural initiatives which first established modern Dubai's trajectory[1] were broadly coincident with the rumblings of dissatisfaction that beset the modernist movement in the early-1960s, most notably voiced in Jane Jacobs' great polemic, *The Death and Life of Great American Cities*. Of most significance here was Jacobs fascination with the processes and structural configuration that are necessary to sustain a vital urbanity, as observed within her native New York, and especially in Greenwich Village, contrasted against deterministic principles of the regimented visual order in modernist town planning that – in her brutal analysis – assumed the 'dishonest mask of pretended order, achieved by ignoring or suppressing the real order that is struggling to exist and to be served.'[2]

Dubai is of course a long way from New York, and the extent to which its large-scale urban grain differs from the focus on more intricate patterns of city life advocated by Jacobs is immediately noticeable. Dubai has flourished precisely by employing the characteristics that Jacobs believed a successful urban realm should avoid at all costs. On deeper reflection, this may not be such a surprise. Jacobs' analysis observed a condition where there was an established cityscape and a relatively mild climate, suitable for an active life on the city street all the year round. Dubai, conversely, sits in the desert with temperatures almost twice those of New York (or its European counterparts) at any given time of the year, and yet has grown from a sleepy regional port to an internationally recognized metropolis in less than fifty years. The adoption of that most American, albeit principally suburban, building type – the shopping mall – as the means of delivering urban space in modern Dubai exemplifies the awkward gap between the theory and practical reality of what a city might be under such circumstances. It is a scenario that clearly perplexes urban theorists in Jacobs' shadow, who recite declamations of a soulless and weak urbanity dominated only by vulgar consumption. Instead, I would argue, these types of statement indicate a reading of the city that – despite its relevance to a Euro/American context – may have reached its limits within an environment whose compressed history and climactic challenges ask a wholly different set of questions of what a city should be. Through an analysis of the shopping mall as a building typology that is hybridized in this extreme context, this chapter will explore its relevance to the making of modern Dubai and the nature of the urban space that results. But first, we must qualify the relevance of the building typology within this context a little further.

Dubai's assumed 'status as the lower Gulf's economic capital'[3] – born out of its free-trade orientated infrastructural gambles, namely through the expansion of Port Rashid[4] and later the opening of Port Jebel Ali[5] – is one that is now proving difficult to sustain. Itself relatively impoverished in terms of ownership of the Middle East's most precious natural resource, oil, yet part of a country, the UAE, which holds the world's sixth largest reserve,[6] Dubai lives in the constant shadow of its neighbouring Emirate, Abu Dhabi, which controls 90 per cent of this resource.[7] Without the self-sustaining financial security of its neighbour, Dubai's ruling al-Maktoum family instead felt compelled to make a 'commitment to invest in their own domestic infrastructure so that Dubai would be able to support and enhance its existing re-export and commercial sector while also facilitating broader diversification away from oil in the future.'[8] It is striking to note that oil and natural gas account for less than 6 per cent of Dubai's economic activity.[9] Rather, it is speculative real estate/construction, trade/re-export, financial services and luxury tourism (attracting around 5 million visitors per year) that now dominate.[10] Dubai's financial security is thus dependant on an openness to foreign investment, necessitating that it adopts a commensurate 'visibility' to the outside world.

While this openness can easily be represented statistically – a staggering 80 per cent of the city's population of 1.7 million consists of expatriates – it is even more explicit in the provenance of architectural forms that represent the modern city. Displayed here is the strategic intersection of capital and skyline commensurate with 'the infrastructure and the servicing that produce a capability for global control'.[11] However, it is hardly sufficient, within this global representation of place image, to reproduce the generic cityscape of elsewhere. Mike Davis observes that:

> … the same phantasmagoric but generic Lego blocks, of course, can be found in dozens of aspiring cities these days (including Dubai's envious neighbours, the wealthy oil oases of Doha and Bahrain), but al-Maktoum has a distinctive and inviolable criterion: everything must be 'world class' by which he means number one in the Guinness Book of Records. Thus Dubai is building the world's largest theme-park, the biggest mall (and within it, the largest aquarium), the tallest building, the largest international airport, the biggest artificial island, the first sunken hotel, and so on … Having 'learned from Las Vegas', al-Maktoum understands that if Dubai wants to become the luxury-consumer paradise of the Middle East and South Asia (its officially defined 'home market' of 1.6 billion people), it must ceaselessly strive for visual and environmental excess.[12]

Captured within Davis's description of the Dubai skyline are those characteristics that have pervasively displayed themselves as the stuff of globalised architecture since Jacobs' polemic half a century ago. It is a process recognized by David Harvey as the 'relation between capitalist development and the state … as mutually determining'.[13] Ostensibly this describes a top-down vision whose autocratic underpinnings are obfuscated by a language of visual spectacle borne of, though far removed from, the core intent of Jacobs' theories. The hegemony of global capital is reinforced by stealth, at the expense of the genuine existence of micro-level processes of urban interaction from which its supporting visual rhetoric is drawn. By superficially harnessing the streams of critical thought that served to undermine the socially progressive aspirations of the modernist project, capital has also hollowed them out, limiting the potency of any new influence that contemporary theory may attempt to produce.

At a global level, the shopping mall is a building typology that is central to this penetration of capital into all facets of modern life under the democratizing auspices of populism. Founded on the generic building block of a spatial formula that was christened the 'dumbbell plan' (the brainchild of the godfather of the shopping mall, Victor Gruen), and which persists due to its devastating financial success, the internalised environment of the mall differentiates itself within a given consumer market via a language of decorative surface that can be tailored to suit any target demographic.[14] Asserting itself as a more desirable alternative to a given lifestyle, the mall, in its 'native' western existence, typically adopts the form of a pastoral alternative to the perceived ills of urbanity – in other words, a self-contained entity accessed by car and predicated on familial values of safety and togetherness. It is a scenario that Kim Dovey describes as 'a collective dream world of mass culture … at once captur[ing] and invert[ing] the urban. It is a realm of relative shelter, safety, order and predictability which is semantically and structurally severed from the city.'[15] Whether the city actually represents the threat implied by the mall, and whether the mall can deliver a genuine alternative to the collective anxiety that it fosters, remain highly questionable.[16]

Transposed to Dubai, however, this strategy of ideological opposition finds a more tangible target: the climate itself. A climatically controlled internal environment provides Dubai's expatriate population and tourists, many of whom are totally unused to the fierce heat of the desert, with a comfortable public space that possesses a deeper significance than the inferred civic benefits within the mall's western context. Rem Koolhaas, in his study of the urban spaces of Singapore, a context whose tropical climate in many ways echoes the challenge of Dubai, describes it thus:

> … [It is] the city as a system of interconnected urban chambers. The climate, which traditionally limits street life, makes the interior the privileged domain for the urban encounter. Shopping in this idealized context is not just the status-driven compulsion it has become "here" but an amalgam of sometimes microscopic, infinitely varied functional constellations, in which each stall is a "functoid" of the overall programmatic mosaic that constitutes urban life.[17]

Onto this scenario, Dubai has even grafted one of its most prominent civic events, the Dubai Shopping Festival, which takes place during February each year in its shopping malls, attracting 3 million visitors to the city.[18] While undoubtedly a commercially driven stimulation of tourist cash, it is also representative of the kind of spatiality in which much of the city's social life takes place, and of the principal activities it offers.

Climatic necessity aside, the need to understand the civic space of the Dubai shopping mall is made even more vital by the less visible role that this typology plays in the general apparatus of globalization within a skyline contrived to attract foreign capital. The shopping mall can thus be understood as assuming, for the foreigners drawn to Dubai, a means by which the inhabitation of a largely alien context is naturalized through more familiar symbols and spatial practices. In mitigating the effects of cultural dislocation that are inherent in the expatriate lifestyle, the mall compresses geographical space as a 'response to desire for fixity and for security of identity in the middle of all the movement and change. A 'sense of place', of rootedness, can provide … stability and a sense of unproblematical identity.'[19]

The implication is that in Dubai there is indeed a transcendence of the consumption-based values that undermine our perception of the western shopping mall, though key questions still remain – such as, what are the civic qualities of the urban space the Dubai mall actually produces, and to what extent are cultural processes also hybridized by the transplantation of the mall into this context?

Our search for answers to these questions begins as the grain of old historic Dubai bleeds into its modern skyline, stewarded from the early-1990s by its ruler, Sheikh Mohammad bin Rashid Al Maktoum. Located at the commencement of Sheikh Zayed Road (the long axis linking Dubai to Abu Dhabi), the Bur Juman Centre – unlike many structures that define the Emirate's brand image – displays its own internal history. As one of Dubai's very first shopping malls, opened in 1991 by the Al Ghurair Group, the centre was soon forced to compete with newer and far more sophisticated malls as expatriates, tourists, and their concomitant money flowed in.[20] Accordingly, the Bur Juman Centre was given a face-lift and relaunched in 2005 as a high-end mall aimed at the luxury market. This six-year-long, AE Dirham 1.4 billion expansion at the hands of an American architect, Eric Kuhne (who also designed the Bluewater mall in the UK) duly doubled the size of the centre to 80,000 m² with 300 shops.

Kuhne believes his work has deeper significance than a straightforward rebranding exercise. Naming his design sphere as that of the 'Civic Arts', and referring to the project as Bur Juman Gardens, Kuhne clearly wishes to be perceived as a socially and contextually conscious architect, above the morass of commercial architecture in which the mall usually sits. In his own words, 'Bur Juman Gardens celebrates the diversity of science, arts, and letters that the Arabic World has contributed to civilization'.[21] Grand words indeed, but what does this vision really deliver? Kuhne's extension avoids the outright pastiche of image and form that undermine so many shopping malls, instead favouring abstracted contextual motifs. These include a pseudo British High-Tech series of laminated timber beams and roof glazing whose references to the designs of Michael Hopkins et al. are robbed of any feeling of integrity by the overbearing sheen of marble and fussy decorative details adorning many of the mall's internal surfaces. While a certain

9.1 Atrium roof in Bur Juman Gardens

9.2 Modern extension to the Bur Juman Centre

9.3   Original mall at the Bur Juman Centre

Arabian flavour in some of these details lends a localized reference over and above one's conventional expectations of shopping mall interiors, the overall result is far from the didactic historical message that Kuhne's rhetoric implies.

The visual tension between the mall's history and its need to suit Dubai's contemporary brand image is particularly problematic. Spatially joined as a seamless figure-of-eight configuration, the visual contrast between the shiny new extension to the Bur Juman Centre and its first phase could not be greater. The resulting disjuncture only serves to reveal that it is the building's underlying plan form which is the key determinant of its spatiality, a point which is worth exploring further. The notion of an instrumental plan as the basis of the shopping mall is not of course a new concept. Victor Gruen's 'dumbbell plan' has, since the earliest days of the typology, exerted an almost unbreakable hegemony over the design process. Comprising a linear shopping route flanked by smaller retail outlets, and terminated at either end by large 'anchor' stores, this spatial formula understands that the 'exposure of all individual stores to the maximum amount of foot traffic is the best assurance of high sales volume'.[22] Functioning as shopping magnets, the two anchor stores draw consumers through the entire range of curiosities and temptations which the mall has to offer, heightening the user's psychological stimulation to engage in acts of consumption. By coupling this pattern of coerced perpetual movement with its internalized plan form, the mall creates an introverted journey of consumption freed from the unplanned distractions and encounters which occur in more traditional urban scenarios. The atomization of the mall's inhabitants forms the bedrock of the sustained consumption-led fantasy on which its financial success depends, though regrettably robs the typology of many of the interactive social processes that Gruen had hoped would be fostered within his creation.

As the scale of global mall developments grew, Victor Gruen's generic formula has developed a number of variants to counteract the fatigue its instrumental axial layout can produce.[23] More than most, Eric Kuhne has realized the importance of balancing the feeling of perpetual movement with manageable chunks of visual information as a subtle means to manipulate the formula. His figure-of-eight plan in the Bur Juman Centre stimulates an effortless, repetitive cycle of movement, different to the more rigid and mechanical qualities of its linear predecessors, plus it uses the curvature of the mall layout to break the consumer's line of site – this becomes a means to divert their attention onto the immediate shopping environment, while the promise of yet further riches, just out of view, stimulates further exploration. While its plan form may thus have changed, it is clear that the coercive tools underpinning the Bur Juman mall are as strong as ever. Ignoring Kuhne's rhetoric, it seems his real talent is to eke a little more life from this deadly equation between plan and profit in the shopping mall. In this sense he is a worthy successor to Gruen, even if the latter was not as aware of the Faustian pact he was making with this spatial formula when it first left his drawing board.

Unfortunately for Kuhne, the success of the mall's spatial formula depends on concealing these manipulative processes beneath a totalizing, immersive surface language that brands the mall experience for its target demographic.

The 'authenticity' of any surface language, however, is undermined by the aforementioned disjuncture between the old and new sections of the Bur Juman Centre. It is an architectural moment that reveals the mall's ephemeral qualities all too clearly, asking some difficult questions of the pseudo-urbanity it seems to offer. Sitting as a symbolic marker at the point where the historical city breaks down to reveal the new Dubai 2.0, the defensive, large-scaled block of the Bur Juman mall neither integrates itself into the grain of the historic city, nor does it offer a credible alternative. Rather, the tired, bland appearance of the original Bur Juman is a depressing reminder of the compressed sense of time from which all malls suffer, and the willfully contradictory dialectic between form and function which are ever-present. The Bur Juman Centre may mark the start of Dubai's new global journey, but is also a cautionary tale of the limits to which branded modernity, constantly required to re-invent itself on no substance at all, is subjected.

If we move onward in search of Dubai 2.0, the dimension of difference between the old and new urbanism becomes quickly apparent. While old Dubai clusters around the creek inlet that extends from Port Rashid, defined by the pedestrian-scaled nuclei of Deira and Bur Dubai, the new city stretches out as a 30-km strip either side of the 12-lane highway of Sheikh Zayed Road. The resulting urban structure is defined visually by a continuous procession of towers lining the edge of the road, falling behind, almost instantaneously, to a low-rise carpet of residential and luxury hotel buildings terminated on one side by the Persian Gulf and on the other by the desert. While it is the symbolic capital invested into the skyline that is meant to be seen, arguably more significant is the road itself. Following the coastline, the combination of linear road and surrounding desert ensure that the new Dubai is a long narrow affair (little more than 4 km wide). It's a linearity rendered even more intense by the impassable barrier that the road itself presents, almost perfectly bisecting the strip development it creates. Moreover, the stretched out, car-oriented scenario explicitly abandons the relational pedestrian networks commonly associated with western conceptions of the 'ideal' city. In the new Dubai, the realm of the pedestrian becomes instead a series of nodes spread out along this immense strip and accessible only by car. These nodes have evolved beyond the fault line between history and modernity on which our western urban precedents precariously sit. With such values left behind, all too quickly, it is to Dubai's image as a burgeoning globalized metropolis that our attention is directed: nowhere is this message encoded more strongly than in our next shopping mall for study.

Situated at the base of the world's tallest structure, the 828 m-high Burj Khalifa Tower, which opened in January 2010, the Dubai Mall apes the lead of its totemic marker by asserting itself as 'the largest shopping space in the world'.[24] The title of the world's largest shopping mall is something which is subject to much competition between emerging global economic hubs, all of whom are vying to outdo one another in the race to supersede the United States within the capitalist framework it defines and, at least for now, still spearheads. Accordingly, the means by which claimants to the title of biggest mall are measured are rather nebulous. In terms of total floor area for all facilities, the Dubai Mall is indeed the world's largest at around 250,000 m^2 – but if one were to look at the gross

9.4   Main
pedestrian
concourse at
the Dubai Mall

lettable area for shops to occupy, it in fact only sits in 7ᵗʰ place (with the top
spot going to the New South China Mall in Dongguan, China).[25] By any standards,
however, the Dubai Mall is truly immense. Designed by the Singapore-based
mall specialists, DP Architects PTE, the Dubai Mall comprises 1.2 million m² of
accommodation arranged over four levels, containing 1,200 shops and also an
aquarium/underwater zoo, 2,000-person capacity ice rink, 22-screen multiplex
cinema, 120 restaurants and cafes, and 14,000 car parking spaces. It attracts
more than 750,000 visitors per week.[26] While this barrage of statistical worthiness
serves to infuse the craving for 'world class' symbolic capital evoked in the
earlier quote from Mike Davis, its scale alludes toward a richer stream of social
capital, which according to Rem Koolhaas, forces us to see that 'in the quantity
and complexity of the facilities it offers it is itself urban'.[27] Echoing this, the Dubai
Mall's designers state that 'it is *sine qua non* that the mall be conceived and
planned as a microcosm of a metropolis, a City within a City, to ensure that the
desired qualities of live [sic], work and play are perpetuated'.[28] The question we
must address is the nature of the physical structure on which this purported 'city
within a city' is founded.

As in the Bur Juman Centre, the Dubai Mall eschews Gruen's traditional
'dumbbell plan' in favour of a triangular layout with gently curving malls. The origin
of this particular configuration comes from Erich Kuhne, Bur Juman's designer,
in his scheme for the Bluewater shopping centre, just outside London, from the
late-1990s. Its Dubai offspring has simply super-sized the concept. In essence, 'the
arduous intermediate stages of commercial evolution have been telescoped or
short-circuited to embrace the "perfected" synthesis of shopping, entertainment,
and architectural spectacle on the most pharaonic scale'.[29] Again, the triangular
plan stimulates a sense perpetual movement, this time with three 'anchors' at the
points, each signified by an event – here it is two large shops and, bafflingly, a public

9.5   Public art installation in the Dubai Mall

art installation. Consumers' motion is broken only at carefully choreographed moments when one is able to interact with a man-made lake, through terraces connected to the mall's many restaurants, and all within the colossal shadow of the Burj Khalifa Tower.

So it might seem in the Dubai Mall that the globally-biased conjunction of plan and profit has prevailed yet again, and that there is perhaps never any other possible outcome. Such an assumption, however, assumes that the mall's inhabitants are reduced to wholly passive bodies capable only of a rigid adherence to the social contract it wishes to define. But that would be an erroneous reading, since it 'leads to an overestimation of the efficacy of disciplinary power and to an impoverished understanding of the individual which cannot account for experiences that fall outside the realm of the "docile" body.'[30] It is thus imperative to acknowledge, and move beyond, the generic physical structure of these Dubai malls to discover the 'relation of subject to discursive formations as an articulation' which are inscribed within them, as part of a far more complex and interesting field of global/local tensions.[31]

Perhaps the most obvious trace of the culturally specific contestation of generic mall space, if one visits at the right time of year, is the change in the mall's psychogeography during the month of Ramadan. To adhere to the pattern of daylight fasting, the mall must close its restaurant amenities until the sun goes down. In one sense, this represents a minor triumph of indigenous cultural practices over the relentless pursuit of profit by the global mall machine. It also temporarily shrinks the size of the mall's 'turf', and in doing so reveals its programmatic limitations. At the Dubai Mall, the response is to excise its lower restaurant level during the daylight hours of Ramadan, effectively reducing the mall to a three-storey affair. Most interesting, however, is the way in which this scenario in the mall plays out the underlying tensions that exist between Dubai's Muslim population (both local and expatriate) and the almost entirely expatriate non-Muslim diaspora. Some malls deliberately blur the boundary of their acknowledgement of Ramadan, and other cultural practices, through subtle manipulation: for instance, it has become common practice for many restaurants to obscure views in and out during daylight hours, to conceal the non-Muslims eating within. For this period, therefore, these restaurants function as 'private' entities that exploit a loophole tacitly accepted by the indigenous population, allowing foreign visitors to follow different cultural values. Both sides are engaged in an uneasy complicity in face of the overarching process of capital accumulation.

Nonetheless, the issue of appropriate dress and behaviour on the part of the non-Muslim expatriate population has led to the launch of an anti-indecency campaign within Dubai's malls. From an Emirati perspective, the scenario is one whereby the indigenous population does not 'want to generalize and say that all expats behave in that inappropriate way. However, many expats who come to our country are either not aware of our cultural norms or are just not respectful of them and choose to behave any way they want to.'[32] But conversely, as one western expatriate was reported as saying: 'I respect Dubai, its religion, culture and people. I come here frequently for business and pleasure, and I was never asked to cover my shoulders or knees until recently … besides I don't have long or covered outfits, and most importantly I didn't do something bad to Dubai or its people.'[33] So if the shopping mall serves to bring Dubai the status of a global entrepot centre, it clearly has some way to go to breach a divide – which in many ways it actively undermines – between cultural practices that appear to exist in relatively autonomous spheres.

Within the Dubai Mall, a far more explicit attempt to integrate a sense of cultural authenticity can be seen. Occupying the central point of its plan, in the void between its three interlinked malls, the Dubai Mall has a beating heart in the form of a fake *souk* which specializes in selling gold. Predictably it is also the world's largest. The mall's designers hoped for an explicit place-specific message to be imparted via this 'symbolic integration of Arabic culture' into its overall fabric.[34] But, unfortunately, this part of the mall is all too easily bypassed by the shopper, being zoned off the beaten track,

9.6   Gold Souk at the centre of the Dubai Mall

rather than integral to the main circulation paths. This is reinforced by the shiny newness of the interiors, whose aesthetic errs toward a generic representation of luxury brand consumption, rather than the more nuanced and culturally hybrid experience the traditional *souk* offers. It is this sheer lack of spatial differentiation that in the end is most problematic. As a destination within a cityscape of the world's biggest things, the Dubai Mall offers little more than the narrow definition of *'world class'* to which it aspires. It is a fleeting moment of being that will soon be superseded by its competitors – and what then? An alternative set of criteria are required to navigate the destinations within this landscape of consumption.

At the extreme end of the scale is the scarcely believable indoor ski-slope whose prosthetic form sticks out of the side of the previous holder of the title of Dubai's largest shopping centre, the Mall of the Emirates. Here one is reminded of Rem Koolhaas description of airports as being 'a concentrate of the hyper-local and hyper-global in the sense that you can get goods there that are not available even in the city, hyper-local in the sense you can get things there that you get nowhere else.'[35] Although clearly successful – the Mall of the Emirates was as busy as any I visited during my research – there is still a hefty environmental price tag required to sustain this fantasy, as well as the others. While the relatively small size of Dubai positions it well behind the USA and China in terms of overall carbon consumption, the city now

9.7   Indoor ski slope at the Mall of the Emirates

holds the unenviable distinction of 'having the highest ecological footprint per capita' anywhere on the planet.[36] Viewed within an understanding of the nature of the economic processes which underpin the cityscape – albeit that the credit bubble on which Dubai's speculative property boom was built was well and truly burst by the global financial crash from 2008 (although it has since recovered somewhat)[37] – it is difficult to imagine a *volte-face* whereby the Dubai of the future could exist without the air-conditioned environments that make the desert habitable for its large expatriate population. Nonetheless, the environmental excess attached to strategies of differentiation in the city's malls is simply unsustainable in the longer term. It is surely more fruitful to engage with forms and spaces that are more demonstrably appropriate to patterns of human habitation in this specific context.

Our next precedent promises a more nuanced blend of global and local ingredients. Conceived as a recreation of 'life as it used to be for residents along Dubai Creek, complete with waterways, abras, wind towers and a bustling souk', the Madinat Jumeirah resort development, opened in 2003 by the architect/developer, Mirage Mile, borrows its imagery heavily from the remnants of the old city preserved in the Bastakiyah Quarter.[38] On first entering the imitation *souk* that forms the centerpiece of this luxury resort, the faithfulness with which these fragments are re-assembled compresses, in psychogeographical terms, the distance from the traditional city. Here the usual 'dumbbell plan' of the shopping mall is abandoned in favour of 'meandering paths [that] lead visitors through a bazaar-like atmosphere in which open fronted shops and intimate galleries spill onto the paved walkways'.[39] Already bounded by Dubai's impassable road structure, this building realises that it doesn't need the forced movement of the mall to stimulate a captive audience into acts of consumption. Rather, this conscientious reconstruction of the spatiality of the *souk* evokes Bernard Tschumi's analysis of the design of the garden as a space of leisure which merges 'the sensual pleasure of space with the pleasure of reason, in a most useless manner'.[40] The Madinat Jumeirah seems therefore to be a refreshing change, though one that requires further investigation to avoid falling into the trap of simple post-structuralist awe which so often prevent meaningful critiques of shopping centres.

It is in the things that are absent (heat, smell, mess, hustle and bustle, unplanned forms of inhabitation) that the superficial conceit of the language of the Madinat Jumeirah becomes apparent. Here again, the muted presence of globalized brand imagery comes to the fore. The quick realisation that its stalls offer not the informal, bottom-up spaces of consumption of Dubai's old *souks*, but instead a cleverly disguised version of the usual suspects from the generic shopping mall the world over, questions the 'reality' we are faced with here. It's a question reinforced by the simulations of Bastakiyah's traditional wind-towers around the mall's exterior. In principle these might be a legitimate way to find a more sustainable means to control the internal climate, but of course these catchers of the wind do nothing of the sort; their presence in form but not function brings any higher sense of aspiration quickly down to earth. It can be read as a representation, as Homi Bhabha notes, that is undermined by the problematic production of a 'recognizable Other, as a subject of a difference that is almost the same, but not quite'.[41]

For the almost exclusively white, wealthy, western clientele who use the Madinat Jumeirah shopping centre as part of their Dubai holiday, it has become a legitimate substitute – during my visit, one well-heeled gentleman was using it enthusiastically to introduce his equally well-heeled girlfriend to

9.8   Historic wind-towers in the Bastakiyah Quarter of Dubai

9.9   Bastakiyah's textile *souk*

9.10   Malls at the Madinat Jumeirah resort development

9.11   Wind-tower motifs at the Madinat Jumeirah in Dubai, UAE, with the Burj Al Arab Hotel beyond

the experience of a 'real' Arabian *souk*. It hence provides a representation of cultural authenticity for a market that wants to believe they are engaging with the locality, but ultimately wants to be able to eat English fish-and-chips rather than try anything more challenging. Once again, a field of difference is opened between the indigenous and expatriate idea of what Dubai is, limiting a more engaged condition of cultural hybridity or any deeper sense of social capital in its structure.

The final stop on our Dubai tour is one that invokes historical narrative to evoke a sense of cultural legitimacy. The Ibn Battuta Mall constructs a story based on the travels of the famous 14th-century Muslim scholar. Structured around a loose 'dumbbell plan', the mall is separated into six 'events' themed to represent a particular stop on Ibn Battuta's travels. Thus under one roof it seems possible to visit Andalusia, China, Egypt, India, Persia and Tunisia. Unlike the Madinat Jumeirah resort, however, there is little attempt to recreate an authentic, robust representation of Dubai's culture. Instead, it is an environment that is unashamedly artificial, revelling in its fantasy narrative.

Situated on the limits of new Dubai, some 30 km away from its historic core, the Ibn Battuta Mall seems to offer little in the way of architectural merit, yet it does encapsulates a number of characteristics of this Emirati state. More than any

9.12 Advert within the malls of the Madinat Jumeirah resort

of the self-conscious environments in other Dubai malls, the spaces convey some sense of the freewheeling trading spirit implicit in the city (see Plate 15). Likewise, the inward, autonomous nature of the Ibn Battuta Mall, by visibly keeping the threat of the adjacent Jebel Ali power plant and the encompassing desert at bay, conveys a more problematic schism underlying Dubai as a whole. This unease is enhanced by the sight, all around this outlying mall, of countless immigrant workers labouring in the ferocity of the desert heat to put up large projects they will never be allowed to inhabit.[42] It is a stark reminder of an apparent global inclusiveness that is in fact being built on the exploitation of an immigrant underclass whose existence is rendered invisible by the autonomous structures they are creating. This inward-looking, capitalist urbanity falls into that most post-modern of traps – a static sense of being, inherently limited in terms of transformative potential by the nature of its built form. The issue then is, from these apparently limited circumstances, what might Dubai become in the years to come?

9.13 'Chinese' section of the Ibn Battuta Mall in Dubai, UAE

9.14 'Indian' section of the Ibn Battuta Mall

9.15 'Persian' section of the Ibn Battuta Mall

CONCLUSION

George Katodrytis describes Dubai as a 'prototype of the new post-global city, which creates appetites rather than solves problems. It is represented as consumable, replaceable, disposable and short-lived ... Dubai may be considered the emerging prototype for the 21st century: prosthetic and nomadic oases presented as isolated cities that extend out over the land and sea.'[43] While this chapter touches on certain characteristics of the geo-political framework and emerging spatiality that go hand-in-hand with this reading of Dubai, it remains the case that it is still a relatively young city whose urban qualities feel wanting in some respects. As Christopher Davidson points out: 'Dubai's remarkable development strategies will never reach their full potential unless ... a civil society exists'.[44] Thus the fundamental obstacles are the separate spheres of existence defined by a patrimonial Emirati ruling class, a moneyed class of expatriate workers and tourists, and a relatively invisible underclass of migrant workers. It is, on the face of it, a highly striated class structure whose lack of genuine interaction is exacerbated by the stretched out, island-like autonomy which defines much of its urban condition. Yet, in concept at least, Dubai defines itself as a culturally hybrid dynamo striding ahead of the more conservative ideals of neighbouring Emirati states.

Dubai's shopping malls visited for this chapter embody this paradox. While each displays characteristics and innovations from its locality, it is also in the nature of this building typology to exhibit its worst traits through its own insularity. It would be all too easy to fall back on westernised urban discourse to interpret this condition as an inherently weak, divisive urban structure in constant denial of its own history, which only leads each successive development in pursuit of an insatiable appetite for being bigger and better than the rest. Rather, I would posit that the different type of urban space that Dubai clearly consists of demands a different – or at least updated – kind of urban theory to understand its fundamental characteristics. The need for this process is even more important as Dubai is being forced to reevaluate its building stock, both in the wake of the current global recession which has temporarily slowed down its real-estate boom, and the opening of a metro system which threatens to liberate much of the stretched-out city for a larger portion of the populace.

It would be folly to believe these two circumstances will in themselves imply an overall shift in terms of what Dubai ultimately becomes. Both however imply a change away from Dubai's present striation toward a 'smoother' type of space, one that is 'identified with movement and instability through which stable territories are erased and new identities and spatial practices become possible'.[45] Accordingly it is in analysing the shopping mall not so much as a 'despotic signifier' of identity, but rather as a field of social interaction within a wider urban structure, that a far more productive understanding of Dubai can be pursued. Far from representing the death of the city, it might yet be that the things we choose to do in shopping centres are capable of producing their own culturally hybrid histories, and in so doing can transcend the apparent limitations of the format. It is even possible that due to Dubai's intense climatic, economic, social and cultural conditions, it could act as one of the crucibles for the future transformation of the shopping mall, should the necessary freedom of expression be allowed.

NOTES

1   Christopher M. Davidson, *Dubai: The Vulnerability of Success* (London: Hurst & Company, 2008), pp. 91–98.

2   Jane Jacobs, *The Death and Life of Great American Cities* (London: Penguin, 1961), p. 25.

3   Davidson, *Dubai,* p. 103.

4   Ibid., pp. 92–93.

5   'Jebel Ali', Wikipedia website, http://en.wikipedia.org/wiki/Jebel_Ali (accessed 5 October 2009).

6   'Oil Reserves', Wikipedia website, http://en.wikipedia.org/wiki/Oil_reserves (accessed 5 October 2009).

7   'Oil and Gas', UAE Government website, http://www.uae.gov.ae/Government/oil_gas.htm (accessed 5 October 2009).

8   Davidson, *Dubai*, p. 106.

9   'Dubai', Wikipedia website, http://en.wikipedia.org/wiki/Dubai (accessed 5 October 2009).

10   Ibid.

11   Saskia Sassen, *Cities in a World Economy* (3rd Edition, London: Pine Forge Press/Sage Publications, 2006), p. 112.

12   Mike Davis, 'Sand, Fear and Money in Dubai', in Mike Davis & Daniel B. Monk (eds), *Evil Paradises: Dreamworlds of Neoliberalism* (New York: The New Press, 2007), pp. 51–52.

13   David Harvey, *The Condition of Postmodernity: An Enquiry Into the Origins of Cultural Change* (Oxford: Blackwell Publishing, 1990), p. 109.

14   Victor Gruen, *Shopping Towns USA* (New York: Van Nostrand Reinhold, 1960). See also: Jeffrey M. Hardwick, *Mall Maker: Victor Gruen, Architect of and American Dream* (Philadelphia: University of Pennsylvania Press, 2004); Alex Wall, *Victor Gruen: From Urban Shop to New City* (Barcelona: Actar, 2005).

15   Kim Dovey, *Framing Places: Mediating Power in Built Form* (London/New York: Routledge, 1999), p. 4.

16   Nicholas Jewell, 'The Fall and Rise of the British Mall', *The Journal of Architecture*, vol. 6, no. 4 (Winter 2001): 317–378.

17   Rem Koolhaas; 'Singapore Songlines', in Rem Koolhaas & Bruca Mau, *S, M, L, XL* (Rotterdam/New York: 010 Publishers/Monacelli, 1995), p. 1073.

18   'Dubai Shopping Festival', Wikipedia website, http://en.wikipedia.org/wiki/Dubai_Shopping_Festival (accessed 5 October 2009).

19   Doreen Massey, *Space, Place and Gender* (Oxford: Blackwell Publishing, 1994), p. 151.

20   'Bur Juman', Wikipedia website, http://en.wikipedia.org/wiki/BurJuman (accessed 5 October 2009).

21   Eric R. Kuhne and Associates, 'Bur Juman Gardens', Civic Arts website, http://www.civicarts.com/bur-juman-gardens.php (accessed 5 October 2009).

22   Gruen, *Shopping Towns USA*, p. 74.

23   Jewell, 'The Fall and Rise of the British Mall'.

24   'Burj Dubai (Dubai Tower) and Dubai Mall, United Arab Emirates', Design/Build Network website, http://www.designbuild-network.com/projects/burj/ (accessed 5 October 2009).

25   'List of the World's Largest Shopping Malls', Wikipedia website, http://en.wikipedia.org/wiki/List_of_largest_buildings_in_the_world#List_of_the_world.27s_largest_shopping_malls (accessed October 2009); It should be noted that the overall floor areas are disputed for a number of malls on the list, and while the New South China Mall currently assumes the mantle of 'largest' based on gross leasable area, it is, at the time of writing largely empty. On this point, see also the Wikipedia entry at http://en.wikipedia.org/wiki/Talk:List_of_largest_buildings_in_the_world#Mall_areas (accessed 5 October 2009), as well as Donohue, M., 'Mall of Misfortune', 12 June 2008, *The National* website, http://www.thenational.ae/article/20080612/REVIEW/206990272/1042 (accessed 5 October 2009).

26   'Dubai Mall', Wikipedia website, http://en.wikipedia.org/wiki/Dubai_Mall (accessed 5 October 2009).

27   Koolhaas, 'Bigness, or the problem of Large', in *S, M, L, XL*, p. 515.

28   DP Architects PTE Ltd, 'Dubai Mall', DP Architects website, http://www.dpa.com.sg/main.html (accessed 5 October 2009).

29   Davis, 'Sand, Fear and Money in Dubai', p. 54.

30   Stuart Hall, 'Who Needs Identity?' in Stuart Hall & Paul du Gay (eds), *Questions of Cultural Identity* (London: Sage Publications, 1996), p. 12.

31   Ibid., p. 14.

32   Fatma Salem, 'Dubai Malls Join Anti-Indecency Campaign', 8 August 2009, *Gulf News* website, http://www.zawya.com/Story.cfm/sidGN_08082009_10338386/Dubai%20malls%20join%20anti-indecency%20campaign/ (accessed 10 November 2009).

33   Ibid.

34   DP Architects PTE Ltd, 'Dubai Mall', http://www.dpa.com.sg/main.html (DP Architects website, accessed October 2009).

35   Koolhaas, 'The Generic City', in *S, M, L, XL*, p. 1251.

36   Landais, E., 'UAE tops world on per capita carbon footprint', 30 October 2008, *Gulf News* website, http://gulfnews.com/news/gulf/uae/environment/uae-tops-world-on-per-capita-carbon-footprint-1.139335 (accessed 10 November 2009).

37   'Shares Hit by Dubai Debt Problems', 20 November 2009, BBC News Online website, http://news.bbc.co.uk/1/hi/business/8381258.stm (accessed 10 November 2009).

38   'Madinat Jumeirah', Wikipedia entry, http://en.wikipedia.org/wiki/Madinat_Jumeirah (Wikipedia website, accessed 10 November 2009).

39   'Souk Madinat', Jumeirah Hotels website, http://www.jumeirah.com/Hotels-and-Resorts/Destinations/Dubai/Madinat-Jumeirah/Madinat-Souk/ (accessed 10 November 2009).

40   Bernard Tschumi, *Architecture and Disjunction* (Cambridge, MA/London: The MIT Press, 1996), p. 86.

41   Homi K. Bhabha, *The Location of Culture* (London: Routledge, 1994), p. 122.

42   Davis, 'Sand, Fear and Money in Dubai', pp. 48–68.

43   George Katodrytis, 'Metropolitan Dubai and the Rise of Architectural Fantasy', Radical Urban Theory website, http://www.radicalurbantheory.com/misc/dubai.html (accessed 18 September 2009).

44   Davidson, *Dubai*, p. 209.

45   Kim Dovey, *Becoming Places: Urbanism/Architecture/Identity/Power* (London/New York: Routledge, 2009), p. 22.

10

Sharjah, UAE

Hassan Radoine

On land and in the sea, our forefathers lived and survived in this environment. They were able to do so because they recognized the need to conserve it, to take from it only what they needed to live, and to preserve it for succeeding generations.[1]

The city state of Sharjah is the result of a complex interaction of environmental, economic, political, and cultural factors across successive periods of time which shaped its particular physical form and social composition. Decisions made in response to multiple fast-changing economic and political pressures have greatly affected the urban planning of Sharjah – the most prominent of these factors being economic boom and the related population growth.[2]

Before the discovery of oil in the 1950s, Sharjah was under the protection of the British Empire. At that point there were only approximately 1,000 people living along the coastline in what is currently known as the 'heritage area'. Economic resources were limited, and so local people were mainly dependent on fishing, pearl diving and sea trading. The British rulers produced a typical outline plan for Sharjah, around its creek, which still forms the basis for the city today. However, if one looks closely at the current formation of Sharjah, one can see that the city has been built without sufficient regulation or sense of urban planning. Due to the availability of land and the relatively low population in past eras, Sharjah was not yet being challenged – as it is today – by problems such as urban sprawl, traffic jams, lack of parking spaces, and an increasingly dysfunctional urban infrastructure.

In the 1960s, once oil extraction had got well underway, the new-found economic prosperity of Sharjah allowed rapid urban change. Oil became the single major source of income for the country. The introduction of modern technology that accompanied oil drilling, along with the advent of extensive trading exchange with the rest of the world, made the means of modern life available to the city's citizens. Sharjah became one of the cities in the Middle East most eager to follow the western model of modernization and urban development. As a consequence, its environment was transformed to accord with the new local ambition to modernize the city as quickly as possible. A foreign workforce was invited to participate in the country's urban development process. Indeed, continuous economic prosperity and the resulting demand for labour soon attracted a large number of non-Emiratis to come to work in Sharjah. This led to a dramatic growth in population: there are now an estimated 890,000 people in Sharjah's metropolitan area, the result of which the ratio has in recent years reached around 20 per cent citizens to 80 per cent foreigners, like in neighbouring Dubai. The population increase has also caused daunting problems with spectacular consequences for the urban planning, not least in terms of the serious disruption of Sharjah's surviving historical fabric.

THE CONSERVATION AND ADAPTATION OF OLD SHARJAH

From 1720 or so, the powerful Qawassim tribe first came to settle along the most strategic Gulf coastline from Ras Al-Khaimah further north down to Sharjah. Later on, in 1820, a general treaty signed with the British imperial forces caused the collapse of Qawassim maritime activity and divided the kingdom up into smaller sheikhdoms. Internal conflicts between members resulted in independence for Sharjah and Ras Al-Khayma as separate emirates by 1914. It is notable that the Qawassim tribe made Sharjah their urban hub, and it was there that the initial settlers survived through fishing, pearl diving and sea trading. Sharjah became in time a typical Arabic and Islamic walled town. Although its urban pattern shows some localized influences, it was the broader ideals and forms of an Islamic city which were predominant. An early map of Sharjah drawn by the British military in 1820 revealed that – while still obviously a small town – it already possessed several important features of a Islamic city that included:

- Al-Sour (defensive city fence/wall): Sharjah's *sour* (1804–1819) was built by Sheikh Sultan I bin Saqr Al-Qasimi to protect it from invaders. The *sour* was constructed out of local materials such as stone reefs and sandstone brought in from the coastline and Abu Musa Island. This defensive wall was around 2.75 m high and 0.5 m thick. It had three main entrances through which Bedouins could enter the city with their camels and goats to sell them in the Al-Arsa market. By 1886, however, there were no parts of the *sour* remaining due to the expansion of the town.
- Palmary area: this was located outside the *sour* next to the water supplies.
- Al-Layyeh area: this was a small fishing village located to the south on the other side of the creek from Sharjah.
- Al-Jubail area: this was located outside the *sour* and had an elevated cemetery at 10–15 m above sea level.
- Coastal *souk*: this market was located along the coastline of the creek but within the *sour*, and it sold fish, gold and various different goods.

Surviving evidence from Sharjah's early development shows that the city consisted of several types of architectural and urban elements. The most

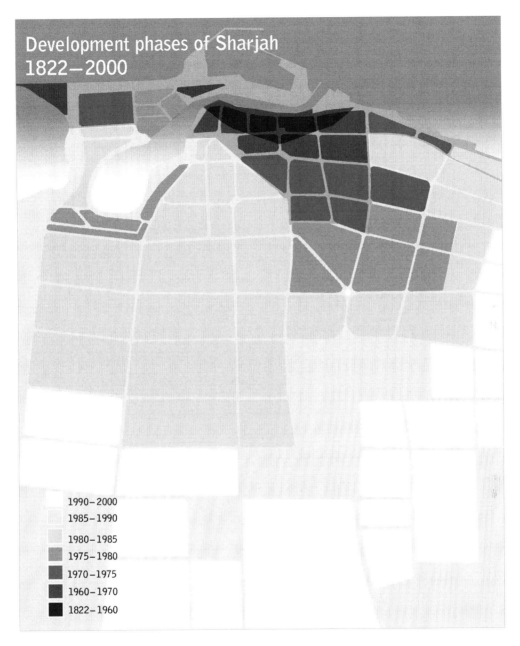

Development phases of Sharjah
1822—2000

1990–2000
1985–1990
1980–1985
1975–1980
1970–1975
1960–1970
1822–1960

10.1   Development phases of Sharjah, UAE, from 1822–2000, showing the
gradual move inland from the old port (top centre of map)

notable houses had clear Persian and Indian influences, and in general the built fabric was of a somewhat 'primitive' nature, called 'arish. The Islamic community was established in several dense residential neighbourhoods. However, the slow growth of Sharjah during the 19th century – a period of decisive internal changes and important external influences – did not enable the city to reach the degree of urban maturity that was the case in other Islamic capitals. It was for this reason that the still-nascent Sharjah found itself unable to resist the pressures of modernizing change that impacted from the beginning of the 20th century (see Plate 16).

Hence, in 1930, Sharjah witnessed the birth of its first airport, immediately altering its urban morphology from the traditional to the modern. The airport was constructed by British military forces as a key transit point on the route between India and the United Kingdom. It brought in new financial income to the city at a time when its pearl trading was declining, and led to the need to form a new gate into the old town, connected by land and sea. This significant piece transport infrastructure underlined Sharjah's strategic geographical position as well as introducing new patterns of technology and urbanism. The airport was created as a small military urban district containing more than 1,200 air-conditioned housing units, water reservoirs, power station and hospital, all protected by an encircling wall. The construction of the military airport and accompanying district influenced the whole traditional setting of Sharjah through the arrival of major new roads (albeit originally as dirt tracks). What is now Al-Uruba Road, currently used by trucks and lorries, was in fact the first landing strip. In 1938, the process of modernizing Sharjah's infrastructure was given a further financial boost when the local government handed out contracts for British oil companies to explore the area for oil reserves.

THE RECTILINEAR AND THE GRID-IRON

In 1968, just when the British military forces were preparing to leave the United Arab Emirates after 150 years of protectorate status, Sharjah had expanded in size to include new districts such as Maysaloon, Al-Falaj, Al-Sharq and Al-Mujarrah. It was therefore decided to draw up a plan that divided Sharjah into a more orderly, western-style grid. This master-plan was devised by the British civil engineering firm of Sir William Halcrow & Partners. From that point on, the city started to have even newer transport infrastructure such as metalled roads, roundabouts and a bridge connecting the old city to Al-Layyeh on the other side of the creek. In addition, with the creek now starting to dry up because of soil deposition, Sharjah's urban form shifted significantly from a localized model to the modern urban archetype. The trend towards a rectilinear, grid-iron layout was stressed by the 1968 master-plan, and had impacted on the ground by 1980. The traditional old town was now stretched out to espouse the linearity of an ordered, westernised urban pattern. Consequently, the historic hub of Sharjah was confined to a series of heritage spots on the map.

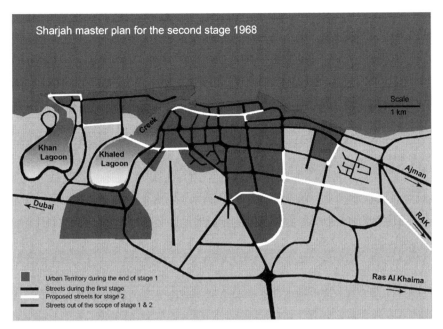

Sharjah master plan for the second stage 1968

Scale
1 km

Creek

Khan
Lagoon

Khaled
Lagoon

Ajman

Dubai

RAK

Ras Al Khaima

Urban Territory during the end of stage 1
Streets during the first stage
Proposed streets for stage 2
Streets out of the scope of stage 1 & 2

10.2   First master-plan for Sharjah as devised by the British firm of Halcrow & Partners in 1968

The emerging grid-iron plan showed the emphasis now being placed on connecting roads at the expense of well-defined neighbourhood zones. The master-plan gave priority to the main avenues shown in red for its first stage, then to other projected urban roads marked in yellow for its second stage; there were also various roads around or outside the periphery (as indicated in white), which were projected to be built during both the first and second stages. The extension of roads served to enlarge the body of the city, creating a more stretched urban territory. Sharjah's old city began to shrink even more under the vehicular pressure of the new road-based infrastructure.

Following Sharjah's independence in 1972, the municipality did not tamper with the emerging westernised urban layout. Instead, it continued to lay out streets and divide the city into districts following the demands of road traffic. New green areas like Al-Zahraa Square were formed. Sharjah's local government also decided to alter the entrance to and general shape of the creek, affecting the maritime commercial activities along the shoreline. By 1977, more houses were beginning to spread across the southern neighbourhoods and the first skyscrapers appeared in Sharjah. The city started to change to an even more modern form of rectangular urban blocks, metalled roads, roundabouts, green squares and landmark buildings (such as schools, hospitals, fire stations, etc). Sharjah now consisted of a series of eclectic urban parts set within a rigid traffic infrastructure.

THE SUBURBAN AND PERIPHERAL

The next key trend – towards suburban and peripheral development – was triggered by a new master-plan in 1980 that imposed an even more absolutist

10.3 Second master-plan for Sharjah drawn up in 1980 for implementation up to 2000

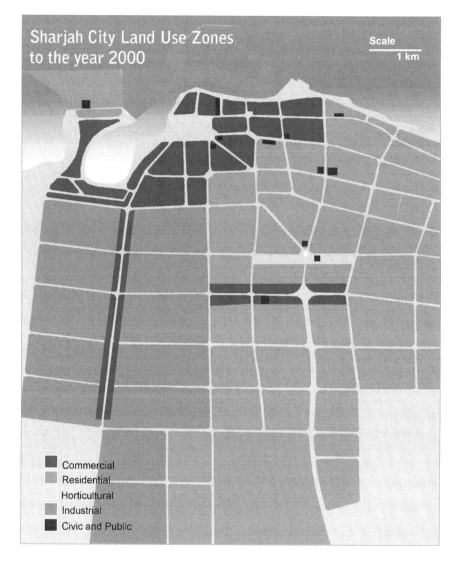

Sharjah City Land Use Zones
to the year 2000

Scale
1 km

Commercial
Residential
Horticultural
Industrial
Civic and Public

traffic map onto the city. Although the city was clearly not fully developed, the new plan allowed the spread of construction in peripheral areas where future roads were projected. And since the early-1980s, this trend has generated a sort of 'urban suburbia' which has heavily impacted on the relevance of having a city centre – or indeed the old core of Sharjah at all – as a point of reference.

In the 1980 master-plan, Sharjah's historic centre became totally subdivided within the overall traffic grid system, and the function of this zone was envisaged as being completely commercial. No regard was paid to the city's heritage or to its role as a cultural focus; hence there are now only a very few civic and public buildings in the old quarter, not at all sufficient for such a large city. Similarly, the industrial district of Sharjah, which was supposed to be kept on the urban periphery, was now allocated a strategic area adjacent to the lagoons, and as a result the industrial

10.4 Drawing showing the dramatic changes to just part of the old historic area of Sharjah by 2008

zone 'invaded' the body of the city in a longitudinal manner, running in a north-westerly/south-easterly direction.

This second master-plan continued to be implemented up to the year 2000 without any rectification or without anyone really questioning its relevance. Although concerns about urban heritage had become a serious issue in the Arab region since 1975, through the actions of UNESCO and other heritage organizations, it appears that the authorities within Sharjah's government were not yet equipped to review the city's past in a constructive way. Only minor restoration works on some selected buildings were undertaken. On the other hand, the implementation of the master-plan was at full gear, which had a great impact on the current shape of the city. Historic Sharjah became a piecemeal collection of heritage spots with the main banking street crossing its main zone. Since 2000, newer traffic plans have been generated but again without any consideration of the continuous disorder being created in the heritage area. Moreover, despite the fact that the old city has always been very active, and still preserves some of its traditional social and commercial activities, urban policy still seems to focus on the historic theme-park aspect.

THE BIRTH OF A NEW CITY CENTRE IN SHARJAH

The call for a new, alternative city centre was prompted by this loss of purpose for the old town and the consequent absence of a civic dimension within the city. The establishment of the three lagoons as an attractive natural feature along Sharjah's southerly coastline – with Al-Khan Lagoon and Al-Mamzar Lagoon now joining the adjacent Khalid Lagoon, the latter being an extension of the old creek – as well as competition from Dubai's well-known tourist and entertainment resources, has created the need for a new urban magnet. Currently, the area around the lagoons is becoming noticeable for high-rise buildings and continuous efforts to design the landscape to create a simile of Dubai. However, this new city centre cannot fully replace the cultural meaning of the historic hub of Sharjah.

Indeed, the disconnected old and new centres in Sharjah generate an urban antagonism. On one hand, the active traditional harbour is still a vibrant seafront with partial heritage remnants occupied by dynamic, multi-ethnic commercial activities. On the other hand, the more artificial aquatic vision of the lagoons represents the contemporary image of Sharjah with its mixed functions. This antagonism ought to be resolved either by merging the two centres into one large whole, or else carefully creating a bi-polar central area for Sharjah that balances its historical and contemporary urban images.

The area around the lagoons is currently driven by a competitive and somewhat random market-led development process, and no master-plan has been set up to face the dilemma of ensuring infrastructural, cultural, and environmental sustainability. The Al Qasba district between Khalid Lagoon and Al-Khan Lagoon is the only macro-project that reflects a clear vision, in terms of a cultural and environmental package, which is worthy of consideration amidst chaotically dispersed government and private buildings. Therefore, the new transportation plan is again an *a posteriori* resolution of urban issues and problems, and is not based on a holistic vision for the future planning of Sharjah. What is needed instead is for us to trace the urban changes in Sharjah to understand its inner strengths and weaknesses within a wider professional lens.

ENVIRONMENT AND WATER IN SHARJAH

Sharjah's history is woven around its main waterfront, and this now includes two of the large artificial lagoons, Khalid and Al-Khan, with the Al-Qasbaa Canal linking them. Hence in order to gain a deeper understanding of the urban fabric and environmental pressures in Sharjah, it is crucial to look at the present *status quo* of its water infrastructure and the waste-water crisis which is now constraining its proper development.

Khalid Lagoon has become one of the most important features of the city and key to its socio-economic status. It is a fair size, with its surface area is about 3,000,000 m², but with a depth of only 3–7 m. Khalid Lagoon is located right in the heart of the city and is surrounded by high-rise buildings, markets, recreational parks, entertainment and cultural centres, and busy commercial districts. The area around the lagoon is widely used by Sharjah residents for recreation and socializing, while the lagoon itself is used for boating, water sports and commercial activity. The lagoon is connected to the Gulf by the narrow channel of the creek, known as Al-Khour, and this is how water is exchanged. The creek is heavily used by ships and boats, and the surrounding land use is predominantly commercial.

Similarly to Khalid Lagoon, the nearby Al-Khan Lagoon is also connected to the Gulf through a narrow channel. Al-Khan Lagoon is used mainly for recreational fishing and boating, and the district is less developed than the area around Khalid Lagoon, although development is increasing rapidly. The Al-Khan Lagoon is easily the smaller of the two main lagoons, with a total surface area of approximately 1,500,000 m^2 and a depth of between 5–7 m. In addition to realising the social and economic benefits of creating the lagoons, the Sharjah government has also invested in constructing the Al-Qasbaa Canal between them in part to help improve the water flow and consequently improve the water quality. First commissioned on 8th November 2000, the canal is now about 1 km long, 5 m deep and just 30 metres wide. A gate is provided at the Khalid Lagoon end of the canal to allow water to flow in one direction from Al-Khan Lagoon into the Khalid Lagoon, but not in the opposite direction.

Despite such improvements, the shortage of water supply and poor waste-water management, which is still overly reliant on septic tank systems, are major issues in Sharjah. Without immediate municipal legislation, and a clear strategy for water provision and management, the city faces tremendous environmental challenges to its rapid urbanization. The steady growth in population, high-rise buildings, industrial zones, tourist activities and public facilities has increased exponentially the usage of both drinking and sewer water. This heavy usage is not being managed properly, challenging the urban authorities to be able to cope with rapidly rising demand for all kinds of water supplies.

URBAN PLANNING AND GOVERNANCE IN CONTEMPORARY SHARJAH

The history of planning in Sharjah has been related mainly to the grid pattern – the main focus for which was the automobile *per se*. The first master-plan for Sharjah in 1968 set out a traffic engineering schemata that impacted on the city's and has only created chaos and disorder up till now. Although Halcrow & Partners claimed at the time to be pioneering the future growth of Sharjah, facts on the ground proved that their plan was mediocre *vis-à-vis* what was being achieved internationally in terms of urban planning. Since the emergence in 1968 of the main road, which stretches from the southern border with Dubai to Ras Al-Khaimah to the north, Sharjah has gone through a number of major urban and geographical transformations based on infrastructural demands: these include Corniche Road along the creek, Port Khalid, and now the three artificial lagoons.

In addition to the unsuccessful master-plan by Halcrow & Partners, the city suffered acutely from not having a sufficiently qualified institutional structure to execute planning policy and follow up with requisite guidelines. As in most Arabic and Islamic countries, the first local municipalities imported by colonialists were rather useless and clashed with traditional systems of social management (*Hisba*, *Qadha'*, guilds, etc.). These municipalities needed time to develop and mature in tandem with the complex nature of contemporary Islamic cities. However, in most cases it is sad to say they are still not fully competent to run the planning and management of their urban spaces.

10.5 Traditional and modern architecture together in Sharjah

This clash between the older and newer styles of city management has resulted in the destruction of old Sharjah, the potential of which does not seem to have been perceived – or, rather, was ignored. Local heritage tended to be regarded as 'primitive' and thus unsuitable for a modern 'developed' city. Therefore, major destruction was undertaken to insert new boulevards into the body of the old town. No real effort was made towards conservation and no concern was shown as to the value of cultural resources. While progressive urbanism worldwide was questioning the validity of centralized planning and the imposition of city forms and concepts onto inhabitants, the international consulting offices were simply having their day in a region where criticism is scarce and a fascination with modern westernised forms blinded all stakeholders involved in the process.

To counter the destructive process of the historical memory and heritage of Sharjah, His Highness Sheikh Sultan – with the foresight of a cultural renaissance – initiated a long-term restoration programme that has thankfully saved the most strategic part of the city from eradication. However, this restoration work is clearly not enough today to meet the planning pressures on the whole city. The sheikh's office is keen to undertake this task, believing that sound planning is required to underscore the value of built heritage in the future Sharjah as a cultural anchor within the UAE. For this reason, Peter Jackson, a architect interested in cultural heritage, was hired since 2007 as the Sheikh's office advisor in order to oversee the planning process.

As such, this revived planning process needs to take into consideration the following aspects:

10.6   New office towers in downtown Sharjah

- Integration: heritage sites and monuments should be an integral part of planning policy.
- Continuity: the need is to establish a new master-plan that can guarantee the historical and cultural continuity of Sharjah.
- Diversity: heritage preservation means not a partial approach, but a holistic one that considers all past or present cultural differences.
- Identity: the planning process should protect the sense of identity and sense of belonging to Sharjah, while also being cosmopolitan and modern.
- Profit: cultural investment must not be about making the city into an absolute museum, but instead needs to rejuvenate Sharjah's history so it remains a sustainable centre of commerce and trade.
- Development: the planning process has to preserve the existing heritage and increase resources to produce new cultural experiences and thus valuable heritage for the future.
- Community: heritage sustains communities and forges their memories of place, meaning that heritage planning empowers a community to define itself, creating greater social and cultural attachment to its living space.
- Environment: heritage has also to include natural and ecological resources that augment the experience of architectural and urban heritage, and

sustaining environment would enable Sharjah to balance its modern development while preserving its ecological dimension.

- Density: the fast-growing population in Sharjah has to be managed to avoid the social chaos found in other Arab cities. For any city to prosper, its planning strategies ought to remain within the capacity to retain a reasonable density and maintain the quality of civic life.
- Traffic: this should be merely a means, and not an end in itself as it is today in planning. Sharjah should not be a transit route through its central zone, but instead should remove all disturbing vehicular influxes to outside its urban territory so that inhabitants and visitors alike can better appreciate its history and cultural resources.

In order to reach these planning goals, Sharjah cannot rely on its current human and technical resources since there are not at the level expected for such an optimistic endeavour. The city's planning authorities are sub-standard, and rampant real-estate development is likewise hindering the planning process. In absence of a clear planning governance and sufficient local technical expertise, the planning authorities are not being challenged enough. Therefore, constructive criticism is usually seen more as a threat rather than something that can help to shape a better future for Sharjah.

CONCLUSION

Rapid economic and population growth in Sharjah has led to a number of unintended consequences. The last master-plan from 1980, which set out a pattern of infrastructure to create urban zones and other features, is not really applicable any more, nor is it guided by clear urban legislation. This lack of sound urban zoning is clearly constraining the city from becoming a functional urban agglomeration, leading to poor accessibility, weak public facilities, unclear urban boundaries, excessive mixed-use areas, and housing sprawl. Traffic flow and parking problems are major urban issues because of the improper planning of transportation circulation networks which are undergoing continuous reformulation and change.

In terms of built-up areas in Sharjah, there is generally a lack of strict rules and regulations in how the land market is operating. It means that the city has reactively grown to follow the demographic increase but has been designed as a series of disconnected parts (at the architectural level) and not as a whole (the urban level). The unidirectional urban extension of Sharjah because of confining boundaries with Dubai, Ajman and the Gulf coastline is placing real pressure on the city centre to grow up vertically through an increase in high-rise buildings. However, these new towers are the result of land speculation without the adequate urban infrastructure appropriate to such building types. Meanwhile, the cultural heritage area in old Sharjah is coming under threat of disappearing altogether from the map of the city, despite the continuous efforts to preserve some the scattered remaining historic buildings.

In addition, due to the critical urban *status quo*, the city is spending a colossal municipal budget just to survive, and there is no adequate planning system to envision tasks and tailor expenditure accordingly. Foreign private consulting companies are still in control, just as they were in the days of the British protectorate, and are not willing to empower the municipal planning authorities or to enhance the skills of civic employees. If one wants, for instance, to conduct a study into the current urban crisis of Sharjah, one finds that most government documents are in fact in the custody of foreign companies, which is also very risky as these companies may leave at any time without prior notice. Hence, for a proper planning process to be established, the following measures are vital:

- Development of municipal leadership and administrative capacities.
- Building up a sound database about Sharjah (such as data on socio-economics, geography, heritage resources, traffic patterns, etc.).
- Establishment of better institutional communication and negotiation.
- Closer management of stakeholders and decision makers.
- Development of sufficiently qualified local professionals.
- Stronger management of private buildings projects in the city.
- Establishment of a sound urban legislation.
- Encouragement of public participation in the planning process.

NOTES

1   As quoted in UAE Ministry of Information and Culture, *United Arab Emirates Yearbook 2002* (London: Trident Press, 2002), p. 19.

2   The account in this chapter is based on the following sources: Nasser H. Abbudi, *Safahat min Athar wa-Turath Dawlat al-Imarat al-Arabia al-Muttahida* (Ain: Zaid Center for Heritage and History, 2002); Hind Al Yousef, 'A Green Legacy', 20 September 2008, *Gulf News* website, http://gulfnews.com/news/gulf/uae/environment/a-green-legacy-1.132208 (accessed 5 October 2009); Graham Anderson, 'The Issue of Conservation of Historic Buildings in the Urban Areas in the Emirate of Sharjah' (Unpublished PhD Thesis, University of Durham, UK, 1991); Jan Assmann & John Czaplicka, 'Collective Memory and Cultural Identity', *New German Critique*, no. 65 (Spring 1995): 125–133; Jane Jacobs, *The Death and Life of Great American Cities* (New York: Vintage Books, 1961/92); Mohamed Mursi Abdullah, *Dawlat al-Imarat al-Arabia al-Muttahida Wajiranuha* (Kuwait: Dar al-Qalam, 1981); Christian Norberg-Schulz, *Genius Loci* (New York: Rizzoli, 1980); John J. Nowell, 'Now and Then: The Emirates', *Arabian Historical Series* (Vol. 1, Dubai: Gulf Printing & Publishing, 1998); Abdullah A. Rahmah, *Al-Imarat fi Dhakirati Abna-iha: al-Hayat al-Iqtisadia* (Sharjah: Manshurat Ittihad Kuttab wa-Udabae al-Imarat, 2005); Ali M. Rashid, *Al-Hussun wal-Qila' fi Dawlat al-Imarat al-Arabia al-Mutthida* (Abu Dhabi: Isdarat al-Mujamma a-Thaqafi, 2004); Mohamed Shakir, *Mawsu'at Tarikh al-Khalij al-Arabi* (Amman: Dar Usama li-Nashr wa-Tawzi, 2003); 'Sharjah, promoting the culture of understanding', *New York Times Magazine* (special advertising supplement produced and sponsored by Summit Communications), 13 May 2007; Salim Zabbal, *Kuntu Shahidaa: al-Imarat min 1960 ila 1970* (Abu Dhabi: Isdarat al-Mujamma' Thaqafi, 2001).

PART II

EASTERN COASTLINE OF PERSIAN GULF

11

Abadan and Khorramshahr, Iran

Nasser Golzari

The histories of some cities are coiled with symbols, legends, economic upheavals, political revolutions, colonial occupations, and such like. The two cities of Abadan and Khorramshahr in the south-western Iranian province of Khuzestan are no exceptions. Both display a hybrid identity which has been forged out of global oil interests and acts of local cultural resistance. Add to this mix their unique climate conditions and the cultural practices of local people, as well as the often confusing old street patterns, and you're in for a treat. The two river ports of Abadan and Khorramshahr – sitting not far downstream from Basra in Iraq – lie on the Arvand River, often referred to as Shatt Al-Arab, this being the Euphrates/Tigris confluence as it flows into its delta at the northern end of the Persian Gulf.

11.1 Map of Abadan and Khorramshahr on the border with Iraq and close to Kuwait

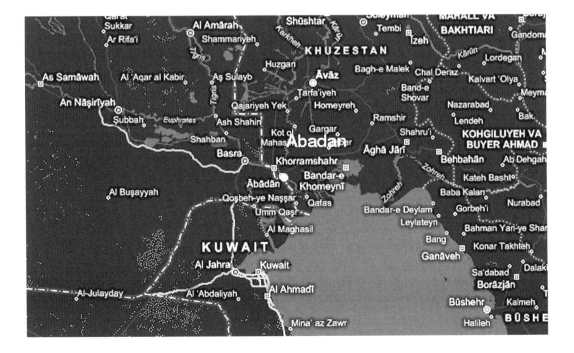

Abadan hence sits 60 km north of the Gulf shoreline. In terms of its local geography, the city is bounded by the Arvand River on its south-to-south-western sides, this forming the Iraqi border, and by the Bahamnshir outlet of the Karun River on its north-to-north-western edges. Flowing off in the south-westerly direction is the aforementioned river to the Persian Gulf. Khorramshahr is the somewhat overshadowed neighbour just 15 km the north-west, and indeed they could on the surface be regarded as a kind of 'twin city'. However, this would be to miss their subtleties. While the historically iconic cities of Abadan and Khorramshahr are geographically so close they remain so different in their cultural practices, urban fabric, housing types and political symbolism. Abadan remains easily the larger of the two, with a current estimated population of around 220,000 persons, compared to just 124,000 in Khorramshahr. Some argue that these differences and the contradictory historical journeys which the two cities have taken – in terms of urban structure, cultural identity and everyday habits – in fact make them complementary. Others might see the links merely in terms of having the same climate, an equal denial of past practices, and thus a casual attitude towards consuming and wasting energy. A closer look at the political history and human habitation of these two fascinating cities on the northern rim of the Persian Gulf offers clues as to how oil-rich cities are shaped both by local climate and the brutal pressures of the global market economy. The presence of oil in this area, especially in Abadan, has totally dominated the lives of local citizens and been instrumental in destroying its older, more climatically responsive, built fabric. An exploration of these tensions will form the substance of this chapter, following a brief background introduction.

THE ARRIVAL OF AMERICAN/WESTERNISING TENDENCIES

11.2   Abadan oil refinery in the early-1950s

Abadan and Khorramshahr both grew steadily in importance after the discovery of oil and gas reserves. The Anglo-Persian Oil Company built its first refinery in Abadan in 1909–1913 and by the 1930s this was the largest in the world. Growth continued to boom after the Second World War, such that for a few decades Abadan was the largest oil-producing city anywhere; Khorramshahr played the role of an important supporting act. More recently, the urban development of Abadan and Khorramshahr has been shaped by their geographic location close to the borders of a number of oil-producing Gulf countries, notably with Iraq to the west and Kuwait to the south-west.

Both cities thus became extremely active economically during the reign of the Pahlavi dynasty (1925–1979), and during the latter stages of which Iran's oil income soared from $22.5 million in 1954 to over $19 billion in 1975–1976.[1] This staggering increase in oil revenue however brought little benefit for local citizens. The economic gap between the local majority and a transient wealthy minority (mainly Americans and Europeans) had become chronically unfair by the end of the 1970s. This situation also needs to be set within the major geopolitical changes of that era. Iran's oil supplies and its strategic location, adjacent to what was then the Soviet Union, now Russia, were vitally important to the USA at all levels. This 'invasion' of Iran by the global market first began to be truly noticeable during the 1960s in all industries and in people's everyday lives. As Hamid Naficy explains in his essay on new Iranian cinema of that era:

> Regional media influences in Iran were replaced by global interests. American companies began selling all kinds of products and services, from feature films to television programmes, from TV receivers to TV studios, from communication expertise to personnel training: in short, they sold not only consumer products but also consumer ideology.[2]

Naficy continues by noting that the first Iranian television station, which was commercially based and privately owned, was established by Iraj Sabet, whose family also happened to be the agents for Pepsi Cola and various US advertising agencies. The new channel imported American programmes as well as dictating all the commercials broadcast on Iranian TV. By the late-1960s and early-1970s, products like Pepsi Cola and Winston cigarettes became a lifestyle image and a symbolic representation of the 'western' world for Iran's upper and middle classes.[3] Indeed, what was particularly alarming about the arrival of American consumer products was their close association with the culture of pleasure being enjoyed by workers and middle-income groups. When the first Pepsi Cola factory opened to the west of Tehran, with its glazed façade exposing the process of bottling the drink, many working-class families went for picnics in front of the Pepsi factory rather than to their usual local park! This intrusion of 'brand' culture and its metaphor of American/westernised desire was vividly described in the work of the controversial female Iranian poet, film-maker and writer, Forugh Farrokhzad (1935–1967). In a poem of 1965 titled *Someone Like No One Else*, she wrote beautifully of her memories as a child.[4] Farrokhzad was one of the most unconventional and sharpest commentators on the socio-cultural transformations being experienced in Iran at the time, bringing in references to everyday mass culture in her work.

The arrival of the American consumer culture and its glittery products primarily benefitted Iran's elite minority, creating a huge economic and cultural gulf with the rest of Iranian society. This was not only visible and tangible in Tehran, Iran's modern capital, but if anything was probably even more representative of and reflected in cities like Abadan and Khorramshahr. Economic inequality, exploitation of local workers, and privileges given to expatriate Europeans and Americans can be seen in some of early Iranian movies. Most notable was the

Abadani director, Amir Naderi, in his masterpieces 'Tangsir' (1973) and 'The Runner' (1985); both films are set in Khuzestan, where the sheer depth of oppression and local anger was bravely and masterfully documented in these films.

Importantly, Khorramshahr and (more specifically) Abadan played critical roles in the movement to nationalise Iran's oil industry in the early-1950s, as well as at the decisive moments of victory by the Islamic Revolution over Shah Mohammad Reza Pahlavi in 1978–1979.[5] Indeed, it is argued that the two key events that were the turning point for the Iranian Islamic Revolution were the oil-workers' strike in December 1978 and the burning down of the Rex Cinema in Abadan on 'Black Friday' in August 1978, with over 350 people killed in the fire. However, after this featuring role for Abadan and Khorramshahr in the late-1970s – with their heroic fight against the Shah's dictatorship and its appalling human rights record – came the devastating physical, human and economic sufferings and losses which both cities experienced during the Iran/ Iraq War (1980–1988).[6] Even after eight years of fighting and occupation by Saddam Hussein's Iraqi Army, backed by America and France, neither Abadan or Khorramshahr ever gave up. Instead, both cities managed to resist until the Iraqi forces were driven out, with the result that they – and this time around even more so in Khorramshahr's case – became the symbol (and indeed reality) for yet another historic Iranian achievement.

Yet despite contributing such rich layers of political and economic meaning within the socio-political fabric of Iran, neither of these two cities was rewarded with much attention or indeed resources with which to celebrate and share its historical importance with local citizens or tourists. Their unique urban planning, spatial characteristics and architectural details – which collectively offer a platform to discuss the relationship of climatic context and cultural identity to models of habitation – are likewise underappreciated, indeed even ignored. Rather, one needs to rely on undocumented local knowledge provided by the older generation of citizens still living in the two cities, often in a sad state of affairs; bizarrely, many older residents adhere to the myth of the pomp and glitter of 'the good old days', even if only for a few elite groups, back in the Pahlavi era. It is therefore important to transcend this condition of historical amnesia and urban neglect by looking more carefully at Abadan and Khorramshahr to find out how people might live in the northern part of the Persian Gulf. However, given that Abadan has for so long been the 'dominant twin', the bulk of analysis in this chapter will by necessity focus on it.

CITYSCAPE

Abadan lies on what is in effect an encircled island of 63km in length and from 3–19 km in width, abutting onto the Arvand River or Shatt Al-Arab. Looking from a bird's-eye perspective when flying in from Tehran, one is fascinated by the regularity of the agricultural land around Abadan. The well-mannered forest of date palms – which still provide a sizeable percentage of world's dates – hugs the city to its northern, eastern and western edges, giving it protection from the desert beyond. It is an unexpectedly pastoral image, given that Abadan is barely known for anything but its oil resources.

The airport to the north-west, just like the main railway station, is a facility shared equally by Abadan and Khorramshahr. On stepping out of the plane, one immediately feels the pleasant dry heat – that is, if you take care to avoid arriving in summer at any time between 12.00 noon and 6.00pm, when temperatures are usually in the mid-40s°C. During these 'boiling' hours in the summertime, when the heat becomes unbearable, you will hardly find anyone around; indeed, the airport itself is closed. However, in the months from November to April, local temperatures become far more agreeable.

In contrast to Tehran, Abadan seems extremely calm and polite. There is a surprising absence of any smell of oil/petroleum, the very thing that modern Abadan is famous for. The city's history predates Islam back to the Sassanid dynasty (224–651AD). Written legends suggest that Abadan was initially known for its salt deposits and mat-making crafts, and it later grew into an Islamic port city during the great Abbasid Caliphate. In Iran, there is never any shortage of legends and unofficial stories which offer more tangible insights into the life of cities than written histories do. Hence it is believed that the Prophet Muhammad and Imam Ali (his son-in-law and Islam's first spiritual leader) somehow made references to Abadan as a place of paradise where 'palm gardens and mosques come together making it ideal – 'God's creation' – as a place of rest for Hajji's, visitors to Mecca, to stay'.[7] Here is important to note that soon after Islam was born, a regular movement by *Hajji* pilgrims took place from Iran across the Euphrates/Tigris River to the Saudi cities of Mecca and Medina. Thus a city like Abadan, positioned on the edge of a river in the desert, also offered a perfect stopping point for Muslim travellers.

The already mature tradition of Iranian urban architecture, based on private mansions, gardens and courtyards, was readily adapted to the new demand to build Islamic mosques. With a central pond celebrating the role of water – an element used as a practical response to the hot climate and hence a staple of songs, poems and daily cultural rituals – the insertion of mosques into gardens was yet another variation on the Persian garden/courtyard typology. Indeed, the mosque came to replace the private mansion as the pre-eminent urban form, with the side benefit also of making traditional Persian gardens more socially inclusive. Hence for the Prophet Muhammad and the new Islamic leaders, the fusion of the emerging mosque typology with a sophisticated form of urban space served as a symbol of the new Islamic paradise-on-earth, as well as fitting easily into climatic conditions and cultural practices. Some of these very early mosques and garden courtyards are still visible in and around Abadan. Sadly, however, Abadan in later centuries has lost this urban continuity. Now, and certainly for the younger generation in the province – as indeed in the rest of Iran – the city is explicitly conceived of in terms of oil/petroleum income and the struggle of the Iran/Iraq War, rather than for its older tradition of shaded gardens, waterways and climatically responsive buildings.

11.3   Flames of
the oil refinery
and petrochemical
complex
dominating
Abadan's skyline

CITY OF FLAME: ABADAN AND OIL/PETROLEUM

The National Iranian Oil Refining and Distribution Company (NIORDC) and the
connected National Iranian Petrochemical Company (NIPC) serve to divide
Abadan visually and physically from west to east. Incredibly, the floor area
of both plants occupies nearly a third of the city's area. So these are the two
elements which constantly remind citizens of the presence of global forces in
Abadan. Whenever one drives or walks around the city, the flames of the oil
refinery and the petrochemical complex are always there, dominating the place
from all directions.

It is worth here tracing the story of the oil industry in Abadan to see how this
situation arose. Back in 1905, the whole region was indirectly controlled by British
colonial rule, and one symbolic manifestation of this was the formation that year
of the Anglo-Persian Oil Company. In 1908, oil and gas reserves were discovered in
the city of Masjed-e-Soleyman – like Abadan, in Khuzestan province, but further
to the north. To be able to export these supplies, by 1913 the Anglo-Persian Oil
Company had built a pipeline to its first refinery in Abadan, thereby instantly
transforming the latter into a globalised city. As noted, within 25 years Abadan
had the largest oil refinery in the world, even if there was still extreme poverty
and inequality for most of its local community. Prior to the nationalisation of
Iranian oil in the early-1950s, around 80–85 per cent of the wealth created was
in British ownership. This contradiction between poverty and elitism remained in
Abadan in different forms even after nationalisation, and exists today in different
forms. None of the British colonial rulers, nor the Pahlavi regime which replaced
them, nor even the subsequent Islamic Republic government, have bothered to
explore the climatic wealth and social potential of Abadan. Instead they have just
exploited the presence of oil and gas to feed Iran, and the wider world, with little
thought about local citizens.

Abadan, as the 'city of flame', seems historically to have always been a transient
city. Its population increased greatly after the discovery of oil, most of whom were
skilled workers and engineers brought in from the rest of Iran, especially Tehran, or
else from abroad. It is believed that during its peak from the early-1950s to the mid-
1970s, less than 10 per cent of the city's population came from Abadan or elsewhere
in Khuzestan province. The other 90 per cent were from elsewhere, including a large
number from Britain, continental Europe or the USA who were only there to work in
the oil industry. This transient community was totally unfamiliar with the climatic

11.4   American oil-worker families arriving in Abadan

condition and everyday cultural habits which over the centuries had created such a strong imprint on the urban character and spatial formation of Abadan.[8]

The extensive use of Europeans and Americans for technical and administrative staff was a deliberate policy on the part of British colonial powers to maintain control over the oil industry. This could be graphically seen in 1951 when Iran suddenly nationalised the Anglo-Iranian Oil Company. Britain immediately imposed economic sanctions and deployed its warships to blockade Abadan and all of Iran's southern ports. Furthermore, they withdraw all of their technical personnel along with 300 administrators from Abadan. Iran's counter-attempt to bring in technicians and consultants from other countries proved a failure, forcing it to turn to US support to run the industry.[9]

Meanwhile, the transient oil community brought its own forms of architecture, urban planning and living habits which in no way related to Abadan or the logic of living in that climate. Its unsuitability was reflected in the street layouts and building types erected during the 1960s and 1970s. Later on, when the city was attacked in 1980 by the invading Iraq Army, it was the non-local oil worker community that was the first to leave, including other Iranians. Moving as far as they could from the war zone, most never came back, meaning that only a few traces of their occupation survive today. I was told by a local shopkeeper who was one of the few from elsewhere in Iran who did return to Abadan:

> People went away partly because the government was too busy trying to fight the war, as well as being extremely surprised by the attack, and so they did not provide any protections or facilities for those fleeing from Abadan. But we had to come back; after all, it is our home. This was not the case for Tehranis, who left Abadan and never returned.[10]

Restoration of full operational conditions at the Abadan oil refinery didn't happen until 1997, and created renewed economic and employment activities.

Once again, however, the oil worker community brought in from other provinces of Iran appears to be a transient one. The Islamic Republican government did introduce a variety of measures, including certain financial incentives, to encourage people to move back to the city to restart the economy. Yet the city of Abadan today seems to consist of displaced souls, with more and more new arrivals from elsewhere in Iran.

There is a mysterious, ominous feel to the oil refinery/petrochemical plant in the way it overshadows the city, rather like in *The Castle* by Franz Kafka.[11] It's an impossible space to penetrate, literally and metaphorically, so one can only imagine the hidden, bureaucratic layers of power within. Citizens talk about it, mentioning the social divisions created in the Pahlavi era, the money it has generated, the foreign managers and engineers implanted from outside, the way which the city has been designed around it in a secretive and inaccessible manner. The stories one hears from locals about the past and present life of the oil refinery invoke a specific image; as an alien object, this global representation is still untouchable in their minds. Industrial plants constitute a huge part of Abadan's identity and yet are unable to identify in any meaningful sense with the city's everyday life.

NON-PLACE?

The pattern of continuous immigration and the sudden gains and losses of population make Abadan a service city – perhaps even a 'non-place' – within the national and global marketplaces. If there continues to be little attention to how to create a sustainable local community, the problem will simply be perpetuated. What, then, ought to be the physical identity of cities of this kind? Other key issues of cultural identity are also being swept under the carpet. Almost all of Abadan's southern and south-western borders are shared with Iraq, reminding citizens of the bitter 1980s conflict in which Abadan was under direct siege for 18 months. Driving around the city, almost every taxi driver tells you of their experience of war as if it was yesterday. Half-demolished buildings likewise offer strong reminders of those moments. This psychological presence of the Iran-Iraq War, which ended 23 years ago, is of great concern, and of course the same problem exists in neighbouring Khorramshahr.

A concerted process of post-war reconstruction would have been the ideal scenario for both these war-damaged cities, and indeed a localised, environmentally-driven regeneration programme on socially sustainable lines would have fitted the stated policies of the Islamic Republic government. Hashemi Rafsanjani, who from 1989–1997 was the first Iranian first president after the Iran-Iraq War, tried to push for extensive rebuilding. He favoured private development and free-market investment linked to the newly introduced concept of real estate, echoing to some extent what was happening in Britain under the Thatcher government. But all that has happened since then is a vague promise of establishing a 'free economic zone' in Abadan, similar to those in Kish

Island or Dubai, which if introduced would simply freeze out local citizens once more and, critically, perpetuate unsustainable forms of development.

In addition, it is not clear why Iran's bold reconstruction projects from the 1990s, including a Californian-style oasis – called Arge-e-Jadid[12] – created from virtually nothing in the middle of the desert, didn't touch upon Abadan and Khorramshahr given their historically important locations on the Arvand River/ Shatt Al-Arab. There is a very real argument that the cities deserve far more attention and investment than has hitherto been offered to them. They could be turned exemplars of urban reconstruction based on specific climatic conditions, use of natural resources, and ways in which cultural identity is reconnected to urban lifestyles. Similarly, it's also unclear why some of the *bonyads* – charity foundations which became devoted to religious purposes following the 1979 Islamic Revolution, and also highly effective in redistributing the wealth of the upper-class minority from the Pahlavi era – haven't been asked to consolidate banks and regenerate empty properties in the Khuzestan region to promote socio-economic reconstruction.[13] Instead, large numbers of properties which once belonged to the elite during the Pahlavi dynasty, some of which reflect imported colonial architecture such as from Britain or the Netherlands, remain unoccupied and left to ruin in Abadan and Khorramshahr. Instead, they ought to be reused as prime examples of how to redesign old dwellings for a new cultural context.

11.5   Half-demolished buildings in Abadan as reminders of the Iran/Iraq War, as photographed in 2009

11.6   Colonial-style dwellings sit empty and left to ruin in the Bawarda garden suburb in Abadan

11.7   1950s Anglo-Iranian Oil Company dwellings by the British
architect, James M. Wilson, in the Bawarda neighbourhood

GOOD AND BAD OLD DAYS – 'THE THEATRE OF SILENCE'

The contrast with Abadan's traditional urban layout posed by the dwellings built for oil-workers, with their incorporation of colonial styles in gated communities, only adds to the surreal nature of the city. 'Alien' forms of pitched roofs, Arts & Crafts cottages, Art Deco mansions – now mostly unoccupied – hint at a theatrical setting. This however is a 'theatre of silence', with little life inside it, as a result not just of the fall in population after the Iran/Iraq War but also the social disconnection of neighbourhoods. Again, this is unfortunate, especially given the vibrancy of Abadan in earlier generations. Indeed, this oil-rich city was the epicentre of political activities in Iran during the 1940s, pushing for workers' rights and the nationalisation of oil. In March 1946 the British Army, aided by a few sections of Iranian forces, killed over 50 left-wing demonstrators protesting against colonial control.[14] This level of grass-roots activism fed into the Liberal Party led by Mohammad Mosadegh, who became Iran's Prime Minister in the early-1950s, as well as the hugely influential Tudeh Party ('Tudeh' in Farsi means 'masses', indicating in effect it was Iran's Communist Party).

The 1950s was also the critical period in Iran when the USA began to muscle its way into Iran, displacing British colonial domination. This carefully orchestrated change in patterns of influence is well documented in memoirs from the time. As one example, Farmanfarmanian observed: 'Jerry Dooher, first deputy of American Embassy in Iran and an influential political figure, was well known for his strong views against the unjust policies of Britain in the British-owned Anglo Iranian Oil Company (AIOC)'. He continued:

> One afternoon, Dooher told me: "You should throw out the British oil company".
> Every time I saw him he would repeat this and would say: "Create new conditions,
> what is wrong with that? Whatever happens, we, the Americans, would send our
> ships and would buy your oil".[15]

George McGhee, the US Assistant Foreign Minister who also happened to be married to the daughter of Everette De Golyer, a Texas oil millionaire, travelled to Abadan specially to create 'fairer' conditions for negotiations with the Anglo-Iranian Oil Company.[16] McGhee was a partner in De Golyer's oil prospecting company and as such had already discovered 'a sizeable oil field in Louisiana'.[17] Blatant financial self-interest was evidently the name of the game.

Iran's initial share of the profit from the oil industry, back in 1910, had been only 15 per cent; this was later increased to 20 per cent, just prior to nationalisation, as an attempt by the British powers to win a longer lease for its extraction. In that period prior to nationalisation, Britain owned over 51 per cent of the Anglo-Iranian Oil Company and exercised total control over the company and its employees. However, following a US-backed *coup d'état* in Iran in 1953, the Iranian share went up to 25 per cent and the controlling ownership of Iran's oil consortium was now to be divided between America, Britain, and France/Netherlands. However, the USA's newly acquired role as chief arbitrator meant that relations between Iran and Britain had been irrevocably changed. During the 1950s America was intent on replacing Britain as the major colonial power in the Middle East, as part of its wider plan for global domination in the Cold War era. Mary Ann Heiss has written of this geopolitical battle for control over Iran's oil resources:

> ... the shifting Anglo-American relationship regarding the Iranian oil nationalization crisis of the 1950s [had three phases] ... the era of US benevolent neutrality; the era of Anglo-American partnership; and the era of US domination.[18]

This neo-imperial activity by America in Iran and the Middle East had of course begun before the Second World War; what was different now, however, was its intensity.[19] The United States played a clever double-edged game in Iran. On one hand, via state officials like Dooher and McGhee, it encouraged Iran to regard British policy towards Iranian oil as wrong and unfair. On the other hand, when it came to critical moments such as in 1951 when Britain was imposing sanctions against Iran in wake of oil nationalization, they helped the British by spying on Mosadegh's government. Indeed, it appear to have been the Americans who planned the 1953 military coup, using the CIA's might, with aid from MI6, thereby bringing down the democratically elected prime minister just because he had nationalized the oil reserves.[20]

THOUGHTS ON REBUILDING ABADAN

Abadan's fertile location and its role as a major river port might suggest more than enough reasons for investors to be interested in the city, but this clearly isn't the case. The current Mayor's slogan – 'Think global, act local' – is a catchphrase that has of course been used often before, but one that needs to be unpacked and readjusted to suit the local conditions. The municipality has, as part of its latest planning policy, designated the northern riverfront in Abadan as a 'family park' for recreational activities, motorcycling, horse riding, etc. It is even being named Jazeereh Shademani, which translates as 'Fun Island', with the hope is that other potential sites for urban regeneration will be incorporated into the city's plan as a result.

11.8 Current state of Arvand River on the edge of Abadan

11.9   Sikh temple presents an appropriate alternative climatic model

To the south, overlooking the date palm forest, is the Arvand River with its potential as a locus for the customary evening promenade of family groups, a veritable social parade similar to that in Italian cities. However, the dusty southern wind from the desert creates a real environmental hazard. It is a problem exacerbated by the continual loss of agricultural land in Iraq and by the refusal of the Saudi Arabian government, ever since the Islamic Republic came to power in Iran, to deal with its own (non-farming) desert areas to reduce the effects of ecological damage through prevailing winds. Iran today doesn't have the same international backing as the Pahlavi dynasty once did to pressurise Saudi Arabia into mitigating this eco-environmental pollution. Instead, layers of southerly desert dust regularly cover much of Abadan as well as other Iranian cities along the Persian Gulf coast.

However, if one continues along this southern edge of the city, there is an important old Sikh Temple which presents a far more appropriate model of how to respond to the climate. It contains a peaceful courtyard with an optimal ratio of courtyard size to height of surrounding walls. In this manner, the width provides adequate protection from the dust and noise from the street while also forming a shaded courtyard. The building's entrance is articulated by a small and delicate 'watch tower' that responds to the city scale. The back of the temple's courtyard faces onto the river and palm trees, with a high wall protecting its interior from dusty desert winds. It's a sensible, passively controlled arrangement which ought to have been used more in the design of hotels and other new buildings in this region. Likewise, a wide platform hovering over the bank of the Arvand River in front of the lively fish market seems an ideal spot for evening promenading. As

11.10   Sikh temple courtyard

a port city, and certainly in the milder temperatures of the non-summer period, it could support a few seafood restaurants or stalls selling dates, pizza and other produce, so as to create a public focus for different age groups. And yet this potential collective space, shaped by local climatic conditions and memories of the old port district, remains a forgotten marginal site.

Maybe the Mayor's new slogan might actually mean something if he were actually to initiate some relevant economic and environmental strategies. Decent public spaces, custom-made to suit Abadan's culture and climate, could be the basis for socio-economic regeneration. Urban strategy needs to help local traders and different communities use the city in an inclusive and environmentally comfortable manner, while also respecting the habits and tastes of different age groups, and of both genders. In Iran today, this is a critical issue, given that the forces of global capitalism have not as yet totally dominated and changed people's lifestyles. Instead, the economic sanctions imposed on Iran by the United States (and some European countries) for the last two decades have forced the country to develop its own industrial base – including oil refining, car manufacturing and building materials, amongst others. It also compels Iran to find alternative passive climatic techniques to reduce energy use. Hence the sanctions have resulted in a return, in some trades at least, to older practices of recycling materials and goods, helping local economies to survive. In most local markets in Iran you will find places to repair every household object. This recycling of objects happens due to economic restrictions, not for environmental reasons. However, this level of self-sufficiency has equally slowed down the pace of entry of global forces; local craft industry is very much still alive (even if to some extent affected by the use of imported machinery). In terms of building materials, for instance, the result is a cultural collage ranging from local Iranian elements to a mixture of Turkish or Chinese products. It makes it hard to assess accurately the relative quality of locally made materials, yet it's also critical that the Islamic Republic government supports Iranian-made products to bolster costumer confidence.

IDENTITY SHIFT FROM GLOBAL TO URBAN SCALE

Despite the obvious cultural and climatic characteristics of Abadan and Khorramshahr, confusion remains about their current and future identities, and how these should be reflected in terms of urban grain and building typologies. Prodigious wealth from oil and gas in the Pahlavi era could easily have brought about intelligent city planning and social reform, reducing the gap between classes, as well as providing decent infrastructure. But this simply didn't happen. Instead there was an imposition of neo-colonial architecture from Europe, growing socio-economic friction, and the almost total destruction of the city fabric in Abadan and Khorramshahr. Similarly, very little of the massive surge in income following the 'Oil Crisis' of 1973–1974 was used for creating economic self-sufficiency or industrial training in the Shah's Iran.

11.11 Private facilities for European engineers, managers and their families in Abadan

11.12 Small one-bedroom houses built by the Anglo-Iranian Oil Company for local workers

Indeed, the excessive reliance on oil revenue during the Pahlavi dynasty, and then to a lesser degree by the Islamic Republic government, has caused Abadan to become divided by extreme wealth and poverty. During the 1960s and 1970s, the surface image of the city changed. But this new 'European look' – with its private bars, nightclubs, discos, cinemas, expensive hotels, casinos, fast cars in wide roads, outdoor swimming pools and western-style villas – was only aimed at elite groups who came from Tehran or abroad. Locals weren't allowed to use these facilities even if they dressed up specially to do so; rather, the new pleasures were for 'members only'.[21] Houses copied from Europe, set within town planning copied from North America, formed residential enclaves for high-ranking managers and engineers in the oil business. Some of these dwellings even had 10–12 bedrooms, whereas lower-ranking technicians and manual workers, especially Iranians, were squeezed into 1–2 bedroom apartments. As in other Persian Gulf cities like Dubai, Manama or Kuwait City, the expatriate managers and engineers were only temporary residents. Most of the new villas were carefully located in the west of Abadan, where the air is cleaner, while workers' apartments were in the dustier and more polluted areas to the south or east. Local workers also had to live continuously in Abadan, whereas the elite groups, being unable to deal with the hot climate, would spend several weeks a year in northern Iran, or abroad, leaving much of the city unoccupied. Today, the larger neo-colonial houses tend either to have been divided into smaller apartments or, as mentioned, are left unoccupied (see Plates 17 and 18).

ABADAN OF THE 1930s AND 1940s: A FAST-MOVING TRANSIENT CITY

In 2009, Abadan and Khorramshahr celebrated the centenary of the discovery of oil in Iran, something which was to have such a great impact on all levels of life. Abadan's population spurt had led to a dramatic expansion of the city by the 1950s, with its urban planning led by British and continental European experts influenced by the Garden City movement or the *siedlungs* that had appeared in cities like Berlin, Frankfurt or Stuttgart in the 1920s. It is thought that a British architect, James M. Wilson, was the mastermind behind the layout and house designs for the Bawarda neighbourhood in Abadan. These mini-cities, known in Iran as *shahraks*, however missed out many elements of the Garden Cities or *siedlungs*, such as social housing, health clinics and nurseries.[22]

The German *siedlungs* were indeed designed for lower-income families, whereas ironically in Abadan the new settlements were intended for the minority upper classes and European expatriates. As highlighted in Murray Fraser's book, *Architecture and the 'Special Relationship'*, the earlier social goals of the British Garden City movement came gradually to be dropped in the post-war period in favour of incorporating Americanising trends such as increased car use.[23] In Abadan, as in present-day Dubai, this use of American-style patterns of suburbanisation led to a similar outcome. Indeed, in Iran, the concept of hybrid Anglo-American town planning was clearly intended to segregate social classes by dividing locals from a wealthier transient community.[24] It was fed by the growing influence of American ideology in the Persian Gulf region, and in most aspect of peoples' daily lives, during the Cold War. Given that the Anglo-Iranian Oil Company was the largest employer in all of Iran, Abadan's layout was pushed in unsustainable directions. The result was wider boulevards, large American cars, gated communities, casinos, bars and off-licences located strategically in main squares, private open-air swimming pools, tennis courts, Pepsi Cola and cigarette adverts, and countless other symbols of Americanisation. In this manner, US-style planning imposed the same canonical pattern onto many Middle Eastern cities.[25] As one local citizen recalls:

> Abadan was like a European city with American Chevrolets, so it resembled a strange mixture. It was like us watching an American movie filmed in American suburbs but the houses looked European. It was confusing but we liked it, yet it was also unreal because of the type of people who were driving the cars. They never walked on the pavements or in the streets. We only had a glimpse of them from a distance, behind their fenced mansions. They represented a maximum of 10–15% of the population, but it was funny to watch them.[26]

As demonstrated by Fraser, this strange cultural hybrid of Anglo-American town planning wasn't unique to Iran, even if did take on notably different forms in other countries such as Britain.[27]

The consequences for Abadan and Khorramshahr were drastic. Cities within cities were created with deep hedges around 'mansions' in exclusive neighbourhoods to protect the elite from poorer locals. Rather than the passive environmental strategies that dwellings had used traditionally, sensible practices were given up in favour of polished stone, reflective surfaces and centrally located entrances just to create a grand image, but one which needed to rely on heavy energy usage to keep occupants cool.[28] Sadly, little has changed since the collapse of the Pahlavi dynasty, and so these gated *shahraks* continue to fragment the different neighbourhoods of Abadan and Khorramshahr.

ZOOMING IN

The urban planning that was applied to Abadan and Khorramshahr in the 1950s and 1960s was manifestly wrong. These American-style boulevards and gated neighbourhoods, with almost no provision for shading or transitional zones between structures, create individual disconnected buildings reliant on expensive air-conditioning and other mechanical systems to allow people to use them. It's total madness, and yet Abadan's local authority, just like every other Iranian municipality, is still busy spending a large portion of its annual budget on road widening rather than serious environmental improvements. If a city with an average summer temperature of 40–50°C is to function effectively, close consideration needs to be given to the scale and proportion of streets, alleyways, external shading, public open spaces, transitional zones, etc.

During the summer siesta hours in Abadan and Khorramshahr, which stretch from 12.00 noon to 6.30pm or 7.00pm, one has no choice but to go to sleep. Outside, one cannot find a taxi. Children are unable to use playgrounds as it is too hot. Office workers therefore tend to work from 7.00 am to lunchtime and then start again in the early evening. Hence cities in this region stop and sleep in sensible ways, according to environmental logic. Practicing the siesta in a hot climate conserves energy and reduces the need for air conditioning in the hottest periods, and the energy that people gain from their midday meal is then released for the 're-launch' of the city in the cooler evening period. It is no accident that, for instance, the local municipalities in Abadan and Khorramshahr provide rooms for employees to take an afternoon snooze.

Poor environmental planning in these two cities has also greatly reduced the amount of external spaces usable in summer. This is problematic, since more time is thus spent indoors in poorly constructed homes, offices and shops, which in turn increase the demand for air-conditioning. A lack of awareness in how to respond to climatic context is not new; instead, what is different is the denial by municipalities about the importance of the issue. They simply refuse to learn from the fabric of the old city with its courtyards and roof-top terraces, some of which are still in operation in Abadan and Khorramshahr. However, perhaps one of the problems is that so little of pre-oil Abadan remains. Instead, one could look at other cities on the northern coast of the Persian Gulf, such as the fishing port of Bandar-e-Deylam – which lies about 150km east of Abadan – to see how street lifestyles and everyday cultural habits can positively influence buildings and urban form. Traditional cities in the Gulf region generally had one main commercial street which contained the bakeries, butchers, teahouses, offices, etc., and also a narrower residential street, off from which were narrow alleyways feeding into a series of courtyard houses. These dwellings had terraces with overhangs, shading devices in front of windows, trees and other kinds of shading devices. The hierarchy of movement from the external public space to the internal private space thus had an environmental as well as a cultural logic, in that the built form reduced the amount of heat gain while also channelling winds in order to cool dwellings. When mapping the movement of children, housewives and old people in such cities, one finds that, for instance, children instinctively play in the cooler narrow alleyways next to where the older citizens locate their seats, and can supervise them. These environmentally efficient urban pockets cannot possibly be achieved by using the wide roads and dispersed suburban dwellings which tend to be favoured today.[29] In other words, there are basic principles for organising urban spaces and building clusters in hot climates which simply cannot be ignored.[30]

11.13 Walled garden courtyard house in Abadan with articulated brickwork and plants for shading

In traditional houses in Abadan and Khorramshahr, the position of courtyards were also carefully related to prevailing sea breezes. North-facing facades had larger non-shaded openings, whereas southern facades had smaller windows with porches and shutters to offer inexpensive passive cooling. Courtyard entrances were located in the direction of the westerly or south-westerly wind, which also dictated the position of doors into rooms. Doors were always positioned to catch as much wind as possible, and cooling was intensified by hanging a thin curtain over the opening which was constantly sprayed with water. A typical courtyard contained trees and plants for cooling as well as a shallow pond, and rooms were raised above ground level. Small bread-making kilns were frequently positioned within the courtyards.[31] In hot climates it made environmental sense to have domestic kilns in the correct place so they can then as a heat exchange system when the weather becomes cooler. These devices, which can also be regarded as strategic features at the urban level, provided the kinds of invisible passive technologies which worked so well to improve the bodily comfort of citizens at a 1:1 scale.

RETURNING TO SOME SIMPLE CLIMATIC DESIGN MOVES

In the context of the 1950s, when environmental awareness and sensitivity to cultural identity weren't seen as such priorities, it is perhaps not surprising that the urbanism introduced by British and American planners was so contrary to the specificity of Abadan. However, today, local bodies such as Abadan Municipality or the Cultural Heritage Office ought to propose more intelligent alterations to historic buildings and urban spaces. Instead, one finds that their designs over the last decade are totally inappropriate: for example, in public parks they just select standard play equipment out of European catalogues and then import it from Dubai! Street furniture and the sorts of materials being used for building envelopes reflect a similar lack of local cultural and environmental awareness.

Clearly, a better way is required to deal with a city like Abadan. This however raises the question of what else than car-based 'gated villages' or the surreal flues of oil and petrochemical plants could be used to characterise Abadan? I would suggest a few other currently undervalued elements of cultural identity:

1. Districts containing fine 1930s Art Deco buildings;
2. The two majestic rivers encircling the city;
3. Two historical cinemas, the Naft and Rex, each symbolic of its political period;
4. Summer roof-top living building features designed by local architects;
5. Typical bakeries, whether in domestic courtyards or outdoors in streets;
6. Traditional brickwork buildings with their careful detailing
7. System of drainage trenches, usually openly exposed.

It is therefore still possible to find individual buildings in neighbourhoods which possess fine detailing similar to that found in Isfahan and Tehran in the 1940s and 1950s. Clearly there were some skilled local bricklayers able to combine intricate

11.14   Brickwork and glazed tiles in the hybrid dwellings of the Bawarda Garden Suburb, as reminiscent of central and southern Iran from the 1930s to the 1950s

tiling with exquisite brick details, creating an important piece of Abadan's cultural heritage. Likewise, the modifications introduced by some Iranian architects and engineers for the '1000 Homes' project, as erected by the Anglo-Iranian Oil Company for local workers in the 1960s, offers a telling example of cultural and environmental identity. Adapting some inadequate designs by the British architect, James M. Wilson, these Iranian architects and engineers altered the housing forms and plans to incorporate roof-top living to take advantage of cooler air in the evening and at night.

Indeed, this powerful older residue in Abadan could be tapped into by looking at other aspects of its built fabric. Most houses in the region were once made of local Marjani stone, which is sadly no longer used for new developments. As noted, these traditional dwellings tended to be raised up by 2–3 metres above the

11.15 View of the '1,000 Homes' project by the Anglo-Iranian Oil Company for Iranian oil workers in Abadan, as modified by Iranian architects from original designs by the British architect, James M. Wilson

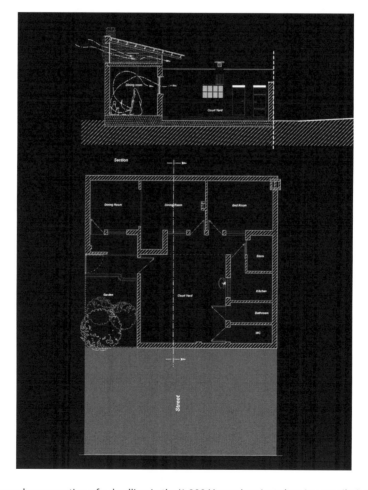

11.16 Plan and cross-section of a dwelling in the '1,000 Homes' project showing ventilation strategies

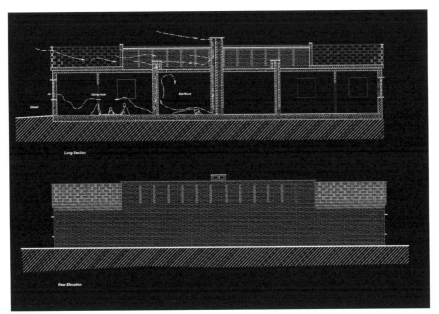

11.17 Elevation and longitudinal section of paired dwellings in the '1,000 Homes' project showing ventilation strategies

ground to catch all the available sea winds. In addition, it protected the houses from rising damp or flooding from seawater, while also marking out the public/private threshold between the courtyard and the house. Rooms within houses, and windows within rooms, were also carefully situated. Sleeping areas/bedrooms were positioned in the direction of cross ventilation from the entrance and across the courtyard. The kitchen, as a source of heat, was placed away from the sitting room and at 90 degrees to it. And best of all, the sitting room was located on the outer wing of the courtyard with its doors and windows be openable onto the latter, facing north rather than south, to reduce heat gain and provide the best conditions for cross-ventilation. Predictably, most of the new buildings in Abadan and Khorramshahr now ignore these practical, invisible technologies, resulting in the loss of air movement and light quality; similarly, their foundations and column plinths are gradually being damaged and eroded because of rising damp and the high salt content in the water. We have forgotten so much that we once knew.

CONCLUSION

My visit to the cities of Abadan and Khorramshahr to carry out research for this chapter involved peeling off a number of invisible layers. What was illuminated was a range of active or inactive global and local forces, many deeply concealed, within this culturally and economically important – yet deeply neglected – region of Iran. In the province of Khuzestan, and in Abadan in particular, there is a close link between the socio-political landscape and people's cultural and environmental needs; likewise, these factors were traditionally manifested in the spatial organisation of cities and individual buildings. In this sense, my study of

Abadan and Khorramshahr demonstrates the crucial interweaving between climatic conditions and cultural practices.

The problem, however, is that contemporary urban planning and methods of building design create a damaging tendency towards over-consumption and wastage. 'Modern' technologies such as air-conditioning are difficult to control and largely ineffective in terms of creating a cool, stable and healthy environment in such a hot region. This over-reliance on air-conditioned houses, cars and working spaces has led to building types (and indeed cities) becoming too similar across Iran, whether they are in the dusty desert heat of Khuzestan, or in the dry cold of Tehran, or the even colder rainy north of the country. Low-quality building envelopes and the forgetting of traditional passive environmental techniques are thus squandering of energy resources and are resulting in the loss of specific physical and spatial identities that buildings and cities once had in different Iranian provinces.

It is vital therefore to record and analyse the older building and spatial practices. If one looks properly in Abadan and Khorramshahr, one can still find many of these 'invisible' techniques; even more importantly, see how they interact with everyday habits and cultural practices. These are small, yet critical, acts which can make living conditions in buildings and cities far more comfortable, affordable and sustainable. Hence the reintroduction to Abadan and Khorramshahr of appropriate street furniture, proper provision of shading and planting, and a smarter urban strategy for open public spaces could encourage the better use of these cities even in the summer period of ultra-high temperatures.

Instead, what we find is that the beautifully shaded and planted courtyards and gardens of traditional Iran, with their cool ponds, are being replaced by unbearably hot and non-shaded spatial models taken from western car-based suburbs. Indeed, the notion of open-air car parks in the baking heat of cities of this kind simply makes no sense. In today's urban planning in Iran, whether for a city in the north or the south, there is now the same standard width used for roads, the same lack of hierarchy from public to private spaces, and the same problems of shortage of shade or transitional zones between blocks. Similarly, at the building scale, thin outer walls with no insulation have in high-rise apartment blocks supplanted the thick earth walls that older houses once had, and so the new dwellings gain and lose heat far too quickly. Metal doors/windows are being used instead of wooden doors/windows, again accentuating problems of excessive heat gain and heat loss. All this is being done for short-term profit by the minority who control building development in cities like Abadan and Khorramshahr. New technology based on cheap source of heating and cooling is thus producing a lazy approach to city planning. But what happens if and when citizens find themselves unable to afford their fuel bills? In such a case, what are they possibly do during the blazing heat of summer or bitter cold of winter?

This is why a clear and suitable urban strategy is urgently required for Abadan and Khorramshahr. Bold infrastructure projects could well include the following: an extension line for the north-south railway that currently ends in Khorramshahr; improved waterways and more intensive use of river banks; the redistribution of essential services to all neighbourhoods; and the reopening of some of the great private schools built under British rule (such as Mehragan School) or in the Pahlavi era, albeit this time making them available to ordinary families rather than just the elites of those earlier periods. Above all, traditional everyday practices and passive building techniques – invisible, but extremely effective and sustainable – have to be reinforced. In my discussions with local citizens and municipal officials in Abadan and Khorramshahr, the importance of better public policies to cut the culture of waste was raised again and again. At the moment, it might seem to some to be a far-off issue, almost a luxury, because of the availability of cheap fuel in Iran. Yet soon enough it will become a matter of survival, especially for the less well-off. Once western sanctions end and Iran opens up once more to the global economy, with its higher inflation levels, then the situation will rapidly become untenable.

Despite the obvious warning signals, the current Islamic Republic government seems less and less interested in developing alternative means to ensure sustainable economic growth. Unlike in 2000, when the Iranian Fuel Conservation Organization (IFCO) was set up by the Ministry of Power and Energy to reduce oil and gas usage by energy-saving measures in building construction, today there is little evidence of any such strategies in the province of Khuzestan.[32] Hence it is now time to act in Abadan and Khorramshahr since there are still traces of low-technology building practices which can cut energy use and create a sustainable environment which is culturally determined. The different levels of Iranian government, whether nationally or locally, need to concentrate on supporting these alternative 'invisible' ways of addressing climatic needs. The present emphasis on developing nuclear energy as the back-up plan might seem on the surface to be a good option for a developing country like Iran, given the global context, but of course opponents

11.18   Beautifully crafted modern tower in the Miras Farhangi building in Abadan

like the United States and Israel see this as just a smokescreen for producing Iranian nuclear weapons. Far less controversial and more logical would be to finance research to improve building practices and energy efficiency; in Iran, as elsewhere, energy consumption in buildings makes up around half of all demand.

If a more enlightened policy was adopted by the Iranian government, then plenty of sources of inspiration could be found. As mentioned above, Abadan and Khorramshahr have histories which are as vital to the emergence of modern Iran as, say, Isfahan, Shiraz or Yazd. While these other cities might be more famous and beautiful, even Abadan and Khorramshahr can be seen to possess valuable architectural and urban assets. Therefore these two major cities of Khuzestan need to celebrate their natural resources other than just plentiful oil and gas deposits. They also possess fantastic varieties of palms, dates, fish, poetry, music and such like; they have a climate which can be used positively, especially during the balmy seasons of spring and autumn; plus they have powerful links to the rivers, sea, sand and desert. In terms of human habitation, both contain fascinating traditions of courtyards, alleyways, roof-top terraces and a host of invisible, ordinary spaces. These older urban traditions need to be reconnected to people's lifestyles and cultural practices in Abadan and Khorramshahr. As Iain Borden writes so evocatively about the relationship between architecture and the everyday:

> We must recognize that, beyond the square, piazza and avenue, cities need hidden spaces and brutally exposed spaces, rough spaces and smooth spaces, loud spaces and silent spaces, exciting spaces and calm spaces. Cities need spaces in which people remember, think, experience, contest, struggle, appropriate, get scared, fall in love, make things, lose things and generally become themselves.[33]

NOTES

1   'During the 1970s, the agrarian reforms of the White Revolution … skyrocketing oil revenues, and Iran's new role as the US's Persian Gulf gendarme combined to bring rapid – and destabilizing – social, political, and economic change. Oil income shot up from $22.5 million in 1954 to over $19 billion in 1975–1976. By mid-decade, nearly half of Iran's people lived in urban areas (up from 30 percent a decade earlier): Quote from Larry Everest, 'The US & Iran: A History of Imperialist Domination, Intrigue and Intervention', *Revolution*, no. 89 (20 May 2007).

2   Hamid Naficy, in Rosa Issa & Sheila Whitaker (eds), *Life and Art: The New Iranian Cinema* (London: National Film Theatre, 1999), p. 15.

3   Ibid. Ironically, similar imagery and products (Coca Cola, hamburgers, etc.) were also used in the film *Goodbye Lenin* (2003) by Wolfgang Becker to show the arrival of global capitalism in East Germany after the fall of the 'socialist' planned economy of the Eastern Bloc.

4   Sirus Tahbaz, *The Life and Arts of Forugh Farrokhzad: Lonely Woman* (Tehran: Zariab, 1998), p. 189.

5   Habib Ladjevardi, *Labour Unions and Autocracy in Iran* (Syracuse, NY: Syracuse University Press, 1985), pp. 173, 328.

6   In 1976, in the last years of the Pahlavi dynasty, Amnesty International reported that Iran had the 'highest rate of death penalties in the world, no valid system of civilian courts and a history of torture which is beyond belief. No country in the world has a worse record in human rights than Iran'.

7   A.K. Lyravi, *The History of the City of Deylam* (Bushehr: Sharo Publishers, 2001), p. 69.

8   'Only a low 9% of managers (of the oil company) were from Khuzestan. The proportion of natives of Tehran, the Caspian, Azerbaijan and Kurdistan rose from 4% of blue collar workers to 22% of white collar workers to 45% of managers. Thus while Arabic speakers were concentrated on the lower rungs of the work force, managers tended to be brought in from some distance.' Quote from 'Abadan', Absolute Astronomy website, http://www.absoluteastronomy.com/topics/Abadan (accessed 14 September 2010).

9   'The United States, Sweden, Belgium, the Netherlands, Pakistan, and Germany all refused to make their technicians available to the nationalized Iranian industry.' Quote from 'Abadan Crisis', Wikipedia website, http://en.wikipedia.org/wiki/Abadan_Crisis#cite_note-4 (accessed 14 September 2010).

10   Interview by the author with Mr Anfi, owner of the photographic shop in Ferdosi Street, Abadan, Iran, 18 July 2009.

11   *The Castle* (1926) is a novel by Franz Kafka. 'In it a protagonist, known only as K., struggles to gain access to the mysterious authorities of a castle that govern the village where he wants to work as a land surveyor. Dark and at times surreal, The Castle is about alienation, bureaucracy, and the seemingly endless frustrations of man's attempts to stand against the system.' Quote from 'The Castle', Wikipedia website, http://en.wikipedia.org/wiki/The_Castle_(novel) (accessed 25 May 2010).

12   Mike Davis & Daniel B. Monk, *Evil Paradises: Dream Worlds of Neoliberalism* (New York: New Press, 2007), pp. 35–36.

13   Ibid., p. 39.

14   'The Oil Workers Union was attacked and banned during Reza Shah Pahlavi in 1930s. By 1946 the unions were still banned under the new Shah. The economic gap between British workers and the local Abadani workers was extensive. The British were not complying with any of their contractual agreements to provide schools, hospitals, services, roads and reasonable above-poverty wages for the local workers. This led to series of strikes by workers in March 1946 by the Oil Workers Union. The British formed a counter union (paying Arab workers in the Oil Company to join it). The plan was to axe Khuzestan province from rest of Iran. Following the massacre of the workers, in which 50 were killed and 170 were injured, the British Navy was on stand-by in Basra and stopped work in the Oil Company.' Quote from Manucher Farmanfarmaian & Roxane Farmanfarmaian, *Blood and Oil: Memoirs of a Persian Prince* (New York: Random House, 1997), p. 217.

15   Ibid., p. 287.

16   Ibid.

17   Daniel Yergin, *The Prize: The Epic Quest for Oil, Money and Power* (London: Simon & Schuster, 1993), p. 452.

18   Essay by Mary Ann Heiss, Department of History, Kent State University website, http://128.36.236.77/workpaper/pdfs/MESV3-6.pdf (accessed 20 August 2010).

19   'Chapter 3: Foreign Policy and Antitrust: The Cartel Case and the Iranian Consortium', taken from *Multinational Oil Corporations and US Foreign Policy Report – together with*

individual views, to the Committee on Foreign Relations, US Senate, by the Subcommittee on Multinational Relations. See: Mount Holyoke University website, http://www. mtholyoke.edu/acad/intrel/oil1.htm (accessed 20 August 2010).

20   Yergin, *The Prize*, p. 470.

21   During my many taxi journeys and discussions with local people in Abadan and Khorramshahr during the course of this research, many stories were painted about the realities of the city. As one taxi driver, Mahmood Rejaei, told me: 'We were able to see the private pools from our roofs and dreamed about swimming in them, but those who died have taken the dreams with them. The clubs were the same. Even if we were able to borrow some nice and clean clothes to go, they would have recognised us and so we were never able to smuggle our way in to them.'

22   Ronald V. Wiedenhoeft, *Berlin's Housing Revolution: German Reform in the 1920s*, Architecture and Urban Design no. 16 (Ann Arbor, MI: University of Michigan Research Press, 1986), p. 10.

23   Murray Fraser (with Joe Kerr), *Architecture and the 'Special Relationship': The American Influence on Post-war British Architecture* (London/New York: Routledge, 2007), pp. 135–145.

24   'Planning was utilized to build the segregated city, in which a European, upper-class quarter was separated from the rest of the city. French Morocco offers the most vivid example of this kind of city planning: European quarters were built separate from the old medinas; important urban cultural sites were preserved; and the European part of the city utilized the most up-to-date urban-planning techniques. Similar practices were followed in Algeria, Tunisia, Libya, and Egypt.' Quote from 'Urban Planning, The Colonial Period 1800–1945', *Gale Encyclopedia of the Middle East and North Africa*, 'Reference Answers website, http://www.answers.com/topic/city-planning (accessed 20 August 2010).

25   'US and British oil companies also established company towns for their workers. The Arabian-American Oil Company (ARAMCO), for example, used Western planners and engineers to lay out company towns such as Dhahran and Abqaiq using a system of blocks with a grid pattern. Similarly in Iran, British planners modeled the city of Abadan on the landscape of suburban England. Middle Eastern countries depended on the West for qualified planners and consultants to carry out urban planning. Consequently, a planning technique then common in the West, the master plan, was imported to the Middle East and soon became ubiquitous throughout the region. Most plans were end-state master plans, in that the ultimate look of the city in the future was already predetermined. Most plans were also unclear about the process of city planning or procedures for implementation. Additionally, the plans were usually static and design-oriented, with little consideration for the social and economic needs of the majority.' Quote from Hooshang Amirahmadi, 'Regional Planning in Iran: A Survey of Problems and Policies', *The Journal of Developing Areas*, vol. 20, no. 4 (1987): 501–530.

26   Interview by the author with Mr Anfi, owner of the photographic shop in Ferdosi Street, Abadan, Iran, 18 July 2009.

27   Fraser, *Architecture and the 'Special Relationship'*, p. 135.

28   Solar radiation on horizontal surfaces being of course at their maximum during summer where there is a use of over-reflective building materials. See: Richard Nicholls, *Low Energy Design* (Oldham: Interface, 2002), p. 131.

29   Mike Jenks & Rod Burgess, *Compact Cities: Sustainable and Urban Forms for Developing Countries* (London: Spon Press, 2000), p. 343.

30   Compact city design principles and the argument for grouping of buildings to reduce heat loss and in the case of Abadan heat gain in individual buildings. See: Nicholls, *Low Energy Design*, p. 49.

31   The traditional earth stove located in the corner of the courtyard gardens or sometimes under the ground is still a very common practice in Iran and some other Middle Eastern countries.

32   'Iranian Fuel Conservation Company (IFCO), a subsidiary of National Iranian Oil Company (NIOC), was established in 2000 with the mission to regiment the fuel consumption in different sectors through review and survey of the current trend of consumption and executing conservation measures nationwide.' Quote from 'About Us', Iranian Fuel Conservation Company website, http://www.ifco.ir/english/index.asp (accessed 27 August 2010).

33   Iain Borden, 'The unknown city of architecture and the everyday', Re-public website, http://www.re-public.gr/en/?p=40 (accessed 27 August 2010).

12

Bushehr, Iran

Semra Aydinli and Avsar Karababa

BUSHEHR:
The City of History
The City of Passion
The Old Friend of the Sun
The Land of Industry, Fishing and Commerce

Bushehr, with its architectural and urbanistic themes dating from the Elamite era of c.2,000 BC, through to the civilization of the Sassanid dynasty and then to its cosmopolitan image of today, is a port that plays an important role in the commercial relations of Iran.[1] As the capital of Bushehr province, it is located on the Persian Gulf on a vast plain along the coastal region of western Iran. The city lies directly across the Gulf from Kuwait. Bushehr is represented both by historical continuity, with its old city reflecting Iranian Islamic identity, and by the image of change, due to the presence of international commercial facilities, trading ports, military bases, nuclear power plants and various contemporary buildings. Continuity and change are opposing yet complementary concepts in a world where global issues and local values have been put on the agenda.[2] Bushehr, because of its geographic location with easy access to international high seas, plus its rich resources of oil/gas/minerals, and its extensive plantations of palm trees – as well as its various tourist attractions – takes full advantage of its valuable economic potential.[3] These geographical and cultural advantages define its idiosyncratic identity, defining thus the configuration of the city.

This urban identity can be readily experienced in the Old Quarter of Bushehr, where there are many examples of traditional Persian Gulf architecture from the period from 1870 to 1920, including ecologically satisfying housing settlements with unique spatial configurations rooted in Iranian Islamic identity. The Old Quarter represents the spirit of time and space, creating an 'aura' that can be experienced as having certain physical factors (narrow streets, rhythmic arrangements of openings, displacement of solids and voids at different scales) as well as the psychological, social and mental forces which are an integral part of lived space. In this context, we will aim in this chapter to interpret the environmental potentials of Bushehr as a narrative with its visible and invisible dimensions emerging from a continuous unfolding of overlapping spaces, materials, technologies and details. Beyond the city's physicality, we have tried to read the environment as a place of events and activities that represents a tension between reality and possibility. For our research, a structure of meaning was composed by unfolding the mutual relationship of interdependent elements such as urban identity, economics, ecology, neighbourhood, public space, and the act of belonging both to Iranian Islamic identity and being a Persian Gulf city in a global world. Although this interwoven whole is like a patchwork of traces constituting a series of spatial images, all our investigatory photographs were deciphered through documents, maps, aerial images, urban master-plans, and statistical data provided by the municipality and regional government. These superimposed images and written documents, including our own notes and urban traces grasped during this journey of discovery, provide access to deeper underlying questions about Bushehr. From this, a broad picture of the city emerged which allowed us to discover these new relations: we have sought to articulate how the network relations of the city are perceived as 'legible', how Bushehr is read in political, social and economic terms, and how the city's image might be represented and promoted in marketing terms.

Our on-site period of personal observation and discovery, carried out without any prior hypothesis or prejudice, helped also to establish the research methods for our visit to Bushehr. The aim was to read the city as a narrative in all its dimensions, hence allowing us to understand its complexities. For

example, Michael Axworthy has drawn attention to the apparent paradox that Iran and Persia are the same country.[4] The image conjured up by 'Persia' is one of romance: roses and nightingales in elegant gardens, fast horses, mysterious, flirtatious women, sharp sabres, carpets with colours glowing like jewels, poetry and melodious music. However, in the clichés of western media representation, the term 'Iran' has a rather different image: frowning mullahs, black oil, women's blanched faces peering, not to their best advantage, from underneath black chadors, grim crowds burning flags and chanting 'Death to …'! It is possible to understand such a paradox when experiencing Bushehr, since it takes its roots from the religious thought of ancient Iranians known as Zoroastrianism (from Zarathustra, or, in Pahlavi, *Zardusht* or *Zardukhsht*). This religion was based on the opposition between order and chaos, good and bad, truth and falsehood, as manifested in the thought, speech, and activity of gods and men. This dualism was also reflected in the configuration of the typology of the houses and the urban pattern, thereby creating its 'aura'. The aim of this chapter is, therefore, to discover the architecture-of-city/city-of-architecture with this specific 'aura' of Bushehr, exhibiting some traces that still today reflect its cultural, social, ecological, spatial and temporal relations.

GENERAL ISSUES COMPOSING THE 'BIG PICTURE' OF BUSHEHR

Bushehr covers an area of 1,442 km², which means it occupies approximately 6 per cent of the entire province, and possessed a population of 205,297 people at the time of the 2006 census (estimates are that the figure has since risen

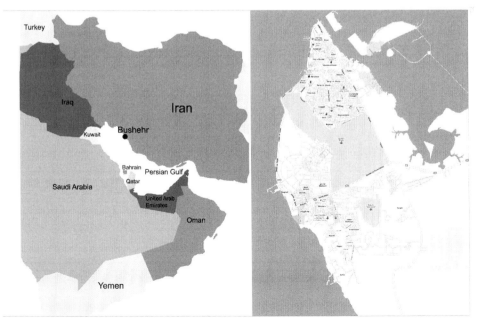

12.1
Geographical
location of
Bushehr at
different scales

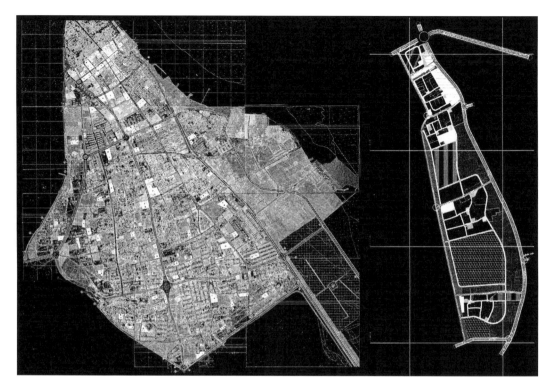

12.2   Current municipal master-plan for Bushehr

to around 225,000). Bushehr is one of the most important ports and transport hubs in the Persian Gulf region. It has a large international airport, and highways connecting it to Ahvaz to the north-west and to Shiraz inland to the east. A secondary coastal road links Bushehr to Bandar Abbas in the south-east of Iran.[5] Furthermore, the Shiraz-Bushehr railroad joins this province into the Iranian railroad network, facilitating land-based distribution to and from the province. The city itself is now brutally divided into two by a large military base and by Bushehr's airport. The centre is located to the north, embracing the Old Quarter, while the industrial part – considered as a developing area in Bushehr Municipality's current master-plan – sits slightly to the south.

This master-plan was prepared by the local authority in 2008, and explains how the city intends to grow towards the east and south-west. Individual housing settlements will be spread amongst the palm groves and other green areas, and small industry is to be kept segregated from facilities such as schools, health centres and coastline recreational areas. Extensive maritime facilities, industrial buildings and nuclear power plants have influenced the development of Bushehr over time, providing opportunities as well as threats. While these more global facilities provide wealth and power for the city, they may also become a threat whenever the balance is not so well defined between global and local issues. Bushehr doesn't appear to be affected by the current international economic downturn, since the Islamic economy, being effectively 'closed', is not integrated with the global economy.[6] This degree of separation that prevents global developments from affecting Bushehr's economic growth can also be considered as an opportunity in terms of its independence.

Bushehr is of course one of the chief ports of Iran, lying at a distance of 1,218 km from the capital in Tehran. It is often called Bandar-e Bushehr because it has both a fishing port and a commercial port. The main reason for establishing these port facilities was the strategic location of Bushehr; in that it is built out into the sea on a peninsula in the shape of an anchor, providing natural protection for ships and boats in its harbour. Bushehr, which acts as an export point for farm produce from the neighbouring fertile Fars province, has long played an important role in the commercial affairs of Iran. Moreover, due to its special geographic location and notable wealth, representatives of foreign companies and foreign consulates – including Britain, Germany, Russia and the Ottoman Empire – were located in the city, and some of whom erected fine buildings which have been preserved to the present time. Because of its key geo-political role, European colonialists were interested in taking control of the region and the city of Bushehr – not least the British Empire.[7] It is possible still to see this British influence on the architecture in the Old Quarter, again making its spatial 'aura' unique within the Persian Gulf region. Furthermore, as noted, the antiquity of the historical region dates back to the Elamite era, two millennia before Christ, when Bushehr was known as Lian.[8]

Bushehr, however, remained economically depressed until the 1960s, when the Iranian government initiated a major redevelopment program. In 1975 the government, in cooperation with a German company, began building a nuclear power plant at Bushehr some 12 km from the centre. This facility was only partially completed when it was bombed by Iraq during the Iran-Iraq War (1980–1988). In 1995 Russia signed an agreement to finish the plant and to supply a light-water nuclear reactor. Although the agreement called for the spent fuel rods to be sent back to Russia for reprocessing, the USA has expressed concern that Iran is reprocessing the rods itself to obtain plutonium to make nuclear bombs. The previous President of Iran, Mahmoud Ahmadinejad, backed by most of the Muslim clergy, followed a somewhat lonely path of resistance to the global influence of western values, and in particular to that of America. This resistance might have been praiseworthy in itself, had it not been for the suffering and oppression, the dishonesty and disappointment that also followed.[9] However, there is a misguided belief by many in Iran that this direct opposition to western values is the way to stop the inevitability of development on a westernised model in the Middle East, but this fails to see that these tensions offer both opportunities and threats. As long as there is no balance between local values and global issues, then by simply closing all doors to the global community in accordance with rigid rules of Islamic doctrine, all the opportunities created by this resistance are transformed into threats. It also fails to see that Bushehr has local power precisely because of its geo-political position – its nuclear power plant is capable of generate over 1000MW of electricity, plus there are plentiful gas supplies – and this in itself creates a dynamic balance between the so-called tension of the local and global. In other words, the very 'locality' of Bushehr can be used as a powerful tool within the globalised world.

During our meetings with the Governor of Bushehr and other government authorities, they confirmed that the current global economic crisis isn't affecting the economy of Bushehr, nor are Iran's political difficulties, since the Iranian Islamic economy is kept independent from the Islamic judiciary.[10] Although foreign investment in Bushehr is still increasing, according to the Governor, the city is being preserved as a recognition of its idiosyncratic Iranian Islamic identity, something which is based neither on capitalism nor on communism. Iranian Islamic identity, which draws its roots from ancient Persian and more recent Iranian cultures, has been hugely influential on the city's architecture. Today's urban designers in Bushehr Municipality seem to be well aware of their social responsibility and environmental sensibility: high-rise buildings are simply not allowed, and all contemporary buildings are required to be designed on a relatively humanistic scale.

Because of Bushehr's attractive geographical location as a port, and its proximity to target markets, industrial infrastructures and marine products, the city is clearly attracting a good deal of foreign investment. Bushehr's industries include seafood canneries, food processing and engineering. This is the background for significant opportunities for investment in various other sectors including oil industries, gas and petro-chemicals, mineral processing, and growing dates, among others.[11] Yet despite these promising future developments, unemployment in Bushehr today is sizeable, around 24.2 per cent of the workforce; this is partly as a result of a sluggish economic performance, but also because of a dramatic demographic growth over the last two decades. According to 1999 statistics, Bushehr's investment value in industry was only

0.3 per cent, but since then investment in both the industrial and tourism sectors in the city have increased, mainly due to globalisation. Accordingly, the human development index in Bushehr was 70 per cent, whereas the human poverty index was 21.7 per cent.[12] In terms of religious belief, around 90 per cent of Bushehr's population are Shi'ite, with the remaining 10 per cent being Zoroastrian, Christian or Jewish (while the latter are very few in number, Iran curiously has the largest Jewish population

of any Muslim-majority country). Historical documents show that prior to the arrival of Aryans in Iran, Bushehr was the residence for many different tribal groups and ethnic communities.[13]

12.3 Saadat High School, Bushehr

Modern Bushehr was the first city in Iran to introduce lithography, and it also developed new industries such as ice-making and electrical production well before many other Iranian cities. The people of Bushehr were amongst the first Iranians to become acquainted with magazines and newspapers, a number of which were printed and published in the city. Education has therefore also been a priority among the people of Bushehr, and the ratio of educated population remains high compared to the rest of the country. There are many buildings consecrated to education in the Old Quarter: one such example is Saadat High School, built in 1899, and the first modern school in all of southern Iran. It was designed by Moin Altujar Bushiri. Many new buildings

12.4 Various cultural centres around Bushehr

12.5 The spatial character of Bushehr's urban pattern and housing typology

in a more contemporary architectural style are built as cultural centres, and also provide religious education within their walls. However, with so many of these unauthorized schools now providing religious instruction, we were told by a member of Bushehr Municipality that the education system has fallen even further back than it was at the beginning of the 20th century: a clear criticism of the present education system. Bushehr today has four colleges and universities: the Persian Gulf University, Bushehr University of Medical Sciences, Islamic Azad University of Bushehr, and Iran Nuclear Energy College. All of this points to the potential of contemporary architecture in Bushehr, full of contradictions and complexities. Both concrete and steel construction techniques are now being extensively used for new housing and office buildings, as part of a familiar global context.

DISCOVERING BUSHEHR'S OLD QUARTER VIA ECOLOGY[14]

The Old Quarter of Bushehr was built from 1810 next to the port, creating one of the rarest and most superior types of coastal architecture in the Persian Gulf region. Thus besides its archaeological relics and historical monuments, there is a high standard of 19th-century architecture in the city. The pattern of settlement in Bushehr's Old Quarter has a unique character with its narrow streets feeding sequentially into squares, creating a rhythm of opening and closing; in other words, its urban character depicts enclosure and spaciousness in a similar way its houses. Furthermore, one of the most striking features of Bushehr is its relationship to water. Since the city sits on a peninsula, the sea surrounds the land and can be seen from every point in the Old Quarter. The topology of the old city and its architecture relate to each other in visible and invisible ways. The result is spatial paradoxes of exteriority and interiority, spontaneity and predictability, tension and resolution, balance and instability, rhythmic coherence and continuous unity. These opposing but complementary attributes of the Old Quarter provide some clues for the design of togetherness, belonging and wholeness, which are necessary for harmonious social and ecological relationships. All these concepts form multi-layered structures of meaning to facilitate the reading of the city as a narrative, as well as to understand how architecture can be truly site-specific.

The spatial configuration of the streets/voids and the houses/solids have emerged in accordance with Bushehr's regional, climatic and cultural conditions, through which the Gulf region's peculiar local spirit brings together man, nature and values of Iranian Islamic identity. Every part of the unified whole relates to the central idea of this identity, which is why the Old Quarter can be considered as an ecosystem in itself, being organized in a way that it takes its roots from multiple layers. It is possible to discover this 'deep ecology' while experiencing and reading the city as a narrative. Its narrow streets are channels both for the movement of people and the movement of air. The narrow streets, opening onto squares, are then usually accompanied by a school, mosque or market, acquiring a specific character due to the colour of these buildings. At the end of a period of darkness created by the shadows cast by the buildings, bright sunlight erupts in the square, which then becomes a landmark. Walking along the streets, it is possible to conceive of daylight in relationship to its seeming opposite, shadow – for, as Louis Kahn observed, shadow belongs to light. This power of contrast makes us think about where we are and what is unique and special about our surroundings, due to its spatial character. The most striking feature of Bushehr's Old Quarter is the fact that the traces of all its buildings could survive just through their perceptual energies.[15]

It is obvious that because of the climate, the lifestyle in the Old Quarter is dependent on patterns of outdoor living, hence making the courtyard the most important component in the configuration of its houses. Apart from these hidden courtyards, an outdoor living area up on the first floor has a similar spatial character, which in the corresponding traditional Turkish house is called *hayat*, meaning 'life'. *Hayat* is a place connecting different rooms, hence it being an in-between space; conceptually, it is neither inside nor outside.[16] Today the lack of outdoor living areas in modern houses (balconies aren't real substitutes for these *hayat* spaces) brings the need for urban spaces where people can come together and socialize. People duly collect together in public spaces in the Old Quarter, especially along the seafront or in courtyards of religious buildings, sitting on the ground without taking into consideration gender differences. Especially on Friday nights, men and women of all ages crowd the streets and other spaces. Open-air markets, entertainment spaces, theme parks, seaside promenades; until the middle of the night, they each play a vital role in the livelihood of the Old Quarter, mixing everyday traditional values with more global influences (see Plate 19).

The modifications and intersections of the volumes between the street level and the first floor of the houses dramatize the composition of solid/massive walls below, which are shaped according to the street. The configurations of the upper floors are based on the spatial organization of the rooms, often exhibiting a variety of triangular bay windows. The narrowness of the streets makes it necessary to arrange these bay windows (called *çıkma*) in accordance with the relationship between the upper floors and ground-floor storey in a given direction, creating hence another urban visual rhythm. Massive wooden doors with their ornaments increase the dramatic contrast of solids and voids. Balconies, which have 1.5m-high wooden parapets constructed from removable wooden boards, provide privacy and shade the interiors without interrupting air circulation. Privacy is an important concept in Iranian architecture, as exhibited here by the high garden walls, first-floor bay windows and massive ground floor walls. The origins of this concept of privacy indeed date back to pre-Islamic periods. There are many spatio/temporal relations of privacy with hidden meanings in Bushehr that can only be understood by experiencing the city. For example, the entrance doors of many houses have different forms of knockers that produce a different sound, through which the residents can discern the gender of the visitor. The ring-shaped door knocker is used by women whereas the pendulous one is

used by men. As another way to promote the separation of sexes, according to the Islamic way of life, the houses are divided into two parts: the *birun*, situated towards the outside of the house, is for men and their male guests; while the *anderun*, situated towards the interior, is for women, their female guests and the domestic helpers.[17]

12.6   Everyday life in Bushehr

It is possible to observe how the quality of life is enhanced in the Old Quarter of Bushehr by analyzing its 'deep ecology': in other words, the mutual relationships in the urban pattern between cultural values, social organisation, climate, traditional lifestyle and housing configuration. The typology of houses and the urban pattern have similar traces rooted in the idiosyncratic Islamic way of life. Wind-catchers, called *badgirs*, are located at the top of the buildings to provide air circulation inside the buildings as a natural cooling system, as distinct from the air-conditioning devices of today.[18] Courtyards, along with other local building techniques, exhibit the interweaving of lifestyles and the physical environment that constitutes the local 'ecology'.[19] Historic water canals in the middle of the street are configured with drainage wells. Today, however, due to the growth in population and increase in new buildings, the city's drainage system doesn't work nearly as well, and these water canals have become open sewers which aren't embedded in the ground, since they are at the same level as the sea.

12.7   The textures and rhythms of the city

The 'ecology' of old Bushehr is not limited to environmental factors, but also perceptual and social relations for the benefit of human beings, such as experiencing the textures and rhythms and indeed vibrant colours of the city. For example, the cool blue-green of the sea creates a real contrast with the buildings in the Old Quarter, built out of limestone covered by mud plaster and painted with warm colours. This unique technique of using limestone with mud plaster applied over it to construct the houses creates a dramatic effect; furthermore, the limestone provides good insulation due to its layered and porous structure. Lime mortar is also used for insulating water in cisterns. Additionally, this colourful built environment becomes a background for women wearing black *chadors*; moreover, occasionally seeing women in colourful dresses walking next to the black-clad women also creates a signal contrast. Colourful windows, called *orsi*, which give a mysterious atmosphere and prevent mosquitoes from entering, have become the symbol of Bushehr. They refer openly to an Iranian Islamic identity, which is also represented by colourful handicrafts and fishing boats.[20]

The Old Quarter of Bushehr has been well supported by Iran's Building and Housing Ministry, which has spent the equivalent of $30 billion on regeneration work. The ministry has several incentives for redeveloping this area through new investment projects, one of these being to restore the coastline wall and transform it into a recreational area. In the regeneration of the Old Quarter, an ecological approach to understanding the whole physical and natural properties is of considerable importance for creating a contemporary livable environment. The past should not be disregarded, and the wheel reinvented, every time a new domestic environment is designed in the name of sustainability. Sustainability can instead best be defined as an integration of local values that require continuity and global issues that relate to change. As a result, a range of cultural, social,

Legend:

☐ Housing
■ Commercial
▨ Commercial - Housing
▦ Tourism-Entertainment-Cultural
▦ Commercial-Tourism-Cultural
▨ Religious-Cultural
■ Educational-Cultural
■ University
☐ Administrative
☐ Service-Tourism-Housing
☐ Green Area
▨ Parking
☐ Cultural Tourism

12.8   Regeneration scheme for the Old Quarter of Bushehr

12.9   Ongoing regeneration work in the Old Quarter

12.10   Major edifices currently being restored

12.11   Omaret-e-Malek, as now owned by M. M. Malekaltujjar

12.12   Sheikh Hossain Chahkutahi Tomb

perceptual, ecological issues can be related to each other to form a unique 'aura'. Yet in spite of the current regeneration agenda of Bushehr Municipality, the restoration of some buildings is being undertaken without proper consideration of the environmental sensibility needed to create balance between the new and old. Other interventions, however, are much more promising. For instance, the steel-frame construction being built as an extension to a building in the Old Quarter will act as the new school of architecture when it's completed, adding a contemporary mark without dominating the general image. Complementary forces can hold together the traditional and contemporary configurations on behalf of the principle of sustainability.

Several fine edifices in the Old Quarter, located along the seafront, have been restored for use as official governmental buildings.[21] Influential facets of Persian identity can be experienced both inside and outside of these grand mansions, in which the typical schema of the courtyard as a common space provides access to all the rooms on the ground floor. Coloured glass windows, wooden doors with ornaments, wooden-beam floors, and other details provide an in-between spatial character for the contemporary reuse of these buildings. Elsewhere, however, a huge derelict building called Omaret-e-Malek, which was built by French architects at the end of the Zand dynasty, is still waiting to be renovated. It is currently occupied by homeless people who are unaware of its value. An extension to the Shaikh Hossain Chahkutahi Tomb is a brutal example of historic preservation with no awareness about environmental sensibility or social responsibility. Concrete columns are being plastered around the existing building, depressing and dominating its original power; one can just imagine how the tomb will 'disappear' altogether once construction is completed. Other cultural changes we observed while in Bushehr may also pose a threat to its cultural heritage, since a lack of environmental awareness may be giving rise to fakery.[22] Interference with the historic environment requires the inclusion of 21st-century life without losing the 'aura' and historical testimony that is being passed from past to present to future. Bushehr represents cultural codes and urban traces that are hidden and waiting to be rediscovered, and so its old buildings should not be 'frozen in time'.

QUESTIONS OF IRANIAN ISLAMIC IDENTITY OF BUSHEHR WITHIN GLOBAL CULTURE

Today, Iranian Islamic identity is a phenomenon of the 'congregation society' type, wherein a close interpenetration of state and society, representation and administration is required. A tendency towards expressing cultural identities exists amongst different political/economic ideologies across the world today, and each cultural sphere needs to generate its own technological systems as a consequence. Iranian Islamic identity needs to be deconstructed in relation to recent developments in the globalised world so that this identity can more easily become materialized. Under the influence of marketing strategies within the context of globalization, cultural dynamics can be said to exist in the exchange market. In order to avoid

12.13   Window
of the Iranology
Institute in
Bushehr, reflecting
some fragments
of Iranian Islamic
identity

falling into the trap of marketing 'locality' in
Bushehr as a meaningless commodity, its
architects, urban planners, political authorities
and decision makers should be aware of the
potential of the idiosyncratic features of Iranian
Islamic identity. It is for instance possible to see
the fragments of the global world in Bushehr
just from the design of a window in its Iranology
Institute, which manages to symbolize locality
and reflect a broader Islamic sensibility.

Preserving the 'locality within globalization'
refers to dynamic spaces that flow, instead of
static places in which the conflicts between
the local values and global issues only create
tension and resistance. Although global issues
represented by change and local values requiring
continuity constitute a paradox, they can also
complete and nourish each other. Locality is
not only a process that constitutes the 'other' of
globalization, but also a specific counter-move
to transform the configuration of a city like
Bushehr. Iranian Islamic identity thus needs to
be rediscovered through the globalization lens;
in lights of this deconstruction of Iranian Islamic
identity, old spaces with new ideas can create unique identities by oscillating
between change/global and continuity/locality (see Plate 20).

Hence the Old Quarter of Bushehr has multi-layered and intangible meanings
just waiting to be discovered. To discover Bushehr's potential to create new
connections, first the city has to be read as a narrative with its unique temporal and
spatial relations drawn from the power of geography, history, cultural variety, social
relationships and lifestyles in relation to each other. The most important issue is to
become aware of cultural codes, which are archetypes; however, they shouldn't be
transformed into stereotypes. In the Old Quarter, windows with coloured glass can
be considered as cultural archetypes produced by specific hand-made techniques.
Whenever they are re-used in new buildings, they lose their invisible character
because of mass production, becoming a stereotype. Superficial imitation and
visual fakery can emerge in new architecture if motivated by marketing strategies,
and not by referring to the collective memory which has for so long played a crucial
role in building Iranian Islamic identity. Ahmedi draws attention here to the role
of narrative, which is defined as an event-network that enables us to understand
how identity is constructed over time and place.[23] At the conceptual level, narrative
functions as a meta-code transmitting the essence of historical and cultural events.

Cultural identity here, having its roots in ancient Persian civilizations and
Zoroastrian values, is specific to the Iranian part of the Gulf region. Bushehr is thus
different from coastal cities in other countries in terms of its historical, religious,

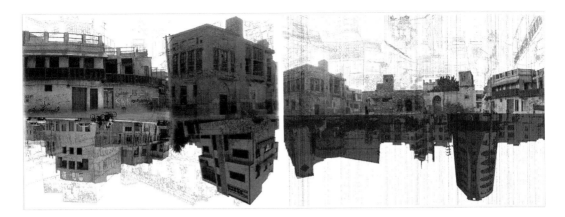

political, economic, psychological and social networks. Besides, the single-party government in Iran, with its congregational religious ideology, is holding up ways for new developments by pressuring the press and mass media into conformism. To understand such as complex network system as exists in Iran, with all its contradictions, things cannot be reduced to the knowledge provided solely by analytical research. Understanding the whole phenomena as a network system requires us also to look around the margins at senses affected by perceptual experiences, and which can create multiple new paths and connections.

12.14   Old Quarter of Bushehr within the context of globalisation

According to the Governor of Bushehr, the Islamic revolution led by Ayatollah Khomeini was the antidote in terms of maintaining Iranian Islamic identity. In the Governor's view, although Shah Mohammad Reza Pahlavi was an admirer of western culture and wanted to destroy Islamic values, he was not successful. Throughout history, Persian (and then Iranian) culture was never greatly influenced by European expansionism, even if the two were in close contact through commercial relations. According to the Governor, the democracy brought in by Khomeini has since played an important role in creating a unique cultural identity based on inexhaustible contrasts. He also emphasized that the Iranian Islamic Republic, by not losing its sense of cultural identity, acts as a role model for other developing Middle Eastern countries. But this, however, is also the paradox of being a closed society. By not imitating western culture, and by strenuously maintaining a sense of locality, it means that Iran has not been so able to be involved in the globalised world, and thus has missed out on opportunities for information exchange and commercial benefits. For instance, Bushehr remains unaffected by the global economic crisis, but similarly it has not yet been able to profit from international booms either. A balance between global issues and local values is needed to get beyond this paradox. Bushehr, sitting on the Persian Gulf coast, has the potential to create a new balance through the power of its natural resources and cultural heritage. These potentials will surely also help the ongoing development of its cultural identity, maintaining its locality within a global context. During the 21st century, Iranian Islamic identity will have to be deconstructed and continually remade, and its rethinking can represent both change and continuity without losing its 'aura'.

CONCLUDING REMARKS

This chapter focused on a holistic understanding of Bushehr in light of Iranian Islamic identity and how this has influenced the configuration of the city – with an emphasis on the need to conceive of future developments through the concept of 'locality within globalization'. Overlapping ideas gained by reading the city as a narrative were strengthened by photographic images we took to show thematic relations. Thus the research process proceeded in a non-linear form, having no beginning or end, so as to remain open to new ideas. This non-linear process, in which all the contradictions were brought together in relation to each other, allowed us to trace the resistance to the global influences of western values while also responding to changes in the city. One can regard this as a reflection of a continuing sense of Iranian uniqueness and cultural significance.

Furthermore, global culture will absorb locality if the process doesn't contain tensions and antagonism, with the locality needing to open up doors for new cultural/spatial relationships within the context of globalization. Cultural identity can thus be defined as a tension between the sameness and difference caused by global fluidity. Iranian Islamic identity should thus be read in accordance with the contemporary and revolutionary possibilities offered by the tension between local and global. Although Iran is a country with an ancient tradition of monarchical splendour, the revolutionary Islamic Republic also has many paradoxes which can be seen as offering the potential for global fluidity.[24]

By considering sustainable living conditions composed of a combination of change and continuity, architecture and urban design should seek to promote cultural development through global fluidity. The 'deep ecology' movement does not propose an entirely new philosophy, but instead revives an awareness which is part of our cultural heritage. The growth of this new awareness relies on the maxim: 'Think globally and act locally'. By looking at the issue from a range of perspectives, it is possible to discover the multi-layered meaning of Bushehr both in its visible and invisible characters; in other words, through the mood of the city. It is possible to create a new Islamic Iranian identity by preserving Bushehr's locality within globalization, if the architects and urban designers, who are responsible for forming livable environments for the 21st century, read the city as a narrative. By doing so, Bushehr as an important Persian Gulf city – with its long cultural heritage, natural resources and idiosyncratic position in the Iranian Islamic worldview – will assimilate its own continuity and change to show how to preserve 'locality within globalisation'.

NOTES

1   Iran is divided into 30 provinces that appointed governors administrate. Bushehr is one of these, and has an area of 23,000 km², being located in western Iran on the eastern shore of the Persian Gulf. The province consists of nine counties – Bushehr (capital city), Tangestan, Jam, Dashti, Dashtestan, Dayyer, Deylam, Kngan and Genaveh. There are then 22 districts, 29 smaller towns and 43 rural districts, all with a population

of 826,412 people according to the 2006 census. See for example: 'Bushehr Province', Irano-British Chamber of Commerce, Industries and Mines website, http://www.ibchamber.org/Magazine%2015/3.htm (accessed 21 August 2009); A. Barzgar, *Bushehr Province: Land of the Sun* (Bushehr: Bushehr Municipality, 2007); 'Bushehr', *Hosban News* website http://www.hosban.ir/module-pagesetter-printpub-tid-1-pid-16635.html (accessed 22 August 2009); 'Cities of Iran: Bushehr', Iran Chamber Society website, http://www.iranchamber.com/cities/bushehr/bushehr.php (accessed 1 September 2009; Iranology Association and Pejvar Advertisement, *Old Bushehr in a Mirror of Pictures* (Bushehr: Iranology Association, n.d.).

2   Semra Aydınli, 'Continuity and Change in the Image of Istanbul', in Martin Edge (ed.), *Old World – New Ideas: Environmental and Cultural Change and Tradition in a Shrinking World*, Proceedings of the Environmental Design Research Association Conference (EDRA 32/001), Edinburgh (2001), pp. 22–26.

3   Bushehr Investment Committee with Commercial Cooperation Organisation, *The Focus of Investment Opportunities, Bushehr Province* (Bushehr: Bushehr Investment Committee, 2009).

4   Michael Axworthy, *Iran, Empire of the Mind: A History From Zoroaster to the Present Day* (London: Penguin Books, 2008).

5   Bushehr is connected to the other parts of Iran by three connective axes. The first one passes through Bushehr-Borazjan-Kazeroun and goes on to Shiraz, which is the first and major axis for land transportation to the central areas of Iran. This axial route is about 320 km long. The second is the connective axis of Bushehr-Mahshahr-Abadan, which runs parallel to the coastline of the Persian Gulf and is 690 km long. The third one connects Bushehr to Kangan and Bandar Abbas, and is 921 km long. See: 'Bushehr Province', Irano-British Chamber of Commerce, Industries and Mines website, http://www.ibchamber.org/Magazine%2015/3.htm (accessed 21 August 2009).

6   Since the Islamic Revolution and the deposition of Shah Mohammad Rezain 1979, as a result of embargos from countries such as the USA, Iran has become a virtually closed economy.

7   The Portuguese invaded the city of Bushehr in 1506 and attempted to take the place of the Egyptian and Venetian traders who were dominant in the region. Since Bushehr was the chief seaport of the country and the administrative centre for all of Bushehr province, it was later used as a base by the British Royal Navy in the late-18th century, becoming after that an important commercial port.

8   During the 1st and 2nd millennia BC, the peninsula of Bushehr was a thriving and flourishing seat of civilization called *Rey Shahr*. Many relics have been found from the Elamite era and the civilization of Shoush (*Susa*). The structures and artifacts of *Rey Shahr* are said to be related to Ardeshir of the Sassanid dynasty, and indeed *Rey Shahr* was formerly known by the name of *Ram Ardeshir*. Over the passage of time the area and its main city came to be called *Rey Shahr*, and hence the name of Bushehr today. See: 'Cities of Iran: Bushehr', Iran Chamber Society website, http://www.iranchamber.com/cities/bushehr/bushehr.php (accessed 1 September 2009).

9   Axworthy, *Iran, Empire of the Mind*.

10   In the course of researching this chapter, several meetings were conducted with the Regional Government, Mayor, Head of Iranology Centre, Head of Anthropology Museum, and other figures in key government offices.

11   Key examples of investment opportunities in Bushehr are infrastructural, such as creating access to Bushehr International Airport, or access to port facilities for unloading and loading, or maritime terminals for freight and passenger transport

to other Persian Gulf states. The presence of huge oil and gas fields in the province has led to the consideration of potential marine-based industries in Bushehr, such as constructing marine structures and investing in shipyards to build and repair fibreglass and timber vessels, etc. There are also potentials and capacities to invest in air/ship/land transportation of goods, and in the fishing and palm-growing sectors. See: Bushehr Investment Committee, *The Focus of Investment Opportunities, Bushehr Province.*

12   Hamid Ahmedi, *Iran: Building National Culture* (Istanbul: Metis Books, 2009).

13   From historical evidence, in addition to native people and various Mediterranean races settling in the Bushehr province, other ethnic communities such as Dravidians, Jews, Elamites, Sumerians, Nordics, and Arabs also lived in the region. Afterwards, especially during the establishment of the provincial cities, and in particular Bushehr, other ethnic and tribal groups from the Iranian hinterlands migrated to the area, and this multi-ethnic mixture resulted in the present ethnic characteristics of Bushehr Province. Among the later arriving groups were Lurs, Turks, Behbahanies and Dehdashties. See: 'Bushehr Province', Irano-British Chamber of Commerce, Industries and Mines website, http://www.ibchamber.org/Magazine%2015/3.htm (accessed 21 August 2009).

14   Here we are specifically referring to the principle of 'deep ecology', which is widely supported by modern science and in particular by the new systems approach. The 'deep ecology' movement recognizes that achieving ecological balance will require profound changes in our perception of the role of human beings in the planetary ecosystem. According to this more holistic approach, not only physical environmental conditions are at stake in ecological approaches: social, cultural, political, economic issues, working in interaction with each other, are also the crucial for understanding and describing ecological problems. See, for instance: Fritjof Capra, *The Turning Point* (London: Flamingo, 1983).

15   The Old Quarter of Bushehr consists in fact of four quarters: Kuti, Behbahani, Shanbedi and Dehdashti. Kuti, which is located on the coast at the head of the peninsula, was begun 150 years ago.

16   Dogan Kuban, *Turk Hayat'li Evi* (Istanbul: Eren Yayincilik, 1995).

17   This is covered well in the various papers written by Sanjoy Mazumdar and Shampa Mazumdar. See for instance: Shampa Mazumdar & Sanjoy Mazumdar, 'Religious traditions and domestic architecture: A comparative analysis of Zoroastrian and Islamic houses in Iran', *Journal of Architectural and Planning Research*, vol. 14, no. 2 (Autumn 1997): 181–208.

18   *'Badgir'* is the name for a Persian architectural element which in English is called a wind-catcher; and is one of the many examples of energy-efficient designs from the ancient world. This *Iranian term for a wind-catcher refers to a tall chimney-like structure which projects above the roof of a building to expel warm air in the day and trap cooler breezes at night. See: Ahadollah* A'zami, 'Badgir in traditional Iranian architecture', *Proceedings of International Conference on Passive and Low Energy Cooling for the Built Environment*, Santorini (May 2005), pp. 1021–1026.

19   *Qanat* is the local Iranian name for underground water transportation channels.

20   In respect to its cultural identity, handicrafts have long had a leading impact on the life style of villagers living in Bushehr. Due to the limitations of the agricultural sector and seasonal unemployment, most of the habitants of rural areas try to benefit from raw materials naturally available to them as a means for earning more income, and to produce items such as carpet, *gabbeh* (the most outstanding domestic handcraft in Bushehr, a long wafted pile-less carpet weaved by wool mixed with goat hair), *aba* (men's loose sleeveless cloak), *gelim* (short napped coarse carpet), straw-mats,

ceramics, *giveh* (light cotton summer shoes), buckets, hampers, baskets, nets, textiles and sewing products. In addition, traditional shipbuilding is one of the oldest and most important handicrafts in Bushehr, dating back to the time of Nadir Shah. The main material used for shipbuilding is teak imported from India, and then used with other materials from Iranian sources. See: 'Bushehr', *Hosban News* website, http://www.hosban.ir/module-pagesetter-printpub-tid-1-pid-16635.html (22 August 2009).

21   The Iranology Building, Anthropology Museum, Customs Building and Art and Architecture School are some examples of buildings which have been restored; in stark contrast, the British Consulate, Haj Reis Mansion and Old Bazaar are examples of those not yet restored.

22   The types of cultural modifications to historical buildings which can be seen around Bushehr vary over a wide spectrum from fakery to imaginativeness.

23   Ahmedi, *Iran: Building National Culture.*

24   For the first ten years after the Islamic Revolution of 1979, the fact of having a charismatic religious leader (Ayatollah Khomeini), plus a widespread application of populist politics, religious symbols and concepts – accompanied by open hostility to external enemies such as Iraq or the USA – helped to sustain the Islamic identity of the new Iranian state. In the following decade, various developments giving rise to changes in the attitude of urban citizens tended to undermine the religious and revolutionary aspects of political, social and economic life, bringing about a division of identity amongst the people. This issue of what is Islamic identity has ever since been one of the basic political conflicts in Iran. The information that we obtained from various sources in Bushehr shows that besides being underdeveloped in economic and technological terms, a growing urban population and poor urban management policies are working to the detriment of the urbanization process in the city.

17   Houses built by the Anglo-Iranian Oil Company for local workers in Abadan, Iran

18 Brickwork and glazed tiles in the hybrid dwellings of the Bawarda Garden Suburb, as reminiscent of central and southern Iran from the 1930s to the 1950s

19 The urban pattern and housing typology in Bushehr, Iran

20   Window of the Iranology Institute in Bushehr, reflecting some fragments of Iranian Islamic identity

21   Traditional house in Banak, Iran, with courtyard built out of local materials

22   Shop window in a brand new store in Kangan, Iran

23 The abandoned casino on Kish Island, Iran

24   Wind-towers on the reconstructed Ab Ambar well on Kish Island, Iran

13

Kangan and Banak, Iran

Reza Shafaei

This chapter will explore the notion of urban identity in a specific locality in Iran, especially in regard to the role of sustainable development within current conditions of globalisation. Urban identity is a theme closely related to the culture, climate and lifestyle of the people who live in that particular town or city. Two settlements will be investigated: Kangan, a coastal port on the Persian Gulf in south-western Iran, and Banak, a smaller inland town that is almost attached to Kangan.[1] As in effect a linked settlement, it sits on the main coastal road that connects two major sea ports, Bushehr (some 210 km to the north-west) and Bandar Abbas (about 400 km south-east).

Iran is one of the most politically significant developing countries in the Persian Gulf. It is also culturally and climatically diverse, and considered to be a family-based and religious society with its own traditional social structures. Iran has an oil-dependent economy and is recognised as one of the major oil producers as well as main fuel consumers in the world. After the Islamic Revolution 1979, the state has tried to establish a democratic-religious system. In doing so, it has adopted a closed policy towards the global marketplace and has encouraged resistance against any cultural, economic and political influences from western nations. Although these conditions have left Iran less influenced by external forces, the country with its very young population has experienced internal unrest in recent years, which can be interpreted as a search for a contemporary identity and a demand for liberal democratic policies. The social movements that spread around Arab countries, and became known as the 'Arab Spring', hint at more changes in the future of the region. Iran will not be immune.

In addressing urban development at the private, public and global scales, this chapter explores themes of cultural identity and climatic comfort as well as economic status in relation to global changes. This will be done by analysing transformations in the socio-cultural environment as well as the physical environment. In particular, the chapter will ask a number of questions. Firstly, how is global capitalism affecting or changing Kangan and Banak, whether as a result of economic boom or recession? Secondly, how are new conditions of globalisation

13.1   Linked cities of Kangan and Banak on the eastern coastline of the Persian Gulf

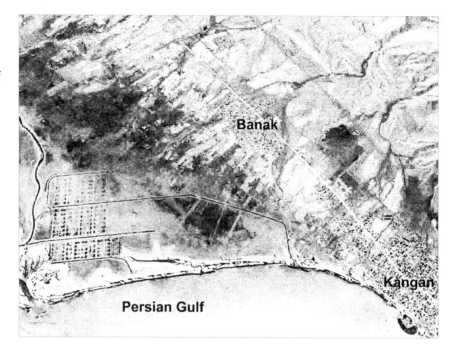

affecting or changing traditional architecture there? How does the local community deal with issues of cultural identity in light of global social changes? How does the community try to represent and symbolise its cultural identity? How does the community use the settlement and what are the everyday patterns of habitation? How do people deal with the local climatic conditions? And lastly, how is climate change affecting or changing the specific town or city, and what steps are being adopted to deal with this problem? (See Plate 21)

LOCATION AND HISTORY

Kangan and Banak are located in the extreme south-eastern end of Bushehr Province, and they form the heart of Kangan County. At an average altitude of just 9 m above sea level, both settlements are very low-lying. Kangan is a port neighboured by the waters of the Persian Gulf to the west and the Zagros Mountains and city of Dashti in Fars Province to the east. Banak, meanwhile, is a town which is now all but linked to Kangan, with the consequence being that both settlements profoundly interact with each other. As a stopping point on the coastal road in southern Iran, as well as a seaport connected to others in the Gulf region, the combined Kangan-Banak settlement acts as a halfway-house for people and products which come, stay or leave. Their combined settlement area is 1,402 km², nestling on the spot where the gentle slopes of the Zagros Mountains meet the sea.[2] The port has a harbour that is 9 m deep, making it one of the most suitable places for sea-related activities in the area. However, large ships cannot land in Kangan, and instead it is used for fishing boats and smaller ships known as *lenj*.

Kangan County is a largely traditional area, with Kangan only being officially a municipality since 1953 (i.e. for only 60 years). It is also one of the most interesting areas along this northern coast of the Persian Gulf due to its natural and cultural attractions. In fact, the settlement of Kangan-Banak 'plays an important historical, economical and strategic role in the region'.[3] As Sani Al-Doleh writes in his invaluable book, *Merat Albaldan*, the historical background of this region dates to 336 BC when Alexander the Great sent food supplies to his troops via the port of Siraf (now Bander-e-Taheri), some 40 km to the south.[4] Siraf was for a long period an important trading and commercial harbour for the Persian Gulf, and, as historians note, Kangan only began to develop after Siraf was heavily destroyed in the 10th century AD. By 1916, albeit still a small settlement, Kangan had grown enough to have its own customs house.[5] As well as the wonderfully fish-populated sea, the beautiful inland mountains are the other key natural resource, along with the Mianloo mineral thermal springs to the north-east and Mond River to the north. Traditionally, the local architecture has adapted itself to the natural environment and climatic conditions: Nasoori Castle in Siraf's old port is one of the most fascinating examples and has survived for hundreds of years.[6]

13.2 Palm trees as the main greenery in the area

GEOGRAPHY, NATURE AND CLIMATE

The climate of the Kangan and Banak area is hot and humid with extreme summers and mild winters. Statistics report that the highest temperature reaches 52°C, and can go as low as 0°C in winter.[7] In the summer, a wind called the '120 Day Wind' blows across the region.

13.3 Impact of recent droughts on the local environment

13.4   Old and new generations reflected in their attitude and clothing

It is a dry and harsh wind described as *Tash Bad* – which means 'Fire Wind' in local terminology – and it sometimes impacts strongly on urban life and human comfort. In addition, earthquakes and floods are two of the major natural threats which need to be considered in designing any development.[8]

Due to its seafront location, Kangan is especially sultry, with high humidity. The region has a low level of precipitation which only lasts for four months from December to March, meaning that Kangan and Banak are constantly confronted by a lack of water resources. There is no surface water or permanent river flowing through the settlements, although, since it is situated between mountains and sea, a number of seasonal rivers do occur, even if they are mostly completely dry. This condition, coupled with physical interventions made to the waterways, has caused seasonal flooding especially in recent years. Mountain trees in the forest park to the east, along with some areas of green croplands to the west, next to the coast, add to the natural potential of Kangan and Banak. Any agricultural production, however, needs to be based on tapping into underground water resources, and indeed local people have traditionally built down water shafts to acquire water. Typical crops include tomatoes, dates, wheat, barley, onions, aubergines and other vegetables. Otherwise, because of the poor soil quality and climatic conditions, the natural vegetation of the area consists of short plants with rough leaves.

POPULATION AND CULTURE

According to the last official statistics from 2006 there were 95,349 people in Kangan County, constituting about 10 per cent of the population of Bushehr Province.[9] Just over half of this population (52 per cent) reside in urban centres in the province whilst the remainder (48 per cent) are in rural areas. In comparison to surrounding counties, agricultural lifestyles thus play a more significant role in Kangan County. In addition, more than 80 per cent of the people, especially men, have only a basic education. The lack of higher-level educational institutions results in a heavy dependence on other cities within Bushehr Province as well as an inability to provide a suitably qualified workforce for local industries. The fact that 44 per cent of the population are between 15–29 years old reveals that Kangan County has the highest proportion of young people in Bushehr Province, creating a real need for proper action to meet their needs in terms of education, jobs, entertainment etc. In addition, it appears from the 2006 census that Kangan itself contained around 24,000 permanent inhabitants occupying 3,035 housing units.[10] A further sizeable number of the local population in Kangan County, around 12,000 men, were temporary skilled and unskilled labourers who worked mostly in the Pars-e-Jonoubi gas field or the industrial zone in the Assalouyeh corridor to the south. Today, it is estimated that Kangan's population is still around the 25,000 mark, thus making it significantly larger than Banak with just 9,000 inhabitants.

The vast majority of the people in Kangan and Banak are Shi'ite Muslims, and a minority are Sunni Muslims, as is usual in Iran. The spoken language is mostly Farsi (Persian) with a local dialect. Due to the close economic relationships with Arab countries on the other side of the Persian Gulf, a fair amount of local people also speak Arabic. Having experienced often volatile histories, a diverse range of ethnic and religious groups have settled in Kangan and Banak at various times, leaving their physical and cultural traces. For example, in Kangan there is an old Jewish temple which has been destroyed recently but which remains a visible trace of other cultures that have marked the place. This multicultural experience in collective memory enables inhabitants to adapt the culture of 'others' with less resistance. In his book on *The Persian Gulf in the Age of Colonialism*, Valara has noted: 'In 1911, two hundred and

13.5   Pottery as a traditional local micro-industry

13.6   National gas industries are turning Kangan-Banak into a heavily industrialised area

fifty new family units settled in Kangan port; while two hundred of them were Jewish and the rest were Arab or non-Arab (Fars).'[11] Today, however, almost all people are Fars, i.e. Persian Muslims, and there are no more Jews at all.

KANGAN'S ECONOMIC AND SOCIAL CHARACTERISTICS

The initial core of Kangan was composed of two main districts: Mahaleh Arabha ('Arab area') and Mahaleh Koozehgari ('Pottery Area'). Despite a generally peaceful relationship between religions, this urban division was apparently based on the grounds that the 'Arab area' was settled by Sunni Muslims and the other by Shi'ite Muslims. According to the latest master-plan for Kangan, once the old town developed, it became divided into six districts, nine urban areas and one urban centre.[12]

Due to its coastal location, the main economic activity in Kangan is fishing and sea-trading – with, as noted, a small amount of agriculture next to the settlement. Industrial expansion in Kangan County generally has already begun to grow due to its close proximity to Iran's largest gas and petrochemical industries. The huge gas facility at Pars-e-Jonoubi is one of the largest energy sources in the world, transforming this region rapidly from sea-based activities to becoming one of the main industrial poles of Iran in recent years. Assalouyeh is one of the 'special economic zones' (SEZ) and it contains the largest concentration of industrial functions in Bushehr Province. A second industrial zone, called the 'Kangan Site', and planned to become twice the size of Assalouyeh, has been started just 10 km from Kangan. Furthermore, one of Iran's most important cement factories, Sarooj-E-Kangan, is situated 12 km from the town, and is heavily involved in exporting to Europe and Asian countries. All these initiatives have attracted huge amounts of economic investment, turning the image of Kangan County into an industrial region. Liberalised trade policies in the free-trade zones along the southern Iranian coast have resulted in a surge in imported foreign products, and indeed the SEZs were set up especially to encourage the transit of goods by freeing them from normal taxation duties.

Bearing in mind the presence of these mega-plants along the coastline, and the fact that about 50 per cent of local people are now involved in related service trades, there are no sizeable industrial activities within Kangan itself. For many years, handicrafts were prevalent in Kangan County, particularly in rural areas, and a few fascinating but small industries such as pottery can be still found in the town. Due to the importance of water in this hot region, pottery production has generally focussed on jugs, water jars, pitchers, and *ghelyan*.[13] But it is still sea-related occupations that form the economic backbone of Kangan, with 35 per cent of its inhabitants being involved in fishing and sea trading, 10 per cent in agricultural activities, and 5 per cent in governmental activities.[14] Yet research also shows that new factors such as consumerism are increasing fast, meaning that productive trades such as pottery, baking and livestock rearing are declining. Recent economic changes have also caused many sea traders to switch to property investment because of the high demand for properties in the area.

The reasons for this investment are clear. Being a port, Kangan has a close relationship with the countries across the Persian Gulf, such as Qatar and the UAE. Given that cities like Dubai and Abu Dhabi are already so developed as economic and business magnets, places like Kangan are bound to be attracted to those power poles: the high proportion of young people in Kangan County provides a ready labour force. This is turning settlements like Kangan and Banak into small-scale consumer markets for Dubai and Abu Dhabi. Furthermore, with the escalating development of energy industries in Kangan County, some companies have begun to buy houses and properties from inhabitants in rural areas. In some cases, they even occupy an entire village with their workers, displacing local people. Instead of creating permanent jobs and sustainable conditions, the companies simply pay people enough to move to new houses elsewhere. This creates a jobless community cut off from its roots, and indeed from real life, once the payouts are spent.

Moreover, due to the huge national-scale industrial developments in Kangan County, a considerable number of ethnic groups from all over Iran, and from nearby countries, have migrated to this area to find jobs and a better life – particularly so during the current economic recession, and with Iran suffering some of its worst-ever droughts. A consequence of migration from rural areas is the proliferation of different ethnic and cultural communities that have not integrated into the host settlement, nor have proper dwellings. One can see the spread of slums in places like Kangan. It is also creating a great deal of social tension. As a result, many of the youths of Kangan and Banak dream of a life in more 'advanced' cities like Dubai or the main Iranian cities such as Tehran or Shiraz. This passion is driving a good many people out of Kangan County, adding to the already tense status of Kangan and Banak.

13.7 Example of a self-made shop built by local merchants

13.8 Newly-built market using concrete and steel which is very quiet during the day as it is so hot

13.9 Vendor creating his shop under the shade of a tree

KANGAN: FROM CULTURE TO ARCHITECTURE

Daily activity in Kangan typically begins at 3.00–4.00 am when the fishermen head out to sea to catch fish for the morning market, held every day starting around 9.00 am or so. The fishermen usually sell their catch in an informal open bazaar along the coastline. However, there is also a special covered fish market beside the main coastal road since a number of people from other regions come to buy fresh fish. All these activities, as well as the other shops in Kangan, usually close down at noon, with people returning to their houses. Some offices that will have started work between 7.00–8.00 am will continue to work on to 2.00 pm by relying on air-conditioning or other mechanical cooling. But because of the extremely hot weather for most of the year, the majority of people go home for a rest with their family when the sun is at its strongest. Social and economic activities restart again around 6.00 pm and continue to 10.00–11.00 pm as the weather is cooler. In the evening, once the sun sets, people often sit in front of their doorways with family members or neighbours to talk and smoke water-pipes. Others will go to places in Kangan to shop and promenade, such as on Vahdat Street in the town centre, or else head for the coastal park for refreshments and entertainment. This form of lifestyle helps to reduce the energy spent on cooling buildings as people go out in the evening when otherwise there would be a peak for lighting their homes or watching television. Public open spaces in the evening also bring natural environmental comforts, creating suitable conditions for social life at the local and urban scales. The selling of foodstuffs such as fish, tomatoes and dates are some of the most important activities.

13.10 Traditional narrow pathway providing shade as well as a human-scaled space for social interaction

Inside dwellings in Kangan, since the houses have no furniture to sit on, people habitually take off their shoes at the entrance, sit down on the carpet, and lean upon special back-rests. Given that heat always rises, the lowest levels of rooms are generally the coldest, and hence the habit of sitting on the floor helps one to breathe and cool down; as such, it again exemplifies a way to use the natural coolness of the ground. Extended families are traditionally common in the Gulf region, and children usually still make their homes in the family house after they marry. Old houses sat next to each other, and indeed neighbours lived so close to each other they could go into the next house via its roof or alleyway. In addition to the environmental role of casting cooling shadows, the narrow alleys also reinforced the community through social interaction within a human-scaled environment. It meant

13.11   A new wide asphalt street which provides no shade and divides the community

that local people acted as a 'neighbourhood watch' scheme, protecting their territory against any perceived social threat. This security, with no need for technology like CCTV, came from the close relationships and sense of belonging in the locality. Recently, however, with the emergence of small nuclear families

13.12   Woman selling fish under a self-made shade in front of the formal marketplace behind

and increasing individualism, the collective structures of traditional communities like Kangan have undergone sudden changes in their social structures and security systems. Likewise, roof terraces – which offer such a large potential surface area – once had a much more specific social function in the built habitat of cities like Kangan. Mr. Koohkan, a 40-year-old municipal employee, told me:

> When we were young we mostly slept at night (except for summer) on the roof of our homes, which was made easy with the use of a kapar [a lightweight structure of textiles and timber]. In the old days, people slept all nights on the roof since there was no cooling system. Some affluent groups built a room called balakhaneh or manzar, but most other people made the simple kapar to use the night wind on the roof against the warm conditions.

Today, this simple and economic way to confront the hot climate is commonly replaced by

13.13   The formal
structure for the
marketplace is
left unused by
local people

problematic and costlier air-conditioning systems, meaning that roof surfaces are now mostly left unused and thus wasted.

THE URBAN FABRIC OF KANGAN

The general urban organisation of Kangan is in a linear pattern along the coastline. The town is composed of a main boulevard in an east-west direction, and from it branch off a number of local streets in a north-south orientation to give access to the residential areas. Today, as noted, this extremely wide boulevard – which also plays a larger role as a transit route that connects Bushehr to Bandar Abbas – divides the growing town into two distinct parts.

Although the main road contains some economic activities, it is in fact one of the branched streets, Vahdat Street, which acts as the pivotal urban centre in social and economic life. It is full of various shops and connects the separate areas on both of its sides which have been settled by Sunnis and Shi'ites respectively. However, the narrow pavements, compared to the width of the road, reduce its importance as a social space for interaction. Moreover, due to increasing traffic, its role seems to be becoming more colourless. Street widening does not lead to sustainable development, but destroys the valuable social structures in cities. Moreover, by giving more respect and hierarchy to vehicles rather pedestrians, it only encourages more traffic and causes worse air pollution. Furthermore, other urban elements such as roundabouts do not represent local cultural identity; all these urban signs need to be carefully reviewed in terms of how appropriate they are.

In Kangan, apart from educational and medical buildings, the key social spaces are generally concentrated in specific public areas which have a clear economic purpose. Aside from the main boulevard and Vahdat Street, it is the morning fish market, evening market and coastal park that are vital for daily life. Whereas Kangan's traditional morning fish market happens along the coast, the evening bazaar is along the side of the main road to catch more passing traffic. Interestingly, although a formal covered market was built by the municipality near to the sea to help the morning market, it is not used by local people; likewise, another market specially built for the evening market is also unoccupied. Instead, because of the lack of shade in these markets, vendors have themselves created a variety of interesting shelters to protect them and their customers. These informal self-built structures tend to be simple, lightweight, temporary and flexible, and are usually of local materials. Such occurrences point to the importance of community participation in the planning of cities.

Apart from the traditional bazaars, other newer commercial outlets have sprung up, mostly concentrated in the town centre or main road, such as the Pardis Trade Centre. The aforementioned influx of foreign goods floods into these new markets from places like Dubai and China, meaning that they have a considerable influence in promoting a consumerist lifestyle – thereby altering Kangan's urban image (see Plate 22). In comparison to traditional markets, their neglect of environmental issues by using air-conditioning and electric lighting poses a threat for urban development.

In addition, the lack of green space in Kangan produces a rather dry and dusty image for the town. In this climate, public green spaces are a social and environmental necessity for urban life. The main green space in Kangan is the long linear coastal park on the waterfront to the south-west of the town with its sea breezes. Used mostly in the evening, it hosts a range of informal social facilities for sports, leisure and picnic areas. Although it is mostly has little shade, local people still use it for picnicking, drinking tea, smoking water-pipes and using the exercise machines in the cooler evenings. However, since these gatherings are mainly based on family or friendship units, these can tend to form into cliques which prevent mixing with other groups. Thus, this park doesn't yet play a fulsome role as a social space compared to Kangan's bazaars. It is also vital there should be more public green spaces at the local level to bind neighbouring communities within a growing town, especially in terms of connecting newer inhabitants with more established ones, as well as mixing classes, genders and ethnicities.

Kangan's natural attractions, along with its fish market, make it a suitable place for tourists to stay, not least as an interim base for Iranian tourists travelling on to destinations such as Bandar Abbas and Kish. But because Kangan doesn't have enough short-term accommodation, travellers usually stay in the coastal park and pitch their own tents. Again, due to the climate, this tourist season only lasts for a short three-month period in winter when the weather is sufficiently mild. It means new public spaces on the seafront, which also get so busy during the *Nowruz* (Persian New Year) celebrations in March, are virtually unused for most of the year. To overcome this problem in summer, proper shading and lighting, along with better paving, could help them to function for other social activities.

Recently, the arrival of new technologies has begun to change the lifestyles of Kangan's inhabitants from their previous dependence on sea to a dependence on industry and machinery. Instead, it would seem that by employing traditional technologies related to people's capabilities, culture and climate it could empower the community more. Likewise, increased water pollution from industrial waste and from urban sewage being discarded into the Persian Gulf – as well as global warming more generally – presents a real threat to the local ecosystem. The danger of epidemic diseases is being spread in Kangan through a lack of drains in the poorer residential areas. There is also in Kangan a virtually non-existent public transport system, creating an over-dependence on private cars and vehicles. Due to the hot climate, people mostly prefer to travel in cars with their cooling systems as opposed to walking. As well as reducing the opportunities for social interactions in urban spaces, it is another cause for environmental pollution and the wastage of fuel resources.

Traditionally, most houses in Kangan were self-built without any supervision by the municipal authorities. Indeed, new residential areas are still being expanded rapidly with little regard to architectural guidelines or urban master-plans. In recent years, due to physical restrictions on space, Kangan's growth has mostly taken place in areas away from the sea to the north-west of the town. These new districts are represented by a grid organisation with wide roads, typical apartment blocks of 3–4 floors in height, some self-built houses and several tall buildings. Hybrid architectural styles are being used that are principally the same as in other Iranian cities with completely different climates and cultures. It means that urban changes are hardly resulting in a proper relationship between new and traditional styles. For example, the courtyards in traditional houses played a crucial role as social spaces where family members gathered, as well as environmental elements to circulate air. Nowadays, people live in apartments that are completely strange to local lifestyles or community needs. The lightweight *kapar* roof structures that were once common devices to deploy wind flows against the hot weather are not being adapted for the new constructions in Kangan.

BANAK'S SOCIO-ECONOMIC COMPOSITION

Due to the location of Banak – and despite its hot and humid climate, its poor soil and water shortage – the main economic activity is agriculture. Activities related to the land have thus been linked to local cultural identity for centuries. Nevertheless, the huge gas resources at Pars-e-Jonoubi are causing massive physical changes in the region, as noted in regard to Kangan, as indeed is the nearby cement factory at Sarooj-E-Kangan. Hence the major local occupations are again agriculture, fishing, sea trading and – increasingly for younger people – either industrial jobs or related service activities. Given that most local people are poorly educated and low-skilled, they often work as labourers for big companies (whereas the higher status jobs go to experts from large cities such as Tehran). Moreover, growing numbers of Banak's inhabitants are amongst those being attracted to Iran's major cities or other centres in the Persian Gulf region, such as Dubai, now that sea transport and visa controls are much easier.

This is a situation which can be found in many other small communities, and this mass-migration is weakening local identity, self-confidence and self-sufficiency. Banak's people, who are keen to stress their own identity, are always having to compare themselves to their more developed neighbour, Kangan, resulting in them competing for a similar lifestyle. Although this could be seen as a dynamic motivation for advancement, it is also a threat which destroys local capabilities. Thus in proposing any development for this small and relatively under-developed community, it has to be emphasised that Banak cannot simply follow the port settlement of Kangan. In fact, Banak is unique in being able to be promoted as an agricultural town, something that is relatively scarce in this hot region. It also suggests that Banak's community should focus on the exchange of goods with Kangan and other sea-based settlements around; taking it back to past traditions when people exchanged, say, dates for onions.

13.14 Elderly resident of Banak smoking his water-pipe in the evening in front of his house

From the clothing style of Banak's inhabitants, one can see how local people have adapted environmentally, culturally and economically to their context through simple techniques. The white colours, lightweight materials and soft textures of the clothes, as well as the shape which enables air to circulate and also allows sufficient covering of the body as people need to follow the Islamic dress code. The main local food was traditionally made of bread and dates; as a case in point, *gamneh* is made from wheat flour. Although the inhabitants of Banak generally carry out some kind of economic activity, such as a bakery, in their private homes, the public focus is in the town centre or either sides of the main road passing through. The rows of shops on this main road tend to have a regional function whilst the bazaar shops in the central area mainly serve local inhabitants. In addition, a weekly market called the Monday Bazaar happens close to the central, permanent market, but according to some local people, the cheap goods sold by its vendors are causing some of Banak's shop owners to shut down their businesses. The central bazaar with its unshaded aisles, and

13.15   Young girls playing in the street in Banak

its attached shops built of steel and concrete, becomes really hot by mid-day on most days. Again this prompts people to go home to rest with their family in the afternoon, meaning that everywhere is usually closed for that time.

Banak has an extremely religious community; once again, the majority are Shi'ite Muslims while a minority are Sunni Muslims. These religions have been historically integrated within the settlement, and today also these different ethnicities continue a peaceful life beside one another. One of Banak's inhabitants, Mr. Jamali, told me that the Sunni minority participates noticeably in the religious and cultural events in the town, whether in public or private. For example, the religious mourning ceremony called *Tasoua-Ashoura*, which is dedicated to Shia, is of great weight in Banak, and most people from different groups take part in it. Other religious events which bind the two religious communities include *Ramadan*, *Eid Fetr* and *Eid Ghorban*. Moreover, national-cultural events such as *Nowruz*, *Sizdah-Bedar* ceremonies and *Yalda Night* play an important role in gathering both religious organisations together, regardless of ethnicity. At a smaller and more private scale, wedding, funeral and circumcision ceremonies also provide a ground for social interaction. Traditionally they were held in a grand manner with many people being present for several days; however, such occasions are now diminishing into smaller events held over fewer days for economic reasons. This does not promise a very interactive social life for Banak's future community.

Moreover, other people – mostly those of a younger age – go further afield, particularly to Kangan, for shopping, promenading, entertainment or refreshments. This can also be attributed to the lack of usable public spaces in Banak. At one time, as Ahmad Rashedi told me, 'there were a mass of date trees in the coastal areas and people used to go to those gardens for picnics and entertainment'. Now, however, this feature is nearly destroyed because of the recent droughts. With the lack of education and poor job prospects, and few sports facilities, the youth of Banak are largely involved in passive leisure activities – for example, motorcycling around the town, leading to a high consumption of fuel which makes the environment more polluted. Therefore, an important priority must be to employ young people in productive activities to create sustainable development. Otherwise there are plenty of temptations. Due to the closeness to Pars-e-Jonoubi, some locals are involved in petrol smuggling, while real social disorders are also emerging, such as drug addiction amongst the younger generation in Banak.

URBANISM AND ARCHITECTURE IN BANAK

Society in Banak is generally family-based and group-based, but apart from the markets and a few other buildings, the town lacks public places or green spaces for social meeting. Apart from a few small children's playgrounds, the main social activity which is vividly visible is an informal gathering called *majles* whereby neighbours gather in front of houses in the evening to chat and smoke their water-

13.16   Traditional house in Banak with courtyard built out of local materials

pipes. Additionally, only the shaded alleyways play a real role in neighbourly relationships or promoting urban livelihoods by offering human-scale spaces. Thus the creation of wider streets by filling in dried up waterways is now separating people (as well as adding to the threat of seasonal floods). In such a small community, it is unreasonable to prefer vehicles to people in urban spaces.

Banak's houses again traditionally used efficient techniques to adapt to their context and provide thermal comfort, including courtyards, thick masonry walls, roof-top *kapars*, etc. Aside from imported timber, building technologies used mainly local materials such as stone, adobe, mud and *sarouj*. The lack of water resources has resulted in using containers for tanks on rooftops. This feature visually impacts on the image of the town, as does the extensive usage of modern cooling systems. In line with local lifestyles, the dwellings in Banak mix agriculture with entertainment and domestic life. As a case in point, the house owned by Haj Abdollah

13.17 New air-conditioned apartments in Banak

Houshiar, aged 70, exemplifies a small self-sufficient settlement. It has a shop as its entrance, a well, a small garden to grow food, a stable, a bakery, several private rooms and a central courtyard. Hence, its inhabitants, an old man and old woman with no children, can easily satisfy most basic needs and even sell some of their products.

As an agricultural community in a baking climate, water is the key to survival. Relying on underground water, the people built wells and then used their livestock to water the croplands. People in Banak also had to bring water from the wells every day for their own use. However, with the arrival of mechanical supplies some years ago now, these patterns of activity have changed, making lifestyles more dependent on machinery. Even less rainfall in recent years causes major droughts, while irregular rainfall patterns, plus the building over of waterways, is leading to worse seasonal flooding that often cuts off places like Banak from other parts of Iran. In other words, water resources need to be vastly improved in efficiency, and changes of habit are required to make people more self-sufficient again. This should be regarded as the priority in the urban development agenda. As Ahmad Rashedi, an educated 74-year-old man known as the 'Banak elder', stated:

> While we can use the free water from rainfall, it has been left useless and instead it only makes floods and consequently droughts. Water, which is our vital need for life, is scarce in this place and so valuable, but it is just wasted and neither can we drink it nor use it for agriculture.

Unlike the scarcity of water, abundant wind energy is a clear potential to be developed. Although storms and severe dusty winds create some problems, the controlled collection of natural wind power offers an economic opportunity for cheap and renewable energy. For example, in Banak there is a simple old windmill, above a well that used to generate the necessary energy to bring up the ground water. In addition, solar energy is another plentiful local resource. As another kind of local renewable energy, it too could reinforce self-sufficiency within the community.

CLIMATE, COMFORT AND PHYSICAL DEVELOPMENT

To pull together what we can learn from Kangan and Banak, a number of traditional environmental solutions at the architectural and urban scales could be combined with new technologies to address climatic issues as follows:

- Urban development does not need to follow the coastline or major roads; instead Banak can continue to grow into its northern foothills with their milder climate, providing that new developments respect the surrounding croplands.
- Given that open-air spaces attract solar heat gain yet closed-off systems block air ventilation, then semi-open urban spaces are more suitable.
- Likewise, since attached buildings block air circulation and detached buildings increase solar gain, then semi-detached dwellings offer the best housing pattern.
- Alleyways should be higher than they are wide to provide shade and funnel the wind in the desired directions.
- Flat roofs are recommended for providing a smaller surface area against sunlight, while also being usable for activities in the milder weather.
- Light constructions and shelters (inspired by 'kapars') can be built on the roof for shade during the daytime and to channel the wind at nights.
- Generous ceiling heights in internal spaces, with openings at high level, help to encourage wind flow.
- Buildings should be constructed above natural ground level against flooding.
- Central courtyards are needed for their social and environmental role.
- Deep balconies, known as eivans, can prevent direct sunlight and help air circulation.
- By providing wind breaks, such as trees, buildings can be protected against dusty winds and be shaded from the harsh sun.
- Windmills can supply energy for airing and cooling, saving on the need for mechanical technologies.
- Using construction materials like timber, rubble, coral, brick and adobe – instead of concrete, steel and glass – can reduce heat gain/transfer, especially if thermal insulation is placed on the outer skin.[15]

13.18   Palm tree with adjacent windmill used
in past times to pump up ground water

CONCLUSION

Urban growth in Kangan and Bandar is now related to new industrial plants as well as more traditional forms of agriculture and port activities, such as fishing and trade between Iran and other Gulf countries. In Kangan, development should follow the coastline to build upon its dependence on the sea and to enjoy the natural breezes. In new projects, the factors of water optimization, wind power and solar energy need to be treated as priorities. Due to the presence of the Assaluyeh gas facilities, as Reza Ahmadian (the consultant for the Kangan master-plan) observed, the town has experienced very high demand for housing immigrants in recent years. However, the physical development of the town is more horizontal rather than vertical, meaning that growth takes place mainly on its outskirts.[16] While the region's energy resources are boosting the national economy, they are also creating serious problems such as flooding.

Banak, as a uniquely green town in a hot locality, has great potential to be managed towards more sustainable development. Due to its location and agricultural basis, Banak is spreading towards the north, away from the coast, into the milder foothill areas. However, urban development is not just about physical issues, as quality of life cannot always be assessed by two-dimensional or quantitative measures. Factors such as socio-cultural and economic conditions need to be balanced with environmental issues. Hence it is necessary to promote cultural attitudes such as user participation, social engagement, urban identity, etc. Jeremy Till writes: 'In order to develop an architecture that is particular to its condition, there are two imperatives – the environmental and the social – that do this.'[17] And according to the UN Commission on Environment and Development: 'sustainable development is the development that meets the needs of present without compromising the ability of future generations to meet their own needs.'[18]

Hence the crucial point is that sustainability is not just about the environment but is also a multi-dimensional concept emphasising quality of life for the future. Current pressures for economic growth in developing cities such as Kangan and Banak are so strong that it is creating a huge need for 'physical development', which in practice leaves less room for 'quality development'. But, given the recent global challenges (including our economic and eco-environmental crises) every localised society is responsible to contribute as much as it can. Since globalisation conditions every innovation, as well as every crisis, any neglect poses a threat for both the developing local community and developed global society. This recognition highlights the role of urban management in social justice and sustainable development. Furthermore, given the recent socio-political protests by the younger generation in Iran, in their search for a contemporary identity, every localised society will be trying to find its own position to survive in the globalising world. We all need to be socially and environmentally responsive to the pressures of urban settlements like Kangan and Banak which are facing the coming changes.

NOTES

1   'Kangan County', Wikipedia website, http://en.wikipedia.org/wiki/Kangan_County (accessed 7 July 2009).

2   Kangan Municipality official brochure (2009).

3   Ibid.

4   Here I am referring to the nineteenth-century book by Sani Al-Doleh, *Merat Albaldan*.

5   Maab Consulting Engineers Co., *Kangan Master-Plan Studies* (2005).

6   'Kangan', Iran Tourism Organisation website, http://www.itto.org/ city/?cityid=126&name=Kangan (accessed 15 August 2009).

7   Kangan Municipality brochure.

8   Maab Consulting Engineers Co., *Kangan Master-Plan Studies*.

9   Ibid.

10   Ibid.

11   As quoted in ibid.

12   Ibid.

13   Kangan Municipality Brochure.

14   'Kangan', Iran Tourism Organisation website, http://www.itto.org/ city/?cityid=126&name=Kangan (accessed 15 August 2009).

15   Vahid Ghobadian, *Solar Building* (Tehran: Iranian Architectural Centre, 2008).

16   Kangan Municipality brochure.

17   Jeremy Till, 'Ethical Imperatives', *RIBA Journal*, vol. 115, no. 5 (May 2008): 50–52.

18   'Brundtland Report', published as World Commission on Environment and Development, *Our Common Future* (Oxford: Oxford University Press, 1987).

14

Kish Island, Iran

Tim Makower

FIRST IMPRESSIONS

My first impression of Kish, as we come in to land, is of a dry plate of stone, sitting in the sea, undercut by the waves. Its baked surface is spotted with low-lying shrubs. Having landed, and as we head into the city, I can see that its urban design owes more to traffic engineers than to anyone else. Although trees are healthy, the grass is green and roads are in good condition, nonetheless its never-ending central reservations serve to prevent intuitive movement. Pedestrian crossings are few and far between, and buildings tend to step back from the street rather than stepping forward to greet visitors. The street edges are amorphous; there is no clear pattern or plan. What is clear is that this will not be an easy place in which to get my bearings. I cannot really see the sea – there is no *corniche* here like in Doha or Muscat or Cannes. But I can tell that this is a tourist resort, both from the zany holiday graphics and the host of hotels wherever I look. It is also clear that this is no 'Earthly Paradise'. Instead, our car moves from roundabout to roundabout, from manicured boulevard to desert scrubland, past lumpy new buildings and half-finished steel and concrete frames. Eventually we arrive at our hotel. It is hot, painfully hot, mainly due to the extreme humidity, but gratifyingly it seems that Kish Island is a place where some people do walk and bicycle, even at midday, even in August, unlike so many cities of the Gulf region. In fact, the weather here is rather pleasant for nine months of the year.

We are now in the main part of the island. 'It doesn't really have a name, so people just call it the city centre', Behzad Shahandeh, the Tourism Promotion Director, tells me the next day. The term 'city centre' certainly appears to be a misnomer. For a start, with a resident population of just 25,000, Kish is at best a town and not a city. And as Mr Shahandeh is the first to point out: 'Kish doesn't have a centre – it has no sense of orientation. It's amorphous; it lacks the classical harmony we are used to in Iran.' However, as I gradually discovered the development potential on the island and realised just how many large projects

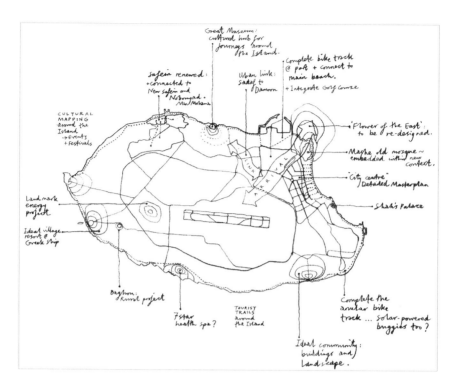

14.1   Author's annotated sketch map of Kish Island

14.2   A typical Kish road scene

14.3   The abandoned casino on Kish Island

are currently underway or in the pipeline, I came to decide that 'city centre' is perhaps an appropriate working title for this area of the island.

Ferdousi Street is the actual main avenue of Kish, but in spite of its line of hotels, amusements and shopping malls, this cannot really be classified as an urban centre, as it fails to give any form to public space. Strangely, as far as I could discover, there is no mosque in the 'city centre'. 'That's because no-one really lives there', claims Majid Karimi, my companion and guide. Instead there is only an abandoned casino, shaped like a spiky crown, at the end of this major axis, backing onto the beach – but more of that later.

14.4   The romance of the Persian Gulf is omnipresent on Kish Island

SOME FACTS ABOUT KISH ISLAND

Kish is a low-lying island of coral rock, 90 km^2 in area, a few kilometres off the Iranian coast in the Persian Gulf. On a clear day you can easily see the mountains of Iran to the north. The island is fairly flat but there is some distinctive topography, with the highpoint at the centre of the island being just 30m above sea level. It is an ancient trading post, part of the famed 'Silk Route' across the Gulf from Bombay to Basra, and it is now one of Iran's primary resorts. The main tourist district is

14.5 Female
visitors to the
Pardis Mall on Kish

situated on the east coast. Kish has a large port in the north-east of the island, which currently handles over 1 m tonnes of cargo each year, with a four-fold increase projected by 2025. All statistics indeed show that Kish is booming. The airport in the centre of the island receives 1.2 million tourists every year, again a figure which has doubled since 2004, and which is predicted to double again by 2025. Likewise, the present population of 25,000 has doubled since 2004, and it too is likely to double again by 2025. Of the population, several thousand are students on courses here, while only about 3,000 citizens (12.5 per cent) are actually native to Kish. The vast majority of people are Iranian nationals but the percentage of foreigners is increasing at a rate some fifteen times faster than that of nationals. Projections are estimating the ultimate population at a maximum of 85,000.

Back in 2004 a third of the surface area of Kish was occupied; today a half of the island is occupied or else committed for development, the majority of it dedicated to new holiday dwellings. By 2025, it is predicted that 60 per cent of the land on the island will be built up. There is a strategic master-plan in place for Kish Island, published in 2005, and an earlier and slightly more detailed master-plan from 1998. Kish is now managed by the Kish Free Zone Organization which has commercial status, although it performs the functions of a municipality. The island is a tax-free zone and, unlike the rest of Iran, visas are not required. Interestingly, Iran's attitudes to women's dress, entertainment and art are also far more relaxed here than on the mainland.

The position that Kish has held within the Persian Gulf for millennia as an international trading post, and as a 'bridge' between Persia and Arabia, accords with its new 'free-zone' status and is reflected in its eclectic architectural identity.

In 1973 the Shah of Iran decided to create a royal resort at Kish, and the long curving beach on the east coast was chosen as the best location. A family of fashionable modern buildings were built between Ferdousi Street and the sea, including villas, palaces, hotels and the now disused casino (see Plate 23). There are also two pre-existing settlements on Kish Island: the first, the aforementioned 'city centre' is along the northern half of the east coast, and the other is the town of Safein up in the north-west corner. A local map reveals that the west side of Safein is older than the rest. 'Yes, that's where the locals live', says Ibrahim our driver. He tells us that the oldest houses there are 45, or maybe 50, years old.

THE NORTH COAST

Before cycling around the island, or before looking in detail at the 'city centre' area or the beach or the new residential neighbourhoods, we decided to use the car to look around to find the roots of Kish. Is there something which makes Kish uniquely the way it is, something which defines its identity? The ruins of Harireh, on the northern coast, between Safein and the 'city centre', are mostly still unexcavated. However, there are still some significant things to see here. A fortified house, a bath-house and the ancient port have each been dug out and reconstructed,

14.6   The old fortified house at Harireh

while work on the old Seljuq Mosque is also now underway. A thousand years ago, Harireh was one of the Gulf's most important centres of pearl diving, fishing and trading. The fortified house is a gem; a small courtyard with simple pointed arcades is surrounded by a set of vaulted rooms. Its simplicity and solidity and the charm of its curved lines makes a lasting impression. The port is a memorable piece of engineering. Built hard against the 3 m-high cliff edge, a natural quayside is created. Vertical loading bays have been cut into the rock, allowing for goods to be lifted from smaller boats at the lower level, which is tucked in under the overhanging cliff.

We then moved on, past the historic walled garden of the Sezham, to the nearby Kariz, one of the most extraordinary ancient water systems in the world. A network of tunnels, 3 km in length, was carved deep underground over 1,000 years ago. Sweet water was collected from aquifers beneath the island, thereby providing all the water the island needed for centuries (water is today piped from a desalination plant on a nearby island). The Kariz is a beautiful place, especially the tree-filled open cut where

14.7　Ruins of Harireh port with new Damoon rising on the horizon

14.8　The ancient Kariz water system

the tunnels meet and a sweeping ramp gives access up to ground level. The enterprising owner of the Kariz has renovated the tunnels and made this into a tourist attraction with a café and small shop at the bottom. However, it is easy to imagine even more use being made of this amazing place. It would make a unique venue for art exhibitions or marketplaces – food for thought perhaps for those who want to raise the profile of Kish as an international tourist destination.

14.9   Wind-towers on the reconstructed Ab Ambar well on Kish Island, Iran

From the Kariz, I could see five wind-towers (*badgirs*) rising above the trees. They serve to cool the Ab Ambar, which is a reconstruction of a traditional domed well with two huge water drums served by galleries and accessed by a long staircase cut into the ground (see Plate 24). The *badgir* is of course one of the great inventions of Persian architecture and is now to be found all around the Gulf region. The cruciform flue catches the wind whatever its direction and the opposite flue creates negative pressure, sucking air naturally through the building. The projecting beams were used to hang wet sheets on so as to cool the incoming air by evaporation.

A little further along the coast we arrived at Safein (pronounced *safeen*, from the Arabic word for 'ship'). Despite its Persian associations, this is clearly a traditional Arab village. Its character is evidence that Gulf regional identity and the Arab Culture are as strong as local identity in other countries which surround the Persian Gulf. Although this village is poor, it is rich in terms of the original thick-walled, mud-built, single-storey houses which are also to be found in

14.10   Traditional house in Safein

varying forms all over the Gulf. I quickly get the feeling that Ibrahim was wrong about these houses being only 45 years old. It is all too easy to imagine this place as a charming fishing village, well looked after and welcoming to tourists, but currently it seems to be sadly unloved. As we explore the narrow lanes and courtyards, certain architectural motifs can be seen again and again. The slightly 'battered' or sloping walls with upturned parapets, the massive conical corner buttresses (*posht*), the recessed panels at high level that were formerly slots to let in air and light but are now blocked up, the projecting *marzam* rain spouts, the elaborated doorways: all of these are designed elements, the product of both technology and aesthetics, developed over generations to make the harsh environment of this region habitable. Does this perhaps offer clues to the local identity and the architectural heart and soul of Kish Island?

The old mosque at the edge of Safein is run-down but as noted it is now being refurbished. It is a beautiful building, with an open arcade and huge buttresses on the seaward side. The crude refurbishment work involves cutting metal air-conditioning boxes into the walls, immediately adjacent to the original natural vents. Between the sea and the mosque a large new park is being built. It is clear that money is being spent on Safein. We are lucky enough to meet Mr Daryobar, who I am told is the 'chief' of Safein. He was coming out of the mosque beside the parade of shops which he owns, along with other properties here and a farm at Baghou (the only rural settlement on Kish). He invited us to his house that evening where we are regaled with stories. In the house's special room for entertaining guests (*majlis*, or *mihman khaneh*), we sit around on floor cushions at the edge of the room while Mr Daryobar's son brings sliced watermelon and fresh dates. The 'chief' continues:

14.11   Safein Mosque in 1980 before the new park was built

14.12   Mr Daryobar in conversation with the author

*When they built New Safein, the eastern part of the village, they didn't explain
why. In 1978, when it was ready, the people from Mashe moved there and nine
months later the Revolution happened.*

I hadn't heard about Mashe at all until then, but I was soon to learn that it had once
been the main village of Kish Island, further along the coast.

*They were not happy to begin with; some of the families had been there for 500
years. Many of them went elsewhere; to the mainland, to Kuwait or Dubai, but
some came here … There are houses in Old Safein which are 300 years old. Just
round the corner is Ali Ebrahimi's house. He died at eighty and his father, who was
100 years old, said that his own grandfather had grown up in the same house.*

At last we were beginning to find out the true value for Kish of these older
buildings in Safein. So I asked Mr Daryobar if he was happy about the new
park that is being built, even though it has moved the shoreline further away
from Safein. He answered with a quote from the *Koran*: 'You can predict that
events will turn out badly but you cannot know what the outcome would have
been if they hadn't happened.' He tells me he is happy about the park: 'The
President [Mahmoud Ahmadinejad] came last year and we asked him to help us
renew Safein. He listened and arranged that work should be done.' The Iranian
government are now building a new fishing port on Kish too: 'Families have been
fishing here for centuries, as well as pearl diving, trading and farming.' Many of
these ancient sources of income have since ceased to be part of community life –
trading is now carried out only on an industrial scale, and pearling stopped here
in 1982 – but fishing is alive and well.

In a later discussion with Mr Shahandeh, I am shown the report on 'New Ideas
and Projects for Investment in Kish 2009'. From this I discover that the prospect of
transforming Safein into a tourist attraction is more than a vague possibility. With a
predicted budget sum of US$ 45 million, plus a construction period of three years
and a period for capital return of five years, this is an ambitious development plan
which runs the danger of 'sanitising' some of the gritty authenticity of Safein today.
Having said that, something clearly has to be done to ensure the town's future
and, provided the local people can stay once it's completed, this project should
hugely enrich Kish Island as a whole. The sprawling modern neighbourhood of Mir
Mohana, which now adjoins Safein, will likewise benefit from having a focal point
of this sort.

Mr Daryobar is also not opposed to change: 'If a bird comes, it stays a while and
then leaves, but it brings good things. Time moves on.' Most of the evening with
him is spent hearing the story of how Kish was founded by Gheish, a man who was
swept there by a great flood from the mountains of Persia. His descendants, living
at Harireh about a thousand years ago, blinded a young female student whose
eyesight was so good that she could spot a man on a camel, on the mainland,
holding honey in one hand and oil in the other. In retribution for this terrible crime
against the young woman, Allah destroyed Harireh and the island lay dormant for
many centuries.

1973 AND ALL THAT

The previous evening I had met another of Kish's old-timers, Mohammad Alavi, an architect who has been working in Kish Island since 1973. He is now refurbishing the low-rise Taban Hotel at the southern end of Ferdousi Street, just next to the 22-storey 'Twin Towers' project which is half-completed. He was involved right from the inception of the Shah's masterplan to turn Kish into a royal resort. In working with the Californian landscape designers, EDAW (part of AECOM) and Mercury Architects from Tehran on that project, Alavi shares responsibility for a part of Kish's legacy which is as significant as (and far more visible than) its older historic fabric.

One of the weak points of the master-plan drawn up for the Shah was its lack of any long-term vision. It didn't anticipate the new centre for Kish becoming the substantial town that it now is, let alone a major city as it could be in future. Ferdousi Street was simply laid out as a feeder road to the line of hotels, villas and the casino, all backing onto the beach. This has contributed to a lack of urban identity and connection to the sea which the growing 'city centre' suffers from, although the EDAW design does have its inadvertent benefits too. The fact that there is no urban *corniche* in Kish is in fact one of its greatest assets, because it means those who are enjoying the sea can escape from the presence of cars. Meanwhile, priority has been given to a remarkable bicycle track which runs around almost the entire island.

As we found when looking into the archives held by the Free Zone Organization, a crucial part of the Shah's masterplan – indeed its proposed 'civic centre' – was never implemented, presumably because of the 1979 Islamic Revolution. This 'civic centre' was intended to be situated at the angle between Ferdousi Street and Iran Street. In the style of its day, the scheme emphasised the 45-degree angle and set up a strong connection to the 'prow'

14.13   Bicycle track at the main beach

of the island at the far north-eastern corner. Today it is a site which is still sitting vacant, waiting for a project called 'The Flower of the East' to take root, as will be mentioned again later. The primary building intended for the Shah's 'civic centre', i.e. a mosque, was never built. Perhaps the lack of this public building and the emptiness of this important corner of the island accounts for much of the placelessness that the 'city centre' exudes in its present-day form.

At the southern end of the beach a steep outcrop of rock, now the site of the Dariush Grand Hotel, marks the division between the world of tourists and that of the old Shah's winter palace. It is significant for the character of Kish that there is still no enclave for the super-rich to develop their mansions, and that the shoreline is fully accessible to the public, except at this one point. The original 1970s master-plan drawings revealed a James Bond-style fantasy of buildings with tectonic concrete fins and sloping walls. Indeed, almost all of the walls seemed to be sloped, either forwards or backwards, and as I progressively got to know Kish I realised that, whether I personally liked it or not, this kind of form is now as much a part of the island's 'vernacular' as are the traditional houses in Safein.

Mr Alavi, who was of course a young man in 1973, attributes the design of many of the key buildings, including the casino, to David Hilliard of Mercury Architects. Perhaps, then, the slopes were meant as a contextual response to the sloped buttresses seen in Safein. To my eye, however, they spoke of fashion rather than timelessness. It is ironic in a way that buildings with this modernist motif are still being designed in Kish today, while the 'timeless' simplicity of traditional Gulf architecture is being ignored. Generally, with a few distinctive exceptions, the diagonals on the latest buildings slope back from the street, which has no logic in terms of casting shade or reducing solar gain. To their credit, however, balconies and deep façades are being commonly used to

14.14 Typical sloped-wall architecture in Kish's 'city centre'

shade window openings. Overall, a sense of solidity prevails. There are not too many buildings of thin glass-and-metal in Kish, although I wonder if things can be kept that way.

My visit to the Free Zone Organization's archive also provided the greatest shock of the trip. Looking at aerial photographs of Kish Island in 1967, I realised that the village of Mashe had been totally obliterated to create the Shah's new resort. For me, this discovery revealed the 1973 master-plan to be one of the greatest acts of cultural vandalism I have known, and also one of the greatest mistakes in urban design and the commercial planning of a tourist resort. Mashe, according to Mr Daryobar, was in fact the lovelier of the two ancient villages on Kish Island. Its wanton destruction by the Shah echoed Allah's attitude to Harireh a thousand years before, but with no good reason. To have refurbished Mashe and made it the heart of the new resort was exactly what was needed to give the Shah's creation the sense of scale, character, urban grain and identity which the area so obviously lacks. It is ironic that if Kish's main shortcoming is its sense of placelessness, the retention of Mashe would have been the answer. It is after all hardly a new discovery that the built heritage has value, both human and economic.

One of Mr Alavi's projects within the Shah's 1970s master-plan was to design New Safein, which, although today it seems just as unloved as Old Safein, is impressive in its urban design. If we compare the plan of Old Safein – an organic plan of soft, 'nearly rectangular' geometries which is highly typical of the Gulf Region – with that of New Safein, they are obviously extremely different. Mr Alavi's plan involved an arrangement of strict rectangular blocks but placed in a very irregular formation to achieve a remarkably similar effect. His buildings are so plain that one hardly knows how old they are, which is

14.15   Map showing the old village of Mashe in 1967

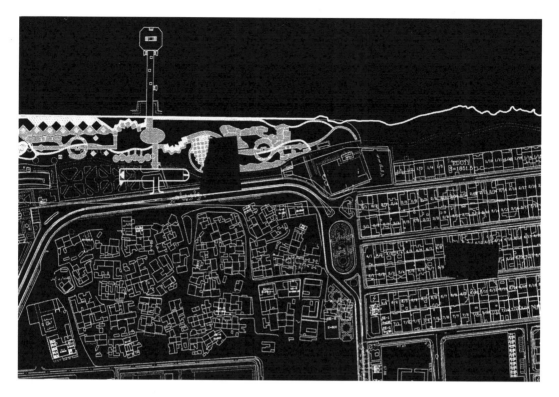

14.16 Urban plan showing the contrast between Old Safein on the left and New Safein on the right

greatly to the architect's credit. New Safein could become a very pleasant place once it has been renewed. The mosque in New Safein, also originally designed by Alavi, was remodelled after the 1979 Revolution to reflect the not-at-all-local architectural style of northern Iran and the Shi'a, as opposed to Sunni, form of Islam.

THE BIKE TRACK

Mr Alavi kindly lent us his bicycles so that we could navigate the whole coastline of Kish Island without using a car. The eastern beach is pleasant but rather patchy – disconnected and unkempt. As we moved south, passing the Dariush Hotel and the former Shah's palace, it is surprising how many derelict structures we found in this otherwise prime part of the island. It seems to be more attractive for landowners to develop virgin sites on the periphery of the 'city centre' than regenerate the existing building stock. If this is the case, they are running the risk of spoiling the whole 'Kish experience'.

It was precisely at this point, as we were cycling towards the looming 'Twin Towers', when I realised that there is now no going back for Kish. The only way to save it from becoming just another resort of mediocre quality (or worse), and to enable it to realise its full potential, will be to encourage more development – but only high-quality development. Meanwhile, its greatest peril is that ongoing development of the wrong kind (as currently underway) will ruin it forever. There is thus nothing to be gained by regretting the loss of the 'unspoilt' natural environment in Kish.

There is little point also in regretting the arrival of lumpy high-rise developments which are sprouting around the island. These too are here to stay. What is of value, however, is to look for the most positive future for new development in Kish; in other words, to think of how buildings and, more importantly, the public spaces between buildings, can achieve an appropriate character and have lasting quality.

South of the 'Twin Towers', there is currently not that much development going on, but yet again the land is not unspoilt. The landscape here is scarred by derelict holiday villas and remains of local infrastructure, so the only realistic answer is to carry on riding the tide of investment in Kish so that one can redevelop with a strategic emphasis on the sites which currently give the place an unfinished feel. We passed the Dolphin Park and the so-called 'Coastal Village of the Persian Gulf', now under construction, which is only the beginning of building up the southern edge of Kish Island. It appears part of an unstoppable process. The long open cycle path along the southern coast is a relief, even in the heat. Strangely the wind was in the opposite direction from the usual prevailing north-westerly, so we were pushed along like sailing ships. Open scrubland with some trees is broken by industrial infrastructure such as the gas plant. The coastline here is mostly of coral rock, undercut by the waves, interspersed with beaches; it's the home of rare sea turtles. The rock is clearly being eroded but no-one seems too worried as it is happening very slowly.

We continued past a derelict hospital – a venture in private healthcare which apparently folded within two years of opening – and moved on towards Keshti Younanie, which translates as the 'Greek ship'. Strangely, along with the beach and the shopping malls and the heritage sites, this is one of Kish's foremost tourist

14.17 The decaying Greek ship

attractions. Most visitors to Kish take a taxi across the island just to be photographed there at sunset. Back in 1966, a Greek ship (which had in fact been built in 1943 in Glasgow) ran aground and it has been here, gradually decaying, ever since. It is indeed very memorable. Perhaps it is a clue to the eclectic spirit which is part of Kish's character and could inform how it develops its 'brand' for the future.

Our cycle ride took us on through Safein and past Harireh to Damoon. The latest phase of development at Damoon is another high-rise hulk, also half-finished. Together with the 'Twin Towers' it acts as a 'bookend' for the coastline development on either side of the 'city centre'. Judging from the hoardings, it looks as though these blocks might have been designed for any resort in the world, which makes me wonder, with these huge forms now emerging, whether the island is indeed 'losing its shape'. However, looking to the future, when Kish will be

14.18   Damoon
rising out of
the ground

developed to maximum capacity, it could be argued that these 'bookends' will
be valuable orientation points. If only they were better designed! Regrettably,
between Damoon and the 'city centre', our coastal path was broken by a large
utilities compound and the industrial port. The fracturing of the northern edge
of the 'city centre' is doubled by the vast (although currently empty) site for a
new golf course, a key part of Kish's future. It puts Damoon in an ambiguous
position; is it part of the 'city centre' or is it in fact part of the separate northern
strip, along with Safein and Mir Mohanna? I feel sure the answer is, or should
be, the former. However the whole unfinished nature of this corner of the island
requires resolution.

After the port we arrived at the 200-hectare wasteland being held in
readiness for 'The Flower of the East' project. We were shown the design later
that day – now, thankfully, put on hold for economic reasons. The project's
layout again reflects the strong 45-degree accent of the Shah's original master-
plan, but the new version would create a stronger presence on the seafront,
plus it is more vulgar and at a much larger scale. Grandiose aspirations of this
kind are not necessarily wrong; in fact, a bold development placed here could
do a lot of good. However, making sure that its design is, firstly, of exceptional,
international and lasting quality, and secondly, that it's relevant and resonant for
Kish – past, present and future – is essential if the island is to fulfil its potential.
Achieving that aim with the current design would be impossible. Then, just as
we finished our bike ride around the site of 'The Flower of the East', we found
the old mosque of Mashe, the only remnant of a community so sadly lost. It is a
small and beautiful building and is now being restored. But how can a project
like 'The Flower of the East' ever be designed to embrace this kind of treasure in
a meaningful, integrated way? How can the 'grand project' and this mosque be
relevant to each other, and, more importantly, in what ways can 'The Flower of
the East' offer a positive contribution to the future identity of Kish?

1989 TO 2005

Apart from Safein and Damoon, where do the people on Kish Island actually live? The 1998 master-plan laid out two new neighbourhoods, Mir Mohanna (adjoining Safein) and Sadaf, the latter which in effect forms the western edge of the 'city centre' area. These communities are both now fully established, with about 10,000 homes between them; they consist of a mixture of low-to-medium-rise houses and apartment buildings. Both have been developed in adherence to strict dimensional guidelines and although none of their architecture is better than mediocre, and the urban design fails to create a memorable environment, nonetheless they are at least urbanistically coherent. What is lacking however are effective connections to the 'city centre' or to Safein and the rest of the road network on Kish Island. A brand new inner-ring road with six lanes won't help in this aim, even if it will certainly speed up further piecemeal development all around the island.

   Sadaf is part of the extension of the 'city centre' which terminates in the site for the 'The Flower of the East' and the proposed golf course, at the centre of which area sits the recently completed Sadaf Tower. This latter building is surely a warning of the cultural demise of Kish over the next few decades unless the tide of poor design can be turned around. Sadaf Tower is a beacon of what Kish mustn't do if it wants to fulfil its potential as a successful place for human habitation. If this building were on an ordinary site in Kish, then it would be unremarkable, since there are many others which are just as bad. However, the problem is that it just happens to sit on one of the most significant landmark sites in the whole topography of the island. The Sadaf Tower sits at a pivotal

14.19   Typical street view in Mir Mohanna

14.20   Sadaf
Tower

point between the 'city centre' and the northern coast, as well as between
'The Flower of the East' site and the airport. How could they have got it so
wrong? The fact that it is ugly and characterless is more than just a missed
opportunity; it sets a general tone of blandness and will do lasting damage to
the development of Kish until it is replaced or at least re-modelled.

Looking more broadly at the role the imminent golf course will have within
the urban plan, this too is problematic. Connection, orientation and legibility
seem to be what are most needed to 'stitch together' the various areas of
development on the island, yet the golf course forms more of a barrier than a
connector. With this part of Kish still unfinished, the outcome cannot be judged
as yet – but I would certainly recommend, given the poor quality of Sadaf Tower,
that a serious review of the whole design for this area is needed before work
restarts on it. In 2004, Drees and Sommer, a firm of German consultants, were
commissioned to produce what Mr Shahande called 'a destination master-plan'
– i.e. a close study of the existing economic, demographic and environmental
conditions, as well as future opportunities for development. Residential trends
formed a major part of their analysis, yet the main emphasis was on tourism.
Given that a dramatic economic growth of 200 per cent is predicted from 2010–
2025, and four times that figure in terms of the expansion of the international
market on Kish Island, their proposal was not unreasonable in suggesting
continued building in already partially developed areas and in open sites
around the perimeter, while also keeping breaks in development along the
southern coast to maintain some of its open character.

The resulting master-plan appropriately focussed on an enrichment of the
'tourist offer' such as sport, conference venues, nature and heritage. Strangely,
neither Safein nor Mashe were even mentioned in the master-plan, nor was the
Kariz, although opening up the Shah's palace to the public, and creating a pearl
museum, and eco-tourist ventures such as the transformation of Mr Daryobar's

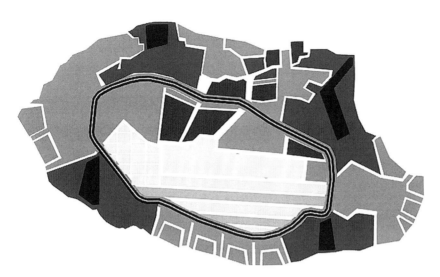

14.21   Urban master-plan by Drees and Sommer in 2004 for Kish Free Zone Organization, indicating the inner-ring road and main development areas

farm at Baghou into a tourist attraction, were all proposed. In the more recently published 'New Ideas and Projects' document, there is also an ambitious plan for the Great Museum of Natural History and Fars Civilisation. This would be the most significant project of all for Kish to define its brand. Anything short of design excellence, however, would only damage its chances of becoming the exceptional place it could be in the future.

Just one page of the 2004 master-plan dealt in any detail with Kish's streetscape and how it might be improved. The document correctly proposed the creation of stronger built edges along Ferdousi Street. However, to ensure that an environment of lasting quality is delivered, a far subtler and more detailed master-plan is required. This should be called the 'quality master-plan', both in the sense of defining the relationships between buildings and public spaces, and in promoting an architectural vernacular for Kish that embodies greater harmony and identity. The 2004 master-plan for Kish Island, meanwhile, is now being branded by Iran as the 'Persian Garden of the Persian Gulf', and although its illustrative drawings are weak, the underlying idea is profound. By making the connection between the Persian root of the word 'paradise' and the man-made idea of the garden, the concept points towards the fact that the design quality of the man-made environment offers the key to the future of Kish.

SO WHAT IS NEXT?

As I take stock of the speed at which Kish Island is changing, and the degree to which it is currently undermining the best aspects of its own character, I find myself wondering what is needed to turn the tide without stopping its development flow, and, should that be possible, which is the best direction for it to go? Let's assume, in the simplest terms, that lasting prosperity, based primarily on long-term success in tourism, is the overriding priority for Kish's future. Currently, since Kish is part of Iran, then the financial model at work here – in terms of catchment area and influence – is going to be more national than global. However, given the Kish Free Zone Organization's international orientation, and its need to compete so as to avoid falling behind other holiday destinations around the Persian Gulf, then Kish's ambition must surely be to increase its global profile as well as its appeal within Iran. How can it do this? Quite simply by making itself into a uniquely memorable, comfortable and delightful place which people will want to come back to year after year – in other words, a real 'Earthly Paradise'. And what might the ingredients be for such a place? In my view, there are four key aspects, which I will now summarise in turn.

Firstly, there is a need for a strong, local cultural identity, particularly in terms of architecture and landscape; it has to be a physical environment which is quintessentially pleasant and harmonious while also being distinctive – in other words, not just a copy of other successful resorts in the Persian Gulf such as Dubai. To this end, a unique local vernacular – indeed a common architectural language – needs to be identified and fostered. A 'base beat' for the built environment is needed; a cohesive backdrop to endow Kish with a strength of character that it currently lacks.

So what, then, is the natural vernacular of Kish? I would argue that it's a combination of several themes, old and new, local and international. Reluctantly, maybe, I would acknowledge that a significant part of the local vernacular is the 'sloped wall' modernist concrete style of the 1970s, originating as it did from the United States. This is to be found all over Kish and, whether one likes it or not, it has become part of the local identity. For a style that was so particular to the 1970s, it is extraordinary how many buildings, some under construction today, still adopt it. Far more significant for me, however, are the traditional buildings of Safein and, formerly, Mashe. These simple, solid vernacular structures have intrinsic value and should be treasured in their own right. But they also have great value as clues for achieving contemporary, contextual design of Kish's unique and distinctive character and its lasting relevance.

A contemporary vernacular therefore needs to reinterpret traditional forms, rather than simply mimicking them. The traditional architecture of the Gulf region has evolved out of structural and environmental challenges, and the availability of particular building materials. Universal solutions were thus refined by particular local influences. To achieve an authentic vernacular, a subtle technical design process is needed, one which can learn from the past but look to the future in dealing with the increasing challenges of global climate change. There will be technical and aesthetic aspects to creating this link between the past and the future. For example, the use of thick walls, shading structures and natural ventilation enhanced by wind-catchers should all be re-assessed in the light of 21st-century technology. The proportions of traditional buildings, their massing and window openings, their special features such as entrances and screens, should be analysed and reflected in contemporary design. The very simplicity of the traditional buildings lends itself well to timeless reinterpretation.

While the traditions of Kish are both local and regional, its aspirations are becoming increasingly international. Indeed its traditional architecture has much in common with other parts of the Gulf region, both Persian and Arabian. So how can any modern vernacular be unique to Kish? It needs to include references to distinctive details from the island – decoded and assimilated in a contemporary way – which can be part of consistent design guidance and ongoing dialogue between designers, developers and statutory authorities. If this is achieved, then universal responses can be made particular. The search for a strong vernacular is not a search for homogeneity. Instead, it is a search for a common language. As with any spoken language, accents will differ and a pleasing level of diversity can still be achieved. Design guidance to promote such a language would touch on topics such as form, composition, surface and detail. It may also be the case that, as with Amman in Jordan or Muscat in Oman, tighter building controls should be imposed on the use of materials, so as to promote cohesion.

The second key ingredient that I would mention is the public realm – that is, the roads, pavements, landscapes and, importantly, building edges. A more detailed master-plan is needed to accompany architectural guidelines that dictate how buildings, particularly within the 'city centre' of Kish, should meet with the streets to achieve clarity, vitality, coherence the prioritisation of giving positive form to the spaces between buildings. This revised master-plan should also highlight every opportunity to develop any currently under-used plots. Tax advantages should be offered to promote buildings on these sites. In my view, Kish could double its density without any new virgin land needing to be developed, and, as long as excellence in pursued in design, the island would be the far better for it. The urban environment would be stronger in character whilst the natural environment could be preserved.

As well as defining codes for new development sites – in terms of massing, street frontage, architectural character, connections and transport – the new detailed master-plan should also make specific proposals for landscape treatment across the island. It should include ways of giving greater priority to pedestrians and cyclists, along with techniques of creating shade for them as they walk or cycle. Simple moves (such as resurfacing every road in a natural 'bound gravel', rather than black tarmac) would be powerful ways of enhancing the identity and feeling of Kish Island. If there is a financial cost to be born here, aside from the fact that such moves would more than pay direct dividends in terms of attracting visitors, then it would be reasonable to tax each new development with the requirement for a 'landscape contribution' to pay for such physical enhancements (on the same basis that a 'Section 106 agreement' requires developers to do so in the UK). A trip up and down Ferdousi Street is enough to show how the pedestrian environment could be improved by the intensification of development. New lines could be set for building frontages, reducing street widths and introducing arcades for shading, and parking could be reallocated to the rear of buildings. Through such measures, a significant increase in density, value, environmental quality and urban character could be realised.

The third ingredient would be to adorn Kish Island, over time, with a series of exceptional landmark projects. Focal points are needed both to attract and delight people, as well as to define the Kish's future identity. Current projects of strategic importance to the island, such as 'The Flower of the East', would however need to be radically redesigned to ensure that they are of international quality and carry a resonance with local cultural traditions. Other projects in the pipeline, such as the proposed Great Museum at Harireh, should be procured through a global design competition, and should become the first in a new era of leading architectural patronage on the island. Kish could make itself world famous for exceptional design. As a parallel, the town of Columbus, Indiana in the USA was made famous as the 'town of architecture' after the Cummins Engine Company developed a policy of subsidising the best up-and-coming young American architects for every new building in the town. The company's chairman bore the additional costs of architects' fees personally in exchange for the right to control the quality of design, and Columbus has reaped the benefits ever since. Kish should do the same.

Landmark projects in energy and environment are also needed on Kish Island, such as a large-scale solar power plant in the centre of the island (which could potentially be a tourist attraction in its own right). Solar-powered initiatives such as electric transport vehicles would then follow, and become part of the positive identity of Kish as a place to live and a resort to remember. Landscape projects should also be required to have landmark status – including tree-planting on a grand scale, innovative approaches to irrigation, perhaps resulting in the actual creation of the 'Persian Garden of the Persian Gulf'. How might all this be achieved? I suggest that a Design Council ought to be established for the island, combining local and international expertise, with the aims of promoting development in accordance with the revised master-plan and of procuring excellence in design. This body should meet regularly to review and approve development proposals and to push forward strategic initiatives. The quality and continuity of the ongoing dialogue and shared vision between developers, designers and the Free Zone Organization would be, above all, a crucial component in securing an authentic, coherent and characterful built environment for Kish in the longer term. Indeed, Kish Island, with its free-zone status, could act as a 'pilot project' for Iran to revive its global reputation as a leading centre of culture.

The fourth ingredient for creating the 'Earthly Paradise' would be a programme of high-profile festivals and events which could set Kish apart from its competitors, creating an annual cycle of activity across the island, potentially with links to universities or other cultural institutions. Initiatives such as an international art fair, or a film festival such as happens at Kassel or Cannes, or a regatta of historic sailing ships as at Klapeida in Lithuania, would draw in specific visitors at different times of the year. High-profile names could then be invited to lead these Kish festivals: for example, the cellist, Yo Yo Ma, with his musical ensemble, the Silk Road Project, and who specialise in the fusion of eastern and western musical traditions, might establish an annual musical event. Festivals of this sort could thus become part of the cultural mapping of the Island, with different events in different locations, such as the Kariz, the 'Greek Ship', Harireh and Mashe. In this way, a strategy for events could influence and be influenced by the place-making strategy that is integral to the revised master-plan. On top of this, local events such as monthly markets ought to be established, plus there is also potential to raise the profile of leisure and sport-related events along with international conferences.

In conclusion, the crucial question is why should Kish aspire to be anything other than the usual high-quality holiday resort? Simply, because tourism is now Kish's *raison d'etre* – as it has been for decades – and this means by definition that it has to compete in the global marketplace. Tourism always thrives best on good design and the creation of remarkable memories; in other words, those memories which shine out from the ordinary ones, and hence memories that really last. To be memorable, a place must be distinctive, and when one looks at the character of most resorts around the Gulf region, so often unremarkable, it is easy to see how Kish could set itself apart. But it is also easy to see how it could fail. There is nothing wrong in the fact that Kish Island is changing so quickly. Much of the groundwork that has been done there is good. However, if Kish really wants to turn itself into an 'Earthly Paradise', then it needs to change direction and push urban, architectural and landscape design right to the top of its agenda.

15

Bandar Abbas, Iran

Widari Bahrin

The term *bandar* in Farsi/Persian means 'port', and indeed the geographical location of Bandar Abbas right on the southern coast of Iran has been its defining character ever since a settlement was founded at some point around 600BC. Positioned strategically on the narrow Strait of Hormuz, the channel of water just 54km wide which separates the Persian Gulf from the Gulf of Oman, Bandar Abbas became the main port city of the great Safavid Empire in the 17th century. Symbolically, it guards the entrance to the Persian Gulf, gazing directly over the Musandam Peninsula in Oman on the other side. Today it remains Iran's most important port and is home to its naval headquarters. Bandar Abbas is also the capital and largest city of Iran's Hormozgan province. However, now that the city's population has risen significantly – it was recorded at around 367,500 people in the 2006 census, and current estimates also suggest a similar amount – urban expansion is drawing even more people in from rural areas, and slums are becoming rife. The city is expanding inland towards the north, building ever more high-rise blocks to deal with its swelling population. Along its historic shoreline, which forms the southern edge of the city, new coastal developments are also radically changing the urban skyline. With urbanisation and port activities lying behind this rapid change, what might be seen as offering a coherent contemporary cultural identity for Bandar Abbas?

As a city, Bandar Abbas exists primarily as a major shipping node, and as such has a very long history of trade via the Indian Ocean with India and East Africa. For the traveller Ibn Battuta in around 1347, it was a fine city filled with busy markets; to the Europeans who visited Bandar Abbas in the 1400s, then known as Hormuz, it was a 'vast emporium of the world'; while to the Chinese admiral, Ma Huan, it was the best managed port anywhere around the Indian Ocean.[1] Today, it remains the most important port in Iran, and its bazaars are replenished daily with fresh sea produce as well as the imported goods that are channelled through neighbouring islands. On top of this, and because of its strategic location on the Persian Gulf, Bandar Abbas has been a major naval base ever since Iran moved its headquarters here in 1977 from Khorramshahr at the northern end of the Gulf. Economically, the major industries in Bandar Abbas include fish processing, cotton milling, textile manufacturing, steel making and aluminium smelting/refining. It is also the export centre for the outputs from the chromium, red oxide, sulphur and salt mines located just outside the city.[2]

At an average altitude of only 9 metres above sea level, Bandar Abbas sits primarily on level ground. Expansion to the city has been mostly along its seafront, resulting in a long and narrow city with major boulevards running in an east-west direction. Nearby elevated points are Mount Geno and Mount Pooladi, each just less than 20 km to the north. As noted, recent urban development in Bandar Abbas has tended to be towards the hillier northern areas of the city. Here, a series of modern multi-storey housing blocks are being rapidly erected next to the Shaheed Rajaee freeway, which acts at the moment as a peripheral ring-road. Some 250 km to the north of the city, a natural pass through the Payeh Mountains facilitates transport via roads to Sirjan and the rest of Iran. Climate-wise, Bandar Abbas is hot and humid with a summer period that lasts for nine months of the year. Maximum temperatures in the summer reach up to 39°C, while the winter is much milder, dropping to only 12°C. This cool winter climate makes Bandar Abbas a busy domestic tourist destination during the festival of *Nowruz* (Iranian New Year) in March each year.

Public spaces play a major part in the life of Bandar Abbas and in shaping the ways in which its inhabitants, coming from their different communities, are able to use and ultimately view the city. Most of its inhabitants seem nostalgic for quieter times and for glimpses of an older identity that inherently belonged to Bandar Abbas in the past, and which still can be seen in various pockets within its urban fabric. This chapter, however, will focus on the external factors affecting daily life in a city that is now experiencing the beginnings of globalisation, with its resultant influx of people from the surrounding countryside.

BANDAR ABBAS: TRADE, TRANSPORT AND TOURISM

As mentioned, economic growth in Bandar Abbas is heavily reliant on its busy port activities – especially from the flourishing flow of trade between Iran and the United Arab Emirates – as well as good transport links on land to the rest of Iran. Also key are the increased levels of domestic tourism.

In terms of trade, the nearby islands of Qeshm and Kish play a major role as points of entry for goods arriving on ships across the Strait of Hormuz (as well as acting as important tourist destinations themselves). Back in September 2003 the Iranian Parliament approved special acts which declared Qeshm and Kish Islands as 'free trade zones', thus liberalising trade and attracting foreign investment. In Kish, for instance, fully overseas-owned firms can now set up their operations, while visitors don't require Iranian entry visas. In addition to this broad-brush initiative for Qeshm and Kish, various 'special economic zones' have been created in the two islands with the sole purpose of promoting the transit and re-exportation of goods without being subjected to normal customs duties and tax regulations.[3]

The port of Shaheed Rajaee, lying some 20 km west of Bandar Abbas, has likewise been declared as an 'special economic zone', and it now handles much of the exportation of Iranian goods. This trading flow in Hormozgan province adds up to a considerable amount given that Iran as a whole in 2003 imported goods to the value of US $22.3 billion and in return exported US $27.4 billion worth.[4] Today these figures are far higher.

Beyond Kish and Qeshm Islands, and just across the Persian Gulf, are of course the Sultanate of Oman and the United Arab Emirates. With Dubai and Abu Dhabi already established as well-connected regional transport hubs, Bandar Abbas is thus in an excellent position to provide cheap land and labour to supplement the growth of those two UAE cities. According to the 2007 International Monetary Fund report on Iran, an estimated 750,000 Iranians enter this labour market each year. With the rates in Iran for skilled and unskilled labourers, and for supervisory foremen, being just half that in the Jebel Ali and Sharjah 'free trade zones' in the UAE, industry in Bandar Abbas is unsurprisingly beginning to see major growth. Furthermore, when it comes to the internal transport infrastructure within Iran, which already has good connections to other countries in central Asia, a draft agreement in 2006 to create the Trans-Asian Railway, nicknamed the 'Iron Silk Road', and linking northern Europe to southern Asia through Bandar Abbas, should in time provide even better export potential, even if progress so far has been slow.[5] This new rail corridor is intended to compete with existing ship traffic passing through the Suez Canal.

Tourism is another major opportunity. Kish Island's unique coral features and Qeshm's natural attractions, coupled with its historic architecture, make both of them very popular destinations for Iranian holidaymakers. As a result, the amount of tourist traffic passing through Bandar Abbas has increased, even if the city itself only serves as a base from which domestic tourists can sail to the two islands by boat. However, because of the region's harsh climate, the tourist season generally happens outside of the long hot nine-month summer. This turns parts of Bandar

15.1   Boats taking visitors to nearby islands during the off-peak season

Abbas which are full to capacity during the busy tourist season into under-used, or often empty, areas for much of the year. The most notable locations are the public seafront spaces that, while packed out for the *Nowruz* celebrations, are far quieter at other times. Plus there are other detractions from the potential for tourist development. With the natural features of the islands of Qeshm and Kish offering the main attraction for eco-tourism, the alarmingly high degree of water pollution in the Persian Gulf is a real threat. The possible causes and implications of this will be discussed again later.

SLUMS AND SMUGGLING

A substantial channel for smuggling in the Persian Gulf currently passes through Kish Island, given that 'export processing zone' duty exemptions are available and are often used to disguise other kinds of imports leaving or entering Iran. The estimated value of illegal imports varies from US $3–8 billion a year. In addition to the smuggling of goods, reports of illegal immigration into Oman and the United Arab Emirates via Bandar Abbas are not uncommon. With the journey time between Bandar Abbas and Ras Al-Khaimah in the UAE being just two hours by speedboat, or else the chance to sail the shorter route to the Musandam Peninsula in Oman and then travel overland into Dubai, this covert movement of people should perhaps not be unexpected.[6] All of these patterns of unauthorised trade and migration via Bandar Abbas is being further fuelled by an influx of people who move to the city seeking work, yet instead find themselves in poverty. As a result, Bandar Abbas now acts either as a refuge where hopeful migrants go to in hope of escaping drought and hardship, or else a temporary transit point for people and goods heading to their final destinations by whatever means possible. The consequence is that various new communities in Bandar Abbas are not fully integrated into the city and often have to live in squalid, hastily erected homes.

15.2   Slum areas in the northern part of Bandar Abbas

15.3   Slums along the coast providing shelter for migrant fishing communities

15.4   Waste-water drainage from slum housing

15.5   A local seller transporting his produce to the bazaar

15.6   Typical public space found under a shaded canopy in a slum area of Bandar Abbas

With busy factories and decent employment prospects for both skilled and unskilled labour forces, rural migration has hence resulted in plentiful informal settlements around the city. Most of these slums remain poorly maintained and serviced, although Bandar Abbas Municipality has partly been successful in providing proper services to these areas. Some slums are found in southern areas of the city close to the seafront, where inhabitants catch and sell fish to provide income for their families. Other slums are located north of the city centre in districts where sanitation is often highly problematic. Outbreaks of illness due to contaminated water supplies are not uncommon in Bandar Abbas. However, a network of large open drains have now been built in an attempt to facilitate the removal of sewage and waste water from dwellings, but this isn't without its own problems as the untreated waste is simply discharged directly into the Gulf, causing concern over rising sea pollution. The occurrence of 'red tide', a phenomenon whereby freshwater algae rapidly accumulate in the sea and result in high mortality rates for marine wildlife, can be seen to occur in waters off Bandar Abbas. The cause of 'red tide' has been attributed to industrial pollutants, the dumping of urban sewage into the open sea, and systematic increases in seawater temperature due to global warming. As reported in *Iran Daily* on 5th August 2009, the Persian Gulf and Oman Sea Research Centre is currently monitoring the situation closely. It would appear their greatest concern is to prevent the effects of 'red tide' as otherwise it so directly harms the livelihoods of local fishing communities and also eco-tourism to Qeshm and Kish Islands.

Another reason for the growing numbers of people migrating into Bandar Abbas has been the severe drought conditions often being experienced in Iran in recent years. A widespread failure of rain-dependent grain crops occurred in 2008–2009, resulting in what the US-based Foreign Agricultural Service described as one of the worst droughts in recent history.[7] Therefore many previously agriculturally-based communities are now choosing to resettle themselves in Bandar Abbas, where the buying and reselling of imported food produce as part of ongoing Gulf trade is seen as a more viable option to growing foodstuffs oneself in such difficult climatic conditions.

PUBLIC SPACE IN BANDAR ABBAS

The increase in population, plus the fact it consists essentially of such poor people, is putting real pressure on public space within the city. The urban layout in the slum areas of Bandar Abbas consists of small winding roads with continuous walled-in houses. These homes are generally self-built and erected without any building permission, often using the large breeze blocks found on major construction sites. Such dwellings are often then added onto as and when required, again without official permission. Houses tend thus to be grouped together according to the township that its inhabitants originated from (for example, much of the large community in the north of the city originally came from Chahestania). This then means that this migrant population remains very

15.7   Typical new public space concentrated along the waterfront

much as outsiders to the city they are now living in. Some steps are being taken to help the situation. The Iranian Housing and Urban Development Organization, sponsored by the World Bank, is undertaking building projects to help the integration of migrant communities with the rest of the inhabitants of Bandar Abbas. The projects include the provision of schools, cultural centres, green spaces and new roads within those communities. However, while the plentiful public spaces that have been created might seem to allow greater intermingling between newer and more established inhabitants, many of the newcomers clearly still prefer to remain close to their homes amongst their own communities. One possible reason for this may be that the majority of the new public spaces are concentrated along the waterfront, and well away from many of the socially fragmented residential areas to the north of the city.

Indeed, public space in Bandar Abbas today largely consists of the parks and promenades along the southern waterfront. Used primarily in the evenings, all year round, these coastal spaces provide ample capacity for a wide range of activities. For most of the year, the warm evening breeze from the sea offers a welcome change from the sweltering heat of the busy bazaars during the day. The new Dowlat and Mellat Park, a 2 km-long strip situated in the east of the city, provides sports grounds and leisure facilities such as the covered picnic areas which have become a common feature along the shoreline. Since it is now

15.8   Bustling public space in the centre of Bandar Abbas

the largest park in Bandar Abbas, yet at some distance from the city centre, a bus terminal has been built to facilitate transport. However, its location so far from the heart of the city means that only local residents or wealthier citizens with cars are really able to utilise the park. Smaller parks closer to the city centre, such as Bustaneh Kish Park and Lavan Park, tend to be more frequented despite the fact they are much smaller and less picturesque, and are not helped by noise from passing traffic. These smaller, brightly-lit spaces are used equally by people going out for evening walks, or by groups who sit smoking *ghalyun* water pipes on concrete plinths, or those who use the purpose-built exercise machines. Nonetheless, social interaction also tends to be minimal in these parks, given that the kinds of activities taking place don't automatically lend themselves to the mixing of different groups.

15.9   Open-air exercise machines in a park at night

Users of the parks in Bandar Abbas are likely to be a combination of tourists and local inhabitants, as well as homeless people, all of whom come for different reasons. This mixed user base also results in an assortment of architectural typologies. For instance, for the tourist in Dowlat and Mellat Park, there is an array of Iranian wind-catchers erected as historical examples from different provinces, as well as a water cistern structure which has been turned into a restaurant. These elements provide backdrops for holiday snaps along the seafront. For local residents there are smaller, less conspicuous picnic huts, and large plinths to sit upon, again mostly located closer to the water so as to provide places for human spectacle. Here the physical space of the plinths suggests an external version of traditional domestic courtyards. Firstly, barriers of light provide a level of privacy for those perched on these small concrete 'islands'. Secondly, given that the coastal walkway paths rarely lead to these plinths, potential 'intruders' from outside would need to walk either along the sand or across uneven rocky ground to reach them.

15.10   Giant television screen for park users

15.11   Local residents smoking water pipes along the shore

15.12   Shading structures for public picnicking

15.13   Fishing boat passing through the breaks in the park network that give access to the water

15.14   Children's play area with inflatable devices

Thus for local Bandar Abbas inhabitants, these are perfect places they can go where they won't be seen by others.

These features of constructed public space are likewise reflective of the small pockets of daily street activity found within urban neighbourhoods (see Plate 25). Often situated on street corners or beneath some form of shading, the occupants and users are generally those living in the immediate area. Keen to watch over the comings and goings in their urban living space, people become more receptive to chit-chat with outsiders, such as me when I visited. One local, Ali Lashgari, who is in his mid-seventies, told me he had a particularly nostalgic view of Bandar Abbas. Noting that most buildings have been erected in the last thirty years, he said that these had replaced older and simpler types of huts where residents once lived. Earlier in his lifetime, public facilities like the Galladari bathhouse were still being utilised as part of community life; today, instead, the baths are a tourist attraction which demonstrates the traditional system for water heating from a different era – that is, not as a part of daily habits but as a novelty attraction.

All over Bandar Abbas, the small meeting places in the streets are wedged between older buildings in the neighbourhood fabric. They are often indicated by the use of more traditional building techniques, generally based on porous sea stones, called *saruuge*, held in place by a mortar mixture of clay, limestone and goat hair. Today these older structures and street spaces are visually lost and often redundant among the new multi-storey apartments built of reinforced concrete and rendered breeze blocks. However, in an attempt to reclaim these lost parts of the city, there has been a strategy adopted to insert multi-purpose sport courts into residential areas. Sport, however, while it might allow the younger generation to mingle and interact, still leaves the older generation of Bandari residents to remain within their own immediate neighbourhoods.

15.15   Display of different wind-catchers near to the seafront picnic areas

15.16   Everyday street life
within neighbourhoods

15.17   Ali Lashgari, septuagenarian
local resident of Bandar Abbas

15.18   Inside the Galladari bathhouse today

15.19   Porous sea stone as a traditional building material that is no longer being used

15.20   Multi-storey apartments under construction in Bandar Abbas

BANDAR ABBAS: TRANSIT CITY

From its surface appearance at least, Bandar Abbas remains a classic transit city. More modern architectural styles are being imported and built along its waterfront to suit the purposes of economic growth, whereas traditional building approaches are now used more casually and seemingly to satisfy the general tourist demand for cultural heritage around the Persian Gulf region. While these poles represent the current trends in the architectural and cultural identity of Bandar Abbas, the segregation of public spaces from the communities that actually need them has been an ongoing problem in the city for decades. As one example, a small Hindu temple in the city centre which features prominently in tourist brochures offers indeed a novel sight within an Islamic city which is otherwise peppered with typical azure-blue mosque domes. However, the Hindu temple remains closed to the public, and can usually only be seen from outside its gates, where some local fruit sellers have set up shop. It possesses large shaded grounds of 100m^2 in area, and yet these are currently cordoned off from the busy bazaar that spills over onto the pavements around, which seems a real waste. These sad remains of a building that was once so alive and yet now sits in this fenced-off section of Bandar Abbas, as with other spaces now confined solely to serving the tourist trade, help to symbolise the relics of a transient population – in this case, a past community from India.

15.21   Disused Hindu temple in the city centre

The municipality in Bandar Abbas needs to pay much more heed to this ongoing problem. Over the years, a number of transient communities have made their home in Bandar Abbas, leaving behind remnants of their inhabitation. Current migration into the city, which is being caused by rapid economic development, is also adding to the already rich ethnographical variety of people that make up its inhabitants. Therefore it is no surprise that Bandari residents always appear to be keen to assert an aesthetic which is adopted from its collective history, even if now it is primarily to attract tourists. Meanwhile the boundaries between the tourists and fleeting visitors, and those who have deeper roots in the city, remain too delineated. In terms of the traditional city residents, the new tourist attractions are kept at arm's length, leaving those now entering the city to live and work unable to penetrate or assimilate into the local social fabric. What this suggests on the part of existing citizens is the keen awareness of – and even a resistance to – the scary prospect of being 'colonised' by the processes of 21st-century globalisation. Certainly many of the people I spoke to during my research voiced such worries.

15.22   A typically busy local street bazaar in Bandar Abbas

In this sense, the recent economic spurt of Bandar Abbas is in many ways detrimental for its different communities, whether older residents or newcomers. Problems caused by rampant smuggling, slum dwellings, poor sanitation and water pollution are posing real threats to people's livelihoods and their health and well-being. The major public spaces that have been built have been designed with visitors and tourists in mind, causing local people to feel ever more marginalised; instead, the latter are now being forced into cavities of unused space within the city. That said, what the new public parks do provide are places within Bandar Abbas that are away from the crowded streets and super-busy roads. If this strategy were now to be taken further into the city, reaching into the older neighbourhoods and the new slum quarters, a series of green public spaces could perhaps help to reinforce communities that are currently being divided by powerful economic factors. With this realisation also comes the possibility of introducing renewed life back into the city centre, improving living conditions for inhabitants and revitalising its architectural character – while of course also building upon the existing delicate and multi-faceted cultural heritage of Bandar Abbas.

NOTES

1   Michael Dumper & Bruce E. Stanley, *Cities of the Middle East and North Africa: A Historical Encyclopaedia* (Santa Barbara, CA: ABC-CLIO, 2006), p. 69.

2   Ibid., p. 70.

3   Saskia Sassen, *Global Networks, Linked Cities* (London: Routledge, 2002), p. 196.

4   'Trade and Transport Facilitation: pre-diagnostic', World Bank website, http://
     siteresources.worldbank.org/INTTLF/Resources/Iran_pre-TTFA_04.pdf (accessed 31
     August 2009).

5   'About the Trans-Asian Railway', United Nations Economic and Social Commission
     for Asia and the Pacific website, http://www.unescap.org/ttdw/index.
     asp?MenuName=TheTrans-AsianRailway (accessed 1 September 2009); 'Trans-Asian
     Railway', Wikipedia website, http://en.wikipedia.org/wiki/Trans-Asian_Railway
     (accessed 20 October 2012).

6   Anna Zacharias, 'Migrants cross strait of dreams', 3 November 2008, *The National*
     website, http://www.thenational.ae/article/20081103/NATIONAL/336260425/1010/
     mcfc.co.uk (accessed 25 August 2009).

7   'Middle East & Central Asia: Continued Drought in 2009/10 Threatens Greater Food
     Grain Shortages', United States Department of Agriculture: Foreign Agricultural Service
     website, http://www.pecad.fas.usdaov/highlights/2008/09/mideast_cenasia_drought/
     (accessed 31 August 2009).

PART III
CONTEMPORARY DESIGN APPROACHES

16

Sustainable Identity: New Paradigms for the Persian Gulf

Nader Ardalan

This essay will address my ongoing academic research and professional applied design studies related to re-conceiving the principles and aesthetic basis of future built environments of Persian Gulf countries, so as to better achieve their potential for phenomenal and cultural sustainability. The study is partially based upon the successful research findings of the 'Year One Pilot' focused on the United Arab Emirates, and which was sponsored by the UAE government. These findings were published in summary in the Winter 2008 edition of *2A Architecture & Art Journal* in Dubai. Furthermore, a Harvard Kennedy School Middle East Initiative Grant by Kuwait Foundation for Advancement of Science for 2009/10 allowed both an anthropological and architectural research continuation of this general topic, as published in our report on 'New Arab Urbanism'.[1] These studies have now culminated in the major new cross-disciplinary Harvard University Research Project for which I am co-editor related to all the eight countries bordering the Persian Gulf. The book, when published, will be titled the *Gulf Encyclopedia for Sustainable Urbanism*, and it is being sponsored by Msheireb, a subsidiary of the Qatar Foundation. This body of research complements my current professional practice in the region and over 40 years of built work in the diverse countries and bioclimatic/cultural zones that surround the Persian Gulf.

My research studies focus upon a series of key research questions that have generated the framework of our exploration, and which still remain to be fully answered:

Q1. How have decision-makers and creators of the new developments in the Persian Gulf made their key decisions? In particular, how have they incorporated concerns for the environment and culture into their programming, planning and design process, aside from the standard considerations of material function, economics and marketability? How has environmental responsibility and cultural relevance been defined and managed in the design/build process?

Q2. Regarding sustainability, is the impetus for its consideration – if it exists at all – just reacting to the chaos caused by contemporary civilizations, resulting in the climate change crisis and some of the ensuing governance requirements or media hype? Is the 'green impulse' popularly supported by the private and public sectors? Is it a direct expression of deeper ethical beliefs? And if so, which ones? How can future developments become effectively more sustainable?

Q3. With regard to cultural consciousness, is there a holistic dimension to be found in the creative process of the architects and planners working in the Persian Gulf? Is there a design quest to convey a 'spirit of place', a Genus Loci, or could the designed work be geographically located anywhere? Does context matter; if so, in what ways?

Q.4. With specific reference to the Gulf Cooperation Council (GCC) countries, do the new developments exhibit a particular cultural character and narrative? One view might be that identity deals directly with a particular civilization's world view of ultimate reality; if that is so, what civilization is being represented in these new developments? If there are shortcomings in this respect, how can they be improved? What role does globalization play in these narratives?

THE CURRENT SITUATION

The topic of 'sustainable human settlements' and the well-being of the marine environment of the Persian Gulf is a vast challenge. It requires considerable, ongoing multidisciplinary research, as well as more in-depth and broader surveys and documentation, detailed analysis, discussions and new public policy initiatives. It also requires a dynamic archival base, which suggests the effort should be institutionalized, funded on a much larger basis and capable of being monitored on some dynamic GIS platform, which the Regional Organization for Protection of Marine Environment (ROPME), a United Nations Environment Programme-related entity in Kuwait and sponsored by the eight Gulf countries, has already started with regard to sea conditions.

It is clear that the two major sides of the Persian Gulf are experiencing completely different levels of economic investment and development. The Gulf Cooperation Council (GCC) side on the west is verging on becoming overly developed with extensive unsustainable built environments, while the Iranian side to the east exhibits just the opposite condition, with extremely under-developed built environments but highly strategic port activities. The Iraqi coastal edge, while very limited in geographical size, nonetheless provides access via the Shatt-al-Arab (Arvand River in Iranian) to the port of Basra, while pouring into the Gulf the entire drained marsh lands and waterways of the Tigris/Euphrates valley. Oman, further removed from the Persian Gulf itself, offers a more benign picture of development, but ironically the most rapid urbanization.

However, all these sides are contributing to the unfortunate pollution of the marine environment through a number of factors: offshore and onshore oil industries that spill or seep vast amounts of oil into the waters; by substantial tanker discharges that also introduce invasive alien predatory species that endanger local fisheries and marine life; by urban dumping of raw sewage and industrial waste; by desalination and power plants; and not least by inter-tidal urban developments that destroy biodiversity and coral resources. Together, these problems cause the Persian Gulf waters to be one of the world's most polluted seas.

16.1   Relief map of the Persian Gulf region

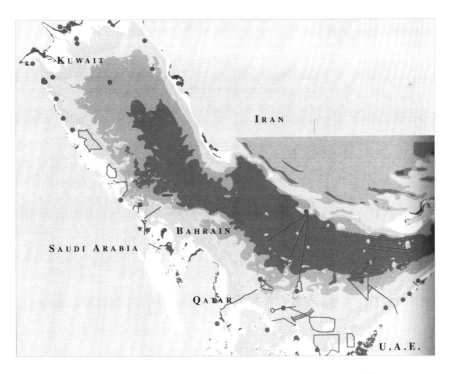

16.2   Bathymetry, ports and oil installations in the Persian Gulf

The current findings of our research and those from an evaluation based on several sustainability criteria such as the 'One Planet Living Principles', indicate that the majority of the current planning, design, construction and real-estate practices and models that have been used – particularly in the GCC part of the Gulf region since the 1990s – now demonstrate serious shortcomings.[2] This working conclusion is principally due to the documented observations by various international agencies and professional critics of the following phenomena:

- The region's high energy and resource consumption that showed Abu Dhabi in 2007 had the world's highest carbon footprint per capita;

- Measures of urban and water pollution in the Gulf, as specifically recorded in the *State of the Marine Environment Report 2003* by ROPME.[3] This showed the four primary causes were:

  1) Oil industries
     - 25,000 tankers, 60 per cent of world oil transported through the Gulf;
     - World's highest oil pollution risk (1.2 million barrels a year spilled);
     - Hydrocarbons in water exceed by 3 times the levels in North Sea.

  2) Wars from 1980 to 2003
     - Iraq/Iran War (1980–1988) = 2–4 million barrels of oil spilled;
     - Iraq Invasion of Kuwait (1990–1991) = 2 million mines, 730 oil well fires, 9 million barrels spilled into Gulf;
     - Iraq War (2003) = Oil well fires in Basra, etc; shipwrecks, oil spills.

  3) Urban development and population growth
     - From less than 34 million people in1960 to 140 million plus in 2008;
     - Inter-tidal zone/biodiversity destruction by offshore construction;
     - Sewage, industrial chemicals and agricultural pesticide discharges;
     - Chlorine, brine & elevated temperatures at desalination/power plants;
     - 66 per cent of Gulf's coral reefs are now at risk;
     - Over-fishing, use of industrial gill nets close to marine nesting areas.

  4) Natural occurrences
     - Shallow water, 50 m average depth, slow moving three-year cycle;
     - Persian Gulf's high water salinity and unusually high temperatures;
     - Red/Green Tides (algae blooms) are disease agents for marine/human life;
     - Invasive marine species due to tanker ballast emptied into Gulf.

- Uneven urban quality and cohesion, lack of human scale in cities, plus traffic congestion that is evident from even a casual drive through any of the Gulf's urban centres now experiencing rapid growth;

- Unresolved socio-demographic dynamics due to the majority of the resident populations of the GGC being expatriates of widely diverse ethnic and economic backgrounds. As a late phase of modernism, globalization magnifies these structural problems by superimposing onto them populations from starkly different backgrounds. The resulting cultural disorientation, alienation and identity crisis remain to be resolved. What is the path forward?

- Identity Crisis: a visual/spatial loss of a vital sense of cultural identity, collective memory, traditional knowledge and values, indigenous narratives, historic textures/patterns, and sense of place. In other words, the intangible elements of heritage.

PROSPECTS FOR THE PERSIAN GULF REGION

The forms of nature are meaningful. They are the resultants of a fit-for-purpose process. Similarly, the forms of the built environment, such as cities and architecture, must ultimately be fit for their bioclimatic/cultural context or else they will not be efficient enough to be maintained, and finally will not survive. This ecological observation can apply to the existing conditions of the Persian Gulf and its surrounding built environments, where the rules of economic determinism have principally dominated development in the last decades with the noticeably retrogressive and destructive shortcomings observed above. Imagine then what the prospect might be for these communities over the next decades if more positive and constructive values – based upon a more holistic ecological fitness and the well-being of human processes – became the motivating rules and forces that governed development in the Gulf region.

Such a model was proposed by Ian McHarg, the acclaimed 'ecological planner', in his seminal 1969 book entitled *Design with Nature*.[4] In it, he proposed that in order to comprehend holistically an ecological bioclimatic zone, for instance the Persian Gulf region, an inventory of all its ecosystems and life processes had be made first to understand the systemic issues involved in that region, and then to determine the most adaptive processes to achieve the solution that offered the least social/ecological cost for the maximum social/ecological benefit. Nine sectors might be considered in such an inventory, which together can provide an integrated picture for future planning and action: Ecosystems; Built Environments; Transportation; Agriculture; Socio-Cultural Patterns; Health; Water; Energy; Economy.

Without having the benefit of such an informative and detailed inventory and analysis available as yet for the Persian Gulf, but based upon our on-going Harvard University investigations to date – and those published by ROPME or reviews of the master-plans for various regional cities and major projects – the following observations and impacts can be made generically about the prospects for the Persian Gulf region:

1. The marine ecosystem will reach its 'tipping point' in terms of pollution in the near future due to the four primary causes discussed earlier.[5] The mitigating steps proposed by ROPME include:

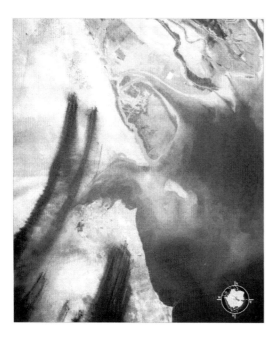

16.3   Fire plumes of Kuwaiti oil fires in 1991

-   Conservation and restoration of the marsh-lands of Lower Mesopotamia
-   Integrated management guidelines for coastal areas and legislation to harmonize development activities in these coastal zones, with its member states pledging to prevent, abate and combat further pollution from land-based building activities.
-   MARPOL Convention to be ratified by member states to prevent further pollution from ships.
-   Legislation for the conservation of biodiversity and the establishment of protected areas to prevent increasing mortality of fish and coral.
-   Attention needed to the rise in sea-level and water temperature which are increasingly threatening the marshes and mangroves that protect coastlines and support healthy ecosystems.

2. Built environments will need to avoid building in the coastal intertidal zones to protect biodiversity, and they must adopt more sustainable development strategies for water desalination, power generation, sewage and waste disposal. The estimated sea-level rises of 600 mm over the next decades and storm surges will only increase the threats to coastal development and infrastructure.

3. Transportation strategies are already under way to build major port facilities and a regional rail system. Within the regional cities, there need to be more mass transit networks and greater use of alternative energy systems for vehicles planned, plus the development of protected, shaded, cooler micro-climates to encourage greater pedestrian movement.

4. Agriculture will face problems from increasing heat, pests, weeds and water scarcity. So there needs to be an encouragement of alternative agricultural systems, such as hydroponics, especially in close proximity to urban settlements. More effective approaches to saving water in agriculture must be legislated for.

5. Socio-cultural patterns exhibit many unresolved socio-demographic dynamics in the Persian Gulf region, and these need to be considered. In the GCC countries, the majority of the residents are expatriates of widely diverse ethnic and economic backgrounds, with more than 70 per cent of the work force being non-nationals. However, in these lands of great prosperity, many of these expatriates live in poverty. Expatriates do not have citizenship status and associated rights, with limits to freely perpetuating their respective social and cultural values and personal dreams of self-

realization, while they are also actively building the global, branded 'Images of Unlimited Prosperity' in these new lands.

6. Public Health and pathology have been proven to correlate closely with environment. In one of the hottest, most arid and humid environments of the world, further stress from increasing heat waves due to global warming will undoubtedly impact on human health and quality of life – this is especially true in cities, where high densities, heat sinks caused by an over-emphasis on 24/7 air-conditioning, atmospheric pollution, noise pollution and urban tensions exist. Mitigation of these impacts need to be encouraged through the creation of naturally cooler micro-climates and more healthy environments by changing current building, urban and transportation patterns.

7. Water has long been an issue of critical concern in this desert region. Iran and Iraq at least have adjacent mountain aquifers to draw upon rivers that traverse their territories, but in the GCC, except for Oman, all the other five states fall into the UN category of having an 'Acute Scarcity' of water. However, water consumption in the GCC zone ranks as the highest per capita in the world at 300–750 litres per day. Aside from these high consumption patterns, other critical areas of concern are: depletion of ground water aquifers; food self-sufficiency policy of GCC aggravates water scarcity because it means agriculture dominates the water supply; prime dependency on sea-water desalination plants has negative impacts on environment; greening of deserts through the planting of indigenous species is not proving sustainable. As a consequence, the GCC established the Water Cooperation Committee in 2002 to understand better its regional water demands, and to enhance water management.[6]

8. Energy demand will increase with population growth in the Gulf, while global warming trends will at the same time increase demands for cooling of buildings. These forces will result in significant increases in electricity use and higher peak demands. New building types which are more energy efficient and more environmentally adapted by using mixed-mode cooling systems need to replace the current unfit-for-purpose models. Once energy demand is reduced, alternative renewable sources (such as solar, wind, bio-fuel and others) need to be developed and used in grid connections to standard power generation networks.

9. Economies have to adapt to create more ecological and sustainable urban settlements, and this goal needs to be encouraged and promoted through incentive programs that will support a more stable and energy efficient pattern of life in this region. Innovative loans and financing for project construction that is based upon long-term energy and water savings can help to promote greater use of sustainable strategies: 'If developing countries and their businesses seize the initiative on energy productivity, they will cut their energy costs, insulate themselves from future energy

shocks, and secure a more sustainable development path – benefits that are all the more desirable given the current global financial turmoil.'[7]

SUSTAINABLE DESIGN: TWO CASE STUDIES

A brief review of the status of sustainability consciousness and mitigating ecological actions indicates that of the eight Persian Gulf countries, it might be said that the UAE, Kuwait and Qatar are most active in developing and supporting environmental issues. The UAE has related more prominently to the land-based aspects of sustainability through the Abu Dhabi ESTIDAMA and the UAE Green Building Council in Dubai, whose programs of sustainability guidelines focus greatly on energy and water consumption. The innovative MASDAR initiative in Abu Dhabi may be the most noted development yet to experiment with the idea of an actual low-carbon, solar-energy-based urban project.[8]

Kuwait through the EPA, KISR and the presence of ROPME, tends to focus more on the sustainability of the marine environment, and have as yet to nurture strong sustainability guidelines for the built environment. However, an important program of waste management has now been initiated. Qatar has recently set up the Qatar Green Building Council; the country's selection to host the 2022 World Cup has prompted the design of sustainable sports facilities; and the Msheireb redevelopment project in downtown Doha is the prime example of sustainable guidelines being applied to a new urban project. The Msheireb Properties sponsorship of Harvard's aforementioned *Gulf Encyclopedia for Sustainable Urbanism* research project also has the potential to generate important scientific and socio-cultural recommendations for more holistically sustainable strategies for future life in the region.

Saudi Arabia has in recent years launched its Saudi Green Building Council, with few projects that have actively incorporated either LEED or BREEAM sustainable standards. Its new Atomic Energy City under design at this time outside of Riyadh based on sustainable standards shows promise. Bahrain and Oman probably have lagged the most in this field; Iraq due to continued internal strife has had little opportunity to consider this subject, with the other countries falling somewhere in between. Iran, due to imposed international sanctions, internal issues, and its more limited public and private investment in urban development, has neither shown great attention to sustainability nor to reducing the apparent excesses in energy or water consumption patterns. Iran, a self sufficient nation in many ways, remains the 'elephant in the room' that hopefully once stirred and released from its encumbrances will become a leader in sustainable development, particularly as aided by UN-Habitat's best practice standards.

Two selected case studies from my own projects will be now discussed here to illustrate the specific characteristics, issues and challenges that projects based upon sustainable principles have considered. The aim is also to discuss what lessons can be gleamed from implementing these kinds of mitigating design approaches in the Persian Gulf region.

DESERT RETREAT, UAE

Client: Aldar Properties, Abu Dhabi, UAE
Professional Team: Architects: KlingStubbins, USA
Design Consultant: Ardalan Associates, LLC, USA

In 2007, when thinking about the Desert Retreat, an intimate, private extended family place for an Emirati national in the remote deserts of the UAE, I came to the conclusion that what can be valuable in the design theme and its architecture is to set a high standard of archetypal significance (see Plate 26). Not just to repeat the historical 'pastiche' version of traditional architecture, nor the aseptic *'avant-garde'* modernity devoid of culture, but to search for what Joseph Campbell called the 'monomythic' and primordial common ground narratives of space, time, forms, signs and symbols from the Persian Gulf region, and from around the world, to be realized in a unified new creation of traditional values and contemporary opportunities.

In keeping with the essential nature of the site, the retreat is to be constructed of architectural concrete made from the red sand of the site, washed and blended with exposed aggregates from the adjacent Hajar Mountains to alleviate its visual heaviness. Teak and sandstone complete a material palette that complements the selection of a site in an ecologically adapted oasis landscape. The place should evoke a primordial sense of the origins of mankind, somewhat as the historic remains of the region give one the awe inspiring sensation of ancient beginnings.

16.4 Desert Retreat aerial view, proposed design for Al Ain in the UAE

West Elevation

16.5   Desert
Retreat elevation

THE INTELLIGENT TOWER, DOHA, QATAR

Client: Gulf Organization for Industrial Consulting (GOIC), Doha, Qatar
Professional Team:
Architects: KlingStubbins, USA
Design Consultant: Ardalan Associates, LLC, USA
Engineers: ARUP, USA/Qatar

The typology of high-rise architecture presents us with a significant design challenge today as we strive to reduce the energy consumption of buildings as a means of achieving sustainable development. High-rise typologies place great value on the occupants' access to natural light and views. To meet this demand, the ratio of perimeter envelope to floor area is typically high. As a consequence, the solar gain per unit of floor area is also high, and the energy required for cooling becomes significant. This is particularly true in the Persian Gulf region where solar gain is extreme and the opportunity for natural ventilation is seasonally limited. While keenly aware of this phenomenon, the project for an Intelligent Tower in Doha which won an international design competition in 2007 also recognizes that architecture, like all complex systems, is the resultant vector of myriad criteria. Beauty, function, land use, financial return, all rightly demand consideration: each one battles for primacy, each seeks optimization.

My vision for this 70-storey tower grew out of our knowledge of and experience with the functional demands on first-class, commercial office towers. So our design proposes a modular, flexible workplace that can support organizational

16.6   GOIC Intelligent Tower for the Doha Corniche, Qatar

and technological change and ensure a high-quality indoor environment for every occupant, while also reducing energy consumption and operational expense. In addition, the building design and the contracting process will facilitate rapid construction. Together, these factors will establish the building as a leader in the Doha office market. Materially, the tower's exterior is a unitized, high-performance, curtain-wall system with non-reflective, minimum-tint glass and top-quality aluminum panels. The exterior is light in colour, as is appropriate to the environment and in harmony with the Qatari traditions of predominantly white architecture. The criteria governing the selection of internal materials and finishes will include: utilization of regionally available and recycled materials; non-endangered natural materials; low-emission paints, carpets, adhesives and sealants; and the use of construction IAQ practices and a 'green housekeeping' program.

The Intelligent Tower will employ a number of energy-generating strategies including wind turbines and photovoltaic panels. Likewise, energy-saving strategies will include: exterior sun-screen devices; triple-layer, high-performance glazing with integral shading device; controlled daylighting; natural ventilation; chilled beams; under-floor air and telecommunication distribution; occupancy

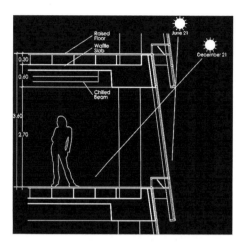

16.7   Typical office floor section for the GOIC Intelligent Tower

16.8   Diagram showing the wind turbines and solar panels on the GOIC Intelligent Tower

lighting controls; efficient lighting and plumbing fixtures; gray water re-cycling; central district cooling; construction efficiency and waste minimization strategies; digital control energy management system; full building commissioning for optimized energy efficient operation. Current computer modeling software affords us the opportunity to simulate the performance of these strategies early in the design process. These simulations are parametric and thereby clearly quantify the relative impact of each strategy. Knowledge of the cost/benefit of these sustainable strategies – in terms of both capital and operating costs – from early on allows the owner to make informed choices prior to the refinement of the contract documents. This reduces the amount of time required for design changes and increases the length of time devoted to producing high-quality project documentation.

In that the mission of the client, GOIC, is to promote industrial development within the wider Gulf Cooperation Council area, it was fitting to incorporate into its headquarters those progressive technologies which can exploit certain characteristics of the climate to generate energy and potentially stimulate greater use of alternative renewable energy systems. Therefore, solar arrays and wind turbines will be located in the tower's two finials. Given the pace of development of such technologies, they are to be located not only where they would achieve optimum output, but also where they could be replaced when more effective models become available. In summary, the Intelligent Tower aims to be at once a beautiful structure resonating with the traditions and aspirations of Persian Gulf states, an effective office building fostering a creative and productive workplace, and an efficient machine minimizing energy consumption and sponsoring innovative sustainable technologies.

These two projects, to name just a few, have not been implemented; they exist as theoretical constructs which are yet to be lived in and tested. But these initiatives are also cutting edge-design proposals to address and directly mitigate both the more tangible energy efficiency and sustainability issues and the equally important, but even less tangible, cultural aspects.

16.9 Lucite concept model of the GOIC Intelligent Tower

VALUES AND DESIGN OPPORTUNITIES

In response to the cultural identity issue raised at the beginning of this essay, it may be instructive to review the basic attitude of Islam to nature. It echoes the same Biblical sources as the Judaic-Christian view, but with a significant difference. Ian McHarg in *Design with Nature* made some very salient observations on this issue.[9] In his view, while Islam emphasized that mankind could metaphorically make paradise on earth and make the desert bloom, the responsibility and relationship to nature was that of stewardship; mankind was both the custodian of nature and the servant of the divine. Moreover, for the settled peoples, the 'garden paradise' metaphor became an ingredient of urban form, while for the nomad the reverence for the earth was so great that mankind was enjoined to leave no trace of having even touched the land. However, McHarg then continued with a somewhat controversial hypothesis:

> *Historically, the Judaic-Christian attitude has been based upon Genesis and, quite contrary to Islam, emphasized the conquest of nature. Man was separate from the temptations of carnal nature and must have dominion over the bestial earth; he must subdue the earth ... With only partial lapses by the European Romanticists of the 18th C., the history of Europeans' attitude to nature has been one of exploitation and conquest.*

If McHarg's theory is valid, it may help explain the history of the last fifty years in the Persian Gulf region and the question of which attitude towards civilization is at work today in the operations of this region, given the observed destructive impacts upon the environment. Due to the intensity of new development in the GCC zone, and looking at the urban forms and architecture being built there today, the predominant models that have been followed seem to be those of Los Angeles and Las Vegas with regard to contemporary urban patterns and zany avant-garde architecture, while often resembling Disneyland wherever pastiche gestures toward the traditions of regional architecture are concerned. So this leads to the key question: are there no more valid design alternatives left?

Of course, Iran and Iraq in this region lag behind in urban development for their own reasons, but the civilizational question as it relates to architectural style remains the same. Can the new generations of Islamic cultures of the Persian Gulf today become the 'visionary stewards of this environment', and rise to the challenges of contemporary opportunities and globalization while remaining true to the values and aesthetic principles of their ancient heritage? The unique identity of each of these places along the Persian Gulf waters, of these millions of new pioneering inhabitants at this time, building these vast testaments of the human spirit in the 21st century, deserves far more meaningful signs of their diversely rich civilizations than what is being realized today. Can then the next phase of development achieve a more authentic, environmentally sustainable and civilizational narrative relevant for the identity images of this region?

Art, architecture, cities, and their relation to the natural environment of the Persian Gulf, offer the major opportunity to the creative decision-maker, be it state institutions, companies or the individual – not only as a vehicle of economic gain, nor only as aesthetic satisfaction, but also a powerful semantic conduit between the microcosm of earthly existence and the macrocosm of timeless existence. In other words, between the myths and profound beliefs of ancient civilizations and our own contemporary times; between the collective unconscious of humanity and the individual psyche.

FURTHER DESIGN EXPLORATIONS

Now, moving onto the issue of the future aesthetics of architectural and urban expression for the Persian Gulf region, it has been said that the functional domain of holistic aesthetics is based upon the simultaneous and profound awareness of the hidden and the manifest aspects of external reality.[10] The artistic search for the deepest mysteries of this awareness is centred upon a personal and direct state of confrontation with reality in its broadest aspects, requiring no intermediaries, and which may lead to an epiphany. In the contemporary secular world in which most architects work, how to express this transcendent, spiritual experience, but not only through the canons of organized religion becomes their prime search. What can we learn from other pivotal historic periods of creative expression to guide our next steps? Research in philosophy, design and the arts can contribute to cross-fertilization of promising ideas. In 1910 Wassily Kandinsky wrote:

> The great epoch of the spiritual which is already beginning, or, in embryonic form, began already yesterday … provides and will provide the soil in which a kind of monumental work of art must come to fruition.[11]

In the world of the artist, the move is away from representational art towards abstraction, preferring instead symbolic colour and form as the means of expression in an attempt to reach a higher and deeper dimension of meaning, the most pervasive of which is that of the spiritual. It is a reaction against the limitations of the pervading rationalist and materialist world views of contemporary society. The role of the artist/architect is thus to free and reinvigorate modern design with greater meaning. Maurice Tuchman's essay in *The Spiritual in Art: Abstract Painting 1890–1985* observes that: 'The five underlying impulses within the spiritual-abstract nexus – cosmic imagery, vibrations, synesthesia, duality and sacred geometry – are in fact five structures that refer to the underlying modes of thought.'[12] To these aspects should perhaps be added three more key impulses.

The first is a silent sense of the unity of existence – at oneness with the infinity of the universe – which was a pervading theme of the earlier 19th-century Transcendental Movement, characteristic of the writings of Ralph Emerson and Walt Whitman in America, and which continues to influence many creative individuals today. This theme is also the core of the *Wahdad-i-wujud* (unity of existence) thinking attributed to the 12th-century Andalusian mystic, Ibn Arabi, which had considerable and direct influence on later metaphysical contemplatives (including Emerson) and can be a vital source of inspiration for those who would taste of its elixir.[13] James Lovelock, author of the *Gaia Theory,* advances the concept of looking at all existence on the Earth as one living organism, thus helping to possibly bridge the beliefs of science and faith.[14]

The second impulse that I would add is the appreciation of alchemy by the artist/ architect as a method of dealing with matter. Alchemy becomes a metaphor not only for the transmutation of external matter from its 'dark heaviness to light', but most importantly for the creative person themselves. The alchemical experience holds for the artist/architect the potential for a complete psychological catharsis that can both illuminate and purify their spirit.

Light releases the energy trapped in matter.[15]

The third impulse is the idea of archetypes, as conceived by Plato and later explored in depth psychology by Carl Jung in what he termed the 'collective unconscious'.[16] Closely related to archetypal thinking is the field of mythology and its pivotal role in human consciousness, as particularly elucidated in the writings of Joseph Campbell and architecturally manifested in the works and thoughts of Louis Kahn.[17]

Architecture is the embodiment of myth.[18]

Through contemplative practice, the resulting comprehension of the above impulses is often characterized by a sense of the universe as a single, living substance of which humans are an inseparable part. Furthermore, inherent in this sense is mankind's role of stewardship of Mother Earth, Gaia. Even if by this effort one is only able to catch but a brief and passing glimpse of an aspect of the systemic unity of existence, the creative attempt is still inspiring and fulfilling. The creative challenge then is how to express most saliently the perfume of this sense.

This approach provides a peculiar kind of 'field' of consciousness or world view as the context for the creative imagination to take place. The activation of the creative imagination may be of an audible nature that transcends mere conventional tonal or linguistic frameworks through music, song, poetry or verse. In a similar manner, it may be of a visual nature in the form of light, colour and matter expressed through art, architecture or movement. In both cases, the imagination is set into vibrations through abstract, transcendent symbols of this 'perfume' that have a propensity to pulsate the heart and thereby to touch the soul.[19] The soul serves here as the *modus operandi* within humans to spontaneously sense the ineffable and the sublime – to go beyond the mere phenomenal to higher levels of realization about the realities of existence. Art and architecture thus have a transcendental potential.

CONCLUDING OBSERVATIONS

Such then is the nature and framework of this quest for holistic, sustainable identity. It is a quest to shift architecture from a kind of machine-inspired functionalist aesthetic to a more ecological and spiritually inspired design approach. The resolutions of these values and aesthetic questions remain elusive, but provide profound inspirations for more meaningful answers that touch the individual soul and collective humanity. As Frank Lloyd Wright wrote:

> *When you become the pencil in the hand of the infinite,*
> *When you are truly creative … design begins and never has an end.*[20]

To truly understand the key issues of sustainability and cultural identity, we need to begin with a cosmic, systemic awareness of the context of human existence on both a tangible, phenomenal level and the less tangible, cultural level. We need to become aware of the particular world views of the indigenous civilization, the *genius loci* of the place, and the optimum ecological fit of proposed developments. The mandate of good design is to elegantly realize this holistic vision in physical reality. Such an approach may provide an important methodology by which common ground can be found between the profound world views of traditional civilizations and the highest aspirations of contemporary innovations in art and architecture. Without such a common ground, the new architectural creations lack a sense of place, are environmentally unsustainable and appear as alien usurpers of an existing civilization, thus causing the identity crisis that is observable in the Middle East as a whole, and particularly in the new developments of the Persian Gulf region. Instead, we urgently need to find new ways of designing in harmony with nature.

NOTES

1   Steven Caton & Nader Ardalan, 'New Arab Urbanism: The Challenge to Sustainability and Culture in the Gulf', Final Report for the Kuwait Program Research Fund, John F. Kennedy School of Government, Harvard University, 2 December 2012, viewable at http://belfercenter.hks.harvard.edu/files/uploads/05_%20New_Arab_urbanism.pdf.

2   'Persian Gulf Research Project on Sustainable Design', *2A Architecture & Art Magazine* (Dubai), no. 7 (2008).

3   ROPME, *State of the Marine Environment Report 2003* (Kuwait: Regional Organization for Protection of Marine Environment, 2004).

4   Ian McHarg, *Design with Nature* (New York: Doubleday, 1971). The book was originally published in 1969 by The Natural History Press.

5   *State of the Marine Environment Report 2003.*

6   Mohammed A. Raouf, *Water Issues in the Gulf: Time for Action* (Washington, DC: The Middle East Institute Policy Brief, 2009).

7   Diana Farrell & Jaana Remes, 'Promoting Energy Efficiency in the Developing Countries', *The McKinsey Quarterly* (February 2009).

8   *ESTIDAMA: Sustainable Buildings & Communities Program for the Emirate of Abu Dhabi* (Abu Dhabi: The Urban Planning Council of Abu Dhabi, 2008).

9   McHarg, *Design with Nature.*

10   Nader Ardalan & Laleh Bakhtiar, *The Sense of Unity: The Sufi Tradition in Persian* Architecture (Chicago, IL/London: Chicago University Press, 1973: Persian translation

by Hamid Shahrokh of Tehran Municipality, 1998; Spanish edition as *El Sentido De La Unidad: La Tradicion Sufi en la Arquitectura Persa*, Madrid: Ediciones Siruela, 2007).

11   Quoted in Kenneth Lindsay & Peter Vergo, *Kandinsky: Complete Writings on Art* (New York: Da Capo Press, 1994).

12   Maurice Tuchman, *The Spiritual in Art: Abstract Painting 1890–1985* (Los Angeles, CA/New York/London: Los Angeles County/Abbeville Press, 1986).

13   Toshihiko Izutsu, *Sufism & Taoism: A Comparative Study of Philosophical Concepts* (Berkeley, CA/London: University of California Press, 1983).

14   James Lovelock, *The Ages of Gaia: A Biography of Our Living Earth* (New York: Bantam Press, 1990).

15   Quoted in Donald W. Hoppen, *The Seven Ages of Frank Lloyd Wright* (New York: Dover Press, 1998).

16   Jolande Jacobi, *Complex Archetype Symbols in the Psychology of C.G. Jung* (Princeton, NJ: Princeton University Press, 1974).

17   Joseph Campbell, *The Hero's Journey* (New York: Harper & Row, 1990).

18   *The Interaction of Tradition and Technology: Report of the Proceedings of the First International Congress of Architects* (Isfahan/Tehran: Ministry of Housing & Urban Development/Government of Iran, 1970).

19   Lindsay & Vergo, *Kandinsky*.

20   Quoted in Hoppen, *The Seven Ages of Frank Lloyd Wright*.

25 Local street bazaar in Bandar Abbas, Iran

26   Desert Retreat aerial view, proposed design for Al Ain in the UAE

27 Masdar City eco-town in Abu Dhabi, UAE, by Foster + Partners

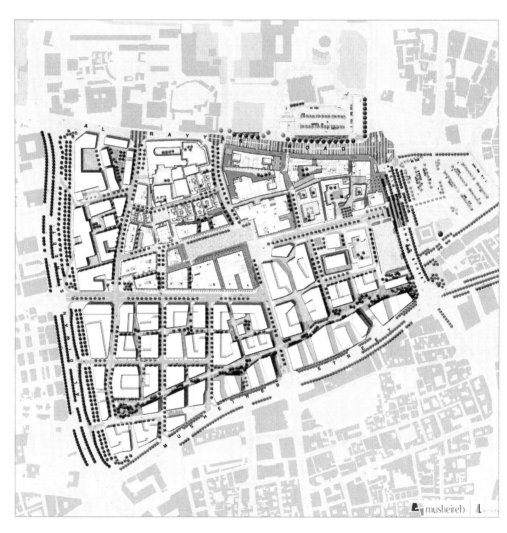

28   Master-plan for the Msheireb project in Doha, Qatar, showing its fine urban grain

29 Organic urban form mixing new and old in the Msheireb project

30   Msheireb project in Doha as seen from the south-east

31   Close-up of 'mashrabiya' screen on the Al Bahar Towers, Abu Dhabi

32   View of chauffeur's house in the Villa Anbar in Dammam, Saudi Arabia (1992–1993)

17

Reflections on a Wind-Catcher: Climate and Cultural Identity

Susannah Hagan

THE WIND-CATCHER (PART 1)

The wind-catcher is part of a natural ventilation system found in certain hot dry climate zones. It is a raised building element either facing in all directions, or facing the prevailing wind, in order to 'catch' it, bring it down into the building, and cool it with moisture from fountains, pools and *salsabils* (carved stone surfaces over which water runs). Once re-warmed by people and their activities, the air rises through a central tower and is pulled out of the top of the building by the same breeze that drove it inside in the first place. If there is no breeze available, wetted hemp mats can be placed over the openings of the wind-catchers. This moistens and cools the air as it enters. The cooling makes the air drop downwards,

17.1 A typical traditional wind-catcher in Iran

Roman
al remains
ı

creating its own breeze. The wind-catcher is thus a very sophisticated piece of low technology and a characteristic element of an architectural style that seamlessly and elegantly combines performance and form, climate and cultural identity: traditional Islamic architecture. In a contemporary context, however, are the same means of preserving and perpetuating architectural identity available to the Gulf States, or to any other region where traditional built culture is colliding with the hegemony of a high and universal technology?

Architecture has been debating identity ever since the 'International Style' hove into view, although of course it was hardly the first international style. Roman classicism reached right across its empire. Islamic architecture spread all the way to the Far East. The connection between built culture and so-called 'globalisation' is not one of style, but of western industrial technology, western financial might and western expertise imposing itself on the rest of the world. Globalisation goes deep economically but, I'd suggest, is only a veneer politically and culturally. The high-rise block housing for an Islamic family and that housing a Christian one neither helps nor hinders their very different ways of life. Human beings are far too entrenched in their ways, and far too adaptable, to allow one stage-set or another to interfere with their habits and traditions – up to a point, at least. The location of that point is the real question. When does the built environment impede the living out of a culture? And which culture are we talking about? Is it the culture of the past, or an emergent culture grappling with enormous external forces? The cities of the southern Gulf have grown so quickly in a few decades, they couldn't possibly have produced a perfect synthesis of disrupted traditions and disrupting economics and technology in that time. The question is where do they go from here?

Once one slows the alarmed gaze, difference proliferates everywhere, and globalisation is seen to be pervasive but limited. There is, for example, an enormous difference between poor developing countries and rich ones. Poor developing countries find it very hard to resist western economic penetration. Rich developing countries have more control over what they do and don't let in. The wealthy countries of the southern Persian Gulf region certainly fall into the second category, although in the realm of the built environment, western industrial technology has obliterated traditional material culture, even if it has to be said that it has done it more totally at home than anywhere else. We have, though, been here before. The discussion going on now in the Gulf States was going on in the 1960s, 1970s and 1980s in the developed and the developing worlds. Then, the architectural reaction to a universalising industrial technology, so-called 'post-modernism', was as heartfelt as it was ineffective. The first call to arms was historicist post-modernism, with its desire to 'enrich' architectural modernism with architectural history. It ranged from the mildly necrophiliac (for example, Phillip Johnson's AT&T Building in Manhattan in 1979) to the entirely necrophiliac (for example, Quinlan Terry's Richmond Riverside development in London in 1987), from pastiche to exact imitation, primarily of classical architecture. The second revolt was called 'Deconstruction', aka 'Deconstructivism', originally a philosophical assault on the construction of meaning in language, translated over-literally into architecture by Peter Eisenman, Coop Himmelblau and others. Both rebellions against architectural modernism operated entirely within modernism's dominant technologies and industrial ways of making, and did nothing to redirect its energies.

THE FIRST WAY: DEEP RETURN

At the same time, however, there was a much deeper resistance that *would* have dented a universalising technology and the global economic system that supports it, had it been able to compete economically. In Vandana Shiva's book, *Monocultures of the Mind,* there is a strong connection made between biological and cultural monocultures, and between biological and cultural diversity:

> *Diverse ecosystems give rise to diverse life forms, and to diverse cultures.*

> *The co-evolution of cultures, of life forms and habitats has conserved the biological diversity on this planet. Cultural diversity and biological diversity go hand in hand.*[1]

For Shiva, ways of making and living arise from particular ecosystems and their particular climates and materials. Hence the existence of traditional vernacular architecture: a human adaptation to a particular ecology, which functions as part of that ecology. A deep return of this kind, with different ways of life contingent upon different physical habitats, therefore requires a return to vernacular craft economies, and in the 1960s and 1970s, just such a return was called for. In the

raditional
d bricks

developed world, it informed what the Luxembourg architects, Leon and Robert Krier, called 'rational architecture' – a name chosen in a deliberate challenge to the rationalism of architectural modernism. In the developing world, the work and writings of the Egyptian architect Hassan Fathy appeared even earlier, in the 1960s. What united these two positions was both valid and unrealistic. If the style wars of architectural post-modernism were a superficial return to a lost past of visual identity, Fathy and the Kriers' work was a return to ways of making and ways of organising space. The deeper the return desired, however, the more elusive it is.

Fathy's intention was to recover, not just an aesthetic, but an entire way of life – the life before Egypt began to modernise under Abdel Nasser, when it lost much of its building craft culture and the identity it provided. The symbol of cultural recovery was, for Fathy, sun-dried brick construction, used in Egypt since the pharaohs, and until the advent of breeze blocks in the 1950s, the basis of every village in the land. The arches, domes and vaults natural to such a material gave rise to an architecture suited to, and characteristic of, its locality, but Fathy was forced to train up builders in the old techniques because there were so few traditional craftsmen left, and the majority of his countrymen weren't with him. The Krier brothers, like Ruskin before them, also condemned the industrialisation of building technology as alienating and unhealthy for its workers, and destructive of the centuries-old fabric of European cities. It was, however, too late to go back, even with patronage of a nostalgic member of the British royal family.

Resistance had, for Fathy and the Kriers, another weapon in its armoury: typology. Almost forgotten now is the amount of heat and light generated in the 1970s by the revival of interest in historical building and urban typologies – the traditional urban grammar that made up the distinctive languages of cities worldwide, which architects like Leon Krier reproduced, much as so-called 'New Urbanism' reproduces them now.

> *Against the anti-historicism of the modern movement we re-propose the study of the history of the city ... The history of architectural and urban culture is seen as the history of types. Types of settlement, types of spaces, types of buildings, types of construction ... The roots of a new rationalist culture are to be found here, as much as in L.N. Durand's Typology of Institutional Monuments.*[2]

Most violently rejected was the Modern Movement's reversal of the relation between solid and void, the erasure of a continuous urban fabric and its replacement by free-standing objects. This rupture was, and is, particularly violent in the Middle East, between a climatically protective urban fabric, and the sizzling open spaces of 'modern' development, which requires unsustainable quantities of air conditioning to achieve acceptable levels of interior comfort, and makes the external spaces hotter than the desert.

Fathy was also at pains to recover not only lost building crafts, but also disappearing urban typologies. The climatically unwise over-scaling and/or gridding of the urban fabric had begun in colonial interventions in the Middle East during the 19th century, and were continued by indigenous rulers in the 20th century (and now in the 21st century), in a desire to modernise and be seen to be modernising. Today's nostrums for 'the sustainable city' are nothing but a rehash of this traditional human-centered life that Fathy, the Kriers and others were demanding in the 1970s, now repackaged as energy-saving because this fabric has mixed uses and more density, and is therefore walkable.

THE SECOND WAY: CRITICAL INTEGRATION

In spite of the relevance of much of the critique that both Fathy and Krier made of the depredations of mid-20th century architecture and urbanism, the rejection of industrialisation within a built context was doomed. The developing world hadn't fully attained an industrialisation to repudiate, and wasn't about to deny it for themselves simply because the west had already experienced the full force of its disruption. The west was also enjoying the full force of an accompanying rise in living standards. And so, in the developed and developing worlds alike, a more complex position of both/and evolved, with varying degrees of success. This is the French philosopher Paul Ricoeur speaking from the developed world:

> There is the paradox: how to become modern and return to sources; how to revive an old dormant civilisation and take part in universal civilisation.[3]

And from inside the region facing this paradox, this is the Iraqi architect, Rifat Chadirji:

> There is no alternative but to bring the cultural development of Iraq into harmony with this process of internationalisation, while at the same time maintaining the nation's traditional characteristics and qualities.[4]

The question was, and still is, *which* traditional characteristics and qualities? Not traditional building technology, which did so much to determine traditional visual identity. Chadirji himself is the epitome of an exchange of equals between a dominant internationalised culture and his own culture, drawing on the long history of Iraqi architecture and on western modern art and architecture to construct a synthesis. In his book, *Concepts and Influences: Towards a regionalised international architecture*, published in 1986, this rapprochement is presented again and again – with, for example, Corbusier's Ronchamp and a traditional Baghdadi house feeding into his design for an administration building for Baghdad's city government.

In abstracting and deploying traditional elements, Chadirji is also deploying traditional means of mediating between climate and interior. The environmental advantages of a climatically differentiated building envelope are energy-efficient as well as culturally grounded – the thick walls and green and watered courtyards effectively modifying microclimate. Chadirji achieves what Kenneth Frampton explicitly argued for in his writings on the developed world's equivalent at the time: a 'Critical Regionalism'. There were many versions of the culturally inflected modernism of 'Critical Regionalism', from the cultural specificity of Carlo Scarpa to the abstraction of Tadao Ando, but the most relevant for this discussion are those architects who focussed more on the relation of the building to physical site than to historical context, based on the assumption that the two are bound up in a dialectical relation anyway. Kenneth Frampton, the best-known theorist and promoter of 'Critical Regionalism', was explicit, and opened up the way for climate to return as an expression of culture:

> *Critical Regionalism is regional to the degree that it invariably stresses certain site-specific factors, ranging from topography … to the varying play of local light across the structure … An articulate response to climatic conditions is a necessary corollary to this. Hence, Critical Regionalism is opposed to the tendency of 'universal civilization' to optimize the use of air-conditioning etc. It tends to treat all openings as delicate transitional zones with a capacity to respond to the specific conditions imposed by the site, the climate and the light.*[5]

This in turn is but a modulated echo of Hassan Fathy, who says:

> *… if you take the solutions to climatology of the past, such as the wind-catcher … and the marble salsabil with carvings of waves on them for the water to trickle over … you will find that they create culture. With today's air-conditioning, you have removed that culture completely.*[6]

In the view of 'Critical Regionalism', air-conditioning should not be 'optimised'. For Fathy's deep return, it should be abandoned altogether, because in losing a place-specific response to climate, you lose a source of differentiation in the built environment.

THE THIRD WAY: CLIMATE AND IDENTITY

The *mashrabiya* has a practical function as a sun-screen in front of an opening that expanded to include a cultural role as well, hiding the women of a Muslim family from public view, while allowing them to see out. The devices of modern technology have long since snapped any such connection between climatic and cultural function. Air-conditioners are not tied to any one set of tectonics, or to any one culture. But we're no longer at the beginning of this trajectory. There have always been architects in the developing world – and within the Modern Movement itself – demanding a synthesis of the regional and the universal, and now there are more. Even more importantly, now *clients* in developing countries are beginning to demand the same.

To give an example, the Msheireb (formerly called the 'Heart of Doha'), a 35-hectare development in the centre of Doha designed by Allies and Morrison, Arup, EDAW/AECOM and others, is to be part of what Sheikha Mozah of Qatar describes as 'a rising homeland that confidently embraces modernisation and proudly observes tradition'.[7] A responsiveness to climate is part of this observation of tradition, and the 'Heart of Doha' masterplan reproduces the dense, tight, self-shading knit of historic Arab cities and towns – albeit with much higher buildings. In several planned large-scale new developments in the Middle East, one sees some form of obeisance to traditional urban solid-void relationships and their traditional climate-adaptive morphologies. The fact that the resulting savings in fossil fuel energy are more often than not paid for with oil revenues is an irony that has yet to work itself out, as is the fact that this return to traditional typology is being achieved with a large contribution from western designers and engineers.

THE WIND-CATCHER (PART 2)

Bioclimatic design in developed countries is effecting its own resistance to the hegemony of high technology, for predominantly environmental reasons rather than cultural ones. Regardless of whether or not one considers global warming to be a conspiracy to undermine Ferrari, the rate of extraction from, and pollution of, a hapless planet overrun by a species that seems rapacious to the point of suicide, means these environmental reasons are now as important as the older cultural ones – especially if you view the cultural and the environmental as bound up with one another. An elegant efficiency of construction and operation is now *de rigueur* at the scale of building and city. In environmental design, this is achieved by any means necessary – whether by active strategies (mechanical and/or digital), or by passive strategies (which use the building fabric to mediate between inside and outside) or by hybrid strategies (mixtures of both active and passive means). Because the building envelope is now often returned to its original protective function, performing some of the work it did before the advent of mechanical engineering, its materiality becomes intensely important again in terms of reducing energy consumption. On so doing, it can then also inflect a contemporary building towards its cultural, as well as its climatic, region.

Traditional vernacular architecture is a treasury of techniques and ideas that are shamelessly borrowed by bio-climatic architects everywhere, so that there is now some exchange: western high technology streaming into the developing world, and low-energy techniques sliding back into the developed one. The reproduction of traditional styles is not involved in this borrowing, but the influence of tradition is pervasive. The circle of fresh air in/stale air out, driven by the buoyancy of hot air – the so-called 'stack effect' – can be seen reproduced in different ways in much

17.4   Torrent Research Laboratories in Ahmedabad, India, by Brian Ford and Associates (1997)

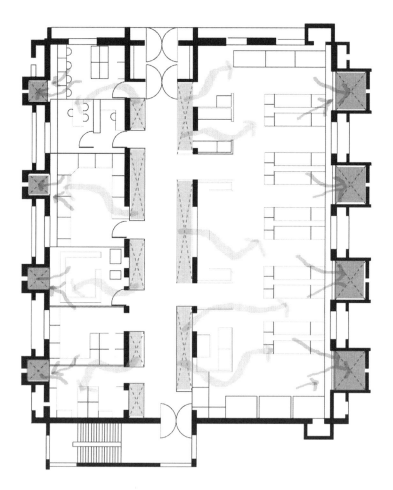

17.5   Plan of Torrent Laboratories showing the PDEC ventilation system

bio-climatically designed architecture in the west. In not only undemanding domestic buildings, but in larger public and commercial buildings with complex programmes, one can see the use traditional, stack-driven passive ventilation techniques. This contemporary air isn't usually entering through wind-catchers; instead it tends to come at the cooler ground level, and is then expelled through atria or special chimneys.

Such techniques have become new bioclimatic typologies in the west, but they are even more applicable to the climates where they originated – within a context of contemporary architecture. In hot humid climates like Malaysia's, for example, where Ken Yeang has developed what he calls 'bioclimatic skyscrapers', these are protected from solar radiation by a series of layers, some built, some grown.[8] Closer to the traditional model are Brian Ford's low-energy cooling designs for the Torrent Research Laboratories in India, completed in the late-1990s. Here, the means of circulating fresh air are virtually identical to the vernacular techniques, but the wetted mats used to cool the air and make it drop on windless days in the traditional system have been replaced by micro-ionisers, which spray the hot air as it enters at roof level. As the sprayed air cools and falls, it pushes down and into the floors below, cooling them in turn. As it is warmed again, the air rises and evacuates through vents. Out of the wind-catcher and the *salsabil* has come Passive Downdraft Evaporative Cooling (PDEC), which can be used at an urban scale as well. The 'cooling towers' in some of the open spaces of the 1992 Seville Expo used the PDEC system.

The borrowing of vernacular environmental techniques, therefore, does not mean the borrowing of vernacular styles, unless the architect and/or client are after such an imitation. The architectural language used in most bioclimatic architecture

17.6   Seville Expo (1992), external areas installed with 'cooling towers'

17.7 Rapid urban development under construction in Dubai, UAE

is entirely contemporary, and most of the materials are industrially manufactured. Environmental design is not an answer to a perceived loss of cultural identity or to totalising modes of production, unless it is deliberately pushed in that direction. Climatic regions are not the same as political or cultural ones. An adobe building could be sitting in the hot dry American south-west or hot dry Syria. On the other hand, if Chadirji is right, then bioclimatic design goes some way to achieving his conciliatory objectives:

> No truly excellent regional architecture can be achieved unless in some sense it blossoms from within its own culture. Iraq must therefore possess its own regional technology before it can have its own [contemporary] architecture.[9]

In building terms, the Gulf States do possess their own regional technology – a traditional, sophisticated low technology – and bio-climatic design is one way of enabling architects to integrate this with a universal high technology. At urban scale, bio-climatic design is also a way of integrating traditional morphologies that were also, among other things, clever responses to climate.

There has been a tendency in architectural discussion to present the part for the whole – for example, the extreme modernist development of Dubai as being representative of the entire and varied Gulf region – whereas something like Foster and Partners' design for the new eco-city of Masdar, on the edge of Abu Dhabi, indicates a culturally and climatically more sophisticated synthesis of old and new on the part of architect *and* client (see Plate 27). If built fabric emerges out of

17.8   Masdar City eco-town on the edge of Abu Dhabi, UAE, by Foster + Partners

established cultural identity, and that established cultural identity is changing, then the built fabric will inevitably change as well. The challenge, surely, is not to resist that change, but to direct it past the crudities of modernist zoning and 'my skyscraper's weirder than yours', past climatic ignorance and democratic deficits. Modernity is emancipatory as well as disruptive. There is nothing to lament in a rise in living standards and an increase in opportunity, as long as everyone and everything (i.e. the environment) can benefit. This is a question of governance, not architecture. Architects can – and indeed should – propose, but governments and clients dispose. There is an emerging desire in the Gulf region to import the new ways of thinking and doing being developed in the west, not those being discarded by the west. If this shift continues to gain ground, then climate can provide a more regionally grounded means of negotiating between an unrecoverable past and new imports.

NOTES

1   Vandana Shiva, *Monocultures of the Mind* (London: Zed Books, 1993), p. 65.

2   Leon Krier, *Rational Architecture* (Gand, Belgium: Archives d'Architecture Moderne/ Snoek-Ducaju & Zoon, 1978), p. 41.

3   Paul Ricoeur, *History and Truth* (Evanston, IL: Northwestern University Press, 1965), pp. 276–277.

4   Rifat Chadirji, *Concepts and Influences: Towards a Regionalised International Architecture* (London: Routledge & Kegan Paul, 1986), p. 41.

5   Kenneth Frampton, *Modern Architecture: A Critical History* (London: Thames and Hudson, 1992), p. 327.

6   Hassan Fathy, *Natural Energy and Vernacular Architecture* (Chicago: University of Chicago, 1986), p. 15.

7   'CEO message', Dohaland/Qatar Foundation for Education, Science and Community Development website, http://www.dohaland.com/company/ceo-message (accessed 29 August 2010).

8   Ken Yeang, *The Skyscraper Bioclimatically Considered* (London: Academy Group, 1996).

9   Chadirji, *Concepts and Influences*, p. 43.

18

Doha Renaissance: Msheireb Reborn

Tim Makower

This chapter is about how to build contemporary architecture in Doha, the fast-changing capital of Qatar. One translation of the word Doha in Arabic is 'a place in the desert which is habitable'. But is the city really habitable, with temperatures in the high-40s°C and even low-50s°C for a few months each year, combined with its dust-ridden air and extreme humidity? Thanks to air-conditioning and the motor car, the answer is 'yes'. However does Doha offer as comfortable a lifestyle as it could, and if we look into the future, can this lifestyle be sustained or, even better, improved for citizens?

I will focus on a project for the rebirth of a significant piece of Doha's city centre, just south of the Amiri Diwan and west of the newly revived Souk Waqif. This ambitious project is being brought about by Msheireb Properties, an offspring of the Qatar Foundation, under the leadership of Her Highness Sheikha Mozah bint

18.1 Location map of Doha, Qatar, within the Gulf

18.2   General city plan of Doha showing the denser old centre next to the *corniche*

Nasser. The project began as the 'Heart of Doha' and indeed, when looking at the city's radiating plan, it lies right at the heart of the old city. Now it is being called Msheireb, the original name of this neighbourhood and which means 'Place of Sweet Water'. The Msheireb project consists of a high-density, medium-rise, mixed-use masterplan, covering about 35 hectares. The masterplan is by Arup and AECOM, the latter company having acquired EDAW, the design firm originally involved the project. My own part in the team, from the early days, as the lead partner on the project with Allies and Morrison was to act as the 'architectural voice' of the project. The discussion in this chapter will be specific to Doha, but it also relevant to the wider region where the rate of change, the level of ambition and the climate are all extreme.

18.3   The tree: rooted in the past, flourishing into the future

So what do I mean by rebirth or 'renaissance'? I am referring to the re-awakening, in a new form, both of a lifestyle and of an architectural language. In the words of Her Highness's brief, we should be 'looking to the future whilst being rooted in the past'. The image of a tree has under-pinned our thoughts. The roots run deep, to a large extent unseen; meanwhile the new growth flourishes; both are connected, and so it is a continuum.

So, looking at the past, were things better in the old days? In some respects, yes, and, in those ways,

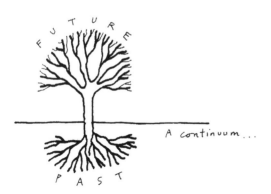

we should learn from and reflect them again now. Apart from the unarguable aim of achieving the highest levels of comfort and well-being for the people of Doha for the long-term future, we are also in search of a strengthened sense of belonging. In terms of the built environment, I would suggest that a sense of identity is a pre-requisite for 'making the most' of urban life, and it is reliant to a large degree on connecting to the past. In Doha this sense of identity seems to be largely dormant, and it is the aim of Msheireb Properties to help to reawaken it.

The identity of Doha is already, in some respects, very strong. If we look from above at the man-made road known as the Corniche, with the landfill area known as West Bay to the north of the city centre – the masterstroke of William Pereira's master-plan in the mid-1970s – we can see how the city is continually 'looking back at itself' across the water in a memorable way. This is surely the single most identifiable feature of the city and it gives a strong sense of orientation, at least when one is down by the water. In every other sense, the Corniche – and the city centre as a whole – offers much room for improvement, both in terms of urban lifestyle and architectural language. Cars currently dominate, and buildings sit as objects in space, rather than forming edges to streets and spaces which at present lack urban definition. It is hard to walk about, even when the weather is good (for at least half the year), as there are not enough pavements, crossings, and, most importantly, there is almost no shade.

18.4   West Bay in Doha from the air

18.5   West Bay at street level

18.6   The
Museum of Islamic
Art by I.M. Pei,
with the new city
rising behind

The Corniche connects two key parts of the city: the old centre, which now contains the Msheireb project, and the new developments in West Bay. They talk to each other across the water and Msheireb definitely has something to teach West Bay. I am a firm believer in West Bay as a place with great potential. I think it is good for Doha, but only at the 'macro' scale, and as just a chapter of an as yet unfinished story. At the moment this is not a place for pedestrians. It is not a place where the street is alive. Indeed in summertime, it is truly uninhabitable unless you are in a car or an air-conditioned building. Nonetheless, it is a highly successful new address within the city, and it is part of the old town/new town dynamic which – with emerging landmarks such as I.M. Pei's Islamic Museum – is setting Doha in a good direction for the future.

The commercial towers of West Bay, whatever one thinks of their individual designs, are spectacular from a distance, particularly at dusk – but that is not enough. They do not cohere: if they were a choir, their music would be a cacophony. As objects they do not make places for people, other than for those inside their glass-clad, air-conditioned forms. Most importantly they do not contribute to a sense of identity which grows out of, or fits into, Qatari tradition. In other words, they are not rooted.

To complement and contrast with this, the Msheireb project envisages a city of arcaded streets and carved-out urban spaces. It offers shade, pedestrian priority and human scale. For Qatari families, it offers an alternative to living in a

18.7   The floating structure of the Msheireb Enrichment Centre,
by Allies and Morrison, with the backdrop of West Bay

18.8   Solidere in central Beirut, Lebanon

box-like villa in the suburbs, surrounded by a wall where, to get anywhere, one has to get in the car. It also aims to offer a harmonious kind of architecture in which, whoever the architect is for a given block, the space between buildings is more important than the buildings themselves, and the common architectural language – in whatever accent it is spoken in – consistently connects this important piece of the city back to its roots. Although from a very different part of the Middle East, the old centre of Beirut is a relevant example of this kind of successful urbanism.

The story of Msheireb begins, as with so much of the history of the city, on 11th October 1939. 'Petroleum Development Qatar. Have had slight show of oil in their test well near Zekrit. Drilling continues' read the telegram sent by the British political agent in Bahrain at the time. If one looks at old photographs of Doha in 1952, one can see clearly the 'old town' of Doha – developed over centuries and based on fishing, pearl diving and trading. Slightly to the west, the 'new town' began to develop fast during the 1950s. The Al Koot Fort and the Eid Ground, which used to be right on the edge of the city, now lie between the older and the newer parts. Al Kahraba Street was laid out then but not yet built up. Legend has it that its soft curve arose from the haphazard rolling out of Doha's first electrical cable (not quite pulled straight) by a British engineer.

The old photographs of Doha also gave essential clues as to how Msheireb could meet Her Highness's brief. Given that our urban site was in the area that was being developed throughout the 1940s and 1950s, modernity was clearly then a driving force; however, there was still at that point a connection between the city of the past and that of the future. Every street held old memories, and, although many of the streets of the Msheireb site are somewhat tired and unloved now, their stories are there to be cherished – and new chapters are still to be told.

The Arup/AECOM masterplan for Msheireb is a *tour-de-force* of how to balance geometry with informality in response to the historic irregularities of the site and to the 'organic' urban tradition of the wider Gulf region (see Plate 28). It is also an exemplar of sustainable urban design at the macro-scale, both in the context of Doha – in terms of the lifestyle changes it will offer – and the degree to which it can serve as a catalyst for urban change in the coming decades. A determining factor in the masterplan has been the local climate, and this led to a number of objectives: how to maximise shade and optimise the use of wind to keep public spaces cool; how in particular to make the 'shoulder months' between summer and winter as comfortable as possible; and how to promote pedestrian movement and minimise reliance on the car. To this end, the strong prevailing wind from the north-west has informed a north-south grain for the block layout, within which the roof forms are used to catch the wind, cast shade and harvest solar energy.

The master-plan is also ambitious in terms of the provision of shared infrastructure and the use of basements. This makes possible a fine urban grain, a traffic-calmed environment and sustainable energy systems on a larger scale. More importantly, however, it is a master-plan based on places and connections, old and new, and of activities and events. It is this complex mix of uses and the framework of carved-out urban spaces which I believe are the key to the plan. These make a

setting for, and a physical manifestation of, memory past and memory future – and thus they make Msheireb a firm part of the continuum of Doha's history.

Msheireb is not the first significant change in the old city centre in the 21st century. Immediately to the east lies the Souk Waqif, an old market which dates back well over a hundred years. In recent few years it has been reborn as a place to shop, eat, drink and promenade, with huge success. Its style and its scale are firmly rooted in the past, without any particular response to the future, and in that respect Msheireb offers something different. However, in terms of urban space and spirit, there is a direct connection, in particular where the southeast corner of Msheireb meets the *souk* and the two worlds are joined to create a continuum.

One of Allies and Morrison's roles within the master-planning team has been to draft the architectural guidelines. These are encapsulated in what we call the 'Seven Steps'; in other words, seven guiding principles for all development in Msheireb project. The first step is 'Continuity'; the general principle that there must be a link between the past and the future. All design has timeless qualities and we are continually reinterpreting the past in new ways. Whether it be the elaboration of a shading screen with the use of patterning, or the proportioning of a solid wall with openings made up of substantial horizontals and verticals, in either case, the new can 'grow out of' the old – and thereby achieve a relevance and powerful resonance with its roots.

18.9   Model of the Msheireb master-plan showing its fine urban grain

18.10   Continuity as expressed by the Al Mana House in Doha

The second step is the 'Balance between Individual and Collective'. If we look at an ordinary street wall around the Souk Waqif, we can see that is made up of many buildings, each touching its neighbours, and together forming the urban backdrop. The elements are all related but, just like a family, every member is an individual. The street image has a visual richness and an engaging informality which seems to balance unity and diversity. None of the buildings shout 'look at me', but together they sing a harmonious song. Part of this particular harmony in the old city, which I believe is also relevant to Msheireb, is the style-less robustness of the everyday architecture; it is something evolved over centuries both for cultural and technical reasons. Step two therefore urges designers, except in selected landmark sites, to emulate this 'team spirit' and promote the primacy of the street wall. In this way, not only will we achieve a coherent piece of city but, in my view, we will realise the particular beauty of a richly variegated but cohesive street frontage – something which would be impossible if we encouraged every building to make its own statement.

Step three is the 'Relationship between Space and Form'. It intends to highlight the soft informality of the 1950s plan of Doha, a pattern of organic growth where the right angle is not dominant. On the basis that, with the occasional exception of object-like buildings such as the Al Koot Fort, the buildings form a kind of 'urban clay' – in that out of them are carved the streets, the narrow alleys (*sikkas*), the informal urban courtyards (*barahas*) which act as sitting places outside houses, and the major spaces such as the market place or the Burial Ground – then it calls for a common spirit to prevail across the site.

18.11   Sketch of Doha in 1952 showing its space and form

18.12   The *fereej* housing cluster redesigned for the 21st century in the Msheireb project

This collective urban spirit is typical of development through the centuries all around the Gulf. Looking again at West Bay, we can see that there is no 'mutual relationship' between its object-like forms and the spaces between buildings. As a result, its urban spaces lack both quality and cohesiveness. If the majority of buildings were 'edges' rather than 'objects', the streetscape would become far more positive. Indeed the same principle applies to the individual dwelling in old Doha, where the interior space of the courtyard is traditionally the focus of activity, and is given a positive form. Even in the making of rooms and the massing of roofscapes, the spirit of 'carved clay' still prevails.

The fourth step deals with 'Aspects of the Home'. We now return to the notion of 'renaissance', or rebirth, of a lost but fondly remembered lifestyle which is reinvented to suit the needs and expectations of the 21st-century Qatari family. The question underlying step four is: 'Can we create a viable and truly appealing alternative to comfortable family life in a suburban villa, transposed into the city centre?' In other terms, will we be able to bring Qatari families – whose parents and grand-parents grew up in the old city – back to the urban centre? Can they enjoy space and comfort that is not just equal to but better than they are now used to? I believe the answer is yes.

As a set of urban principles, this step ranges from the macro-scale to the micro. It sets out a direction for how neighbourhoods will be organised, how outdoor space (both private and communal) will be configured, how new homes should be arranged, and how entrances and rooftops can be made the most of. These ideas apply to apartments as well as family houses. One of the unusual, indeed groundbreaking, aspects of the Msheireb project is the rebirth of the urban *fereej*, the cluster of private family houses in a neighbourhood which share a

18.13   Communal gardens as part of the new Qatari urban living

communal courtyard garden and a communal meeting/entertaining building (*majlis*) for neighbours to use, which is also a place to receive male guests, and rooftop sitting areas. Much work has therefore been done on this aspect, looking at traditional Qatari courtyard houses as well as other house types. The smallest houses in the Msheireb are similar in size to a typical suburban villa in Doha, and many indeed are larger. Every house will have its own integral private garage, at the lowest level, beneath the main entrance floor and the communal garden. Meanwhile, the key to achieving the levels of privacy which residents will expect – in spite of living in closer proximity to their neighbours than they are used to – is the courtyard design. Houses will therefore be relatively

18.14   Solid walls provide privacy in the dwellings, yet the interiors are still flooded with light

closed to the outside street, with carefully modelled walls used to bring in daylight while maintaining privacy. On the inside, however, the courtyards will be very open, and will give residents the ability to open up the house for indoor/outdoor living when the weather is good.

Specific building details are also set out in the guidelines, such as ways of using *mashrabiya* screens to achieve privacy and shading, while also separating the formal part of the house from the family zone. As a lifestyle offer, this is certainly something very new for Doha, as well as for the wider Gulf region. To be able to live in an ample house of 700 m² with a swimming pool on the roof, private courtyard and a communal garden with a shared *majlis* – and all within a few minutes' walk of Doha's best shops, hotels, cultural buildings, schools and public spaces, and the Souk Waqif, National Eid Ground and Amiri Diwan – will for some soon become a reality. To have a three-car garage at the bottom of your house, but then to find that you hardly need to use your car, it means less time spent in traffic jams and more time spent at home or out enjoying the city. It is hence a sustainable vision in a deeper sense than just reducing carbon footprints.

To return to the 'Seven Steps', the fifth step relates to 'Aspects of the Street'. This refers to how one can create a successful continuum of urban spaces, connected to each other and to the surrounding context, in terms both of movement, activity and design character. The guidelines discuss the ways to reflect a strong urban hierarchy; how to manifest and celebrate differences such as between the grand public square of the project (Barahat al Nouq) and the quiet *sikkas* nearby, with an appropriate architectural eloquence. Step five also asks an important question: 'How should buildings meet the ground, how do people relate to the new street frontages as they walk by, and, bearing in mind the heat, will they be comfortable on the streets?' The designs suggest ways in which buildings and the spaces between buildings can make the street a positive place to be in, through the use of extensive shading, arcades and carefully tuned frontages.

If one goes today to Souk Waqif on a warm Thursday night and remember that, only five years ago, people wouldn't have been out and about in the city centre in this manner (except perhaps on the Corniche), then one can see that this desire to meander, and to flow – be it for shopping, eating out or just watching people and bumping into friends – is very much alive and wanting to

18.15   Privacy and shade are achieved with the use of *mashrabiya* screens

18.16   The dwellings have ample space for cars but are set within a walkable city

18.17   Al Kahraba Street North, Msheireb, by Adjaye Associates and Burton Studio

expand its territory. At the western end of the *souk*, where it currently comes to a dead end, is precisely where Msheireb will connect and pick up the flow of people that is already happening. It is from this point that a new set of journeys will begin; whether on the large scale or small scale, busy or quiet. These are journeys that will join up important new places such as Nakheel Square (the location for the new metro station at the south-western corner of the scheme), with old places re-born such as Kahraba Street or Al Rayyan Road.

Continuing the theme of creating a comfortable and sustainable environment – one that will be successful in the longer term – the theme of step six is 'Designing for Climate'. This brings us back to being rooted in the past while looking to the future. New technology is opening up extraordinary horizons for low-energy design, especially when applied on the infrastructural scale of Msheireb project. However the old tricks are often the best ones and indeed 'designing for climate' is nothing new in Qatar. Old techniques such as the 'breathing wall' (*malqaf*), the shaded buffer zone (*liwan* or *shanasheel*), or simply the use of high thermal mass in buildings, are still highly relevant today. Whether such techniques are used as direct references or are reworked in new approaches to design, they represent a basic human impulse: 'How do I achieve the most, or the best, out of the least'. Hence a significant part of step six goes beyond the basic need to deliver optimum performance with minimum energy and minimum waste. It simply seeks to offer choice to users. Can I open the window? Am I able to control my own environment? Can I enjoy being outside when the weather is good?

18.18   *Malqaf*, or 'breathing wall', in a traditional Qatari house

Finally, the seventh step is that of a 'New Architectural Language', an echo of the Italian Renaissance nearly 600 years ago. When Brunelleschi designed the Pazzi Chapel in Florence

in1429, we only have to look at the column details to see that he was learning from ancient buildings such as the Pantheon in Rome, built thirteen centuries before. However, he was not copying them. Brunelleschi's architecture was something radically new, both for his own age and in relation to his ancient sources. He had decoded the 'architectural DNA' of his culture and reconstructed it for his own time. The timespan of the Italian Renaissance was far longer than Doha's more recent architectural history, but nonetheless it is a relevant parallel to the aims of Msheireb. The fact that there had been a loss of continuity between the architecture of ancient Rome and that of the Italian Renaissance is echoed by the fact that there has been a gap between the 'timeless' architecture of Qatar in the pre-oil era, and the metal-and-glass architecture of Doha today. The architecture of Msheireb seeks to bridge this gap.

So what aspects of traditional Qatari architecture does step seven highlight as forming the basis for the grammar and vocabulary of a new language, and what will make this uniquely Qatari? Taking our key references from buildings such as Souk Waqif, the heritage houses already on the Msheireb site, and the coastal town of Al Wakrah just south of Doha, some clear themes emerge. The robust, simple architecture of the thick wall, with predominantly rectangular openings, is the dominant theme; this is then enriched with layers, recesses and the 'split wall' detail of the wind-catchers (*malqafs*) and the projecting *danshals* of mangrove wood, so valuable in those days that the poles were allowed to project, rather than being sawn flush. Within this overall design, areas of patterning are then used either as gypsum reliefs, to highlight important elements such as inner linings and doorways, or as *mashrabiya* screens for privacy and shade. Together it creates an architecture which comes alive in sunlight and shadow.

18.19   The play of shadow and light on old Qatari buildings

(*above left*)
18.20   A traditional *naqsh* pattern as a screen

(*above right*)
18.21   New door motif based on a Qatari mangrove pattern

(*below*)
18.22   Model of the Msheireb Mosque by Allies and Morrison

The thick wall thus acts as the 'clay' out of which the softly irregular urbanism of step three can be carved. It is also the medium for sculpting the asymmetrical but balanced forms of the traditional Qatari skyline. But is this specifically a Qatari feature, or is it simply part of the architectural tradition of the wider Gulf region? It is clear that over the centuries, maritime communities all around the Gulf have been sharing many aspects of an architectural language. If we look at a *sikka* in Kish Island in Iran or a *sikka* at Al Wakrah in Qatar, they are almost indistinguishable. However it is the subtle differences which are most telling and hence the seventh step also calls on designers in the Msheireb project to find inspiration in the particular characteristics of Qatari sources.

In the three main zones (base, middle and top), architectural elements are illustrated as being potential roots and seeds from which the new branches and leaves of an authentic contemporary language can grow. Proportional details are examined, as is the use of arches within a predominantly post-and-beam language to emphasise entrances. The deep colonnade or balcony (*liwan*), the projecting bay window (*shanasheel*), the projecting beam (*danshal*) and the expressed rain spout (*marzam*) are all illustrated as potential references in the guidelines, as are the use of external stair cases with solid balustrades and the carved joinery elements for doors, windows and shutters. Materials and colours are other important parts of the guidance given for the Msheireb designers,

18.23   Msheireb Enrichment Centre by Allies and Morrison

18.24   Organic urban form mixing new and old in the Msheireb project

since they are a key to achieving the level of cohesion described in step two, balanced with richness and diversity. Stone – albeit never traditionally used in Doha in the form of smooth-cut dressed ashlar – is also being encouraged, particularly on primary street frontages. The selection of stone, however, has to be held within the traditionally tight palette of soft whites, light greys and sand colours, and this also includes the most typical traditional Qatari finish, hand-smoothed white render. In terms of composition and hierarchy, we are seeking a spirit of asymmetrical balance which is found throughout traditional Qatari architecture. The modelling of roofscapes, or the modulation of parapet lines, or the positioning of entrances, are all informal but controlled. Doha's skyline will thereby be enriched. This three-dimensional characteristic goes hand-in-hand with the 'softened geometry' of the traditional house plan and the 'organic' urban grain of historic towns and villages around the Gulf region generally (see Plate 29).

Different designers will thus come to Msheireb with different philosophies, and this indeed will be part of the quality and character of this new piece of city. It is essential that the emphasis on the past is used to add to, not detract from the authenticity and integrity of individual new works of architecture. Pastiche is out of the question. Our series of underlying principles of construction, building organisation and climatic response will surely form a primary link between the past and the future but, in a contemporary way. Direct quotations or references (literal or non-literal) can also be used to make the link, be they in terms of architectural elements or from other Qatari archetypes. For example, the language of *dhows* or tents may inform the roofscape of buildings, with timber and canvas being used for shading structures. Putting together this language is indeed an exercise in cultural decoding and, as with any such code, the solution is not obvious but the result should be meaningful.

The intention of these seven steps is therefore to establish a 'base beat' for diverse architectural approaches within the project; a 'Qatari Contemporary' vernacular. As with any vernacular, a common language can bring cohesion without suppressing diversity, expression or accent. Our intention as foreign designers working in Qatar is to prepare fertile ground for a 'home-grown', indigenous architecture to evolve. As gardeners we do not brings the seeds but we do help them to grow into healthy and deeply rooted plants.

Allies and Morrison's major project within the Msheireb exemplifies many of the above principles, and is currently on site. It is known as the Diwan Amiri Quarter and it comprises three government buildings: the Diwan Annex, the Amiri Guards Headquarters and the National Archive of Qatar. Together they form one of the primary frontages of the whole project, and a link between the site and its surrounding urban context. Our site is rich in memory and in terms of clues for a design response which can grow out of the location. To the north lies Al Rayyan Rd with the existing Amiri Diwan and the Majsid al Sheikh opposite, and the Corniche road beyond. To the east are the Burial Ground, the Al Koot Fort and Souk Waqif. To the south, the National Eid Ground and the low-lying heritage houses – recently reconstructed – provide a direct inspiration and a backdrop for the new buildings we are proposing. The site is 300 m long and irregular in shape, and these

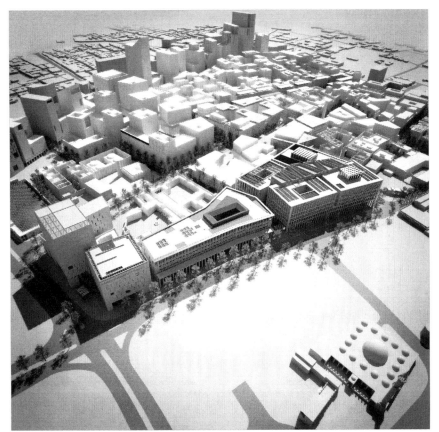

18.25   Diwan Amiri Quarter (Msheireb Phase 1), by Allies and Morrison, seen from the north-east

irregularities, which stem from its history, have generated the particular forms of our design. The siting of each building falls naturally into place, with the Diwan Annex at the western end, facing the southern axis of the Amiri Diwan; the Guards Headquarters in the middle, controlling the security of the site; and the National Archive at the eastern end, facing the Corniche, and turning eastwards also to face the Burial Ground and the Souk Waqif.

The brief for each of the three buildings by Allies and Morrison is unique, bringing its own response. Each building is rooted in a particular Qatari archetype: the fortified tower for the National Archive: the fort and courtyard dwelling for the Guards Headquarters; and the *liwan*-encased small palace (*diwania*) for the Diwan Annex. They act as a family of buildings, all related, but each one is seen as an individual. Beginning with the requirement that all office windows should be openable, the Diwan Annex has been given a double-layer *liwan*, made of simple post-and-beam stone construction, on all its external facades. This forms a security buffer and gives privacy and shade, while making useable balconies for each office and giving clear views. The outer layer of each facade differs in design in response to its particular solar exposure. The Diwan Annex is large – its footprint is about 130 m in both directions – and so to bring it back into scale with the grain of the Msheireb master-plan, it has been sliced into four pieces. Each of these four blocks

18.26   Covered street within the Diwan Annex

has its own rectilinear geometry, but due to the non-rectangular street pattern, they sit at four different angles. Where they meet an irregular space is created, which we call the 'Covered Street'. This is an enclosed and cooled space, providing a buffer space to the offices, but its facades have also been treated as if they were external, with galleries on every level and bridges connecting between the blocks. The roof of this space oversails the cornice line, helping to maintain its street-like feel. The 'Covered Street' runs through the heart of the building and will be the place of social interaction for the thousands of people working there.

18.27   New colonnade along the Al-Rayyan Road

The primary street frontage for all three buildings is along Al Rayyan Road to the north, forming a new backdrop to the Amiri Diwan, and the Masjid al Sheikh. Al Rayyan Road is one of the oldest streets of Doha, as witnessed by the line of existing *diwania* which form its strongly defined edges at the western end. It is being transformed into a ceremonial street with the ability to be closed to traffic for public promenading or for civic events. Meanwhile, the all-important security control mechanisms are integrated into ceremonial gateways. Part of the challenge of placing high-security government buildings in the context of an urban street has been met with the colonnades which run the full length of the site, joining the three buildings in our quarter. Unlike the arcades elsewhere in the Msheireb, these will not have shops and cafes; rather, they make a place where citizens can enjoy the 'Lyric History', an anthology of ancient poetry on the theme of Qatar's history, which will be carved into the white marble-fluted walls running between the main entrances – while also forming a security cordon to vehicles.

The main entrances front onto Al Rayyan Road as part of this colonnade, and each one is elaborated with a language of patterning. Areas of pattern are used in bold and simple ways to highlight doorways, gates and inner linings. These patterns are not reproductions from elsewhere. They are uniquely generated from a number of Qatari motifs; from natural features such as the waterways of Al Khor, from archaeological treasures such as the ancient carvings of Jebel al Jessassiyah, or from found objects that are part of the site's history. Together, these patterns combine ancient Arabic traditions of pattern-making based on an underlying rectilinear grid, with modern digital techniques, both in terms of drawing them out and also for production in stone and metal. This is another way in which the link is made between the past and the future, and between contemporary architecture and its context.

The main VIP entrance to the quarter sits between the Diwan Annex and the Guards Headquarters. The Guards block is set back behind the colonnade,

18.28   CNC-cut pattern in marble, which is then photographed, hand-traced and digitized to create the stone finish for the Diwan Annex

18.29   North facade of the Amiri Guards Headquarters by Allies and Morrison

18.30 Courtyard of the Amiri Guards Headquarters

while the facade of the Diwan Annex is brought to the front line. The Guards Headquarters is a carved and moulded building, both inside and out. Its low courtyard form is a contextual response to the history of the site and to the traditional houses immediately to the south, as well to the brief. Three floors of accommodation (one for each company of soldiers) wrap around the central parade ground, with communal spaces at ground level and the officer's mess and roof terrace at the top. The stone facades of the Guards Headquarters echo the layered thick walls of the neighbouring traditional buildings. On the south side, white render is used rather than stone, in response to the historic Company House on the other side of the Sikka Mohammed, the winding lane which runs between the Diwan Amiri buildings and the heritage cluster of the masterplan. While the courtyard follows the irregular shape of the site, the building's roof oversails the central space, with a rectangular cut-out that follows the primary geometry. This ambitious roof structure serves as a support for photovoltaic cells and a wind-catcher, while also shading the fabric of the building itself to reduce solar gain.

At the eastern end, the design for the National Archive brings the theme of the historic urban patterns of Doha to a climax. This building wraps around the smallest of the three heritage houses, Radwani House, a remnant of the old city when this area was densely covered with houses, tightly packed together in

18.31   National Archive of Qatar seen from the Eid Ground

an organic pattern, evolved over time. The site's informal three-part geometry is extruded into three carved blocks built of stone and of differing heights to accommodate the three functions of the brief. The archive stack, held between the public wing and the support building, forms a focal point for views from the Corniche, the Burial Ground and the Eid Ground. The Radwani House is seen as a piece of 'treasure', both symbolic and actual, which becomes the oral history department for the Archive. The book stack is then raised above a grand columned portico, framing views of the old house, and making connections with the narrow *sikkas* and *barahas* found in the heritage and cultural quarters.

The National Archive is scaled to speak urbanistically from a distance and to reveal further layers of story-telling at closer range. Traditional details are reflected in contemporary ways. Carved stone cills project, echoing the traditional rain spout (*marzam*) detail, and casting changing shadows on the facades as the sun moves through the day. The National Anthem is carved at a large scale onto the east facade, to be read from far off, while calligraphy is used throughout the building to embody Qatar's narrative traditions. In summary, the building is regarded both as a durable container and a lasting symbol for Qatar's archive – the memory of a nation, past, present and future.

In conclusion, these three buildings – along with the other designs that are now on the drawing boards of a range of architects for the subsequent Msheireb phases

18.32   Msheireb seen from the south-east, above Souk Waqif

– while being contemporary are also rooted in the past. They grow out of the place where they come from and they thus fit into the tapestry and identity of that place, with its memories, its forms, and its idiosyncratic character. In that sense, although our buildings, when completed soon, are going to be new, we hope that they will feel natural, resonant and harmonious (see Plate 30). The vision of Msheireb Properties is to create a lasting piece of city, and it is our hope that Msheireb will indeed become the starting point for a new Renaissance in Doha – both in terms of urban lifestyle and architectural language, and one which will continue to be enjoyed by future generations.

19

The Scale of Globalisation

Murray Fraser

What the previous chapters each show, in their different ways, is the complex relationship between architecture, urbanism, cultural identity and globalisation. There can be little doubt that the cities around the Persian Gulf have undergone a process of urbanisation and modernisation over the past few decades; they are clearly not the same places they used to be. But as previous accounts of urban modernisation reveal – with the classic still being Marshall Berman's *All that is Solid Melts into Air* – it is far from being an even or consistent process.[1] The effects of uneven modernisation around the Gulf have been discussed throughout the chapters of this book. Today there are now the almost tired older centres of development such as Abadan/Khorramshahr or Kuwait City or Dammam; as well as busy newcomers like Manama or Doha or Abu Dhabi or Sharjah, epitomised above all by Dubai; or indeed the places in Iran where modernisation has the most potential to rush ahead in future, including Bushehr, Kangan/Banak, Bandar Abbas, Qeshm, and, above all, Kish Island. In general, the cities on the western Arabic coastline are larger and more central to their own country's economic and cultural life, while those on the eastern side tend to be far smaller and more marginal within Iran, at least for the present. This final chapter will not attempt to force any simple conclusion, especially given that modernising processes and their effects are still so uncertain in the Persian Gulf. Instead, I will set out some thoughts about the subject of architectural globalisation and also point to new tendencies, drawn from a critical perspective, which can suggest other ways to design for Gulf cities in the years ahead.

From the outset, I should make clear that I am not a fan of the usual definitions of globalisation within architectural discourse. Critics have rightly warned of the danger of treating globalisation as if it were somehow a natural and inevitable process.[2] But it seems equally dangerous to portray globalisation as if it were merely a construct of neo-liberal economics which architecture have then to decide whether to 'react against', 'work within', etc.[3] What is needed instead is to find ways of talking about globalisation that do not simply play into the hands

of the powerful elites which currently dominate global capitalism – instead, the aim ought to be to pull apart the material and ideological mystifications of globalisation.

We have to do this because globalisation, however it is defined, is the crucial transformation of our age. All other issues, including our widespread worries about climate change and loss of biodiversity, follow in its train. Yet it is equally obvious that architecture still has a difficult time in adapting its discourses and practices to suit global conditions. What is often referred to as architectural globalisation often doesn't have that much to do with it, or else stems from its least interesting or appealing aspects. Instead, there needs to be fresh thinking about architectural globalisation, something I will attempt in this essay by arguing for a change in conceptions of scale away from the *dimensions* of form and space, to the *dynamics* of form and space. It is a process already happening through

19.1   Hong Kong and Shanghai Bank in Hong Kong by Foster + Partners (1983–1986)

the emerging conditions of globalisation, as will be seen later when referring to some of the architectural initiatives now underway in the Persian Gulf – i.e. in a region of the world, as this book has shown, which offers an exemplar for studying the impact of globalising processes.

First, however, it is worth spelling out some of the problems with normal views about architectural globalisation. This can be done by considering three canonical buildings: the Hong Kong Shanghai Bank in Hong Kong, designed by Foster & Partners (1983–1986), the Guggenheim Museum in Bilbao by Frank Gehry (1993–

19.2
Guggenheim
Museum in Bilbao
by Frank Gehry
(1993–1997)

1997), and the Chinese Central TV Headquarters in Beijing by Rem Koolhaas/OMA (2004–2012).They have often been cited as icons of architectural globalisation from each of the last three decades. Yet in fact they are but part of a far older pattern of dominance whereby a few countries – firstly in Europe and later the USA – held cultural sway over what were regarded as relatively undeveloped or 'backward' places. Thus these three iconic buildings exist because of the imposition of supposedly 'superior' ideas and values from outside, and thus from above. It is certainly noticeable that none of the buildings picked up anything from engagement with its context that went on to change the subsequent designs of their respective architects in any meaningful way. It is the old pattern of imperialism and colonisation by any other name, once again making a fetish out of the public display of power and wealth.

Rem Koolhaas, the CCTV's designer, is one of the smartest architects around, and as such is more than aware of that key tactic of the avant-garde, which is to declare a contradictory position to what one is actually doing while also showing one is aware of doing this. Hence we find an astonishingly self-conscious quote from Koolhaas in *Der Spiegel* when he says:

19.3   CCTV Building in Beijing by Rem Koolhaas/ OMA (2004–2012)

> *I have a very hard time with the expression "star architect". It gives the impression of referring to people with no heart, egomaniacs who are constantly doing their thing, completely divorced from any context ...* [4]

And if that were not an astute piece of auto-critique, Koolhaas goes on to talk of the consequences for the 'star architect' in designing too quickly for yet another contentious brief in a place they know little about:

> *... There is less time available for research, so a tendency toward imitation develops. One of our theories is that one can offset this excessive compulsion toward the spectacular with a return to simplicity. That's one effect of speed.* [5]

From such a statement it is only a step to the empty symbolism of buildings such as the so-called 'peace pyramid' in Astana by Foster & Partners, opened in 2006 for the autocratic ruler of Kazakhstan, or Zaha Hadid's 'space age' concoction for the SOHO Galaxy offices in Beijing (2010–2012). If this really were to be the end-goal of architecture after all those millennia of human society, then we might as well pack up and go home. But if we remind ourselves that what Koolhaas, Foster, Gehry, and now Hadid, are up to has relatively little to do with globalisation as such, then there can be another way forward.

19.4   SOHO
Galaxy in Beijing
by Zaha Hadid
(2010–2012)

A similar problem exists in writings about architecture and globalisation. These texts tend to be rather limited in conception, and focus on one particular aspect such as the architecture associated with global finance (Anthony King), the internationalisation of design practices (Donald McNeill), or the possibility of an alternative regionalist approach (Liane Lefaivre and Alexander Tzonis), rather than attempting to write about the subject in a more rounded manner.[6] A more in-depth analysis of contemporary globalisation has been published recently by Robert Adam, although his book too approaches the subject from what is an overly specific viewpoint, being largely concerned with how cultural identity can or cannot be expressed visually in architecture under globalising conditions.[7]

The resulting problem is that when we read accounts of architectural globalisation we tend to find authors lazily falling back onto one or more of the usual myths – one could even call them fallacies – about globalisation. Although each contains a trace of truth, as myths generally do, the net effect is to diminish the discussion of the subject. To tease this point out further, the five common fallacies can be categorised as follows:

1.   **The economic fallacy**: i.e. that globalisation is essentially all about the working of multinational capitalism and its concomitant financial markets, money flows, and digitalised data transfers. This is of course an ideologically driven reification of globalisation which only ultimately serves corporate interests, stripping the term of any broader validity and reducing it to its most utilitarian tendencies. It is an attitude which also beleaguers even much of the best critical writing on globalisation, such as by Joseph Stiglitz or Hardt and Negri.[8] And what the reductive economic viewpoint conceals above all is that cultural globalisation is by far the most vital component in the whole process,

and indeed happens irrespective of problems with financial flows – as has been revealed during the worldwide recession that began in 2008 and which as yet shows little sign of ending in most countries.

2. **The homogenisation fallacy**: i.e. that globalisation is about smoothing out everything and creating a single world order, whereas in actuality it is constantly creating new kinds of difference and heterogeneity, and in ways that will never be uniform or consistent. As Henri Lefebvre once remarked, definitively: 'No space disappears in the course of growth and development: the worldwide does not abolish the local.'[9] Hence the dyspeptic vision of global uniformity has to be viewed instead as a symptom of deeper cultural anxiety about social change. Liane Lefaivre and Alexander Tzonis are particularly representative of this condition, for instance having written:

> As globalization increasingly enters every facet of our lives, its homogenizing
> effects on architecture, urban spaces and the landscape have compelled
> architects to embrace the principles of critical regionalism, an alternative theory
> that respects local culture, geography and climate.[10]

As an observation it is totally wrong, of course, and as Mark Crinson and others point out too easily, critical regionalism is an inherently conservative viewpoint in which the original sense of a political critique of capitalism is lost, leaving only backward-looking romanticism.[11] One could also voice the same point by taking another quote:

> Some fear that the world is coming to dreadful uniformity and monotony. If so,
> this day is yet far off. At present we may shudder at the terrific, often senseless,
> variety of it all.[12]

The only problem is that the quote happens to be over 70 years old! It comes from Richard Neutra, an émigré Austrian architect in the USA back in the 1930s, and could be used word-for-word as a response to the doomsayers today.

3. **The origination fallacy**: i.e. that it is only about 'Americanisation' or 'Westernisation', when in fact globalisation is far more precisely defined as the condition that has arisen because of the ending of the post-war era of US hegemony. To many outside observers, America is now a quasi-empire in decline, as can be shown by economic figures: whereas in the mid-1960s the USA was estimated to account for about half of the world's combined economy, today that figure is only about 25 per cent, and is falling. Although the US still possesses the biggest economy in the world, recent UN data shows that China overtook America in 2010 as the largest manufacturing nation, following a meteoric rise over the previous five years.[13] As with Britain a century ago, America is now in the process of being economically eclipsed by other countries, with particularly China, India, Brazil and Russia forging a more complex balance of global power. This is why it is so important to keep in mind a broader historical

account of globalisation, rather than sloppily confusing it as being equivalent to modernity, or to post-war American hegemony in the Cold War era. Instead, those might well have been its preconditions, but what we now conceive as globalisation emerged after the 'Oil Crisis' in the mid-1970s, along with other early signals of fading US hegemony.[14]

4.   **The novelty fallacy**: i.e. that globalisation is an entirely new phenomenon, whereas of course it is being built on top of centuries-old structures of world trade and imperial conquest, and if anything is somewhat patched up and shaky. Indeed, the global movement of people seems the normative condition for humankind, and hence concepts of nationality or cultural fixity – as dominated during the age of 'high' capitalism – were perhaps more of a blip in history. Even the briefest glimpse at the Taj Mahal or Oxford's Radcliffe Camera or the Hospital of Santo Antonio in Porto or Le Corbusier's designs for Chandigarh – to cite just four of the countless examples available – shows that many seminal buildings are designed in complete contrast to indigenous traditions, yet have been welcomed and adopted as belonging to a place. Or to put it another way, if we believe geneticists like Steve Jones, then the mixing together of the global gene pool has always the main driving force for human societies, and modern technological lifestyles simply accelerate the process.[15] It this is indeed the case, then the current fascination with multicultural cities and hybrid architecture echoes this underlying genetic trend.

5.   **The technological fallacy**: i.e. that globalisation is driven by trans-spatial technology and thus is essentially about information flows, digital telecommunications, the internet, long-haul air travel, etc. These technologies have even invented their own fictions such as cyberspace or the global internet map. But while these trans-spatial technologies undoubtedly aid the spread of globalisation, again they remain something different. So whenever one hears that globalisation is failing because of technical problems with the internet, such as viral attacks or cyber wars, it is entirely misguided. Technology can only ever be a concretization of existing social relations, never a major driver in itself, and therefore globalisation occurs irrespective of technology. Let us also not forget that technology tends never to be used in the ways it was intended, nor in the end can it offer solutions as such, only different methods of organising things. As David Edgerton usefully reminds us, in general it is older forms of technology which work better.[16]

Having identified the five fallacies which prevail in normative discourse about architectural globalisation, it becomes obvious that we need a far more dynamic and nuanced formulation. If one looks at other academic disciplines, there has been a more searching effort to define globalisation, thereby revealing aspects that are extremely relevant to architectural production. Here, for example, is a definition from the German social philosopher, Jurgen Habermas:

> By 'globalisation' is meant the cumulative processes of a worldwide expansion
> of trade and production, commodity and finance markets, fashions, the media

*and computer programs, news and communication networks, transportation
systems and flows of migration, the risks engendered by large-scale technology,
environmental damage and epidemics, as well as organised crime and
terrorism.*[17]

Analysed in this way, globalisation is revealed as a complex and intertwined network in which multiple points of influence impact on each other, and these in turn are influenced by interaction with countless other nodes. Globalisation can thus be conceived as a field in which a multitude of actors and agencies are constantly operating, rather than the linear process with unmediated flows of influence under 'classic' imperialism. This suggests a cultural model that rejects binary divisions such as centre/periphery, global/regional or global/local – or indeed any notion that a single ethnic group or country can hold some kind of truth which they then 'diffuse' or 'disseminate' to others via colonisation or other means. Instead, what do exist are complex trans-cultural networks of exchange in which any attempt to posit a hierarchy is futile. The result of all this, as many observers point out, is that the defining basis of globalisation is the hybrid.[18] Above all, global hybridity creates and also thrives in a condition which is heterogenic, fluid and fissured.

Hence what architecture requires is a deeper vision of globalisation closer to what Stuart Hall terms 'globalisation from below', by which he refers to the mass movement of people across the world and the opening up of cultural practices like architecture at a fundamental level.[19] Much of this human movement is of course driven by desperation and fear, and is deeply traumatic and exploitative; it can also be said to do little to alter existing imbalances of power in societies. Yet nonetheless it opens up greater opportunity and hope than existed previously for the majority of the world's people. Globalisation is therefore not at all synonymous with the tough invisible processes of top-down 'economic globalisation' as described by analysts like Saskia Sassen, although such factors are indeed part of it.[20] Instead it is the cultural changes deriving from the migration of people and their ideas which offer the greatest creative potential for architecture in a rapidly transforming world. As one example, a few years ago the British building press reported, somewhat excitedly, that a third of people in architectural offices had been born overseas: yet there wasn't even a flicker of concern – with most believing the figure was probably higher, especially in London. If British architecture can be seen as healthier than ever, which certainly appears the case, to a large extent this is a product of those who were not born British. One only has to look at Zaha Hadid (Iraq) or David Adjaye (Tanzania/Ghana) or Niall McLaughlin (Ireland), and so on, or at buildings by the likes of Herzog and de Meuron (Switzerland), designers of the Tate Modern, to realise just how vital non-Brits are in energising the scene.

What is required is a time-sensitive conception of globalisation that connects us both to 'deeper history' and, as far as possible, to futurology. What, for example, will globalised architecture look like in the 22nd century? Here, however, I prefer to draw out the creative potential of globalisation by examining its spatial dimensions, and thereby to question the whole notion of scale. In this regard, it is essential to recall that the term 'globalisation' operates both as a reference to a direct observable process that we can see happening in contemporary cities, and at the same time as a cipher or metaphor (in a similar way to the term 'architecture'). Globalisation possesses many fascinating spatial characteristics, with the most commonly cited being the diminution, indeed erasure, of previous conceptions of distance and time. Yet equally important is the inner dimension which is created by our subjective experience of living in the world. After all, globalisation is also something which occurs inside us as an internalised process as we inhabit our everyday living spaces, and therefore it is not just a big nebulous entity that occurs somewhere 'out there'. In other words, we experience an interior globalisation. As a historical precursor, Mies van der Rohe observed the emergence of what he called a new kind of 'global feeling' in the 1920s. This, Mies noted, was not to do with the vast infinite scientific cosmos of Copernicus and Newton, but rather was happening because mankind was running out of space to expand into, hence a need to expand inwards into our own minds:

> *This again is a cosmos, but in a new sense we see it as being without astronomical limits. It is a cosmos seen from a human perspective as the living room that we have been assigned as a field related to our own specific powers of knowledge and creation.*[21]

Such recognition immediately poses a problem for imagining the scale of globalisation. We can no longer rely on the vague idea of a balancing out between larger-scale global forces and smaller-scale local forces. We need to think beyond the clichés (i.e. global = big, local = tiny) to devise some more fluid conceptions of scale. In part, my interest in this topic stems from the frequent criticisms by architectural practitioners of the imprecise use of scale by students when drawing using CAD software, since it gives them the ability to morph their designs continuously, thereby sidestepping (or indeed ignoring) the traditional references of standardised architecture scales such as 1:1 or 1:20 or 1:1000. It is a worry that is now being intensified by the advent of parametric design techniques, and by recent tropes of emergence and environment, which are usually backed up by some kind of attempt to explain architecture as a system or network or rhizome, in a post-humanist sense.[22] In reaction to these more fluid conceptual schemata, with their seeming preoccupation with complex curvilinear surfaces, many architects seem keen to reassert the principle of fixity of scale as an instinctive mechanism that can give physical form to invisible trans-spatial systems and processes. But although one can understand anxieties about misconceptions of scale, all it really does is to voice deep unease about contemporary cultural changes.

A more productive approach is to unpick the way in which architects have hitherto tried to conceptualise scale. Linked closely to the objectification of dimensional measurement, which began with bodily or musical scales and was then abstracted in Enlightenment tools such as the metric system, by the twentieth century a definite sense had evolved of the hierarchy of different architectural scales and what these meant.[23] Eliel Saarinen, for one, declared: 'Always design a thing by considering it in its next larger context: a chair in a room, a room in a house, a house in an environment, an environment in a city plan.' Louis Kahn, in his celebrated acceptance speech when receiving the American Institute of Architects'

Gold Medal in 1971, made the observation that 'the building is a society of rooms … the street is a room or agreement … [and the] city from a simple settlement became the place of institutions', positing a clear conceptual difference between each of these scales.[24] Advances in astrophysics and magnification/quantum physics were the source for the Eames' celebrated 'Powers of Ten' film in 1968.[25] Rem Koolhaas was later to repackage the same hierarchical schema – this time using the language of fashion design – in his book *S,M,L,XL* in the mid-1990s.[26] The problem, however, was that a structured belief in categorical differences of physical scale was also introduced into thinking about globalisation through the idea of local-versus-global, with its patently false binary premise. This has created many adverse effects, not least the frequent and banal use of skyscrapers as the grand motif for globalisation, with the current fascination being focussed on the world's tallest building – the Burj Khalifa tower in Dubai at 828 m high – but with that likely to be overtaken soon.

Urban theorists like Doreen Massey or Manuel Castells have long argued that there is always a complex interlinking process, and indeed a wrapping together, of the local and global in every city.[27] Yet for some reason this message still hasn't quite penetrated into architectural thinking. Hence I would suggest that it is better for us now to drop the schemata of local/global, or 'glocal', or whichever term, and instead start to conceive of globalisation in terms of an absence of restraints rather than something that possesses any specific scalar properties. If globalisation can thus seen more as a void or vacuum which provides spaces for things to happen in, then differentiated notions of scale collapse, becoming endlessly intertwined and superimposed on each other. As a concept, it seems closer to space-time in advanced physics, or to Deleuzian assemblages, or indeed the highly mutable software of contemporary computer-aided design. It also allows for the fact that there will continue to be endless urban variations across the world, as well as myriad smaller urban variations within every city, and never patterns of

19.5   Burj Khalifa in Dubai by SOM (2004–2010)

fixity. The dropping of the binary terms of local and global also gets us around the impossibility – indeed danger – of trying to define what might be classified 'local' or 'global' today in a multicultural city like London, or indeed the thorny problem of deciding who can legitimately claim the authority to be able to give phenomena one of these binary classifications.

Crucially, a more fluid approach also enables us to sidestep the 'big building syndrome' of starchitects like Foster or Koolhaas, and look with equal if not even more interest at the creative possibilities of smaller or medium interventions as elements of 'globalisation from below'. What are needed are new constellations of meaning, new groupings, and interlinked research networks to investigate global architectural phenomena. It is also vital to note that small-scale and medium-scale designs probably offer more interesting and vital tools for creative architectural practice, for four reasons:

1.   Architectural innovation mostly arises from the faster and subtler inter-changes which happen across different cultures, rather than from within established cultural blocks with their entrenched power structures.

2.   The smaller scale of operations and uneven patterns, fissures and fractures made possible today by globalisation also offer more fertile sites and opportunities for inventive design.

3.   Buildings can no longer hope to be symbolic or iconic, given that developed societies don't hold any fixed and readily agreed social meanings; buildings are still of course representational, albeit now representative of the values of ordinary everyday life as opposed to the unique and powerful, as in the past.

4.   Small-scale projects can respond more subtly and directly to the ecological consequences of globalisation, especially if ones looks at the issue of social sustainability, which today has become the key design challenge facing any developed society.

With this more critical view of architectural globalisation in mind, the rest of this essay will look at creative possibilities within the architectural and urban conditions of the Persian Gulf – a context described so vividly in the previous essays. The first point to make, when looking at different kinds of architectural practice in the region, is that so far there has been very little exploration of the collapsed-scale view of globalisation that would enable more fluid readings of forms and spaces in buildings. It is noticeable for instance that, just as in the case of Zaha Hadid, Jean Nouvel and Frank Gehry in their grandiose cultural institutions for Saadiyat Island in Abu Dhabi, Rem Koolhaas only ever seemed to be thinking at the very largest global scale when producing his design for 'Waterfront City' in Dubai.[28] OMA's vast masterplan envisaged an entire new urban district for 1.5 million inhabitants, although due to the economic recession it stands almost no chance of being built. Koolhaas nonetheless set out his design approach:

My goal is to establish a section of the city in Dubai that is a true metropolis. That includes, most of all, a true public space – not the caricature of a public space, meaning shopping malls. I am very grateful to the government in Dubai for the fact that we will have a court there, hospitals and the terminus stations for two subway lines. In other words, this space will have a recognizable identity, ingredients of what characterizes Dubai, but also a real urban life … [which] isn't lacking, but it is confused. We have a neighborhood there called Deira, which is completely urban. It's unbelievably dense, mixed, exciting and beautiful – the type of beauty that will probably need our protection soon. In fact we, as city planners, will have to spend more time in the future thinking about how to plan and preserve at the same time.[29]

His concern to mesh into the existing fabric of Deira, as an older part of Dubai, and thus to reactivate its downtown areas – not through a typical shopping mall, but by street-based mixed-use urban design – echoes the approach of Allies and Morrison outlined by Tim Makower in his essay on the Msheireb project in Doha. Unlike Allies and Morrison, however, there was never any indication from Koolhaas of how the smaller and more intimate details of his Dubai masterplan might fit into, or modify, daily patterns of urban life. OMA's design for Waterfront City remained at the broad-brush level of urban iconography.

The limitation inherent in conceptualising and designing at a single scale is something which is also all too common among indigenous architectural practices on both sides of the Persian Gulf region. Thus while most of these firms almost always claim to work with existing architectural and urban forms, in reality this is never really done using a fluid engagement with different scales of design. A very well known Arabic architect in the region is Ibrahim Jaidah, the energetic force behind the Arab Engineering Bureau (which has offices in Doha, Abu Dhabi, and Kuala Lumpur). Typical projects tend to be the office towers and luxury apartments found in so much new development in cities along the Gulf's western coastline. Jaidah claims his approach is to evoke traditional urban motifs while also embracing western-style modernity.[30] One outcome is the Barzan Tower in West Bay in Doha – nominated for an Aga Khan Award in 2004 – which meshes together a quasi-Arabic facade at its base and a mirror-glass tower above, in a manner that seems reminiscent of 1980s post-modernism. Elsewhere, Jaidah's interest in evoking traditional design, while also equipping it with the latest servicing standards, is exemplified in his award-winning Al-Sharq Village and Spa, again in Doha. It is an Arabic-style hotel and resort for wealthy Qatari residents and overseas visitors. Yet this kind of project, of the kind so often validated by the Aga Khan Trust Award, and which fits in well with the demands of culturally conservative clients, is only fixated with visual references to the forms and symbols used in traditional Arabic architecture, never its spatial meanings and relationships. There can also be little doubt that this approach is holding back the emergence of subtler, more hybrid contemporary architecture in the Persian Gulf. A similar limitation applies to the traditional-style housing estate on Amwaj Island in Muharraq, or the Al Zamil office tower in Manama (winner of an Aga Khan Award), or the Novotel Al Dana Resort in Manama (another Aga Khan Award winner), all of them designed by the team led by Souheil El-Masri of Gulf House Engineering in Bahrain.[31] Nor is this stasis in design ambition limited to Arabic countries along the Persian Gulf. The same problem is mirrored all too often along the eastern side of the Gulf, where a variety of pseudo-traditional Iranian buildings are being constructed with non-functional wind-catchers and other superficial historical symbols, again squeezing out the possibility of more creative thinking.

This is not to deny that there are younger and hungrier practices appearing on the radar within the Persian Gulf region. X-Architects were founded in Dubai in 2003 by Ahmed Al-Ali and Farid Esmaeil with the express intention of being more critical and innovative in approach, as can be seen for instance in their Xeritown master-plan for a 60-hectare sustainable city in the desert close to Dubai (2007), or on the Ain Al-Fayda National Housing Proposal for Al Ain in Abu Dhabi (2009).[32] Furthermore, in a recent issue of *Architectural Design*, Michael Hensel and Mehran Gharleghi put together a fascinating survey of innovative projects by younger Iranian architects, although notably none of those featured operate in cities along its Persian Gulf coastline.[33] Given therefore the stifled quality of so much of the architectural design culture in the Gulf region – a condition which seems entirely at odds with the dramatic globalising changes taking place – the new result is that much of the best new thinking comes from at least some of the western architects who are designing projects for the region. This in itself is perhaps not that surprising, since it accords with my previous observation that innovation takes place more readily at the intersections and crossovers between cultures, and not from within cultural blocks. Soon of course the architects of the Persian Gulf region will be driving the new creative ideas, yet for the moment of cultural transition it appears to be these external agents who are breaking the moulds.

Although the amount of work being done by western practices has declined substantially since economic recession started to bite in 2008, there are notable ongoing activities especially in terms of low-energy sustainable design. Aside from the aforementioned Msheireb project, which is reshaping a sizeable portion of downtown Doha, the most famous is Foster & Partners design for Masdar City.[34] This project sits slightly to the south-east of the city of Abu Dhabi, close to its international airport and main university, and in essence is creating a new suburban university quarter. The buildings are focussed on the Masdar Institute of Science and Technology (MIST), which is being run in conjunction with the Massachusetts Institute of Technology. The project is largely funded by the Abu Dhabi government through various companies set up for the purpose. The initial phase of Masdar City is due for completion in 2015, and is already receiving wide publicity for its mass transportation system, electric cars, emphasis on walkability, low-energy prototype buildings, and extensive use of solar panels and other high-tech applications. However, Masdar can equally be criticised as being an expensive, top-down, government controlled, commercialised approach that has eradicated any genuine sense of experimentation from the equation. If the future of energy-efficient building really needs to have so much money spent on it, then we are left with a real conundrum about how global resources should be used.

Far more innovative is another major research initiative set up in the rival city of Doha, called the Qatar Pilot Plant; it forms one of the initial stages of the much larger Sahara Forest Project, which hopes to find ways to farm the desert lands of North Africa and the Middle East. The ideas for the Qatar Pilot Plant are coming from an international research consortium with partners in the UK and Norway, including Bill Watts from Max Fordham LLC in London.[35] Operational from December 2012, this experimental low-energy centre in Doha is being built on land owned by a leading fertiliser company. Its express intention is to remain as open and flexible and creative in its thinking by incorporating elements such as algae, sea plants, saltwater greenhouses, etc within its integrated system of renewable fuel sources. Already crops have managed to be grown in an otherwise hostile setting. A different attempt to find a more responsive method of energy-conscious design, this time at the level of building detail, is a new environmental technique to shade all-glass office towers which has been devised by Aedas under the lead of its former research director, Peter Oborn[36] (see Plate

31). In a new pair of blocks in Abu Dhabi, called the Al Bahar Towers, the office towers are wrapped with a series of aluminium-framed folding screens faced with polytetraflouroethylene (PTFE). The screens are carefully monitored and controlled by computers to open and close in response to the sun's movement. It transforms

19.6   Al Bahar Towers in Abu Dhabi by Aedas Architects

19.7   Close-up of 'mashrabiya' installation on the Al Bahar Towers

19.8   Villa Anbar in Dammam, Saudi Arabia by Peter Barber (1992–1993)

19.9   Entrance pool in the Villa Anbar

what are otherwise standard towers into exquisitely encrusted examples of performance art, in effect by deploying a mechanical *mashrabiya* screening. At an even bolder sculptural level, the dramatically curvilinear Qatar Faculty of Islamic Studies, located in Doha's Education City, is now being completed on site by the Anglo-Spanish practice of Mangera Yvars. Also part of their scheme is a mosque to serve the wider university campus.

19.10   View of chauffeur's house in the Villa Anbar

However, probably the most interesting attempt as yet to introduce transformative architectural ideas into the Persian Gulf region comes from an older project, back in the early-1990s, for the Villa Anbar in Dammam, Saudi Arabia.[37] It was the first project designed by Peter Barber, now a leading housing designer in the UK. Barber lived on site and worked with local craftsmen for a year to deliver what is an undeniably beautiful modernist house with many nods to Le Corbusier, Luis Barragan, etc. (see Plate 32). In addition, Barber's design also expresses the power relations contained within the dwelling, firstly by giving dramatic form to the chauffeur's apartment in the front courtyard, through a sweeping roof, and secondly by playing on the gender politics inside the house. The client was a leading Saudi female novelist, and hence while the internal planning conforms to the usual separation of male and female spaces, the twist is that there is a small slot with a sliding shutter that links the two living rooms – with the latch for this shutter placed on the female side so they can look into the male spaces if desired, but not the other way around. Overall it represents an elegant and thoughtful piece of architecture, which was shortlisted for an Aga Khan Award but in the end possibly proved too radical for some tastes.

19.11   Rooftop view to the local mosque

19.12   Interior of maid's room on the rooftop

Intriguing as these innovative projects are, they are all somewhat expensive examples, rather than truly nimble creative explorations. Instead, what would most help architectural practice for countries along both sides of the Persian Gulf is the spread of small-scale innovative projects which respond to, and thereby capture, the possibilities presented by rapid global change. Here the best exponents are probably the more experimental architectural teachers and researchers working in the Gulf, such as George Katodrytis of the American University of Sharjah. The projects that Katodrytis sets his students require them to unravel and record the hidden daily activities of Dubai, and at the same time look for chances to design according to emerging socio-economic trends in the city. It is an approach based less on formal aspects of design and more on the reading the hidden urban networks and systems in these Gulf cities, seeing the latter as constantly in flux. Rather than being held in sway by the apparent novelties of computer design, or the fixed visual symbols of past Arabic or Iranian architecture, the inspiration comes from everyday lived practices. Intellectual support for this position is given through the argument offered by Teddy Cruz – a Guatemala-born architect who operates in San Diego and Tijuana on either side of the US/Mexican border – when discussing the tasks for architects today:

> Architectural practice needs to engage in the re-organization of systems of urban development, challenging political and economic frameworks that are only benefiting homogenous large-scale interventions managed by private mega-block development. I believe the future is small, and this implies the dismantling of the LARGE by pixilating it with the micro: an urbanism of retrofit.[38]

Teddy Cruz's projects are themselves deeply ambivalent and fertile in their reading of scale, allowing for the kind of user input to architectural design as hinted at by earlier schemes like Corbusier's Plan Obus for Algiers, while avoiding the level of state control or physical megastructures that such modernist projects seemed to require. Cruz's neighbourhood-level projects also chime closely with the complex hybridity created by what Lefebvre described as 'planetary urbanization', rather than the outdated notion of treating cities as single distinctive entities. This is not to make the argument that somehow 'small is beautiful', but rather to recognise and welcome the sheer intricacy of contemporary urban conditions. A generation ago, Kenneth Frampton wrote of oppositional projects like these as being 'urban enclaves' which sought to resist but could never grapple with the increasing domination of consumerist culture, as if their small scale had to be recognised as an inherent problem.[39] But now with increasingly relevant theories of the cumulative and disproportionate power of 'small change', as proposed by theorists like Nabeel Hamdi, we no longer need to believe in Frampton's implicitly pejorative reading of the issue of architectural scale.[40] Thus we can see that the designs by George Katodrytis through his Sharjah students, and also his practice, StudioNova, try to tap into these everyday flows.[41]

19.13   Dubai Hub project by StudioNova Architects

19.14   View from within the Dubai Hub

These last examples hint at the kinds of explorations which can be made possible by problematising the concept of scale within globalisation. By avoiding any sense of privilege for large-scale projects, and transferring our attention instead to the social dynamics of scale, the situation contains far more design hope than the deathly monuments of Foster, Gehry and Koolhaas. Smaller projects might not be seen to change the world, and of course always run the risk of being dismissed as marginal: but this ignores the fact that they can be equally as powerful in their design ambitions, and above all, they don't close down creative possibilities. Network connections such as through the internet are also expanding their influence immensely. We therefore have to stop thinking of globalisation as something vast. Perhaps instead we should try to imagine it as the smallest thing we can possibly conceive of. Globalisation does not have to be about the mega-project, the ostentatious, or the shallowly symbolic. It is certainly not the preserve of profit-hungry multinational corporations, or would-be powerful states, nor is it a vast nebulous entity that is out of control and trying to control us. Rather its essence lies at mutable scales, in the fluid, the unfinished, the fissured and the everyday, as opposed to the generalised. Or to borrow a maxim, globalisation is in the details.

NOTES

1   Marshall Berman, *All That is Solid Melts Into Air: The Experience of Modernity* (London/ New York: Verso, 1983).

2   Antoine Picon, 'What has happened to territory?', in David Gissen (ed.), *Territory: Architecture Beyond Environment – Architectural Design Special Issue*, Profile no. 205 (May/June 2010), pp. 94–96.

3   This kind of conceptual error is typified in the comments on Middle Eastern architecture by Cynthia Davidson, which posit architecture as a separate object in relation to 'global capital'. See: Cynthia C. Davidson (ed.), *Legacies for the Future: Contemporary Architecture in Islamic Societies* (London: Thames & Hudson/Aga Khan Award for Architecture, 1998), pp. 8–9.

4   'Rem Koolhaas: An Obsessive Compulsion towards the Spectacular', quote taken from interview in *Der Spiegel*, 18 July 2008, viewable at the *Der Spiegel Online International* website, http://www.spiegel.de/international/world/rem-koolhaas-an-obsessive-compulsion-towards-the-spectacular-a-566655.html (accessed 16 November 2009)]

5   Ibid.

6   Anthony D. King. (ed.), *Culture, Globalization and the World-System* (London: Macmillan, 1991); Anthony D. King, *Spaces of Global Culture: Architecture, Urbanism, Identity* (London/New York: Routledge, 2004); Donald McNeill, *The Global Architect: Firms, Fame and Urban Form* (London/New York: Routledge, 2009); Liane Lefaivre & Alexander Tzonis, *Architecture and Regionalism in the Age of Globalization: Peaks and Valleys in the Flat World* (London/New York: Routledge, 2012).

7   Robert Adam, *The Globalisation of Modern Architecture: The Impact of Politics, Economics and Social Change on Architecture and Urban Design since 1990* (Newcastle-upon-Tyne: Cambridge Scholars Publishing, 2012).

8   Examples include: Thomas Frank, *One Market Under God: Extreme Capitalism, Market Populism, and the End of Economic Democracy* (New York: Anchor Books, 2000); Michael Hardt & Antonio Negri, *Empire* (Cambridge, MA/London: The MIT Press, 2000); David Held et al., *Global Transformations: Politics, Economics and Culture* (Cambridge: Polity, 1999); Joseph Stiglitz, *Globalization and its Discontents* (London: Allen Lane/Penguin, 2002); Joseph Stiglitz, *Making Globalization Work* (London: Penguin Books 2006); Joseph Stiglitz, *Freefall: America, Free Markets, and the Sinking of the World Economy* (New York: W.W. Norton, 2010).

9   Henri Lefebvre, *The Production of Space* (Oxford: Blackwell, 1974/91), p. 86.

10   Liane Lefaivre & Alexander Tzonis, *Critical Regionalism* (Munich/Berlin/London/New York: Prestel, 2003), p. 164: See also the discussion in Lefaivre & Tzonis, *Architecture and Regionalism in the Age of Globalization*.

11   Mark Crinson, 'Singapore's moment: Critical regionalism, its colonial roots and profound aftermath', *The Journal of Architecture*, vol. 13, no. 5 (2008): 585–605.

12   Richard Neutra, 'Regionalism in Architecture' (1939), in Vincent B. Canazaro, *Architectural Regionalism: Collected Writings on Place, Identity, Modernity and Tradition* (New York: Princeton Architectural Press, 2007), pp. 276–279.

13   'Top Ten Countries for Manufacturing Production in 2010', *Curious Cat Investing and Economics Blog* website, http://investing.curiouscatblog.net/2011/12/27/top-10-countries-for-manufacturing-production-in-2010-china-usa-japan-germany/ (accessed 12 September 2012).

14   This historical argument is made more extensively in Murray Fraser (with Joe Kerr), *Architecture and the 'Special Relationship': The American Influence on Post-war British Architecture* (London/New York: Routledge, 2007), pp. 14–17.

15   Steve Jones, *The Language of the Genes* (London: Flamingo, 2000).

16   David Edgerton, *The Shock of the Old: Technology and Global History since 1900* (London: Profile Books: London, 2008).

17   Jurgen Habermas, *The Divided West* (Cambridge: Polity Press, 2006), p. 175.

18   See, for example, the discussions in: Jan N. Pieterse, 'Globalization as Hybridization?', in Mike Featherstone et al. (eds), *Global Modernities* (London/Thousand Oaks, CA/New Delhi: Sage, 1995), pp. 45–68; Jan N. Pieterse, *Globalization and Culture* (Lanham, MD: Rowman & Littlefield, 2004). For another interesting study: Sheila L. Croucher, *Globalization and Belonging: The Politics of Identity in a Changing World* (New York: Rowman & Littlefield, 2004).

19   Stuart Hall, 'Globalization from Below', in Richard Ings (ed.), *Connecting Flights: New Cultures of the Diaspora* (London: Arts Council/British Council, 2003), pp. 6–14.

20   Saskia Sassen, *Cities in a World Economy (4ᵗʰ Edition)* (Thousand Oaks, CA/London: Pine Forge Press, 2011).

21   Ludwig Mies van der Rohe, 'On the Preconditions of Architectural Work' (1922), in Fritz Neumeyer (ed.), *The Artless Word: Mies van der Rohe on the Building Art* (Cambridge, MA: Harvard University Press, 1991), pp. 299–303.

22   The boldest statement about parametric design as an aspect of cybernetic systems theory is Patrik Schumacher, *The Autopoesis of Architecture* (2 vols, London: John Wiley, 2010/12): in response, and for an elegant dismantling of the misunderstanding of Deleuzian concepts and systems thinking in the design projects of Hadid and Schumacher, see Douglas Spencer, 'Replicant Urbanism: The

Architecture of Hadid's Central Building at BMW, Leipzig', *The Journal of Architecture*, vol. 15, no. 2 (2010): 181–207.

23   Rudolf Wittkower, *Architectural Principles in the Age of Humanism* (London: Academy Press, 1948/98); Robert Tavernor, *Smoot's Ear: The Measure of Humanity* (New Haven, CT: Yale University Press, 2007).

24   Louis I. Kahn, 'The Room, the Street, and Human Advancement', his acceptance speech for the 1971 AIA Gold Medal, viewable on the Louisiana Technical University website, http://www2.latech.edu/~wtwillou/A310_410_IDES_Images_sum04/Kahn_1971_AIA_Gold%20Medal.pdf (accessed 19 November 2010).

25   Charles and Ray Eames, 'Power of Ten' (1968), viewable on the *YouTube* website, http://www.youtube.com/watch?v=0fKBhvDjuy0 (accessed 18 January 2011).

26   Rem Koolhaas & Bruce Mau, *S,M,L,XL* (New York/Rotterdam Monacelli Press/010 Publishers, 1995).

27   Manuel Castells, *The Rise of the Network Society – Information Age: Economy, Society and Culture* (2nd Edition, Oxford: Blackwell, 2009); Doreen Massey, 'A Global Sense of Place', in Doreen Massey, *Space, Place and Gender* (Oxford: Blackwell, 1994), pp. 146–157; Doreen Massey, *World Cities* (Cambridge: Polity, 2007).

28   Office for Metropolitan Architecture, 'Waterfront City, Dubai, UAE', viewable on the OMA website, http://oma.eu/projects/2008/waterfront-city (accessed 12 September 2012).

29   'Rem Koolhaas: An Obsessive Compulsion towards the Spectacular', quote taken from interview in *Der Spiegel*, 18 July 2008, viewable at the *Der Spiegel Online International* website, http://www.spiegel.de/international/world/rem-koolhaas-an-obsessive-compulsion-towards-the-spectacular-a-566655.html (accessed 16 November 2009).

30   Arab Engineering Bureau website, http://www.aeb-qatar.com/ (accessed 15 July 2012): Ibrahim Jaidah, 'Exploring Urban Identity in the Gulf Region', paper presented to the *Human Habitation: Architecture, Settlement and Cultural Identity in the Persian Gulf Region* international conference organised by the University of Westminster's Department of Architecture, held at the Royal Institute of British Architects, London, 5–6 October 2009.

31   'Gulf House Engineering', viewable on the ArchNet Digital Library website, http://archnet.org/library/parties/one-party.jsp?party_id=12018 (accessed 15 July 2012); Souheil El-Masri, 'Urban Transformations of Manama and Muharraq', paper presented to the *Human Habitation: Architecture, Settlement and Cultural Identity in the Persian Gulf Region* conference.

32   X-Architects website, http://www.x-architects.com/index.php (accessed 28 November 2012).

33   Michael Hensel & Mehran Gharleghi (eds), *Iran: Past, Present Future (Architectural Design special issue)*, vol. 82, no. 3 (May/June 2012).

34   Masdar website, http://www.masdar.ae/en/home/index.aspx (accessed 15 July 2012); 'Masdar Development', Foster + Partners website, http://www.fosterandpartners.com/Projects/1515/Default.aspx (accessed 15 July 2012).

35   'Qatar Pilot Plant', Sahara Forest Project website, http:// http://saharaforestproject.com/projects/qatar.html (accessed 31 January 2013); 'Desert Blooms', *RIBA Journal* (December 2012/January 2013), p. 14.

36   Peter Oborn (ed.), *Al Bahar Towers: The Abu Dhabi Investment Council Headquarters* (Chichester, Sussex: Wiley, 2013); 'Al Bahar Towers', viewable on the Aedas website, http://www.aedas.com/Al%20Bahar%20Towers (accessed 12 September 2012).

37   'Villa Anbar, Saudi', Peter Barber Architects website, http://www.peterbarberarchitects. com/03_Villa.html (accessed 20 January 2013); Peter Barber, 'Villa Anbar, Dammam, Saudi Arabia', in Murray Fraser (ed.), *The Oxford Review of Architecture – No1: Culture and Technology Issue* (Oxford: Oxford Brookes University, 1996), pp. 10–19.

38   Teddy Cruz, 'Mapping Non-Conformity: Post-Bubble Urban Strategies' (2009), Hemispherica website, viewable at: http://hemisphericinstitute.org/hemi/en/e-misferica-71/cruz (accessed 21 March 2011).

39   Kenneth Frampton, *Modern Architecture: A Critical History* (London: Thames & Hudson, 1980), p. 297.

40   Nabeel Hamdi, *Small Change: The Art of Practice and the Limits of Planning in Cities* (London: Earthscan, 2004); Nabeel Hamdi, *The Placemaker's Guide to Building Community* (London: Routledge, 2010).

41   George Katodrytis/StudioNova Architects website, http://katodrytis.com/main/ (accessed 21 June 2012).

Index